Data Structure and Basics of Algorithms

DATA STRUCTURE AND BASICS OF ALGORITHMS

Dr. Chandan Jyoti Kumar

Assistant Professor,
Department of Computer Science and IT, Cotton University

Dr. Sangita Baruah

Assistant Professor,
Department of Computer Science and IT, Cotton University

Dr. Mayuri Sharma

Lecturer
NIELIT, Guwahati

Supriya Borah

Faculty Member,
Machine Learning and Data Science, Pragjyotishpur University

ACADEMIC ENCLAVE

First Edition, 2025

ISBN: 978-93-48642-40-0

Published by
ACADEMIC ENCLAVE™
House No. 10/15, Ground Floor,
Block-A, Street No. 14/3, Kamal Vihar,
Kamal Pur, Burari, Delhi-110084
Email: info@academicenclave.com
Mobile: +91-7042423166
Website: www.academicenclave.com

Printed at Replika Press Pvt. Ltd.

Preface

In the rapidly evolving world of technology, the cornerstone of computer science remains firmly rooted in the logic of data structures and algorithmic design, which continue to serve as the foundation for solving diverse problems in computer science, information technology, and the emerging domains of Artificial Intelligence (AI) and Machine Learning. As educators and lifelong learners, we have observed and experienced how a sturdy grasp of these fundamental concepts is crucial to not only shape a student's academic journey but also develop the ability of a problem-solving mindset.

Born from a deep passion and a strong sense of purpose, this book unfolds through well-structured chapters that are meticulously designed to guide learners on a clear and enriching journey through the foundations of data structures and algorithms. The book prioritizes accessibility and advancement, making it suitable for a wide range of readers, from beginners to aspiring learners to professionals in the field of computer science.

Each chapter of this book is equipped with theoretical concepts, illustrative examples and diagrams for easy understanding, algorithmic programs and codes to give learners a clear and crisp conceptual and practical knowledge about a specific topic in hand. Additionally, each chapter is enriched with constructive and thoughtfully crafted questions over every single domain to check the progress of the learner. The book begins by offering an Introductory overview in *Chapter 1* that lays the foundation of the importance of data structures and algorithms with prerequisites for the later chapters. *Chapter 2* delves into Arrays, focusing on representation and operations of Linear and Multidimensional arrays, and additional concepts of arrays with functions and pointers. Moving forward, *Chapter 3* introduces linked list, explaining dynamic memory allocations and different types such as singly, doubly and circular linked lists. *Chapter 4* discusses about Stack and Queue data structures, with their representation, implementation and applications. *Chapter 5* covers the concept of a hierarchical data structure Tree, its different types and traversal methods. *Chapter 6* expands into Graph data structure, showcasing how relationships and networks are modeled, along with traversal and different pathfinding algorithms. In *Chapter 7,* the focus shifts into Design and Analysis of algorithms, introducing the core paradigms of problem-solving approach - brute force, divide and conquer, greedy techniques, dynamic programming, branch and bound, backtracking, paired with concepts of time and space complexity analysis. Finally, *Chapter 8* addresses Sorting and Searching algorithms, covering different types of searching and sorting algorithms along with discussing their performance trade-off.

Through this book, we aim to nurture the analytical mindset and strengthen the algorithmic logics essential for crafting efficient solutions to various problem-solving task in the realm of computer science. By guiding learners from basic foundational principles to advance problem solving strategies, we aspire to inspire a deeper appreciation for the power and productivity of computational world of logic.

Whether you are discovering the topic for the first time or revisiting them to refine your mastery over the foundations to a bigger and greater world of algorithms and logics, we hope this book serve you as a reliable companion-illuminating your path through the elegant and ever-aspiring world of computer science.

AUTHORS

Contents

About the Authors

Dr. Chandan Jyoti Kumar received his Ph.D. in Computer Science from Gauhati University, Assam. He holds an M.Tech from NIT Jalandhar and a B.Tech from NIT Silchar. Dr. Kumar is currently an Assistant Professor in the Department of Computer Science and IT at Cotton University, Guwahati. He previously served at Assam Don Bosco University and has over a decade of experience in academia and research. His interdisciplinary work spans Machine learning, Deep learning, Bioinformatics, EEG signal analysis and AI in agriculture. His ICSSR-funded research on alcohol use behavior among university students using machine learning highlights his commitment to socially relevant innovation. He has published widely in high-impact journals, edited books and chapters, and guided Ph.D., M.Tech, and BCA/MCA scholars. He actively contributes as reviewer to reputed journals like *Scientific Reports*, *Journal of Big Data*, and *BMC Neurology*, and serves on the technical committees of major national and international conferences. His invited talks and leadership in academic events underline his standing as a researcher and educator.

Dr. Sangita Baruah is the founding Head and Assistant Professor of the Department of Computer Science and Information Technology at Cotton University. She completed her Master of Computer Applications (MCA) from Dibrugarh University and obtained her Ph.D. in Cyber Security from Gauhati University. Her areas of interest span across Cyber Security, Machine Learning, Computer Vision, and the application of Artificial Intelligence in healthcare systems. She is passionate about exploring the intersection of emerging technologies to solve real-world problems.

Dr. Mayuri Sharma is currently serving as a Lecturer at NIELIT Guwahati, Assam. She holds a Bachelor's degree in Computer Science and Engineering from Gauhati University (2015), an M.Tech degree in Artificial Intelligence (CSE) from Assam Don Bosco University (2017) and a PhD (2023) in Machine Learning (CSE) from Royal Global University, Assam. Her research interests lie at the intersection of Machine Learning, Image Processing and Deep Learning, with a particular focus on ML-based agricultural applications and Generative AI domains. She has 6 years of experience in teaching UG and PG students.

Supriya Borah is currently serving as a Faculty Member, AI/ML and Data Science, Pragjyotishpur University, Assam. She holds a Bachelor's degree in Computer Science from Cotton University (2022), where she was awarded the Gold Medal for academic excellence, and a Master's degree in Computer Science from Gauhati University (2024), graduating with a Gold Medal as the top rank holder in her programme. In 2024, she qualified the UGC-NET examination in Computer Science and Applications, further validating her academic and professional dedication to the field. Her research interests lie at the intersection of Machine Learning, Natural Language Processing (NLP), and Medical AI, with a particular focus on the application of artificial intelligence in psychological and mental health domains. In her teaching role, she is passionate about guiding students in core areas of computer science, including Data Structures, Design and Analysis of Algorithms, Theory of Computation, Graph Theory, and Machine Learning.

1

Introduction and Overview

1.1 INTRODUCTION

This chapter presents an introduction to the subject data structure and also presents an overview of various concepts of data structure.

Data structure is an important concept in programming. They are the building blocks of a program. Data structure means organized collection of data. It is sometimes also termed as an extension of data type.

Data type = Data values + Operations

Data structure = Organized data + Operations

Data structure is the structural representation of the logical relationship existing between individual elements of data. In other words, data structure is a way of organizing all data items that considers not only the element stored but also their relationship to each other. We can also define it as mathematical or logical model of particular organization of data items.

Data structures are used in almost every program or software system. Some commonly used data structures are: array, linked list, stack, queue, binary tree and hash tables. Data structures are widely used in various areas, such as: Compiler design, Operating system, Statistical analysis package, DBMS, Numerical analysis, Simulation, Artificial intelligence, Graphics, etc.

The selection of a particular data structure in a program depends on the following two things:

a) The data structure must be rich enough in structure to reflect the relationship existing between the data.

b) The structure should be simple to process data effectively whenever required.

1.2 ELEMENTARY DATA ORGANIZATION

Data structure is categorized into two broad categories. These are:

a) Primitive Data Structures

b) Non-Primitive Data Structures

Primitive Data Structures

Primitive Data Structures are the basic data structures that directly operate upon the machine instructions. They have different representations on different computers. Integers, floating point numbers, character constants, string constants and pointers come under this category. Primitive data structures form the foundation of all data storage and manipulation.

Integers (int) store whole numbers, both positive and negative, making them ideal for counting and indexing (e.g., int num = 10;). Floating-point numbers (float, double) handle decimal values, which are essential for precise calculations in scientific and financial applications (e.g., float pi = 3.14;). Characters (char) represent single symbols, such as letters or numbers, and are commonly used for text processing (char letter = 'A';). Boolean values (bool) store true or false, often used for decision-making in conditional statements (bool isReady = true;). Finally, pointers (available in languages like C and C++) store memory addresses, enabling dynamic memory management and efficient data handling (int *ptr = #).

Example: We will see declaration and initialization of the different primitive data structure in C++ format:

1. For Integer(int) :

   ```
   int num = 10;
   ```

2. For Floating Point (float):

   ```
   float pi = 3.14;
   ```

3. For Character :

   ```
   char letter = 'A';
   ```

4. For Boolean:

   ```
   bool isReady = true;
   ```

5. For Pointer:

   ```
   int num = 20;
   int *ptr = &num; // Pointer stores the address of num
   cout<< "Address: " <<ptr<< ", Value: " << *ptr;
   ```

Non-primitive Data Structures

Non-primitive data structures are more sophisticated data structures and are derived from primitive data structures. They emphasize on grouping same or different data items with relationship between each data item. Non-primitive data structures are again categorized into linear and non-linear data structures.

Linear Data Structures: In linear Data Structures data items are organized sequentially or linearly. In linear Data Structures data can be accessed sequentially in an order. Data elements in a linear data structure are traversed one after the other and only one element can be directly reached while traversing. All the data items in linear data structure can be traversed in single run. These kinds of data structures are very easy to implement because memory of computer is also organized in linear fashion. Examples of linear data structures are Arrays, Stack, Queue and Linked List.

Non-Linear Data Structures: The data structures where data items are not organized sequentially are called non-linear data structures. The data elements stored in such data structures cannot be accessed in a sequential or linear order. There is no particular order to access the elements. In other words, the data elements of the non-linear data structure could be connected to more than one element to reflect a special relationship among them. All the data elements in non-linear data structure cannot be traversed in single run. Examples of non- linear data structures are Trees and Graph

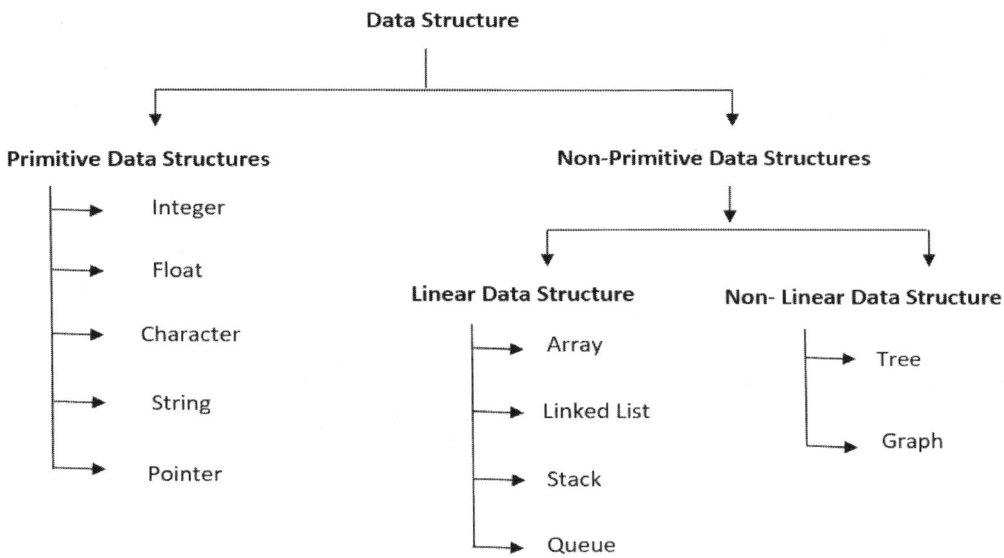

Figure 1.1: Classification of data structure

1.3 DATA STRUCTURES AND OPERATIONS

In the above section we have discussed about classification of data structures. In this section we will present a brief introduction of various primitive and non-primitive data structures.

1.3.1 Array

An array is a non-primitive linear data structure. It is a finite list of homogeneous elements stored in contiguous memory blocks. By finite list we mean that the list should have limited n number of elements which is predefined. By homogeneous we mean that all the elements of the list should have same data type. More precise, we cannot accommodate integer data, floating point data, character data etc on the same list. If the array is declared as integer, we can only store integer data in that list. We can have separate list for separate data types. By contiguous we mean that the data or elements in the list will be stored in successive or adjacent memory blocks. An array can be declared as:

```
int A[50];
```

where int (integer) specifies the data type of the array, 'A' is the name of the array, 50 written inside square brackets specifies the size of the array, i.e. the maximum number of elements the array can hold.

1.3.2 Linked List

Like an array, a linked list is also a linear data structure. However, unlike an array, the elements of a linked list are not stored at contiguous memory locations. Instead, they are scattered in memory and linked to each other using pointers.

In a linked list, data is stored in a structure called node as shown below:

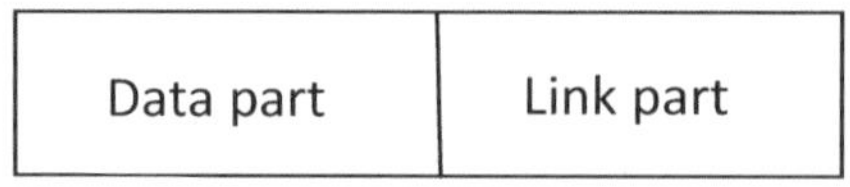

Figure 1.2: A Node

Each node of a simple linked list comprises of two parts:

a) Data part

b) Link part

The data part stores the data value to be stored on the node. The link part is a reference to the next node, *i.e.* the linked part stores the address of the next node.

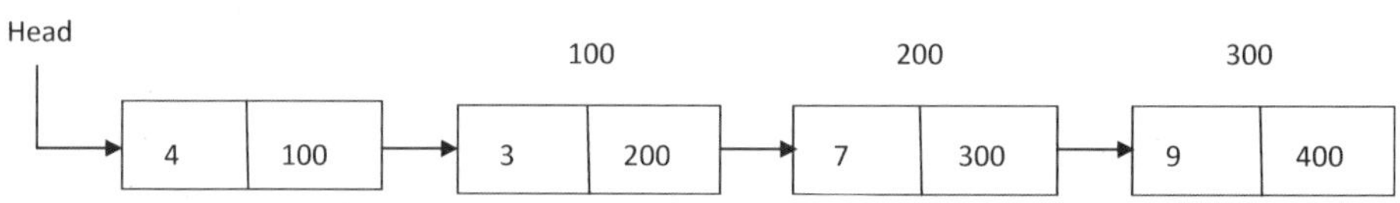

Figure 1.3: A Linked List

1.3.3 Stack

A stack is a non-primitive, linear and homogeneous data structure, where insertion and deletion take place at only one end, called the top of the stack. Since all the insertion and deletion operations in a stack takes place only at one end, *i.e*, from the top of the stack, so the last element to be inserted, will be the first element to be removed from the stack. Therefore, stacks are also called last-in-first-out (LIFO) lists.

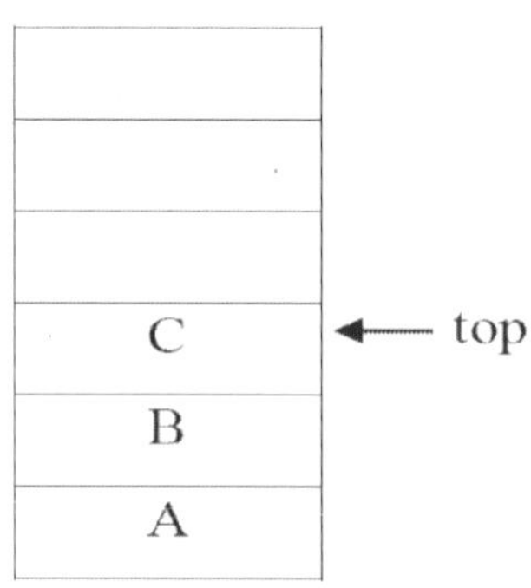

Figure 1.4: A Stack

1.3.4 Queue

A queue is a non-primitive, linear and homogeneous data structure, where insertion and deletion take place at two ends, called rear and front. Rear is the position through which insertion takes place and front is the position through which deletion takes place.

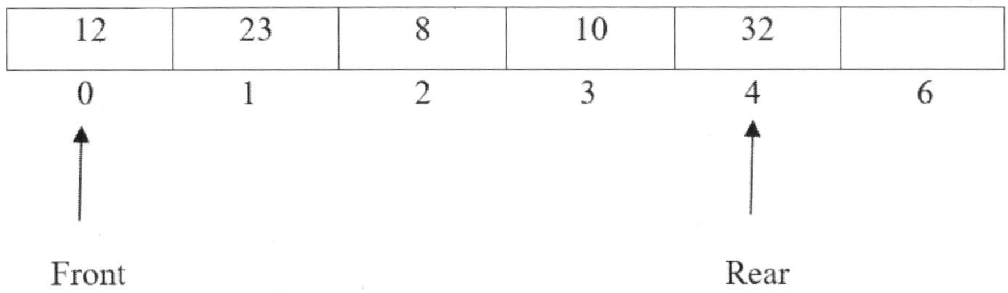

Figure 1.5: A queue

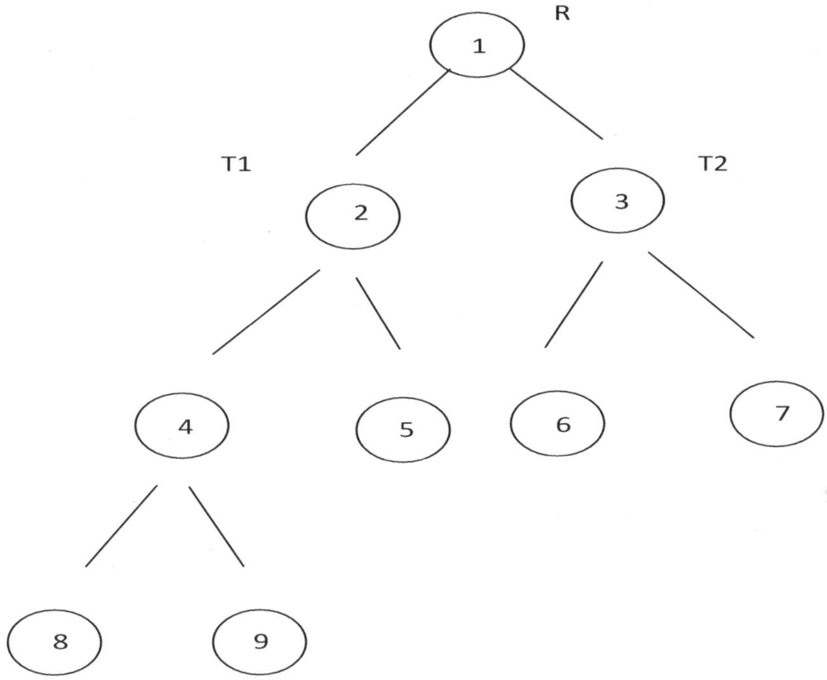

Figure 1.6: A binary tree

1.3.5 Tree

A tree is a non-linear data structure which consists of a collection of nodes arranged in a hierarchical order. One of the nodes is designated as the root node, and the remaining nodes can be partitioned into disjoint sets such that each set is a sub-tree of the root. The simplest form of a tree is a binary tree. A binary tree consists of a root node and left and right sub-trees, where both sub-trees are also binary trees. Each node contains a data element, a left pointer which points to the left sub-tree, and a right pointer which points to the right sub-tree. The root element is the topmost node which is pointed by a 'root' pointer. If root = NULL then the tree is empty.

The above figure shows a binary tree, where R is the root node and T1 and T2 are the left and right subtrees of R. If T1 is non-empty, then T1 is said to be the left successor of R. Likewise, if T2 is non-empty, then it is called the right successor of R. In the above figure, node 2 is the left child and node 3 is the right child of the root node 1. Note that the left sub-tree of the root node consists of the nodes 2, 4, 5, 8, and 9. Similarly, the right sub-tree of the root node consists of the nodes 3, 6 and 7.

1.3.6 Graph

A graph is a non-linear data structure which is a collection of *vertices* (also called *nodes*) and *edges* that connect these vertices. A graph is often viewed as a generalization of the tree structure, where instead of a purely parent-to-child relationship between tree nodes, any kind of complex relationships between the nodes can exist. In a tree structure, nodes can have any number of children but only one parent, a graph on the other hand relaxes all such kinds of restrictions. The following figure shows a graph with five nodes.

A node in the graph may represent a city and the edges connecting the nodes can represent roads. A graph can also be used to represent a computer network where the nodes are workstations and the edges are the network connections. Graphs have so many applications in computer science and mathematics that several algorithms have been written to perform the standard graph operations, such as searching the graph and finding the shortest path between the nodes of a graph.

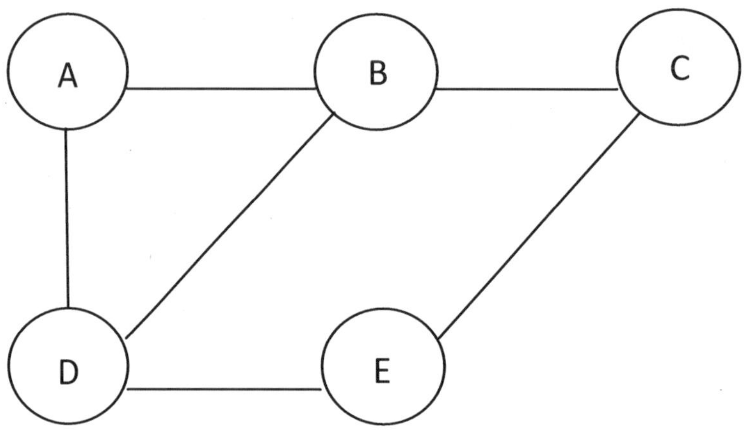

Figure 1.7: Graph

Unlike trees, graphs do not have any root node. Rather, every node in the graph can be connected with another node in the graph. When two nodes are connected via an edge, the two nodes are known as neighbours. For example, in the above figure, node A has two neighbours: B and D.

1.3.7 Operations

In this section we will discuss about various operations that can be performed on the different data structures. Some of the frequently used operations are:

Traversing: Traversing means to go to each data item and access it exactly once so that it can be processed. For example, to display the marks of all the students stored in a data structure.

Searching: Searching means to find whether a particular element is present in the data structure or not. It is also used to find the location of the data item in case it is present.

Inserting: Insertion means to add a new data element to an existing list. For example, to add the roll no. of a new student.

Deleting: Deletion means to remove or delete a particular data item from a given list of items. For example, to delete the roll no. of a student who has left the course.

Sorting: Sorting means to arrange the data items in some order like ascending order or descending order depending on application. For example, arranging the marks of students from low to high.

Merging: Merging means to combine the data items of two separate lists and form a single list of data items. Data items of the two list may be sorted or may not be sorted.

1.3.8. Selection of Correct Data Structure

Selecting an appropriate data structure is very crucial for optimizing performance and ensuring efficient data management. The choice depends on multiple factors, including access speed, memory efficiency, and the type of operations performed on the data.

1. **Access Time Requirement:** Access time indicates how quickly data can be retrieved from a data structure. Some structures provide direct access to elements, while others require traversal.
2. **Memory Constraint:** In memory-constrained environments like embedded systems, mobile applications, or cloud computing, selecting a data structure that minimizes memory overhead is crucial. Optimizing memory usage can significantly improve the performance and cost-effectiveness of an application.
3. **Frequency of Insertions and Deletions:** Some applications require frequent insertion and deletion of elements, and not all data structures handle these operations efficiently. For applications requiring dynamic updates (e.g., priority queues), a structure like a linked list or queue is preferable.
4. **Scalability and Future Expansion:** A scalable structure avoids bottlenecks and preserves system efficiency without performance degradation as data volumes increases. Dynamic arrays, balanced trees, or linked lists are more appropriate than static arrays for applications that are expected to develop dynamically.
5. **Application-Specific Operations:** Different applications demand specific operations such as searching, sorting, and traversal. Selecting a data structure tailored to the core operations of an application ensures maximum efficiency and performance.

1.4 ALGORITHM

An algorithm is defined as a step-by-step procedure or method for solving a problem. It also defines a set of finite instructions to be executed in a certain order to get the desired output. Algorithms are generally created independent of any underlying languages. We can implement it in any programming language of our choice.

Steps of an algorithm may include branching or repetition depending upon what problem the algorithm is being developed for. Besides merely being a finite set of rules which gives a sequence of operations for solving a specific type of problem, a well-defined algorithm has five important features:

- **Finiteness.** An algorithm must always terminate after a finite number of steps.
- **Definiteness.** Each step of an algorithm must be precisely defined; the actions to be carried out must be rigorously and unambiguously specified for each case.
- **Input.** An algorithm has zero or more inputs, *i.e.*, quantities which are given to it initially before the algorithm begins.

- **Output.** An algorithm has one or more outputs *i.e.,* quantities which have a specified relation to the inputs.
- **Effectiveness.** An algorithm is also generally expected to be effective. This means that all of the operations to be performed in the algorithm must be sufficiently basic that they can in principle be done exactly and in a finite length of time.

1.4.1 Characteristics of an Algorithm

All procedures cannot be called as an algorithm. An algorithm should have the following characteristics:

- **Unambiguous** – An algorithm should be clear and unambiguous. Each step, including its inputs and outputs, must have a single, well-defined meaning.
- **Input** – An algorithm should have zero or more well-defined inputs.
- **Output** – An algorithm must have at least one well-defined output that corresponds to the desired result.
- **Finiteness** – An algorithm must terminate after a finite number of steps.
- **Feasibility** – The algorithm should be practically executable with the available resources.
- **Independence** – An algorithm should consist of step-by-step instructions that are independent of any specific programming language or code syntax.

1.4.2 How to Write an Algorithm?

There are no well-defined standards for writing algorithms. Rather, the style of writing an algorithm is problem-specific and depends on the available resources. Algorithms are never written to support a particular programming language.

As we know, all programming languages share basic constructs like loops (do, for, while), and flow-control statements (if-else, etc.). These common constructs can be used when writing algorithms.

Although algorithms are generally written in a step-by-step manner, this is not always the case. Algorithm writing is a process that takes place only after the problem domain is well-defined. In other words, we must clearly understand the problem domain before designing a solution.

Now, let us try to learn how to write algorithms through some examples.

Example 1: Write an algorithm to add two numbers and display the result.

Step 1: Input two integers a and b

Step 2: Add values of a & b

Step 3: Store output of step 2 to sum

Step 4: Print sum

Step 5: End

Example 2: Write an algorithm to swap two numbers.

Step 1: Input two numbers a and b

Step 2: Set temp = a

Step 3: Set a = b

Step 4: Set b = temp

Step 5: Print a and b

Step 6: End

Example 3: Write an algorithm to find largest of two numbers.

Step 1: Input two numbers a and b

Step 2: If a > b

then print a

Else if a < b

then print b

Step 3: End

Example 4: Write an algorithm to calculate the factorial of a number.

Step 1: Input a number n

Step 2: Set fact = 1

Step 3: Repeat steps 4 and 5 from i = 1 to n

Step 4: fact = fact * i

Step 5: Increment i

Step 6: Print fact

Step 7: End

Example 5: Write an algorithm to check whether a number is even or odd.

Step 1: Input a number n

Step 2: If n % 2 == 0

Then print "Even"

Else

Print "Odd"

Step 3: End

Example 6: Write an algorithm to find the sum of the first n natural numbers.

Step 1: Input a number n

Step 2: Set sum = 0

Step 3: Repeat steps 4 and 5 from i = 1 to n

Step 4: sum = sum + i

Step 5: Increment i

Step 6: Print sum

Step 7: End

Example 7: Write an algorithm to reverse a number.

Step 1: Input a number n

Step 2: Set rev = 0

Step 3: Repeat while n != 0

a. Set rem = n % 10

b. Set rev = rev * 10 + rem

c. Set n = n / 10 (integer division)

Step 4: Print rev

Step 5: End

1.5 ALGORITHM ANALYSIS

Algorithms tell the programmers how to code the program. Algorithms are very useful for programmers as well as for the program analyst. A programmer or analyst can observe what operations are being used and how the process is flowing.

We design an algorithm to get a solution of a given problem. A problem can be solved in more than one way.

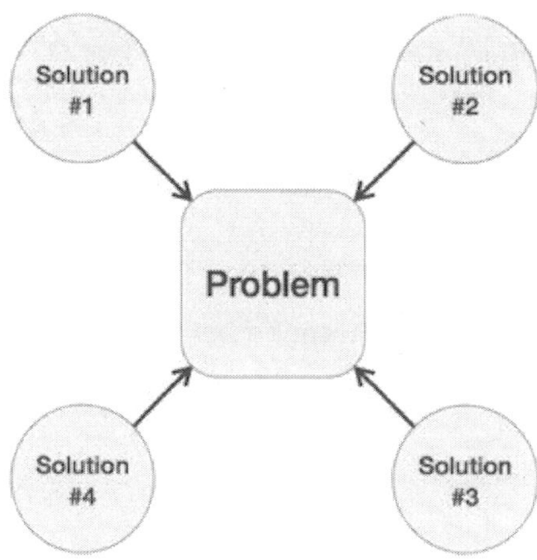

Hence, many solutions(algorithms) can be derived for a given problem. Therefore, the next step is to analyse those proposed solutions(algorithms) and implement the best suitable solution.

Efficiency of an algorithm can be analysed at two different stages, before implementation and after implementation. They are:

- **A Priori Analysis:** This is a theoretical analysis of an algorithm. The efficiency is evaluated assuming all other factors—such as processor speed—are constant and do not affect the implementation. It focuses on analyzing the algorithm based on logic and structure, without actually executing it.
- **A Posteriori Analysis:** This is an empirical analysis of an algorithm. The selected algorithm is implemented using a programming language and executed on the target computer system. During this analysis, actual statistics such as running time and memory usage are measured and collected.

Algorithm analysis primarily concerns the execution or running time of various operations involved. The running time of an operation is generally defined as the number of computer instructions executed during its execution.

1.5.1 Complexity of Algorithm

Suppose **A** is an algorithm and **n** is the size of input data, the time and space used by the algorithm A are the two main factors, which decide the efficiency of A.

- **Time Factor:** Time is measured by counting the number of key operations such as comparisons in the sorting algorithm.
- **Space Factor:** Space is measured by counting the maximum memory space required by the algorithm.

The complexity of an algorithm **f(n)** gives the running time and/or the storage space required by the algorithm in terms of **n** as the size of input data.

However, running time requirements are more critical than memory requirements.

1.5.1.1Time Complexity

Time complexity of an algorithm represents the amount of time required by the algorithm to run to completion. Time requirements can be defined as a numerical function T(n), where T(n) can be measured as the number of steps, provided each step consumes constant time.

For example, addition of two n-bit integers takes **n** steps. Consequently, the total computational time is $T(n) = c * n$, where c is the time taken for the addition of two bits and n is the number of steps. Here, we observe that T(n) grows linearly as the input size increases.

We can have three cases to analyze an algorithm:

1) Worst Case Running Time – Maximum time required for program execution.
2) Average Case Running Time – Average time required for program execution.
3) Best Case Running Time – Minimum time required for program execution.

Worst case Running Time: It is the behaviour of the algorithm with respect to the worst possible case of the input instances. The worst-case running time of an algorithm is an upper bound on the running time for any input. We must know the case that causes maximum number of operations to be executed. For Linear Search, the worst case happens when the element to be searched is not present in the array. When the element is not present, the search() functions compares it with all the elements of the array one by one. Therefore, the worst case time complexity of linear search would be $\Theta(n)$.

Average case Running Time: It is the expected behaviour when the input is randomly drawn from a given distribution. The average-case running time of an algorithm is an estimate of the running time for an "average" input. Computation of average-case running time demands knowing all possible input sequences, the probability distribution of occurrence of these sequences, and the running times for the individual sequences. Often it is assumed that all inputs of a given size are equally likely.

Best-case running time: It is used to analyse an algorithm under optimal conditions. For example, the best case for a simple linear search on an array occurs when the desired element is the first in the list. However, while developing and choosing an algorithm to solve a problem, we hardly base our decision on the best-case performance. It is always recommended to improve the average performance and the worst-case performance of an algorithm.

For example: Time complexity of some sorting and searching algorithms

Quick sort

Worst case = $O(n^2)$

Average case = $O(n \log n)$

Merge Sort, Heap Sort

Worst case = $O(n \log n)$

Average case = $O(n \log n)$

Bubble sort

Worst case = $O(n^2)$

Average case = $O(n^2)$

Binary Search Tree: Search for an element

Worst case = $O(n)$

Average case = $O(\log n)$

1.5.1.2 Space Complexity

Space complexity of an algorithm represents the amount of memory space required by the algorithm in its life cycle. The space required by an algorithm is equal to the sum of the following two components:

- The fixed part refers to the amount of space required to store data and variables that are independent of the size of the input. This includes space for constants, simple variables, fixed-size control variables, and the program code itself.
- The variable part refers to the space required by data structures and variables whose size depends on the size of the input. This includes dynamic memory allocations, recursion stack space, and input-dependent data structures such as arrays, linked lists, etc.

Space complexity S(P) of any algorithm P is S(P) = C + SP(I), where C is the fixed part and S(I) is the variable part of the algorithm, which depends on instance characteristic I. Following is a simple example that tries to explain the concept:

Algorithm: SUM(A, B)
Step 1: START
Step 2: C ← A + B + 10
Step 3: Stop

Here we have three variables A, B, and C and one constant. Hence S(P) = 1 + 3. Now, space depends on data types of given variables and constant types and it will be multiplied accordingly.

1.6 ASYMPTOTIC NOTATIONS

When analysing the complexity of an algorithm in terms of time and space, we usually cannot provide an exact number for the time or space required. Instead, we express the complexity using standard notations, known as *Asymptotic Notations*.

When we analyse an algorithm, we often derive a formula to represent the time taken for execution or the space consumed. This may include the number of memory accesses, comparisons, temporary variables, or the total number of instructions executed. These formulas often include terms that become insignificant for large input sizes and do not meaningfully impact the overall runtime.

For example, suppose an algorithm has a time complexity expressed as:

$T(n) = n^2 + 3n + 4$

This is a quadratic expression. For large values of n, the terms $3n$ and 4 become insignificant compared to n^2.

For instance, when $n = 1000$:

- $n^2 = 1{,}000{,}000$
- $3n + 4 = 3004$

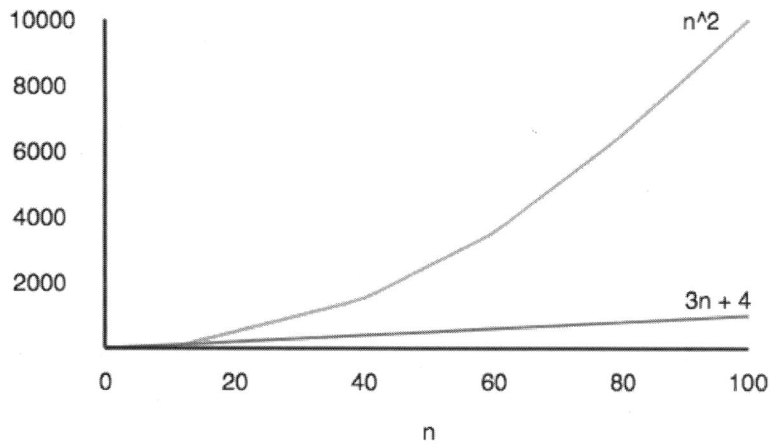

As seen above, the lower-order terms have negligible impact on the overall growth.

Moreover, when comparing the execution time of two algorithms, we also ignore the constant coefficients of the highest-order term. For example:

- An algorithm with time complexity $200n^2$ will be more efficient than one with n^3, for values of n greater than 200.

Since we are mainly concerned with the *asymptotic behaviour*—how the algorithm performs as input size approaches infinity—we ignore constants and lower-order terms.

The word asymptotic refers to behaviour that approaches a particular value or pattern arbitrarily closely, usually as a limit is approached. The main purpose of asymptotic analysis is to measure algorithmic efficiency in a way that is independent of machine-specific factors, without needing to implement the algorithm or measure actual execution time.

Asymptotic notations are mathematical tools that help represent the time or space complexity of algorithms in a standardized form for large input sizes.

1.6.1 Types of Asymptotic Notations

We use three types of asymptotic notations to represent the growth of any algorithm, as input increases:

- Theta Notation(Θ)

- Big Oh Notation(O)
- Omega Notation(Ω)

Theta Notation

The notation Θ(n) is a formal way to express both the lower bound and the upper bound of an algorithm's running time. It defines the exact asymptotic behavior of a function, meaning the algorithm grows at the same rate in both best and worst cases (within constant factors).

A simple way to find the Theta notation of a function is to drop the lower-order terms and ignore leading constants. For example, consider the following expression:

$3n^3 + 6n^2 + 6000 = \Theta(n^3)$

Dropping lower-order terms is justified because, beyond a certain input size (n_0), the highest-order term dominates the growth of the function. In other words, there will always be a value of n_0 such that:

$\Theta(n^3) > \Theta(n^2)$

regardless of the constant multipliers involved.

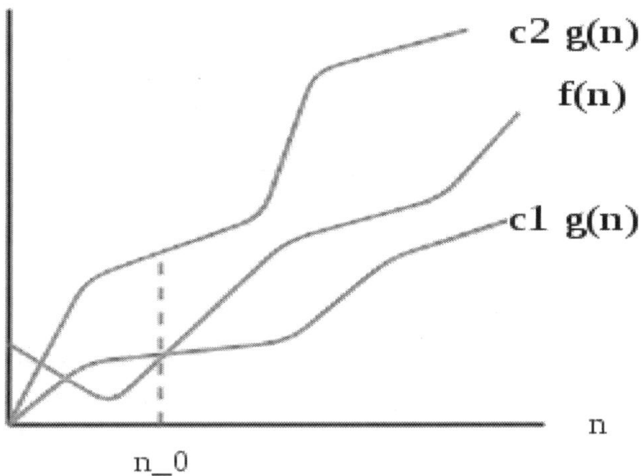

f(n) = theta(g(n))

Formally, for a given function *g(n)*, the set of functions that belong to Θ(g(n)) is defined as:

Θ(g(n))={f(n): there exist positive constants c1,c2, and n0 such that

$$0 \le c1 \cdot g(n) \le f(n) \le c2 \cdot g(n) \text{ for all } n \ge n0\}$$

This definition ensures that *f(n)* grows asymptotically at the same rate as *g(n)*, bounded both above and below by constant multiples.

Big O Notation

The notation O(n) is the formal way to express the upper bound of an algorithm's running time. It measures the worst-case time complexity, representing the maximum amount of time an algorithm can possibly take to complete.

For example, consider the case of Insertion Sort.

- In the best case, it takes linear time: $\Theta(n)$.
- In the worst case, it takes quadratic time: $\Theta(n^2)$.

Therefore, we can safely say that the time complexity of Insertion Sort is $O(n^2)$, as this notation covers all lower growth rates as well (including linear time).

If we use Θ (Theta) notation to represent the time complexity of Insertion Sort, we must specify both best and worst cases separately:

- Best case time complexity: $\Theta(n)$
- Worst case time complexity: $\Theta(n^2)$

The Big O notation is especially useful when we want to describe an upper bound on the time complexity of an algorithm. Often, we can determine an upper bound just by examining the structure of the algorithm.

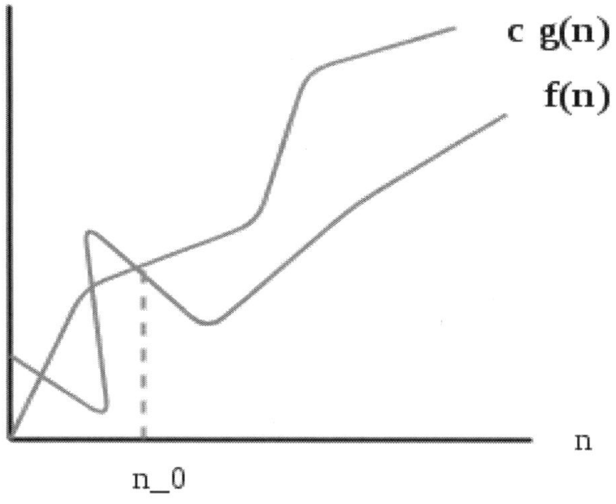

f(n) = O(g(n))

The formal definition of Big O is:

$O(g(n))=\{f(n)$: there exist positive constants c and n0 such that

$$0 \le f(n) \le c \cdot g(n) \text{ for all } n \ge n0\}$$

This means that f(n) does not grow faster than g(n) beyond a certain point, up to a constant factor.

Omega Notation

The notation $\Omega(n)$ is the formal way to express the lower bound of an algorithm's running time. It measures the best-case time complexity, or the minimum amount of time an algorithm can possibly take to complete.

Just as Big O notation provides an asymptotic upper bound on a function, Ω notation provides an asymptotic lower bound.

Ω notation can be useful when we want to establish a lower bound on the time complexity of an algorithm. However, it is the least commonly used among the three major asymptotic notations (Big

O, Theta, and Omega), as we are often more concerned with worst-case performance.

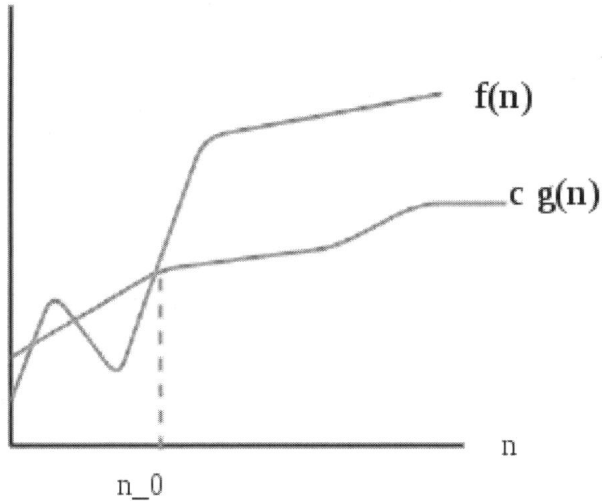

f(n) = Omega(g(n))

For a given function g(n), we denote Ω(g(n)) as the set of functions:

$\Omega(g(n))=\{f(n)$: there exist positive constants c and n0 such that

$$0 \le c \cdot g(n) \le f(n) \text{ for all } n \ge n0\}$$

This means that f(n) grows at least as fast as g(n) for sufficiently large values of n, up to a constant factor.

1.7 LET US SUM UP

- Data structure is the structural representation of the logical relationship existing between individual elements of data.
- Data structure is categorized into two broad categories: Primitive Data Structures and Non-Primitive Data Structures
- Primitive Data Structures are the basic data structures that directly operate upon the machine instructions.
- Non-primitive data structures are more sophisticated data structures and are derived from primitive data structures.
- Non-primitive data structures are categorized into linear and non-linear data structures.
- In linear Data Structures data items are organized sequentially or linearly.
- The data structures where data items are not organized sequentially are called non linear data structures. The data elements stored in such data structures cannot be accessed in a sequential or linear order.
- An array is a collection of similar data elements which are stored in consecutive memory locations.
- A linked list is a linear data structure consisting of a group of elements (called nodes) which together represent a sequence.

- A stack is a last-in, first-out (LIFO) data structure in which insertion and deletion of elements are done at only one end, which is known as the top of the stack.
- A queue is a first-in, first-out (FIFO) data structure in which the element that is inserted first is the first to be taken out. The elements in a queue are added at one end called the rear and removed from the other end called the front.
- A tree is a non-linear data structure which consists of a collection of nodes arranged in a hierarchical tree structure.
- A graph is often viewed as a generalization of the tree structure, where instead of a purely parent-to-child relationship between tree nodes, any kind of complex relationships can exist between the nodes.
- Selecting the correct data structure ensures efficient data access, optimal memory usage, and improved performance based on application requirements.
- Selecting the right data structure depends on access speed, memory efficiency, update frequency, scalability, and application-specific operations for optimal performance.
- An algorithm is defined as a step-by-step procedure or method for solving a problem.
- The time complexity of an algorithm is basically the running time of the program as a function of the input size.
- The space complexity of an algorithm is the amount of computer memory required during the program execution as a function of the input size.
- The worst-case running time of an algorithm is an upper bound on the running time for any input.
- The average-case running time specifies the expected behaviour of the algorithm when the input is randomly drawn from a given distribution.
- The time and space required by a algorithm, is expressed in a standard notation, known as Asymptotic Notations.
- There are three types of asymptotic notations: Theta Notation, Big Oh Notation and Omega Notation.
- The notation Θ (n) is the formal way to express both the lower bound and the upper bound of an algorithm's running time.
- The notation $O(n)$ is the formal way to express the upper bound of an algorithm's running time.
- The notation $\Omega(n)$ is the formal way to express the lower bound of an algorithm's running time.

1.8 CHECK YOUR PROGRESS

1. Define data structures. Give some examples.
2. What are the ways we can categorize data structures? Explain each of them.
3. What are the ways we can categorize non primitive data structures? Explain each of them.
4. Discuss the applications of data structures.

5. Write a short note on different operations that can be performed on data structures.
6. Make a comparative analysis on array and linked list.
7. Explain the different types of data structures. Also discuss their merits and demerits.
8. What are the important components of a graph.
9. What are the factors influencing the selection of an appropriate data structure.
10. Define an algorithm. Explain its features.
11. Explain the characteristics of a good algorithm.
12. Write an algorithm to find the smallest of two numbers.
13. Explain the criteria that you will keep in mind while choosing an appropriate algorithm to solve a particular problem.
14. What are the stages where efficiency of an algorithm can be analyzed?
15. What are the factors that decide efficiency of an algorithm?
16. What do you understand by the efficiency of an algorithm?
17. How will you express the time complexity of a given algorithm?
18. What are asymptotic notations?
19. Discuss the significance of the Big O notation.
20. Discuss the best case, worst case and average case of an algorithm.

2

ARRAY

2.1 INTRODUCTION

Before studying array, readers should have a brief knowledge on variable. A variable is a type of memory container where we can store our data. A single variable allows us to store a single value at a time. If we want to store the roll no. of a single student then we do it by declaring a variable. But what if we want to store roll no. of 20 students? To do this, we need to declare 20 variables. The situation will be trickier if we are asked to store roll no. of 100 or 1000 or more students. As you can see declaring so many variables for a single entity is not easy and sometimes we may fall short of combinations for variable names. Also accessing all those variables for different purposes is also not an easy job. In such a situation array provide a better way to store data.

Array is basically an abstract data type which is linear in nature. Arrays are broadly classified in two categories:

a) One dimensional array

b) Multi dimensional array

Arrays are very easy to implement. But, insertion and deletion operations of data are very time consuming because it requires lot of shifting activities. Therefore, arrays are used for storing data that are permanent in nature, which means there is less insertion and deletion operation.

2.1.1 Array Definition

An array is a finite list of homogeneous elements stored in contiguous memory blocks.

By finite list we mean that the list should have limited n number of elements which is predefined. By homogeneous we mean that all the elements of the list should have same data type. More precise, we cannot accommodate integer data, floating point data, character data, etc. on the same list. If the array is declared as integer, we can only store integer data in that list. We can have separate list for separate data types. By contiguous we mean that the data or elements in the list will be stored in successive or adjacent memory blocks.

For simplicity or for the ease of keeping track of adjacent memory blocks of an array we assume that each element of the array is referenced by an index value. Therefore an array of n elements will also have a set of n index values respectively. Index number is always an integer value as it designates the location of a data in the memory (though not physical location). Thus a list of n numbers will have a corresponding set of index values which are referenced as 1,2,3,4,5......,n. From all these discussions we can conclude that index of a particular element in an array is its relative position in that array.

2.1.2 Properties of an array

Let's sum up the properties of arrays as:

- An array can store n number of elements i.e. length of an array is predefined and static.
- An array can store homogeneous data i.e. data belonging to same data type.
- The elements of an array are stored in contiguous memory blocks i.e. in adjacent memory blocks.
- Each element of an array is referenced by an index value, i.e. a list of n elements will have a corresponding set of n index values.

2.1.3 Length of an array

Length or size of an array is the number of elements present in that particular array. Thus, if an array has 10 elements than the length or size of that array is also 10. If the list is small then, we can find the length by physical verification also. But if the list is large enough then by physical verification it would be difficult for us to determine its length. In general the length is calculated by the following formula:

Length = UB – LB + 1

Where UB or upper bound is the largest or the last index value and LB or lower bound is the smallest or the first index value.

A one-dimensional or 1D array is represented as: A[N]

Where A is the name of the array and N is the number of elements present in that list.

If we want to represent the array A in terms of its index values, than it will be represented as:

A[1], A[2], A[3],A[4],.........,A[N]

Or

$A_1, A_2, A_3, A_4, \ldots\ldots\ldots\ldots, A_N$

Suppose A is an array of 10 elements than it will be represented as A[10].

The above example means that the array A has 10 elements which can be represented as:

A[1], A[2], A[3], A[4], A[5], A[6], A[7], A[8], A[9], A[10]

Or

$A_1, A_2, A_3, A_4, A_5, A_6, A_7, A_8, A_9, A_{10}$

Example 1: The lower bound of an array 'A' is 2013 and the upper bound of the array is 3114. Find the length of the array.

Solution: LB = 2013, UB = 3114

Length = UB – LB + 1

= 3114 – 2013 + 1

= 1102

Therefore, the length of the array = 1102. That is, the array 'A' contains 1102 elements.

2.1.4 Declaration of one-dimensional array

We can declare a one-dimensional array in C/C++ as:

data_type array_name[size]

Here data_type means the type of the data such as int, char, float, etc.

Array_name means the name of the array. Size is the number of elements or data the array can hold.

For example: A one-dimensional array or simply array is declared as: int X[10];

Here are some more examples of array declarations:

int A[50];

float sum[80];

char name[100];

Here, A is an array of type int, which can only store 50 elements of type int.

sum is an array of type float, which can store 80 elements of type float.

name is an array of type char, which can only store 100 elements of type char.

The individual elements in these arrays would be:

A[0], A[1], A[2],............., A[49]

sum[0], sum[1], sum[2],..............., sum[79]

name[0], name[1], name[2],................, name[99]

2.1.5 Accessing the elements of an array

The elements of an array can be accessed by specifying the name of the array followed by its subscript, which is its index written inside square brackets (*i.e* []). Array subscript or index starts at 0 or 1. If the size of an array is 10 then the first element is at index 0, while the last element is at index 9. The first subscript is its lower bound, while last subscript is its upper bound.

For example, in the array int student[10]; there will 10 elements starting from subscript or index 0 to 9. Array subscript or index is always an integer value.

To assign a value to a particular location of the array, we use its index value.

For example: student [3] = 56;

To read a value of an array stored in a particular index, we use the following statement:

cout << student[3] << endl; // 4th element of the array

In the array student, the last element is at student[9]. Now if we try to access elements beyond the last valid index of the array, what will happen?

```
cout << student[10] << endl;  // Accessing out-of-bounds index
cout << student[20] << endl;  // Accessing out-of-bounds index
cout << student[-1] << endl;  // Accessing negative index (invalid)
cout << student[-11] << endl; // Accessing negative index (invalid)
```

Indexes 10, 20,-1 and -11 are not valid index values of the array student. But when we run the program, C compiler will not show any error message, instead some garbage value will be printed.

The C language doesn't check bounds of the array. It is the responsibility of the programmer to check array bounds whenever required.

Example 2: The following program shows how to read and write array elements in C++ language.

```
#include <iostream>
using namespace std;

int main() {
  int A[10]; // Declare an array of size 10

  cout << "Input elements of the array: " << endl;

  // Taking input from the user
  for (int i = 0; i < 10; i++) {
    cout << "Enter A[" << i << "]: ";
    cin >> A[i];
  }

  cout << "\nPrint the elements of the array: \n\n";

  // Displaying the elements of the array
  for (int i = 0; i < 10; i++) {
    cout << A[i] << " ";
  }

  cout << endl;
  return 0;
}
```

Output :

```
Input elements of the array:
Enter A[0]: 2
Enter A[1]: 3
Enter A[2]: 5
Enter A[3]: 12
Enter A[4]: 45
```

Enter A[5]: 56

Enter A[6]: 78

Enter A[7]: 23

Enter A[8]: 47

Enter A[9]: 10

Print the elements of the array:

2 3 5 12 45 56 78 23 47 10

2.2 LINEAR ARRAY AND MEMORY REPRESENTATION

Computer's memory is partitioned into smaller units called memory cells. For simplicity each memory cell is referenced by a number which uniquely defines the cell and is known as memory address. The address of a particular element(A[i]) of an array(A) will be the memory location(Loc A[i]) where it is stored.

Loc(A[i]) = address of the element A[i] in the array A

We can represent an array (int A[10]) diagrammatically also as:

207	301	23	12	0	456	111	890	999	123
A_1	A_2	A_3	A_4	A_5	A_6	A_7	A_8	A_9	A_{10}

Base Address

The address of the first location (A_1) of an array is known as ***base address*** of an array. We can start an array with index 1 or 0. It is not possible to remember addresses of all the elements of an array especially when the array is very large. But if we know the base address of the array than we can keep track or find out the address of all other elements of the array. The name of an array is a symbolic reference to the address of the first element of the array. Therefore, whenever we use the array name, we are actually referring to the first element of that array.

The formula for finding out the address of any element of an array A with the help of base address is as follows:

Address of element A[k] = B + W (K – lower_bound)

Where B is the base address of the array, W is the storage size of each element stored in the array (in byte)and K is the index value of the required element in the array.

Example 3: An array is given as A[ ] = {89, 34, 60, 12, 90, 54, 78}, calculate the address of A[3]. The base address is given as 2000 and each element occupies 2 bytes of memory space.

Solution: The elements of the array A can be represented as:

89	34	60	12	90	54	78
A[0]	A[1]	A[2]	**A[3]**	A[4]	A[5]	A[6]
2000	2002	2004	**2006**	2008	2010	2012

Address of element A[k] = B + W (K – lower_bound)

A[3] = 2000 + 2 (3 – 0)

= 2000 + 6

= 2006

Therefore, the address of A[3] = 2006

2.3 OPERATIONS ON ONE-DIMENSIONAL ARRAY

There are a number of operations that can be performed on an array (as discussed in chapter 1). Some of these operations are the following:

- Traversing an array
- Searching an element in an array
- Inserting an element in an array
- Deleting an element from an array

2.3.1 Traversing an array

Traversing an array means accessing each and every element of the list exactly once and processing it, starting from the first element of the list upto the end of the list. While traversing, starting from the first element of the list, each element is visited once and processed, till the last element of the array. Suppose we want to print the elements of a list or want to count the number of elements present in a list, in such conditions we traverse the list or apply traversing algorithm.

Algorithm for traversal of array: Here 'A' is a linear array. 'LB' is the lower bound and 'UB' is the upper bound.'PROCESSS' is the operation that is applied to each element of the array.

Step 1: [Initialize counter] Set i = LB

Step 2: Repeat steps 3 and 4 while i <=UB

Step 3: [Visit element] Apply PROCESS to A[i]

Step 4: [Increment counter] Set i = i + 1

[End of step 2 loop]

Step 5: Exit

To be more precise with the operation PROCESS, let us redo the above algorithm where PROCESS is the display operation of each and every element of the list.

Step 1: [Initialize counter] Set i = LB

Step 2: Repeat steps 3 and 4 while i <=UB

Step 3: [Visit element] Display A[i]

Step 4: [Increment counter] Set i = i + 1

[End of step 2 loop]

Step 5: Exit

Let us consider the following array to explain the algorithm better.

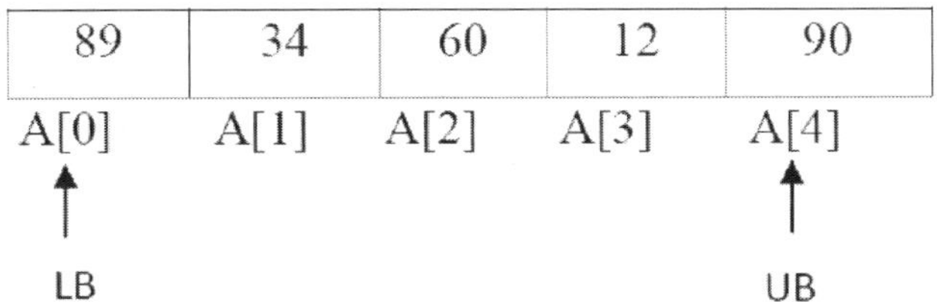

In step1, counter variable 'i' is set to the lower bound (LB). In step2, while loop is taken to set the condition of traversal. The elements will be traversed starting from the first cell (LB) to the last cell (UB). In step3 the data of each visited cell is displayed. In step4 the counter variable 'i' is incremented to go to the next node.

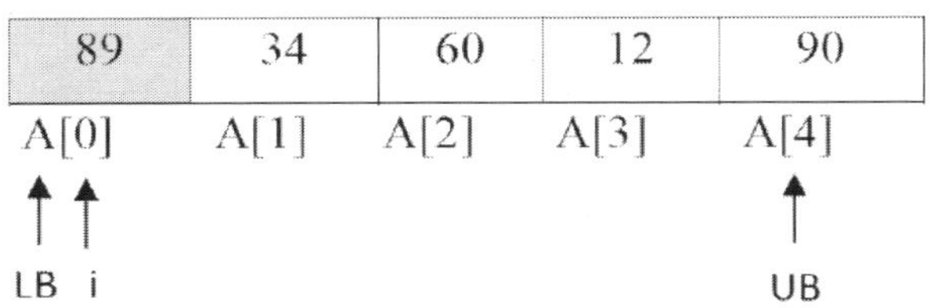

Here i <=UB, so A[0] element is displayed and i is incremented to go to the next element of the array.

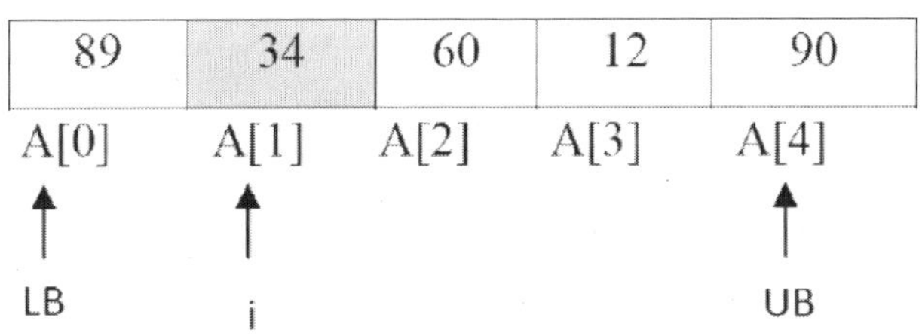

Here i <=UB, so A[1] element is displayed and i is incremented to go to the next element of the array.

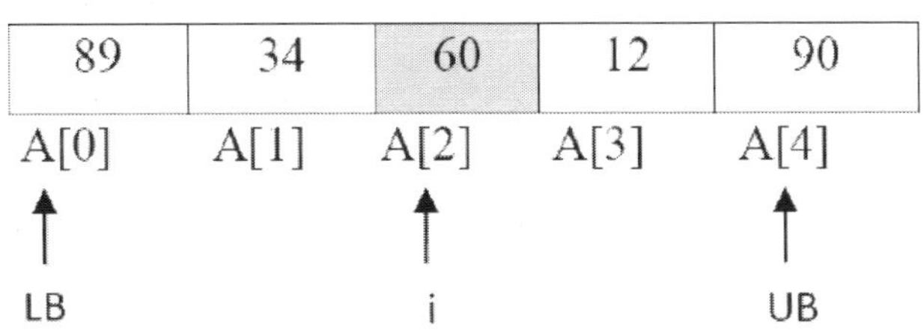

Here i <=UB, so A[2] element is displayed and i is incremented to go to the next element of the array.

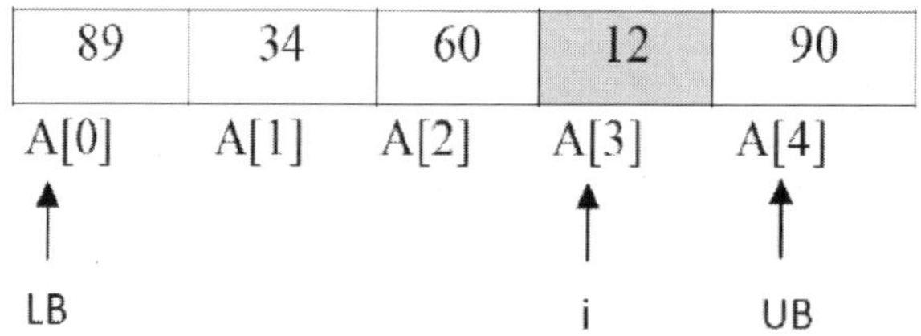

Here i <=UB, so A[3] element is displayed and i is incremented to go to the next element of the array.

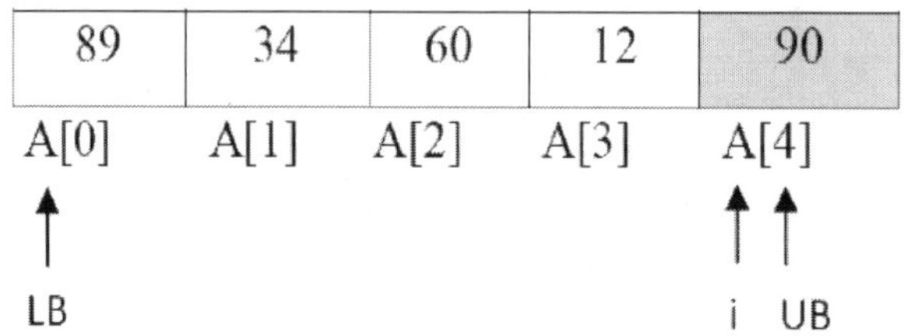

Here i <=UB, so A[4] element is displayed and i is incremented. But after incrementing i the while loop condition will be false. So, the control will come out of the loop.

Example 4: The following program shows how to traverse array elements in C++ language.

```
#include <iostream>
using namespace std;

void traverseArray(int A[], int LB, int UB) {
  int i = LB; // Step 1: Initialize counter

  while (i <= UB) { // Step 2: Repeat while i <= UB
    cout << A[i] << " "; // Step 3: Visit element (Display A[i])
    i++; // Step 4: Increment counter
  }

  cout << endl; // Step 5: Exit
}

int main() {
  int n;

  // Asking the user for array size
  cout << "Enter the number of elements in the array: ";
  cin >> n;
  int A[n]; // Declare array
```

```
    // Taking user input for array elements
    cout << "Enter " << n << " elements: ";
    for (int i = 0; i < n; i++) {
        cin >> A[i];
    }

    int LB = 0, UB = n - 1; // Lower and Upper Bound

    cout << "Array elements: ";
    traverseArray(A, LB, UB); // Call the traversal function

    return 0;
}
```

Output :

Enter the number of elements in the array: 5

Enter 5 elements: 2 3 5 6 7

Array elements: 2 3 5 6 7

2.3.2 Searching an element in an array

Searching refers to the operation of finding whether a particular element is present in the list or not. There are several types of searching algorithms. Which algorithm is to be applied on a particular data set depends on the arrangement of the data. In this section we are going to discuss one of the simplest and common type of searching algorithm known as linear search or sequential search. Searching in details will be discussed later in chapter 8.

Linear Search

In this operation the key element (the element to be searched) is compared with all other elements of the list sequentially starting from the first location till the end of the list. If the key element is present anywhere in the list, than the search is said to be successful and the location in which the element is present is displayed or printed. If the key element is not present till the end of the list, than the search is said to be unsuccessful.

Suppose we have a linear array A with n elements and we have to search whether the element 'key' is present in the list or not. If no other conditions are given than we simply apply the simplest algorithm of searching, that is linear search.

Algorithm of Linear Search: Here 'A' is a linear array with 'n' elements. 'Key' is the given item to be searched. This algorithm finds whether the key is present in the list or not. If the key item is present then this algorithm finds the location 'loc' of the key in the linear array A. And sets loc = 0 if the key item is not present in the list.

Step 1: [Initialize counter] Set loc = -1

Step 2: [Initialize counter] Set i = 1

Step 3: [Search for item] Repeat step 4 while i < = n - 1

Step 4: If A [i] = Key

Set loc = i

Print loc

Go to step 6

[End of If]

[Increment counter] Set i = i + 1

[End of step 3 loop]

Step 5: If loc == -1

Print "Search is unsuccessful"

[End of If]

Step 6: Exit

Let us consider the following array to explain the algorithm better. Suppose the key element to be searched is 12.

89	34	60	12	90
A[0]	A[1]	A[2]	A[3]	A[4]
↑ i				

Here i < = n - 1, so A[0] element is compared with the key, which is 12. Since there is no match so, the counter 'i' is incremented to go to the next element of the array.

89	34	60	12	90
A[0]	A[1]	A[2]	A[3]	A[4]
	↑ i			

Here i < = n - 1, so A[1] element is compared with the key, which is 12. Since there is no match so, the counter 'i' is incremented to go to the next element of the array.

89	34	60	12	90
A[0]	A[1]	A[2]	A[3]	A[4]
		↑ i		

Here i < = n - 1, so A[2] element is compared with the key, which is 12. Since there is no match so, the counter 'i' is incremented to go to the next element of the array.

89	34	60	12	90
A[0]	A[1]	A[2]	A[3]	A[4]

↑
i

Here i < = n - 1, so A[3] element is compared with the key, which is 12. Since there is a match so, the value of counter 'i' is the location of the desired element, which is displayed.

Example 5: The following C++ program shows the implementation of linear search in an array.

```
#include <iostream>
using namespace std;

void searchElement(int A[], int n, int Key) {
  int loc = -1; // Step 1: Initialize loc
  int i = 0;   // Step 2: Initialize counter

  // Step 3: Search for the item
  while (i <= n - 1) {
    if (A[i] == Key) { // Step 4: If found
      loc = i;
      cout << "Element found at index: " << loc << endl;
      return; // Exit after finding the element
    }
    i++; // Increment counter
  }

  // Step 5: If loc is still -1, search is unsuccessful
  if (loc == -1) {
    cout << "Search is unsuccessful." << endl;
  }
}

int main() {
  int n, Key;
  cout << "Enter number of elements in the array: ";
  cin >> n;
```

```
    int A[n];

    cout << "Enter " << n << " elements:\n";
    for (int i = 0; i < n; i++) {
        cin >> A[i];
    }

    cout << "Enter the element to search: ";
    cin >> Key;

    searchElement(A, n, Key);

    return 0; // Ensure the program exits properly
}
```

Output:

Enter number of elements in the array: 5

Enter 5 elements:

2 4 5 6 7

Enter the element to search: 6

Element found at index: 3

Binary Search

In this operation, the key element (the element to be searched) is compared with the middle element of the sorted list. If the key is found, the search is successful, and the location of the key is displayed. Otherwise, the list is divided into two halves, and the search continues in the appropriate half. This process repeats until the key is found or the list is exhausted.

Algorithm for binary search: Here A is a sorted linear array with n elements. Key is the given item to be searched. This algorithm finds whether the key is present in the list or not. If the key item is present, the algorithm finds the location loc of the key in the linear array A. It sets loc = -1 if the key item is not present in the list.

Step 1: [Initialize search space]
Set low = 0, high = n - 1, loc = -1.

Step 2: [Start searching]
Repeat Step 3 while low ≤ high

Step 3:

Compute mid = (low + high) / 2.

If A[mid] = Key, set loc = mid, print loc, and Go to Step 6.

Else if A[mid] > Key, set high = mid - 1.

Else set low = mid + 1.

[End of Step 2 loop]

Step 4: If loc = -1, print "Search is unsuccessful".

Step 5: Exit.

The algorithm begins by initializing three variables: low, which represents the first index of the array, high, which represents the last index, and loc, which is set to -1 initially and will store the index of the target element if found. The search process continues as long as low is less than or equal to high. At each step, the middle index (mid) of the current search space is calculated using the formula (low + high) / 2. The element at this index (A[mid]) is then compared with the target value (Key). If A[mid] matches the key, the element is found, loc is updated with mid, and the search terminates. However, if A[mid] is greater than the key, it means the target must be in the left half of the array, so high is updated to mid - 1, effectively eliminating the right half from further consideration. Conversely, if A[mid] is smaller than the key, then the search continues in the right half by updating low to mid + 1. This process of halving the search space continues until either the key is found or low becomes greater than high, indicating that the element is not present in the array. If the search completes without finding the key, loc remains -1, and the program prints "Search is unsuccessful", signaling that the element does not exist in the given array. Finally, the algorithm exits, having either successfully located the element or confirmed its absence.

Let us consider the following array to explain the algorithm better. Suppose the key element to be searched is 12.

89	34	60	12	90
A[0]	A[1]	A[2]	A[3]	A[4]

First the array will be sorted in ascending order.

12	34	60	89	90
A[0]	A[1]	A[2]	A[3]	A[4]

↑ low ↑ high

Initially, low = 0 and high = 4 . So, mid (0+4)/2 = 2. A[2] = 60 is the mid element

12	34	60	89	90
A[0]	A[1]	A[2]	A[3]	A[4]

↑ low ↑ mid ↑ high

As, key = 12 and 12< 60 i.e key < A[mid] , so search in the left subarray. Update high = mid - 1 = 1.
Now, low = 0, high = 1

12	34	60	89	90
A[0]	A[1]	A[2]	A[3]	A[4]
↑ low	↑ high			

Now, mid = (0+1)/2 = 0. A[0] = 12 which matches the key 12. So, the key is found at index 0 which binary search algorithm will return.

12	34	60	89	90
A[0]	A[1]	A[2]	A[3]	A[4]
↑ mid				

Example 6: The following C++ program shows the implementation of binary search in an array.

```
#include <iostream>
using namespace std;
int binarySearch(int arr[], int n, int key) {
  int low = 0, high = n - 1, mid, loc = -1;

  while (low <= high) {
    mid = (low + high) / 2;

    if (arr[mid] == key) {
      loc = mid;
      return loc; // Key found, return index
    }
    else if (arr[mid] > key) {
      high = mid - 1; // Search in the left half
    }
    else {
      low = mid + 1; // Search in the right half
    }
  }
  return loc; // Key not found
}
```

```
int main() {
  int n, key;

  // Input array size
  cout << "Enter the number of elements: ";
  cin >> n;
  int arr[n];
  // Input sorted array
  cout << "Enter " << n << " sorted elements: ";
  for (int i = 0; i < n; i++) {
    cin >> arr[i];
  }
  // Input key to search
  cout << "Enter the key to search: ";
  cin >> key;
  // Perform binary search
  int result = binarySearch(arr, n, key);
  // Display result
  if (result != -1)
    cout << "Element found at index: " << result << endl;
  else
    cout << "Search is unsuccessful. Element not found." << endl;
  return 0;
}
```

Output :

Enter the number of elements: 7

Enter 7 sorted elements: 2 4 5 7 8 9 10

Enter the key to search: 5

Element found at index: 2

2.3.3 Insertion in an array

Insertion operation refers to adding a new element to an existing array. While inserting a new element to an existing array, we assume that the array has enough space to accommodate a new item. Suppose an array is declared as A[10], that means the array A can accommodate 10 elements and at present it is holding 8 elements, then it is obvious that there are 2 locations that are free and can accommodate 2 more elements. But if the same array is already holding 10 elements than any additional element cannot be inserted as there is no space. If it tries to do so it will be an overflow condition.

When we insert a new element in an existing array two situations may arise:

1. We may like to add a new element at the beginning of the list.
2. We may like to add a new element at the end of the list.
3. We may like to add a new element at any desired location.

To insert an element at the beginning of an array, first check if it's full; if not, shift all elements one position to the right, place the new element at index 0, increment the array size, and exit. Insertion at the end of the list is very easy and simple. If there is enough space in the existing array, than we just have to increment the size of the counter by 1 and insert the new item in that location. But if we like to add a new element at any desired location such as the first location or any other location in the middle than we have to shift all the elements from the desired location towards right by one position to make space to insert the new element.

Let us assume an array A[10] which is stored as:

12	54	6	10	86	89	30	77		
A_1	A_2	A_3	A_4	A_5	A_6	A_7	A_8		

In the above array if we want to add a new item 50 at the end of the list i.e. at the 9th position it is very simple and easy. We just need to increment the size of the array by 1. New size of the array is 9, now insert the item 50 at the 9th location.

So the new array will be:

12	54	6	10	86	89	30	77	50	
A_1	A_2	A_3	A_4	A_5	A_6	A_7	A_8	A_9	

There is still one location free in the array A and we can insert one more element. Suppose we want to insert the new element 199 in 4th location which is already occupied. In such a situation we have to vacate the 4th position by shifting all the elements from the 4th position towards its right by 1 position.

12	54	6		10	86	89	30	77	50
A_1	A_2	A_3	A_4	A_5	A_6	A_7	A_8	A_9	A_{10}

Now as the desired location (in this case 4th position) is empty, so we can insert a new element in that location.

12	54	6	**199**	10	86	89	30	77	50
A_1	A_2	A_3	A_4	A_5	A_6	A_7	A_8	A_9	A_{10}

Algorithm to insert a new element at the beginning of the list: Here 'A' is a linear array with 'n' elements. 'Item' is the new element that is to be inserted in the list.

Step 1: If the array is full, exit.
Step 2: Shift all elements one position to the right (A[i] = A[i - 1] for i = n to 1).
Step 3: Insert the new element at A[0] = item.

Step 4: Set n = n + 1.
Step 5: Exit.

Example 7: The following C++ program shows insertion of a new element at the beginning of an array.

```
#include <iostream>
using namespace std;
void insertAtBeginning(int A[], int &n, int item, int capacity) {
  if (n >= capacity) {
    cout << "Array is full. Cannot insert." << endl;
    return;
  }
  // Shift elements right
  for (int i = n; i > 0; i--) {
    A[i] = A[i - 1];
  }
  // Insert the new element at the first position
  A[0] = item;
  // Increase the size of the array
  n++;
  cout << "Updated array: ";
  for (int i = 0; i < n; i++) {
    cout << A[i] << " ";
  }
  cout << endl;
}
int main() {
  int A[10], n, item, capacity = 10;
  cout << "Enter the number of elements in the array: ";
  cin >> n;
  if (n > capacity) {
    cout << "Array size exceeds capacity!" << endl;
    return 1;
  }
  cout << "Enter " << n << " elements:" << endl;
  for (int i = 0; i < n; i++) {
```

```
        cout << "A[" << i << "]: ";
        cin >> A[i];
    }

    cout << "Enter the element to insert at the beginning: ";
    cin >> item;
    insertAtBeginning(A, n, item, capacity);
    return 0;
}
```

Output:

Enter the number of elements in the array: 4

Enter 4 elements:

A[0]: 12

A[1]: 23

A[2]: 45

A[3]: 56

Enter the element to insert at the beginning: 100

Updated array: 100 12 23 45 56

Algorithm to insert a new element at the end of the list: Here 'A' is a linear array with 'n' elements. 'Item' is the new element that is to be inserted in the list.

Step 1: Set n = n + 1

Step 2: Set A [n - 1] = item

Step 3: Exit

Example 8: The following C++ program shows insertion of a new element at the end of an array.

```
#include <iostream>
using namespace std;
int main() {
    int n; // Current number of elements
    cout << "Enter the number of elements in the array: ";
    cin >> n;

    int A[100]; // Define an array with a maximum capacity of 100
```

```
    // Input existing elements
    cout << "Enter " << n << " elements:" << endl;
    for (int i = 0; i < n; i++) {
        cout << "A[" << i << "]: ";
        cin >> A[i];
    }

    // Inserting a new element at the end
    int item;
    cout << "Enter the new element to insert at the end: ";
    cin >> item;

    // Step 1: Increase the size
    n = n + 1;

    // Step 2: Insert the new element at the last position
    A[n - 1] = item;

    // Display the updated array
    cout << "\nArray after insertion: ";
    for (int i = 0; i < n; i++) {
        cout << A[i] << " ";
    }
    cout << endl;
    return 0;
}
```

Output :

```
Enter the number of elements in the array: 5
Enter 5 elements:
A[0]: 12
A[1]: 23
A[2]: 45
A[3]: 56
A[4]: 78
```

Enter the new element to insert at the end: 10

Array after insertion: 12 23 45 56 78 10

Algorithm to insert a new element at any desired location: Here 'A' is a linear array with 'n'elements. 'Item' is the new element that is to be inserted in the list. 'Loc' is the position at which a new element item is to be inserted.

Step 1: [Initialize counter] Set i = n

Step 2: Repeat steps 3 and 4 while i >= loc

Step 3: Set A [i + 1] = A [i]

Step 4: Set i = i - 1

[End of step 2 loop]

Step 5: Set n = n + 1

Step 6: Set A [loc] = item

Step 7: Exit

Example 9: The following C++ program shows insertion of a new element at a desired location of an array.

```
#include <iostream>
using namespace std;
int main() {
   int n, loc, item;
   // Input array size
   cout << "Enter the number of elements in the array: ";
   cin >> n;

   int A[100]; // Define an array with a maximum capacity of 100

   // Input existing elements
   cout << "Enter " << n << " elements:\n";
   for (int i = 0; i < n; i++) {
      cout << "A[" << i << "]: ";
      cin >> A[i];
   }

   // Input the new element to be inserted
   cout << "Enter the element to insert: ";
   cin >> item;
```

```
    // Input position to insert (0-based index)
    cout << "Enter the position (0 to " << n << ") where you want to insert: ";
    cin >> loc;

    // Validate position
    if (loc < 0 || loc > n) {
        cout << "Invalid position! Exiting program." << endl;
        return 1;
    }

    // Step 1: Shift elements to the right
    for (int i = n; i > loc; i--) {
        A[i] = A[i - 1];
    }

    // Step 2: Insert new element at the desired location
    A[loc] = item;

    // Step 3: Increase the size
    n++;

    // Display the updated array
    cout << "\nArray after insertion: ";
    for (int i = 0; i < n; i++) {
        cout << A[i] << " ";
    }
    cout << endl;
    return 0;
}
```

Output :

Enter the number of elements in the array: 5

Enter 5 elements:

A[0]: 12

A[1]: 34

A[2]: 56

A[3]: 67

A[4]: 10

Enter the element to insert: 100

Enter the position (0 to 5) where you want to insert: 2

Array after insertion: 12 34 100 56 67 10

2.3.4 Deletion from an array

Deletion operation refers to the operation of removing elements from an already existing array. Just like insertion operation, deletion operation also involves a lot of shifting.

When we delete a new element from an existing array these situations may arise:

4. We may like to delete an element from the beginning of the list.
5. We may like to delete an element from the end of the list.
6. We may like to delete an element from any desired location.

To delete an element from the beginning of the list, shift all elements one position to the left to overwrite the first element, then decrease the size of the array by one, effectively removing the first element. Deletion from the end of the list is very easy and simple. We simply decrement the size of the list by 1. But deletion of an element from a desired position is tricky and involves lots of shifting operations.

Let us assume an array A[10] which is stored as:

12	54	6	10	86	89	30	77	50		
A_1	A_2	A_3	A_4	A_5	A_6	A_7	A_8	A_9		

In the above array if we want to delete the last item (item = 50) i.e. item stored at at the 9th position, it is very simple and easy. We just need to decrement the size of the array by 1. New size of the array is 8, as we have deleted the item 50 stored at the 9th location.

So, the new array will be:

12	54	6	10	86	89	30	77		
A_1	A_2	A_3	A_4	A_5	A_6	A_7	A_8		

Suppose we want to delete the element stored at the 6th location. If we delete the element 89 stored in the 6th location than a vacant space will be created at that location.

12	54	6	10	86		30	77		
A_1	A_2	A_3	A_4	A_5	A_6	A_7	A_8		

As we know that, array is a continuous block of data, so there cannot be any vacant slot inside the array. In such a situation we have to fill up the vacate slot by shifting all the elements stored towards the right of the deleted element by 1 position towards its left.

12	54	6	10	86	30	77			
A_1	A_2	A_3	A_4	A_5	A_6	A_7	A_8	A_9	A_{10}

Algorithm to delete an element from the beginning of the list: Here 'A' is a linear array with 'n' elements.

Step 1: If n == 0, exit.

Step 2 : Shift elements left: A[i] = A[i + 1] for i = 0 to n - 2.

Step 3 : Set n = n - 1.

Step 4: Exit.

Example 10: The following C++ program shows deletion of an element from the beginning of an array.

```
#include <iostream>
using namespace std;
void deleteFromBeginning(int A[], int &n) {
  if (n == 0) {
    cout << "Array is empty. Cannot delete." << endl;
    return;
  }
  // Shift elements left
  for (int i = 0; i < n - 1; i++) {
    A[i] = A[i + 1];
  }

  // Reduce size
  n--;

  cout << "\nArray after deleting the first element: ";
  for (int i = 0; i < n; i++) {
    cout << A[i] << " ";
  }
  cout << endl;
}

int main() {
  int n;

  cout << "Enter the number of elements in the array: ";
  cin >> n;
```

```
    if (n <= 0 || n > 100) {
        cout << "Invalid array size!" << endl;
        return 0;
    }

    int A[100]; // Array declaration

    cout << "Enter " << n << " elements:\n";
    for (int i = 0; i < n; i++) {
        cout << "A[" << i << "]: ";
        cin >> A[i];
    }
    deleteFromBeginning(A, n);
    return 0;
}
```

Output :

```
Enter the number of elements in the array: 5
Enter 5 elements:
A[0]: 12
A[1]: 34
A[2]: 76
A[3]: 87
A[4]: 98
Array after deleting the first element: 34 76 87 98
```

Algorithm to delete an element from the end of the list: Here 'A' is a linear array with 'n' elements.

Step 1: Set n = n - 1

Step 2: Exit

Example 11: The following C++ program shows deletion of an element from the end of an array.

```
#include <iostream>
using namespace std;
int main() {
    int n;
    // Input array size
    cout << "Enter the number of elements in the array: ";
```

```
    cin >> n;

    int A[100]; // Define an array with a maximum capacity of 100

    // Input existing elements
    cout << "Enter " << n << " elements:\n";
    for (int i = 0; i < n; i++) {
        cout << "A[" << i << "]: ";
        cin >> A[i];
    }

    // Step 1: Check if the array is empty
    if (n == 0) {
        cout << "Array is empty! Deletion not possible.\n";
        return 0;
    }

    // Step 2: Decrease the size of the array
n = n - 1;

    // Display the updated array
    cout << "\nArray after deleting the last element: ";
    for (int i = 0; i < n; i++) {
        cout << A[i] << " ";
    }
    cout << endl;
    return 0;
}
```

Output :

Enter the number of elements in the array: 5

Enter 5 elements:

A[0]: 12

A[1]: 23

A[2]: 45

A[3]: 56

A[4]: 67

Array after deleting the last element: 12 23 45 56

Algorithm to delete an element from any desired location: Here 'A' is a linear array with 'n' elements. 'Loc' is the position from which the element is to be deleted.

Step 1: [Initialize counter] Set i = loc

Step 2: Repeat steps 3 and 4 while i <= n

Step 3: Set A [i] = A [i + 1]

Step 4: Set i = i + 1

[End of step 2 loop]

Step 5: Set n = n - 1

Step 6: Exit

Example 12: The following C++ program shows deletion an element from a desired location of an array.

```
#include <iostream>
using namespace std;

int main() {
  int n, loc;

  // Input array size
  cout << "Enter the number of elements in the array: ";
  cin >> n;

  int A[100]; // Define an array with a maximum capacity of 100

  // Input existing elements
  cout << "Enter " << n << " elements:\n";
  for (int i = 0; i < n; i++) {
    cout << "A[" << i << "]: ";
    cin >> A[i];
  }

  // Input the position to delete
  cout << "Enter the position (1-based index) to delete: ";
  cin >> loc;
```

```
    // Step 1: Check if the array is empty
    if (n == 0) {
        cout << "Array is empty! Deletion not possible.\n";
        return 0;
    }

    // Step 2: Check if position is valid
    if (loc < 1 || loc > n) {
        cout << "Invalid position! Please enter a position between 1 and " << n << ".\n";
        return 0;
    }

    // Step 3: Shift elements to the left
    for (int i = loc - 1; i < n - 1; i++) {
        A[i] = A[i + 1];
    }
    // Step 5: Decrease the size of the array
n--;

    // Display the updated array
    cout << "\nArray after deleting the element at position " << loc << ": ";
    for (int i = 0; i < n; i++) {
        cout << A[i] << " ";
    }
    cout << endl;
    return 0;
}
```

Output:

Enter the number of elements in the array: 4

Enter 4 elements:

A[0]: 12

A[1]: 34

A[2]: 56

A[3]: 78

Enter the position (1-based index) to delete: 2

Array after deleting the element at position 2: 12 56 78

2.4 MULTIDIMENSIONAL ARRAYS

The arrays that we have studied in the above sections are one-dimensional. These arrays have only one dimension, i.e. the array expands or shrinks in one dimension only. There may be arrays that have multi-dimension or more than one dimension. Such arrays are known as multi-dimensional arrays. These arrays are also known as array of arrays. The simplest multi-dimensional array is the two-dimensional (2D array) array. There may be three-dimensional and n-dimensional arrays as well.

2.4.1 Two-dimensional Arrays

A two-dimensional array has two dimensions, i.e. it expands or shrinks in two dimensions. A 2D array is also known as a matrix. A matrix is a table of rows and columns. A 2D array A has m rows and n columns. These rows and columns are referenced by a pair of indices [i, j]. Therefore a 2D array or matrix of m rows and n columns is a collection of m x n elements where $1 \leq i \leq m$ and$1 \leq j \leq n$.

A two-dimensional array 'X' with 3 rows and 3 columns is shown below:

	Column 0	Column 1	Column 2
Row 0	x[0][0]	x[0][1]	x[0][2]
Row 1	x[1][0]	x[1][1]	x[1][2]
Row 2	x[2][0]	x[2][1]	x[2][2]

Figure 2.1 A 3X3 2D array or matrix

2.4.2 Size of a two-dimensional array

Size of a two-dimensional array is the total number of elements that can be stored in the array and can be calculated by multiplying the size of all the dimensions. For example: The array **X[3][3]** can store total (3X3) = 9 elements (as it is very much clear from figure 2.1).

2.4.3 Declaration of two-dimensional array

We can declare a two-dimensional array in C/C++ as:

data_type array_name[m][n]

Here data_type means the type of the data such as int, char, float, etc.

Array_name means the name of the array. M and n are the dimensions of the array which are nothing but number of rows and columns.

For example: A two dimensional array is declared as:int X[4][5];

2.4.4 Memory Representation of two-dimensional array

The elements of a two-dimensional array are stored in continuous memory locations. There are two ways of representing a two-dimensional array in the memory. These are:

- Row-Major Order
- Column-Major Order

Row-Major Order

In row-major ordering or representation the elements of a two-dimensional array are stored row wise, i.e. m elements of first row are stored in first m locations, m elements of second row are stored in next m locations and so on. A 3 x 4 array stored in row-major ordering is shown below:

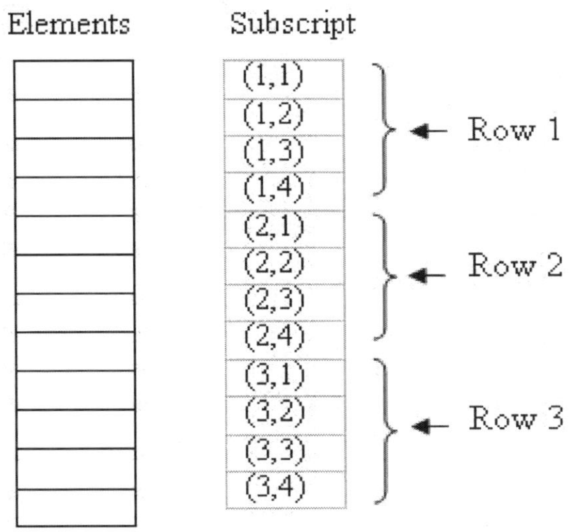

The Location of an element A[i, j] can be obtained by evaluating the expression:

LOC (A [i, j]) = Base_Address + W [N (i) + (j)]

Here,

Base_Address is the address of first element in the array.

W is the number of bytes occupied by each element in the array.

N is number of columns in the array.

Suppose we want to calculate the address of element A [1, 2]. How to do it? Let us show how to calculate the address or memory location of a particular element in the array with the help of an example.

Example 13: The base address of a two-dimensional array A [10] [12] is 1000. Given that each element occupies 2 bytes of storage space. Calculate the address of an element at location A [7, 2] assuming that the elements are stored in row major order.

Solution: Here Base Address = 1000, W= 2, M=10, N=12, i=7, j=2

LOC (A [i, j]) = **BaseAddress + W [N(i) + (j)]**

LOC (A[7, 2]) = 1000 + 2 *[12*(7) + 2]

= 1000 + 2 * [84 + 2]

= 1000 + 2 * 86

= 1000 + 172

= 1172

Example 14: A two-dimensional array defined as A [6...12, 1...5] requires 2 bytes of storage space for each element. The base address of the array is 2000. Calculate the address of an element at location A [6, 3] assuming that the elements are stored in row major order.

Solution: Here Base Address = 2000, W = 2

Lower bound of row L1 = 6

Lower bound of column L2 = 1

Upper bound of row U1 = 12

Upper bound of column U2 = 5

Therefore the number of columns N = UB – LB + 1

= 5 – 1 + 1

= 5

LOC (A[6, 3]), = 2000 + 2 *[5*(6) + 3]

= 2000 + 2 * [30 + 3]

= 2000 + 2 * 33

= 2000 + 66

= 2066

Column-Major Order

In column-major ordering or representation the elements of a two-dimensional array are stored column wise, i.e. n elements of first column are stored in first n locations, n elements of second column are stored in next n locations and so on. A 3 x 4 array stored in column-major ordering is shown below:

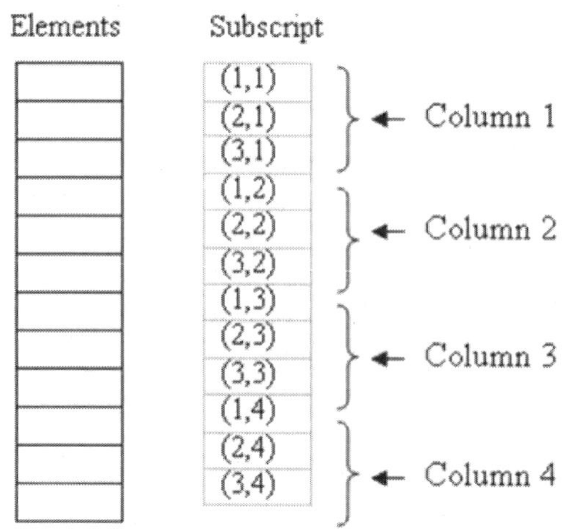

The Location of element A[i, j] can be obtained by evaluating expression:

LOC (A [i, j]) = Base_Address + W [M (j) + (i)] Here,

Base_Address is the address of first element in the array.

W is the number of bytes occupied by each element.

M is number of rows in array.

Suppose we want to calculate the address of element A [1, 2]. How to do it? Let us show how to calculate the address or memory location of a particular element in the array with the help of an example.

Example 15: The base address of a two-dimensional array A [10] [12] is 1000. Given that each element occupies 2 bytes of storage space. Calculate the address of an element at location A [7, 2] assuming that the elements are stored in column major order.

Solution: Here Base Address = 1000, W = 2, M = 10, N = 12, i = 7, j = 2

LOC (A [i, j]) = **Base Address + W [M(j) + (i)]**

LOC (A[7, 2]) = 1000 + 2 *[10*(2) + 7]

= 1000 + 2 * [20 + 7]

= 1000 + 2 * 27

= 1000 + 54

= 1054

Example 16: A two-dimensional array defined as A [6...12, 1...5] requires 2 bytes of storage space for each element. The base address of the array is 2000. Calculate the address of an element at location A [6, 3] assuming that the elements are stored in column major order.

Solution: Here Base Address = 2000, W = 2

Lower bound of row L1 = 6

Lower bound of column L2 = 1

Upper bound of row U1 = 12

Upper bound of column U2 = 5

Therefore the number of rows M = UB – LB + 1

= 12 - 6 + 1

= 7

LOC (A[6, 3]) = 2000 + 2 *[7*(3) + 6]

= 2000 + 2 * [21 + 6]

= 2000 + 2 * 27

= 2000 + 54

= 2054

2.4.5 Accessing Elements of Two-Dimensional Arrays

Elements in two-dimensional arrays are accessed using the row indexes and column indexes. As it is a two-dimensional array we will be using two subscripts or indexes to represent its two dimensions i.e. rows and columns.

Example: int x [2][3];

The above example represents the element present in third row and fourth column.

Note: In arrays if size of array is N. Its index will be from 0 to N-1. Therefore, for row index 2 row number is 2+1 = 3. Similar is the case of a column. For column index 3 column number is 3+1 = 4.

To access all the elements of a two-dimensional array we can use nested for loops. We will require two for loops; one to traverse the rows and another to traverse the columns.

Example 17: The following program shows how to read and write array elements in C++ language.

```
#include <iostream>
using namespace std;

int main() {
  int A[3][2]; // 3 rows, 2 columns

  cout << "Input elements of the array:\n";

  // Taking user input for a 3x2 array
  for (int i = 0; i < 3; i++) {
    for (int j = 0; j < 2; j++) {
      cout << "Enter A[" << i << "][" << j << "]: ";
      cin >> A[i][j];
    }
  }

  cout << "\nThe elements of the array:\n";

  // Printing the array in matrix form
  for (int i = 0; i < 3; i++) {
    for (int j = 0; j < 2; j++) {
      cout << A[i][j] << " ";
    }
    cout << endl; // New line after each row
  }
```

```
  return 0;
}
```

Output:

```
Input elements of the array:
Enter A[0][0]: 23
Enter A[0][1]: 24
Enter A[1][0]: 25
Enter A[1][1]: 26
Enter A[2][0]: 27
Enter A[2][1]: 28

The elements of the array:
23 24
25 26
27 28
```

2.5 OPERATIONS ON TWO-DIMENSIONAL ARRAY

There are a number of operations that can be performed on a two-dimensional array. Two-dimensional arrays are usually used to implement matrices. In mathematics, a matrix is a collection of numbers, arranged in rows and columns. Thus, using two-dimensional arrays, we can perform the following operations on an mxn matrix:

- **Sum:** Addition is possible when two matrices are compatible. Compatible matrices can be added together and the result can be stored in the third matrix. Two matrices are said to be compatible when they have the same number of rows and columns. The elements of two matrices can be added by writing: C [i] [j] = A [i] [j] + B [i] [j]

Example 18: The following C++ program shows how to find the sum of two matrices.

```
#include <iostream>
using namespace std;
int main() {
  int m, n, i, j;
  int A[10][10], B[10][10], sum[10][10];

  cout << "Enter the number of rows and columns of the matrix: ";
  cin >> m >> n;

  cout << "Enter the elements of the first matrix:\n";
```

```
    for (i = 0; i < m; i++) {
        for (j = 0; j < n; j++) {
            cin >> A[i][j];
        }
    }

    cout << "Enter the elements of the second matrix:\n";
    for (i = 0; i < m; i++) {
        for (j = 0; j < n; j++) {
            cin >> B[i][j];
        }
    }

    cout << "Sum of the entered matrices is:\n";
    for (i = 0; i < m; i++) {
        for (j = 0; j < n; j++) {
            sum[i][j] = A[i][j] + B[i][j];
            cout << sum[i][j] << " ";
        }
        cout << endl;
    }

    return 0;
}
```

Output :

```
Enter the number of rows and columns of the matrix: 2 2
Enter the elements of the first matrix:
1 2
4 5
Enter the elements of the second matrix:
4 6
6 1
Sum of the entered matrices is:
5 8
10 6
```

- **Difference:** Two compatible matrices can be subtracted and their difference can be stored in the third matrix. Two matrices are said to be compatible when they have the same number of rows and columns. The elements of two matrices can be subtracted by writing: C [i] [j] = A [i] [j] – B [i] [j]

Example 19: The following C++ program shows how to find the difference of two matrices.

```
#include <iostream>
using namespace std;
int main() {
  int m, n, i, j;
  int A[10][10], B[10][10], difference[10][10];

  cout << "Enter the number of rows and columns of the matrix: ";
  cin >> m >> n;

  cout << "Enter the elements of the first matrix:\n";
  for (i = 0; i < m; i++) {
    for (j = 0; j < n; j++) {
      cin >> A[i][j];
    }
  }

  cout << "Enter the elements of the second matrix:\n";
  for (i = 0; i < m; i++) {
    for (j = 0; j < n; j++) {
      cin >> B[i][j];
    }
  }

  cout << "Difference of the entered matrices is:\n";
  for (i = 0; i < m; i++) {
    for (j = 0; j < n; j++) {
      difference[i][j] = A[i][j] - B[i][j];
      cout << difference[i][j] << " ";
    }
    cout << endl;
  }
```

```
    return 0;
}
```

Output

Enter the number of rows and columns of the matrix: 2 2

Enter the elements of the first matrix:

5 6

9 8

Enter the elements of the second matrix:

4 2

3 3

Difference of the entered matrices is:

1 4

6 5

- **Product:** Two matrices can be multiplied with each other if the number of columns in the first matrix is equal to the number of rows in the second matrix. If A is a mxn matrix and B is a pxq matrix, than matrices A and B can only be multiplied if n=p.

Example 20: The following C++ program shows how to find the product of two matrices.

```
#include <iostream>
using namespace std;
int main() {
    int m, n, p, q, i, j, k, sum;
    int A[10][10], B[10][10], multiply[10][10];

    cout << "Enter number of rows and columns of matrix A: ";
    cin >> m >> n;

    cout << "Enter elements of matrix A:\n";
    for (i = 0; i < m; i++) {
        for (j = 0; j < n; j++) {
            cin >> A[i][j];
        }
    }

    cout << "Enter number of rows and columns of matrix B: ";
    cin >> p >> q;
```

```
    if (n != p) {
        cout << "The matrices can't be multiplied with each other.\n";
    } else {
        cout << "Enter elements of matrix B:\n";
        for (i = 0; i < p; i++) {
            for (j = 0; j < q; j++) {
                cin >> B[i][j];
            }
        }

        // Matrix multiplication
        for (i = 0; i < m; i++) {
            for (j = 0; j < q; j++) {
                sum = 0;
                for (k = 0; k < n; k++) { // n instead of p
                    sum += A[i][k] * B[k][j];
                }
                multiply[i][j] = sum;
            }
        }

        cout << "Product of the matrices is:\n";
        for (i = 0; i < m; i++) {
            for (j = 0; j < q; j++) {
                cout << multiply[i][j] << "\t";
            }
            cout << endl;
        }
    }
    return 0;
}
```

Output:

Enter number of rows and columns of matrix A: 2 2

```
Enter elements of matrix A:
2 4
5 6
Enter number of rows and columns of matrix B: 2 2
Enter elements of matrix B:
1 2
5 6

Product of the matrices is:
22    28
35    46
```

- **Transpose:** Transpose of an mxn matrix A is given as a nxm matrix B, where B [i] [j] = A [j] [i]

Example 21: The following C++ program shows how to find transpose of a matrix.

```
#include <iostream>
using namespace std;
int main() {
  int m, n, i, j, A[10][10], transpose[10][10];

  cout << "Enter the number of rows and columns of the matrix: ";
  cin >> m >> n;

  cout << "Enter elements of the matrix:\n";
  for (i = 0; i < m; i++)
    for (j = 0; j < n; j++)
      cin >> A[i][j];

  // Compute the transpose
  for (i = 0; i < m; i++)
    for (j = 0; j < n; j++)
      transpose[j][i] = A[i][j];

  cout << "Transpose of the matrix:\n";
  for (i = 0; i < n; i++) {
```

```
        for (j = 0; j < m; j++)
            cout << transpose[i][j] << "\t";
        cout << endl;
    }
    return 0;
}
```

Output :

Enter the number of rows and columns of the matrix: 4 4

Enter elements of the matrix:

2 3 5 6

5 6 7 8

1 3 4 6

2 7 6 9

Transpose of the matrix:

```
2   5   1   2
3   6   3   7
5   7   4   6
6   8   6   9
```

2.6 PASSING ARRAYS TO FUNCTIONS IN C++ LANGUAGE

Arrays can also be passed to functions. Just like we pass variables to a function, in the similar manner we can pass an array to a function. We can pass a single element of an array or an entire array to a function. Passing an array to a function is possible for both one-dimensional and multi-dimensional arrays.

Example 22: The following C++ program shows how to pass the data value of a single element of an array to a function.

```
#include <iostream>
using namespace std;
void display(int roll_no) {
    cout << "Selected element: " << roll_no << endl;
}
int main() {
    int A[6];

    // Taking user input
    cout << "Enter 6 elements of the array: ";
```

```
    for (int i = 0; i < 6; i++) {
        cin >> A[i];
    }
    int index;
    cout << "Enter the index (0 to 5) of the element to display: ";
    cin >> index;

    // Checking valid index
    if (index >= 0 && index < 6) {
        display(A[index]);
    } else {
        cout << "Invalid index! Please enter a value between 0 and 5." << endl;
    }
    return 0;
}
```

Output:

Enter 6 elements of the array: 3 4 5 6 7 8

Enter the index (0 to 5) of the element to display: 2

Selected element: 5

Example 23: The following C++program shows how to pass the address of single element of an array to a function.

```
#include <iostream>
using namespace std;
void display(int *roll_no) {
    cout << "Selected element: " << *roll_no << endl;
    cout << "Memory address: " << roll_no << endl;
}
int main() {
    int A[6];

    // Taking user input
    cout << "Enter 6 elements of the array: ";
    for (int i = 0; i < 6; i++) {
        cin >> A[i];
    }
```

```
    int index;
    cout << "Enter the index (0 to 5) of the element to display: ";
    cin >> index;

    // Checking valid index
    if (index >= 0 && index < 6) {
        display(&A[index]);  // Passing address of the selected element
    } else {
        cout << "Invalid index! Please enter a value between 0 and 5." << endl;
    }
    return 0;
}
```

Output:

```
Enter 6 elements of the array: 3 4 5 6 7 8
Enter the index (0 to 5) of the element to display: 4
Selected element: 7
Memory address: 0x7fff0a79e230
```

When we pass an entire array (as arguments) to a function, only the name of the array is passed. That is because the array name is a pointer to the first element of the array or the starting address of the memory area, which is passed as argument. Let us explain it more clearly with the help of an example.

Example 24: The following C++ program shows how to pass an entire array to a function.

```
#include <iostream>
using namespace std;

void display(int A[], int size) {
    cout << "Array elements: ";
    for (int i = 0; i < size; i++) {
        cout << A[i] << " ";
    }
    cout << endl;
}

int main() {
```

```
    int A[6];

    // Taking user input
    cout << "Enter 6 elements of the array: ";
    for (int i = 0; i < 6; i++) {
        cin >> A[i];
    }

    // Passing the entire array to the function
    display(A, 6);

    return 0;
}
```

Output :

Enter 6 elements of the array: 3 4 2 1 5 6

Array elements: 3 4 2 1 5 6

Example 25: The following C++ program shows how to pass a two-dimensional array to a function.

```
#include <iostream>
using namespace std;
void display(int a[2][3]);
int main() {
    int a[2][3];

    // Taking user input
    cout << "Enter the numbers:\n";
    for (int i = 0; i < 2; i++) {
        for (int j = 0; j < 3; j++) {
            cin >> a[i][j];
        }
    }

    // Passing multi-dimensional array to function
    display(a);
```

```
    return 0;
}
// Function to display 2D array
void display(int a[2][3]) {
    cout << "Display the numbers:\n";
    for (int i = 0; i < 2; i++) {
        for (int j = 0; j < 3; j++) {
            cout << a[i][j] << " ";
        }
        cout << endl;
    }
}
```

Output:

Enter the numbers:

1 2 3

4 5 6

Display the numbers:

1 2 3

4 5 6

2.7 POINTERS AND ARRAYS

When an array is declared in a program, the compiler immediately allocates sufficient amount of memory to hold all the data elements of the array. The base address or address of the first element of the array is also allocated by the compiler. Suppose we declare an array arr, such that array arr holds the following data elements.

int arr[5] = { 2, 5, 6, 12, 9};

Assuming that the base address of array arr is 1000 and each integer requires two bytes, the five data elements of the array will be stored as follows:

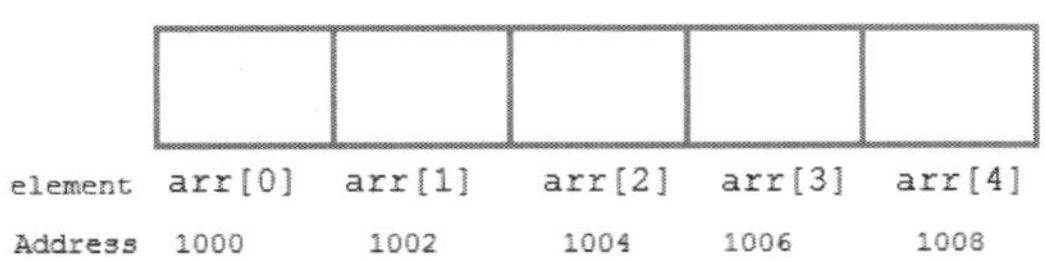

Here variable arr will give the base address, which is a constant pointer pointing to the first element of the array, arr[0]. Hence arr contains the address of arr[0]i.e. 1000.

The name of the array, arr has two purposes: it is the name of the array and it acts as a pointer pointing towards the first element in the array. By default arr is equal to &arr[0].

We can also declare a pointer of type int to point to the array arr.

```
int *p;
p = arr;
```

Alternately, we can also write the following statements:

```
int *p;
p = & arr[0];
```

Both the statements are equivalent.

Now we can access every element of the array arr by incrementing the pointer variable p (p++) to move from one element to another. We can increment a pointer variable but we cannot decrement a pointer once incremented (p-- won't work).

As discussed above, we can use a pointer variable to point to an array, and then we can use that pointer to access the array elements. Let us see this with the help of an example.

Example 26: The following C++ program shows how to access all the array elements using pointer.

```
#include <iostream>
using namespace std;

int main() {
  int arr[6];
  int *p = arr; // Pointer to the array

  // Taking user input
  cout << "Enter elements of the array: ";
  for (int i = 0; i < 6; i++) {
    cin >> arr[i];
  }

  // Displaying elements using pointer
  cout << "The array elements are: ";
  for (int i = 0; i < 6; i++) {
    cout << *p << " ";
    p++; // Moving the pointer to the next element
  }
```

```
  return 0;
}
```

Output:

Enter elements of the array: 2 3 4 5 6 7

The array elements are: 2 3 4 5 6 7

In the above program, the pointer *p will print all the values stored in the array one by one. We can also use the Base address (arr) to act as a pointer and print all the values.

Pointers to Multidimensional Array

Pointers can be used to traverse multidimensional arrays by treating each row as a 1D array. Pointer arithmetic allows us to access elements of a multidimensional array. To understand this, let's consider a 2D array arr[3][4], which represents a matrix with 3 rows and 4 columns. The base address of the array points to the first element of the first row represented by arr[0][0]. We can use a pointer to point to the entire array or to individual rows. When we declare a pointer like int (*p)[4], it can point to an entire row (an array of size 4 integers), and we can use pointer arithmetic to access each element.

Pointer arithmetic in C++ provides a way to navigate through the array by incrementing the pointer. Incrementing the pointer p++ moves it to the next row, and within the row, elements can be accessed by incrementing the pointer by an index, i.e., *(p + i) + j. Let us see this with the help of an example.

Example 27: The following C++ program shows how to use pointers and pointer arithmetic to traverse a 2D array (multidimensional array) and access its elements.

```
#include <iostream>
using namespace std;
int main() {
  int rows, cols;

  // Ask the user for the dimensions of the 2D array
  cout << "Enter the number of rows: ";
  cin >> rows;
  cout << "Enter the number of columns: ";
  cin >> cols;

  // Dynamically allocate a 2D array
  int **arr = new int*[rows];
  for (int i = 0; i < rows; i++) {
    arr[i] = new int[cols]; // Allocate memory for each row
  }
```

```
    // Taking user input for the 2D array
    cout << "Enter the elements of the 2D array:" << endl;
    for (int i = 0; i < rows; i++) {
        for (int j = 0; j < cols; j++) {
            cout << "Enter element [" << i << "][" << j << "]: ";
            cin >> arr[i][j];
        }
    }
    // Accessing and displaying elements using a pointer to a row
    cout << "\nAccessing elements of the 2D array using pointers:" << endl;
    // We can use a pointer to the first element of each row (int*)
    for (int i = 0; i < rows; i++) {
        int *p = arr[i];  // Pointer to the i-th row (an array of size 'cols')
        for (int j = 0; j < cols; j++) {
            // Accessing elements using pointer arithmetic
            cout << *(p + j) << " ";  // Access element at [i][j]
        }
        cout << endl;
    }

    // Free dynamically allocated memory
    for (int i = 0; i < rows; i++) {
        delete[] arr[i];  // Delete each row
    }
    delete[] arr;  // Delete the array of row pointers
    return 0;
}
```

Output :

```
Enter the number of rows: 2
Enter the number of columns: 2
Enter the elements of the 2D array:
Enter element [0][0]: 3
Enter element [0][1]: 4
Enter element [1][0]: 5
Enter element [1][1]: 6
```

Accessing elements of the 2D array using pointers:

3 4

5 6

2.8 APPLICATIONS OF ARRAY

Arrays are widely used in programming due to their efficiency and simplicity. Some key applications include:

a) Mathematical Computation and Data Storage

- Arrays are fundamental in implementing vectors, matrices, and multi-dimensional tables used in numerical computing.
- Many databases store records in one-dimensional arrays, where each element represents a structured data entry containing multiple attributes.

b) Implementation of Other Data Structures

- Arrays serve as the foundation for various data structures, including:
- Lists, stacks, and queues (for efficient data management).
- Heaps and hash tables (for optimized searching and sorting).
- Strings (which are typically stored as character arrays).
- Array-based implementations are often space-efficient and simple but may become inefficient when frequently modified, compared to tree-based structures.

c) Control Flow in Programming

- Arrays can be used for controlling program execution, serving as a compact alternative to repetitive IF statements.
- They are often used in control tables, where an interpreter reads array values to determine execution flow dynamically.
- Example: An array of function pointers can replace large switch-case or if-else blocks, improving code clarity and efficiency.

d) Real-World Applications of Arrays

- Image Processing: A 2D array can store pixel values for image manipulation.
- Machine Learning: Arrays are used in deep learning frameworks (e.g., NumPy arrays in Python).
- Game Development: Arrays store player positions, game maps, and object states efficiently.
- Networking: Routing tables and IP packet processing use arrays for fast lookup operations.

2.9 LET US SUM UP

- An array is a collection of homogeneous data elements.
- The elements of an array are stored in consecutive memory locations and are referenced by an index (also known as the subscript).

- We cannot accommodate integer data, floating point data, character data, etc. on the same list. If the array is declared as integer, we can only store integer data in that list. However, we can have separate list for separate data types.
- While declaring an array three parameters needs to be specified: data type, array name and its size.
- Length of an array is predefined and static.
- The length of an array is given by: Length = UB – LB + 1
- To access all the elements of an array we must use a loop.
- The elements of an array are stored in contiguous memory blocks i.e. in adjacent memory blocks.
- Each element of an array is referenced by an index value, i.e. a list of n elements will have a corresponding set of n index values.
- The name of an array is a symbolic reference to the address of the first element of the array. Therefore,whenever we use the array name, we are actually referring to the first element of that array.
- A two-dimensional array is a collection of data elements stored in tabular form, often known as matrix.
- A two-dimensional array is specified using two subscripts where the first subscript denotes the row and the second subscript denotes the column of the array.
- Using two-dimensional arrays, we can perform different operations on matrices, such as: transpose, addition, subtraction, multiplication.
- A multi-dimensional array is an array of arrays. Like we have one index in a one-dimensional array, two indices in a two-dimensional array, in the same way we have *n* indices in an *n*-dimensional or multidimensional array. Conversely, an *n*-dimensional array is specified using *n* indices.
- Passing an array to a function is possible for both one-dimensional and multi-dimensional arrays.
- Pointers can be used to traverse through 1D array or multidimensional array and also help in accessing elements from an array.

2.10 CHECK YOUR PROGRESS

- What is an array?
- What is the importance of an array?
- How is an one-dimensional array represented in the memory?
- Differentiate between one- dimensional and two-dimensional arrays?
- What are the limitations of an array?
- How is a two-dimensional array represented in the memory?
- Mention some applications of array.
- What is the use of multi-dimensional arrays?

- What is a 2D array (matrix) and how is it stored in memory?
- How do you find the transpose of a matrix and why is it useful?
- Explain the difference between row-major and column-major order storage in a matrix.
- How do you pass a 2D array to a function in C++?
- How are pointers used to access two-dimensional arrays?
- Consider an array int a[50].Calculate the address of a[22], if base address of a = 1000 and each element occupies a storage space of 2 bytes.
- Consider a two-dimensional array A[10][8]. Compute the address of the element A[7][5], assuming that the elements are stored in column major order. The base address of the array is 1085 and each element occupies a storage space of 2 bytes.
- How are arrays related to pointers?
- Briefly explain the concept of array of pointers.

2.11 EXERCISES

Q1. Given an array A[] = {35, 10, 15, 20, 25} of size 10, insert the element 30 at index 2. What is the updated array?

Q2. Given an array A[] = {123,134,145,167,189} of size 10, insert the element 300 at the end of array. What is the updated array?

Q3. Insert an element 50 at the beginning of the array D[] = {20, 30, 40, 60}. What will be the final array?

Q4. Given an array A[] = {2,4,5,6,7} of size 10, insert the element 30 after element 4. What is the updated array? In which index position is the new element inserted.

Q5. Given an array A[] = {21,42,53,64,75} of size 10, insert the element 98 before element 53. What is the updated array? In which index position is the new element inserted.

Q6. If an array C[] = {3, 6, 9, 12} is full with static declaration of array size as 4, can we insert a new element 15? If yes, how? If no, why?

Q7. Given an array G[] = {17, 14, 21, 28, 35}, delete the element at index 3. What is the updated array?

Q8. Given an array I[] = {77, 44, 22, 88, 55}, delete the element after index 2. What is the updated array?

Q9. Given an array J[] = {12, 13, 14, 15, 16}, delete the element before index 4. What is the updated array?

Q10. If an array H[] = {5, 10, 15, 20, 25} undergoes deletion at index 1, what will be the resulting array?

Q11. Consider an array B[] = {9, 18, 27, 36, 45}. Delete the first element. What is the new array?

Q12. If an element 50 is to be deleted from an array J[] = {20, 30, 50, 70, 90}, how will you perform the deletion?

Q13. If an array S[] = {125, 100, 115, 200, 225} undergoes deletion of the last element, what will be the resulting array?

Q14. Given an array A[] = {10, 20, 30, 40, 50}, find the index of element 30 using linear search.

Q15. Search for the element 25 in an unsorted array A[] = {12, 14, 25, 30, 7, 9} using linear search.

Q16. Given a sorted array A[] = {5, 15, 25, 35, 45, 55, 65}, find the index of element 35 using Binary Search.

Q17. Consider an array A[] = {3, 6, 9, 12, 15, 18, 21}. Search for element 18 using Binary Search and determine its index.

Q18. Given a sorted list A[] = {1, 4, 7, 10, 13, 16, 19}, find whether element 14 is present using Binary Search.

Q19. The base address of a 2D array A[8][6] is 2000. Each element takes 4 bytes. Find the address of A[5][3] in column-major order.

Q20. The base address of a matrix B[5][10] is 1500, and each element occupies 2 bytes. Find the memory location of B[2][6] if stored in column-major order.

Q21. Consider a matrix C[7][9] stored in column-major order starting at address 3000. Each element requires 1 byte. Compute the address of C[6][4].

Q22. The base address of a 2D array A[8][6] is 2020. Each element takes 2 bytes. Find the address of A[5][3] in row-major order.

Q23. The base address of a matrix B[3][10] is 1500, and each element occupies 4 bytes. Find the memory location of B[2][6] if stored in row-major order.

Q24. A matrix D[4][4] is stored in row-major order, with a base address of 500. Each element takes 8 bytes. Determine the memory address of D[3][1].

Q25. Given two matrices:

$$A = \begin{bmatrix} 2 & 4 \\ 3 & 5 \end{bmatrix}, \quad B = \begin{bmatrix} 1 & 3 \\ 2 & 6 \end{bmatrix}$$

Find A + B and A-B. What is the resultant 2D array after both operations. Also, write a C++ program showing the implementation of the operations performed.

Q26. Given two matrices

$$P = \begin{bmatrix} 5 & 7 & 9 \\ 2 & 4 & 6 \end{bmatrix}, Q = \begin{bmatrix} 1 & 3 & 5 \\ 0 & 2 & 4 \end{bmatrix}$$

Compute P + Q and P-Q. What is the resultant 2D array after both operations. Also, write a C++ program showing the implementation of the operations performed.

Q27. If

$$X = \begin{bmatrix} 10 & 20 & 30 \\ 40 & 50 & 60 \end{bmatrix}, Y = \begin{bmatrix} 5 & 15 & 25 \\ 35 & 45 & 55 \end{bmatrix}$$

Find (X+Y) and (X-Y) . What is the resultant 2D array after both operations. Also, write a C++ program showing the implementation of the operations performed.

Q28. Given two matrices

$$A = \begin{bmatrix} 3 & -1 & 5 \\ 7 & 4 & 2 \end{bmatrix}, B = \begin{bmatrix} -3 & 2 & -5 \\ -7 & -4 & -2 \end{bmatrix}$$

Verify if the resultant 2D array is a null matrix or not. Also, write a C++ program showing the implementation of the operation performed.

Q29. Find the product of the matrices:

$$M = \begin{bmatrix} 1 & 2 & 3 \\ 4 & 5 & 6 \end{bmatrix}, N = \begin{bmatrix} 7 & 8 \\ 9 & 10 \\ 11 & 12 \end{bmatrix}$$

What is the resultant 2D array. Also, write a C++ program showing the implementation of the operation performed.

Q30. Compute X × Y

$$X = \begin{bmatrix} 2 & 4 & 6 \\ 1 & 3 & 5 \end{bmatrix}, Y = \begin{bmatrix} 1 & 2 \\ 3 & 4 \\ 5 & 6 \end{bmatrix}$$

What is the resultant 2D array. Also, write a C++ program showing the implementation of the operation performed.

Q31. Find A^2

$$A = \begin{bmatrix} 2 & 0 \\ 1 & 3 \end{bmatrix}$$

What is the resultant 2D array. Also, write a C++ program showing the implementation of the operation performed.

Q32. Given a matrix

$$A = \begin{bmatrix} 1 & 2 & 3 \\ 4 & 5 & 6 \end{bmatrix}$$

Write a C++ program to display the transpose of the matrix A.

Q33. Write a C++ program to pass a 1D array to a function and print its elements.

Q34. Write a C++ program to pass a 2D array to a function and display it.

Q35. Write a C++ program to access the elements of a 2D array using pointers.

3

LINKED LIST

3.1 INTRODUCTION

Like an array, a linked list is also a linear data structure. However, unlike arrays, the elements of a linked list are not stored in contiguous memory locations. Instead, they are scattered across memory and connected to each other using pointers.

3.1.1 Definition

In a linked list data is stored in a structure called node as shown below:

Data part	Link part

Figure 3.1: A Node

Each **node** of a simple linked list consist of two parts:

- Data part
- Link part

The data part stores the data value to be stored on the node. The link part is a reference to the next node, i.e. the linked part stores the address of the next node. The following figure shows a linked list of four nodes.

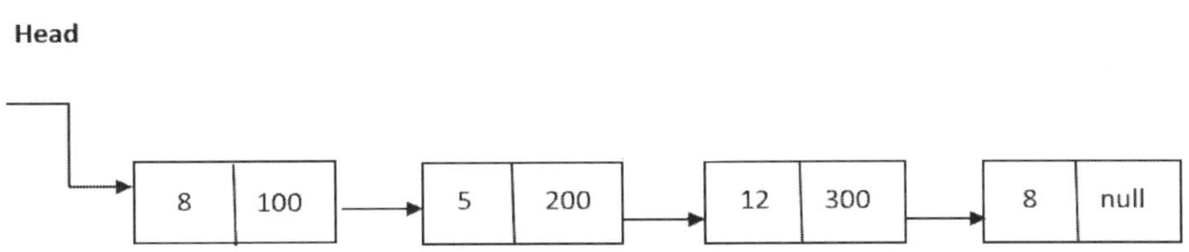

Figure 3.2: A Linked list

The entry point into a linked list is called the **head** of the list. It should be noted that head is not a separate node, but it is a reference to the first node. If the list is empty then the head is a null reference. The first node stores data value 8 and its address part stores 100, which is the reference to the second node. This means that the second data value is stored in the location 100. Similarly, reaching on the second node we get data value 5 stored in the data part and 200 in the address part. This means 200 is the address of the third node. Traversing in a similar manner we reach to the fourth node which is the last node in the linked list. The last node has a reference to null. Null is any invalid location. This means there is no valid node after is location or symbolizes end of the list.

Another fact about a linked list is that it is a dynamic data structure. Unlike array linked list is not a static data structure. The number of nodes in a linked list is not fixed and can grow and shrink on demand. Any application which has to deal with an unknown number of objects will need to use a linked list.

3.1.2 Why Linked List?

You might be wondering why do we need an additional data structure when the same job can be done using arrays. Well, the answer is though arrays can be used to store linear data of similar types, but arrays have certain limitations which are discussed below:

- **Static Size Limitation:** Array is a static data structure, i.e. the size of an array is fixed. Due to this static nature there is often overflow or underflow of memory locations. While doing an array operation we must know the upper limit of the array in advance. Generally, the allocated memory (size of an array) is equal to the upper limit irrespective of the usage. Suppose the size of an array (upper limit) is 100 and we are storing 20 data elements, then 80 memory locations are wasted. In another scenario the size of an array (upper limit) is 100 and we want to store 200 data values; the array will not be able to accommodate data more than its size and there will be overflow.
- **Costly Insertion and Deletion Operations:** Inserting and deletion operations on an array are very expensive. Because while doing inserting and deletion operations lot of shifting of elements has to be done. As in an array all the elements are stored in contiguous memory blocks therefore when an element is deleted, all other elements stored towards the right side of the deleted element has to be shifted towards the left side by one position. Similarly, to do an insertion operation room has to be created for the new element, so to create room all the existing elements from the location of the insertion have to shifted towards right side by one position. Now if the elements stored in the array are more than insertion and deletion operations are tedious.

3.1.3 Advantages of Linked List

- Linked list are dynamic in nature which means memory is allocated in the runtime, whenever required.
- Insertion and deletion operations can be easily implemented.

Drawbacks of Linked List

- In linked list random access is not allowed. Elements of a list are accessed sequentially starting from the first node. Therefore, it is not possible to implement binary search with linked lists.
- Extra memory space is required with each element of the list to store pointers. We need extra 4 bytes (on 32-bit CPU) to store a reference to the next node.
- Reverse Traversing is difficult in linked list.
- It's very time consuming to get to the last element.

3.1.4 Linked List vs Array

Both Array and Linked List are linear data structures capable of storing homogeneous data. But both of them are not same and have certain advantages and disadvantages over each other.

Following are some differences between linked lists and arrays:

- Linked list is a dynamic structure whereas array is a static structure.
- Memory is allocated in a linked list in the run time whereas memory is allocated in an array in the compilation time.
- The size of an array is fixed. We cannot store data more than its upper limit. Whereas the size of a linked list is not fixed and memory is allocated as and when needed.
- In an array the allocated memory is equal to the upper limit irrespective of the usage, and in practical uses, upper limit is rarely reached. So there is usually a chance of overflow as well as under flow in case of an array where as there is no issue of memory overflow and underflow in case of a linked list.
- Inserting and deletion operations in an array are expensive, as they involve lot of shifting. Whereas in a linked list inserting and deletion operations are done very easily and does not involve any shifting work.

3.2 MEMORY REPRESENTATION OF LINKED LIST

To store a linked list in the memory, it requires two contiguous arrays. The first array stores the data values and the second array stores the pointer or address of the next node. To explain this concept properly, let us consider the following linked list:

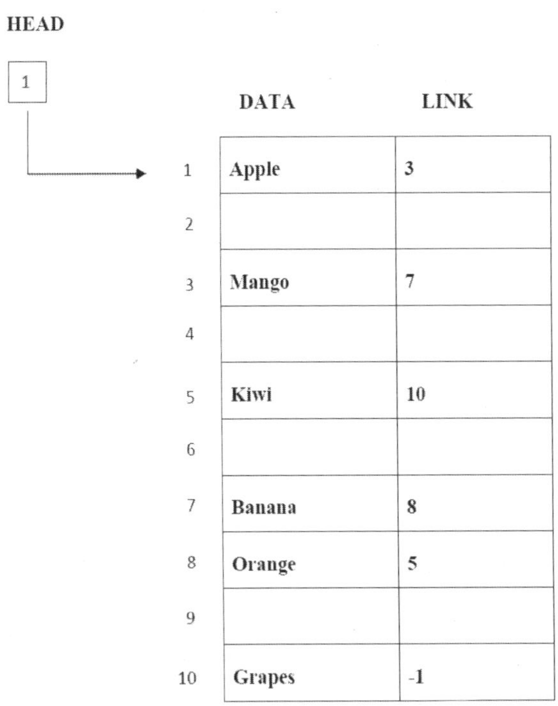

Figure 3.3: A linked list in the memory

In order to maintain the above linked list in the memory, two arrays are used namely --- DATA and LINK. The array DATA stores the data elements of the linked list and the array LINK stores the address or pointer to the next node or data. In this arrangement it is very important to recognize the first data of the list. That is, if the first data is found than the rest of the data of the list can be easily found by means of pointers. But if the first data is not found than the entire list will be lost. Therefore, in a linked list it is very important to mark the first node of the list. The first node of every list is marked by a special pointer usually termed as **start or head**. In our above example, this pointer is named as 'HEAD' and it always points to the beginning data of the list. That is, the variable HEAD is used to store the address of the first node. In this example, HEAD = 1, so the first data is stored at address 1, which is Apple. The corresponding LINK stores the address of the next node, which is 3. So, we will look at address 3 to fetch the next data item. The second data element obtained stored at address 3 is Mango. Again, we see the corresponding LINK to go to the next node. From the entry in the LINK, we get the next address, that is 7, and fetch Banana as the data. We repeat this procedure until we reach a position where the LINK entry contains –1 or NULL value, as it denotes the end of the linked list.

3.3 DECLARATION OF LINKED LIST

Every node of a linked list stores two different types of data. Therefore it is only possible to declare such a node with the help of structure. The declaration is done as follows:

```
struct node
{
  data-type data;
  struct node *link;
};
```

Suppose we want to store integer data in the linked list, than the structure will be declared as:

```
struct node
{
  int data;
  struct node *link;
};
```

3.4 TYPES OF LINKED LIST

- **Singly Linked List:** Singly linked lists contain nodes which have two parts, a data part and an address part i.e. link, which points to the next node in sequence of nodes. The operations we can perform on singly linked lists are insertion, deletion, traversal, searching, sorting, etc.

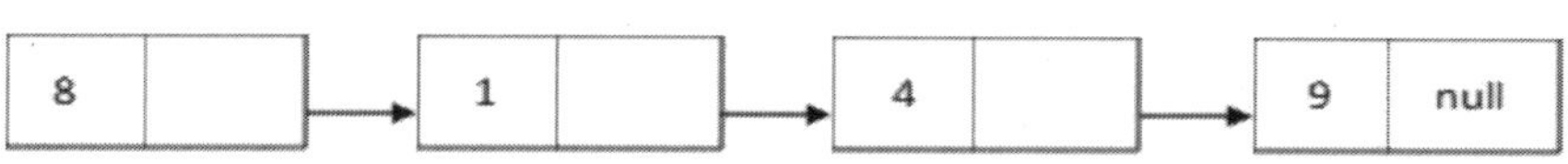

- **Doubly Linked List:** In a doubly linked list, each node contains three parts, two link parts and one data part. The first link points to the previous node and the next link points to the next node in the sequence.

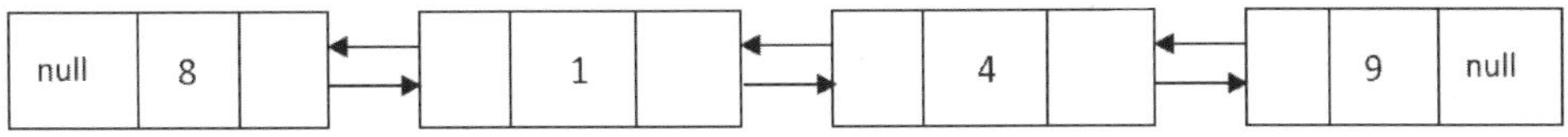

- **Circular Linked List:** In the circular linked list the last node of the list contains the address of the first node, instead of null and thereby forming a circular chain.

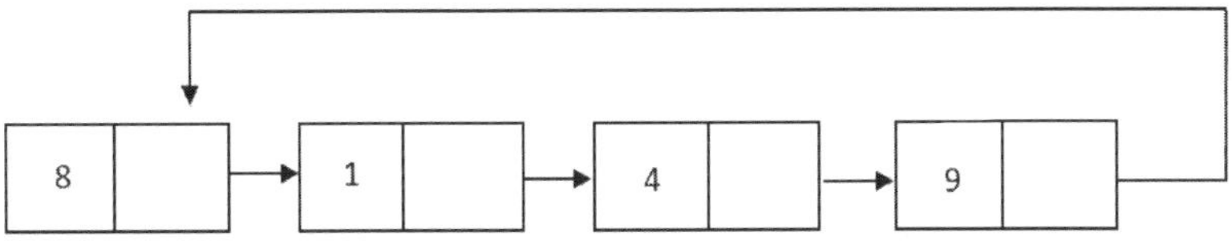

3.5 BASIC OPERATIONS OF LINKED LIST

Following are the basic operations supported by a list.

- **Create** – Creates a linked list.
- **Traversal** – Going to each node and processing it.
- **Insertion** – Adds an element at the beginning/end/desired location of the list.
- **Deletion** – Deletes an element at the beginning/end/desired location of the list.
- **Display** – Displays the complete list.
- **Search** – Searches an element using a given key.

Note: All the above operations will be discussed with reference to the singly linked list.

Before we describe the algorithms to perform various operations in a linked list, let us first discuss an important term called overflow. Overflow is a condition that occurs when avail = null or no free memory cell is present in the system. When this condition occurs, the program must give an appropriate overflow message.

Creating a linked list

Creating a linked list means constructing a new linked list. Insertion is different from create. Insertion means adding a single node to an existing list where as create means to construct a linked list of some desired nodes.

Algorithm to create a linked list: Here 'p' and 'q' are two pointer variables. Pointer variable 'p' is used to store the address of the first node of the list and 'q' is used for traversing. Variable 'item' is the data value to be inserted in the data or information part of the node. 'temp' is a temporary variable, 'n' is the number of nodes to be created.

Step 1: If avail = null, then Print "Overflow"

Go to Step 10

[End of if]

Step 2: Set p = malloc size of struct node

Step 3: Set p->data = item

Step 4: Set p->link = null

Step 5: Set q = p

Step 6: Repeat Step 7 to while i < n

Step 7: Set temp = malloc size of struct node

Step 8: Set temp -> data = item

Step 9: Set temp ->link = null

Step 10: Set q ->link = temp

Step 11: Set q = temp

[End of loop]

Step 12: Exit

In step1, first it is checked whether there is available memory in the system or not. If there is no available memory, then an overflow message is returned. Otherwise, a node 'p' is created and data is stored in the data part and null is stored in the link part. This job is done from step 2 through 4. In step 5, another pointer variable 'q' is made to point to the node 'p'. This additional variable is taken for traversal purpose.

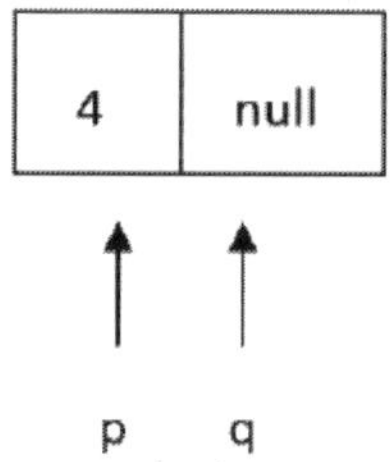

From step 6 through 11remaining nodes of the list is created as per the requirement. Suppose we want to create a list of 3 nodes, then a new node 'temp' is created in step 7. In steps 8 and 9, data 5 is stored in the data part of temp and null is stored in the link part of temp.

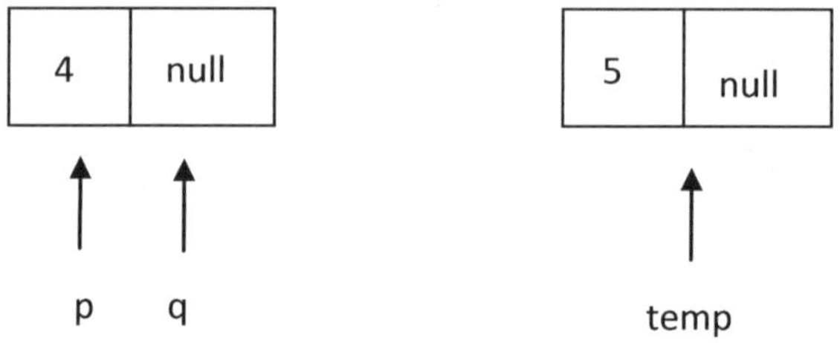

As you see two nodes have been created, but that are not connected. Now its time to update the links. In step 10, q ->link is made to point temp, so that the address of temp is stored in the link part of the node q.

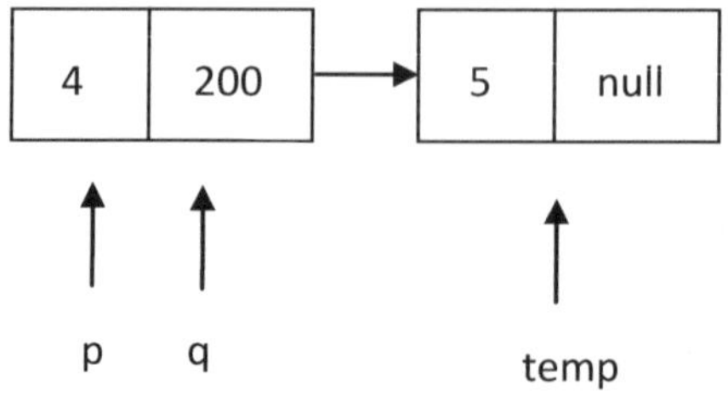

In step 11, pointer q is made is point to the node temp. This is done in order to make temp free, so that a new node can be created using temp.

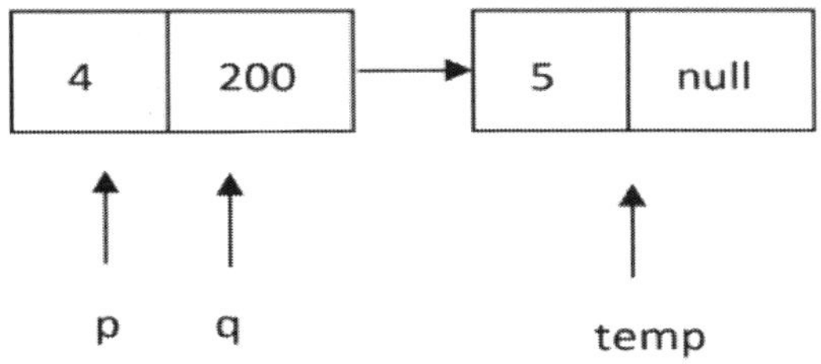

Similarly, other nodes can be created.

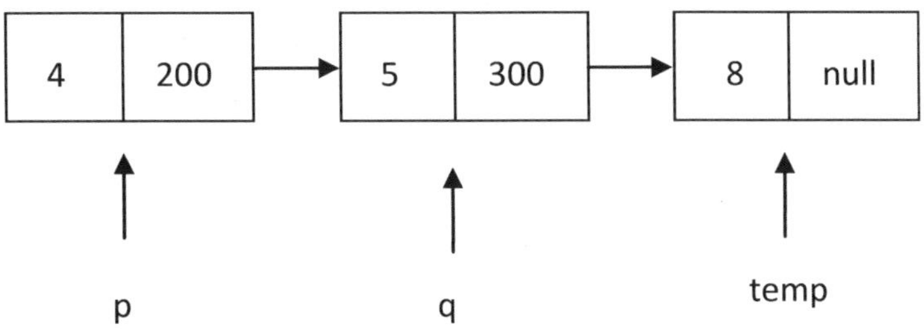

Example 1 : The following program shows creation of a linked list using C++ language

```
#include <iostream>
using namespace std;

struct node {
   int data;
   node* link;
};

void createList(node** p, int n) {
   int item;
   node* temp, * q;

   if (*p != NULL) {
      cout << "Overflow" << endl;
      return;
   }

   *p = (node*)malloc(sizeof(node));
```

```
    cout << "Enter value for node 1: ";
    cin >> item;
    (*p)->data = item;
    (*p)->link = NULL;
    q = *p;

    for (int i = 2; i <= n; i++) {
        temp = (node*)malloc(sizeof(node));
        cout << "Enter value for node " << i << ": ";
        cin >> item;
        temp->data = item;
        temp->link = NULL;
        q->link = temp;
        q = temp;
    }
}

void printList(node* p) {
    if (p == NULL) {
        cout << "The list is empty!" << endl;
        return;
    }

    cout << "Linked List: ";
    node* temp = p;
    while (temp != NULL) {
        cout << temp->data << " -> ";
        temp = temp->link;
    }
    cout << "NULL" << endl;
}

int main() {
    node* head = NULL;
    int n;
```

```
    cout << "Enter the number of nodes: ";
    cin >> n;
    createList(&head, n);
    printList(head);
    return 0;
}
```

Output

Enter the number of nodes: 3

Enter value for node 1: 4

Enter value for node 2: 5

Enter value for node 3: 8

Linked List: 4 -> 5 -> 8 -> NULL

Traversing a Linked List

Traversing a linked list means accessing the nodes of the list in order to perform some processing on them. A linked list always contains a pointer variable, usually referenced as START/ HEAD/p which stores the address of the first node of the list. End of the list is marked by storing NULL or –1 in the LINK field of the last node. For traversing the linked list, we also make use of another pointer variable, usually referenced as PTR/q which points to the node that is currently being accessed. The algorithm to traverse a linked list is shown below:

Algorithm for traversing a linked list: Here 'p' and 'q' are two pointer variables. Pointer variable 'p' is used to store the address of the first node of the list and 'q' is used for traversing. 'data' is used to store the data value of the node and 'link' stores the address of the next node.

Step 1: [Initialize] Set q = p

Step 2: Repeat Steps 3 and 4 while q != null

Step 3: Apply Process to q->data

Step 4: Set q = q->link

[End ofloop]

Step 5: Exit

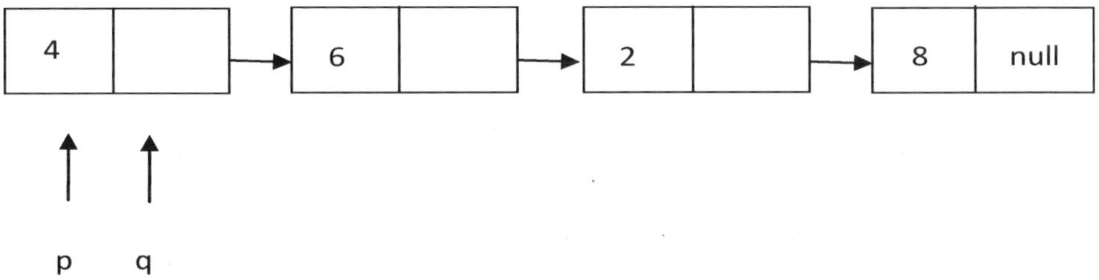

In step1, pointer variable q is set to point to the first node, which is also pointed by p. In step2, while loop is used to go to each node starting from the first node till null value is not encountered. In step3, required operation is performed on the data of each node. In step4, q is updated to move to the next node of the list.

Example 2: The following program shows traversing of a linked list using C++ language.

```
#include <iostream>
using namespace std;
struct node {
  int data;
  node* link;
};
void traverseList(node* p) {
  node* q = p;
  while (q != NULL) {
    cout << q->data << " ";
    q = q->link;
  }
  cout << endl;
}

int main() {
  node* head = NULL;
  int n, data;

  cout << "Enter the number of nodes: ";
  cin >> n;

  for (int i = 1; i <= n; i++) {
    node* temp = new node;
    cout << "Enter value for node " << i << ": ";
    cin >> data;

    temp->data = data;
    temp->link = NULL;

    if (head == NULL) {
      head = temp;
    } else {
```

```
        node* last = head;
        while (last->link != NULL) {
          last = last->link;
        }
        last->link = temp;
      }
    }

    cout << "Traversing the Linked List: ";
    traverseList(head);
    return 0;
}
```

Output :

Enter the number of nodes: 4

Enter value for node 1: 4

Enter value for node 2: 6

Enter value for node 3: 2

Enter value for node 4: 8

Traversing the Linked List: 4 6 2 8

Searching for a key in a Linked List

Searching a linked list means to find a particular element (usually referred as key) in the linked list. As already discussed,a linked list consists of nodes which are divided into two parts, the information part and the linkpart. So, searching means finding whether a given value is present in the information part of the node or not. If it is present, the algorithm returns the address of the node that contains the value.

Algorithm to search an unsorted linked list: Here 'p' and 'q' are two pointer variables. Pointer variable 'p' is used to store the address of the first node of the list and 'q' is used for traversing. 'key' is the required element to be searched. 'data' is the value stored in the information part of the node and 'link' stores the address of the next node. Variable 'pos' stores the position or location of the key.

```
Step 1: [Initialize] Set q = p
Step 2: Repeat Steps 3 and 4 while q != null
Step 3:         If key = q->data
                        Setpos = q
                        Go To Step 5
                Else
```

                Set q = q->link

        [End of if]

    [End of loop]

Step 4: SET pos = null

Step 5: Exit

In step1, pointer variable q is set to point to the first node, which is also pointed by p. In step2, while loop is used to go to each node starting from the first node till null value is not encountered. In step3, the key is matched with the data of every node. If the match is successful than the position of the node is displayed. In step4, position is displayed as null, if the key does not exist in the list.

Let us take the following linked list to explain the algorithm. Suppose the key to be searched is 7.

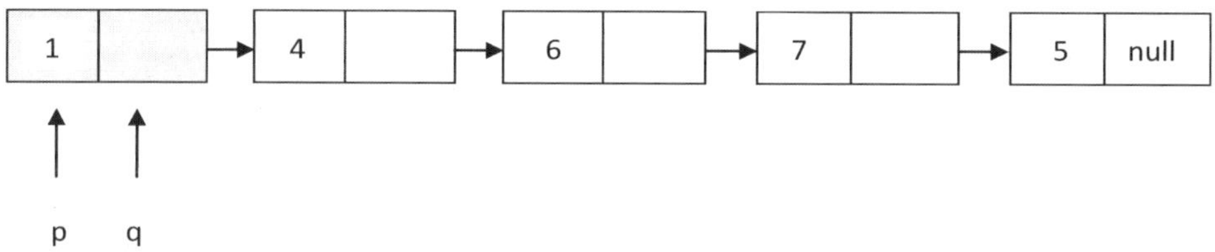

Here q->data = 1. Since q->data ! = 7, so we move to the next node.

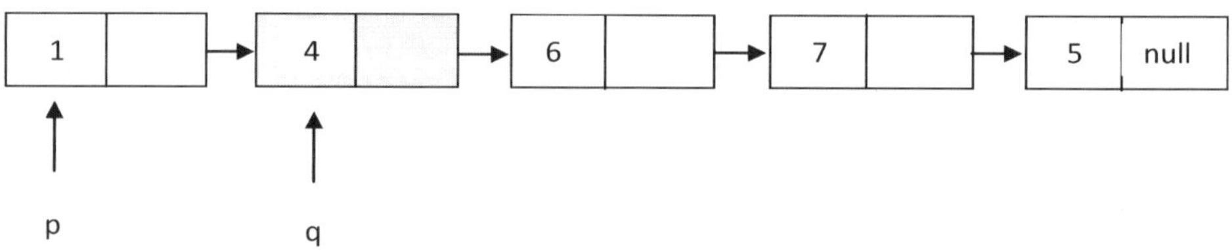

Here q->data = 4. Since q->data ! = 7, so we move to the next node.

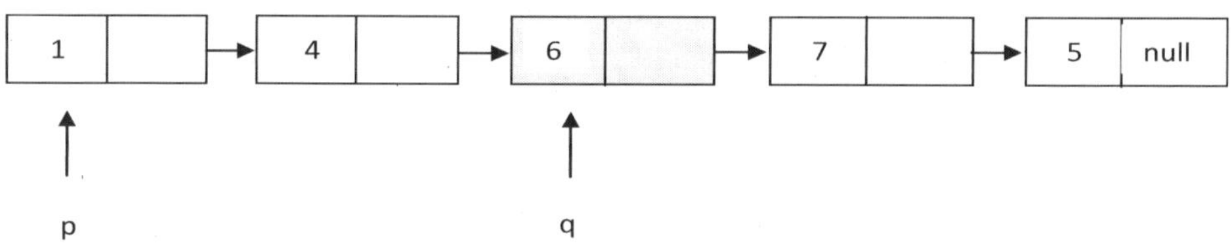

Here q->data = 6. Since q->data ! = 7, so we move to the next node.

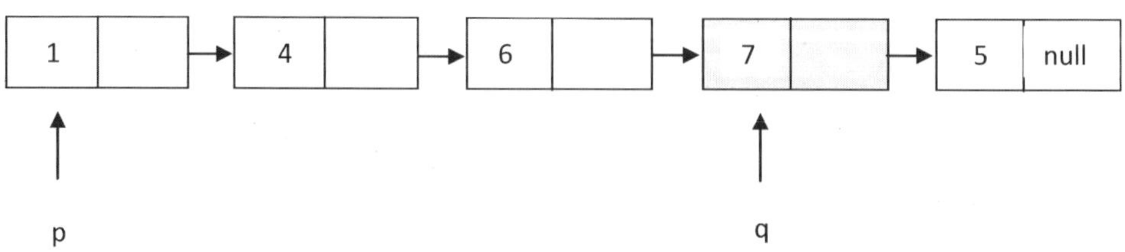

Here q->data = 7. Since q->data = 7, which is the desired key. So, pos = q. Variable pos now stores the address of the node that contains the key.

Example 3: The following program shows searching operation in an unsorted linked list using C++ language.

```
#include <iostream>
using namespace std;

struct node {
   int data;
   node* link;
};

void searchList(node* p, int key) {
   node* q = p;
   node* pos = NULL;

   while (q != NULL) {
      if (q->data == key) {
         pos = q;
         break;
      }
      q = q->link;
   }

   if (pos != NULL) {
      cout << "Element " << key << " found at memory address: " << pos << endl;
   } else {
      cout << "Element " << key << " not found in the list." << endl;
   }
}

void traverseList(node* p) {
   node* q = p;
   while (q != NULL) {
      cout << q->data << " ";
      q = q->link;
   }
```

```
    cout << "NULL" << endl;
}

int main() {
    node* head = NULL;
    int n, data, searchKey;

    cout << "Enter the number of nodes: ";
    cin >> n;

    for (int i = 1; i <= n; i++) {
        node* temp = new node;
        cout << "Enter value for node " << i << ": ";
        cin >> data;

        temp->data = data;
        temp->link = NULL;

        if (head == NULL) {
            head = temp;
        } else {
            node* last = head;
            while (last->link != NULL) {
                last = last->link;
            }
            last->link = temp;
        }
    }

    cout << "Linked List: ";
    traverseList(head);

    cout << "Enter value to search: ";
    cin >> searchKey;
```

```
    searchList(head, searchKey);

    return 0;
}
```

Output :

Enter the number of nodes: 5

Enter value for node 1: 1

Enter value for node 2: 4

Enter value for node 3: 6

Enter value for node 4: 7

Enter value for node 5: 5

Linked List: 1 4 6 7 5 NULL

Enter value to search: 7

Element 7 found at memory address: 0x1e4a6b30

Inserting a New Node in a Linked List

Inserting a new node means to add a new node into an already existing linked list. Insertion operation involves three things – (a) create a node (b) Assign data to the node (c) Update the pointers.

While doing insertion operation, we have to keep in mind the position of insertion. In general, we have three instances of insertion operation. These are:

- Insertion at the beginning of the list.
- Insertion at the end of the list.
- Insertion after a desired location of the list.

Insertion at the beginning of a Linked List

Insertion at the beginning means to add a new node at the first location of an already existing linked list. Unlike array insertion operation in a linked list does not require shifting of the previously occupied nodes.

Algorithm to insert a new node in the beginning of the linked list: Here 'p' is a pointer variable that is used to store the address of the first node of the list. 'temp' is the newly created node. 'item' is the data to be stored in the new node.

Step 1: If p = null, then Print "Overflow"

Go to Step 6

[End of if]

Step 2: Set temp = malloc size of struct node

Step 3: Set temp->data = item

Step 4: Set temp->link = p

Step 5: Set p = temp

Step 6: Exit

In step1, first it is checked whether there is available memory in the system or not. If there is no available memory, then an overflow message is returned. Otherwise in step2, a node 'temp' is created and data 'item' is stored in the data part and the link part is connected to 'p' which is the first node of the linked list. In step5 temp is set as p, so that the new node temp is marked as the first node.

Consider the linked list shown below. Suppose we want to add a new node with data 8 and add it as the first node of the list. Then the following changes will be done in the linked list.

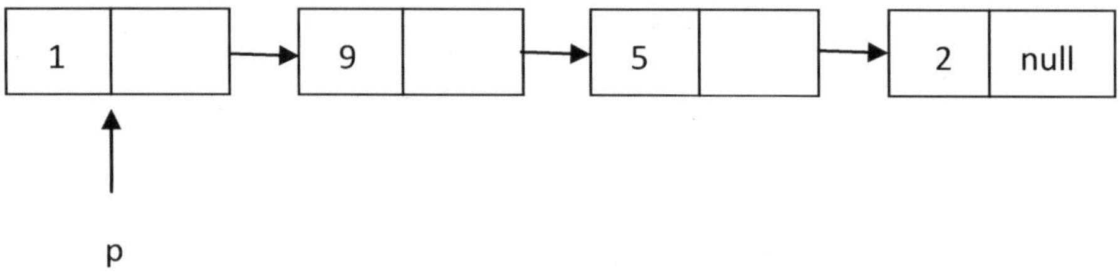

Already existing linked list.

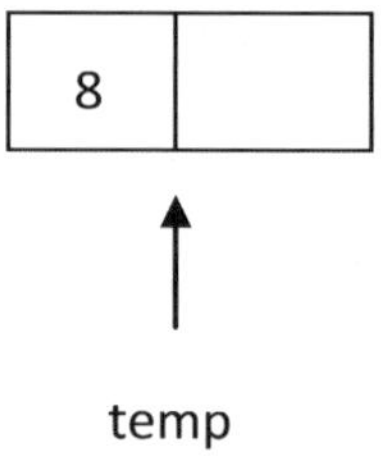

A new node temp is created and 8 is stored in its data part.

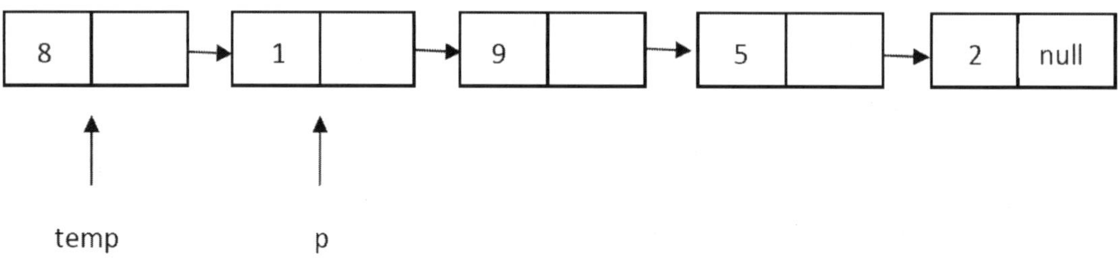

The link part of temp is connected to p.

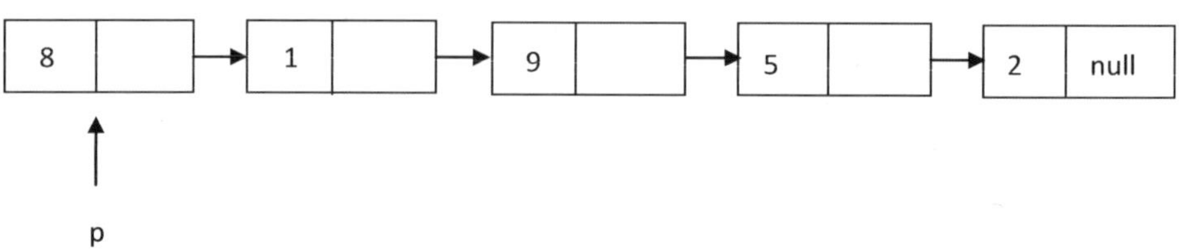

Now temp is set as p.

Example 4: The following program shows inserting a new node in the beginning of a linked list using C++ language.

```
#include <iostream>
using namespace std;
struct node {
  int data;
  node* link;
};

void insertAtFront(node** p, int item) {
  if (*p == NULL) {
    cout << "Overflow\n";
    return;
  }

  node* temp = (node*)malloc(sizeof(node));

  if (temp == NULL) {
    cout << "Memory allocation failed\n";
    return;
  }

  temp->data = item;
  temp->link = *p;
  *p = temp;
}

void printList(node* p) {
  node* q = p;
  while (q != NULL) {
    cout << q->data << " ";
    q = q->link;
  }
  cout << endl;
}
```

```
int main() {
    node* head = NULL;
    int n, data;

    cout << "Enter the number of nodes in the list: ";
    cin >> n;

    // Creating the linked list
    for (int i = 1; i <= n; i++) {
        cout << "Enter data for node " << i << ": ";
        cin >> data;

        node* temp = (node*)malloc(sizeof(node));
        temp->data = data;
        temp->link = NULL;

        if (head == NULL) {
            head = temp;
        } else {
            node* last = head;
            while (last->link != NULL) {
                last = last->link;
            }
            last->link = temp;
        }
    }

    cout << "Original Linked List: ";
    printList(head);

    // Insert a new node at the front
    cout << "Enter data for the new node to insert at the front: ";
    cin >> data;
    insertAtFront(&head, data);
```

```
    cout << "Updated Linked List after insertion: ";
    printList(head);

    return 0;
}
```

Output

Enter the number of nodes in the list: 4

Enter data for node 1: 1

Enter data for node 2: 9

Enter data for node 3: 5

Enter data for node 4: 2

Original Linked List: 1 9 5 2

Enter data for the new node to insert at the front: 8

Updated Linked List after insertion: 8 1 9 5 2

Insertion at the end of a Linked List

Insertion at the end means to add a new node after the last location of an already existing linked list.

Algorithm to insert a new node at the end of the linked list: Here 'p' is a pointer variable that is used to store the address of the first node of the list. 'q' is another pointer variable that is used while traversing the list. 'temp' is the newly created node. 'item' is the data to be stored in the new node.

Step 1: If p = null, then Print "Overflow"

Go to Step 9

[Endof if]

Step 2: Set temp = malloc size of struct node

Step 3: Set temp->data = item

Step 4: Set temp->link = null

Step 5: Set q = p

Step 6: Repeat Step 7 while q->link != null

Step 7: Set q = q ->link

[End of loop]

Step 8: Set q->link = temp

Step 9: Exit

In step1, first it is checked whether there is available memory in the system or not. If there is no available memory, then an overflow message is returned. Otherwise in step2, a node 'temp' is created. In step3 'item' is stored in the data part and in step4 null is stored in the link part. In step5 another pointer variable q is set as p, so that the both p and q points to the first node. This is done so that the link to the first node could be saved for other purposes such as displaying the list. If the link to the first node is lost than it won't be possible to fetch the entire linked list later. So, p will be fixed and q will be used for traversing the list. In step6 while loop is used to set the condition of traversing. Till we do not get null value in the link part of the node we have to traverse. Step7 is to go the next node while traversing. Once our condition is fulfilled, i.e. we get null value in the link part than the control will come out of the while loop and in step8 the newly created node (temp) will be connected to the last node.

Consider the linked list shown below. Suppose we want to add a new node with data 6 and add it after the last node of the list. Then the following changes will be done in the linked list.

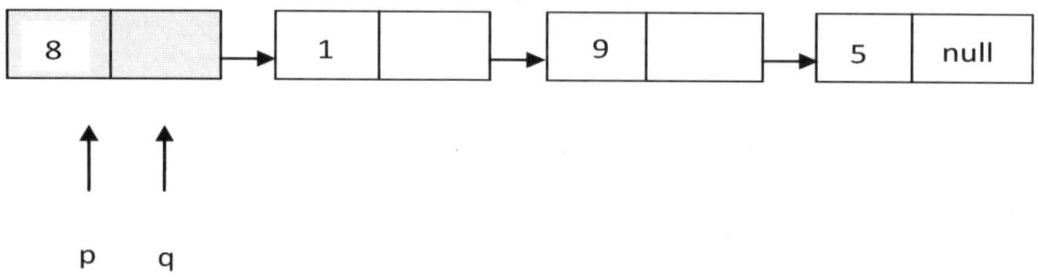

Already existing linked list.

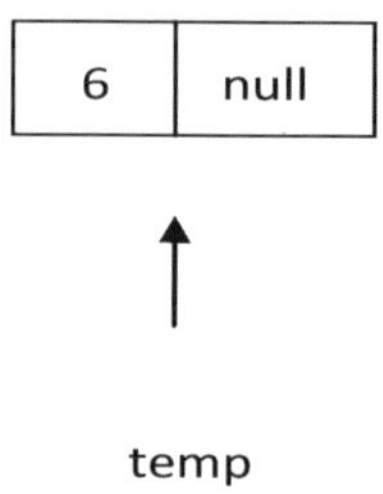

Here q-> link != null. So, it moves to the next node, i.e. q = q ->link

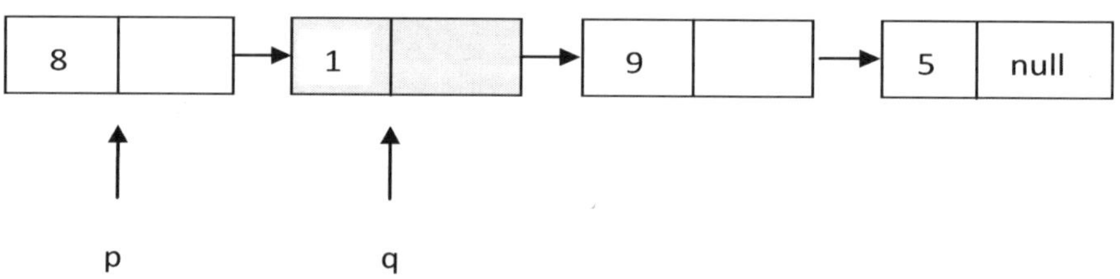

Here q-> link != null. So, it moves to the next node, i.e. q = q ->link

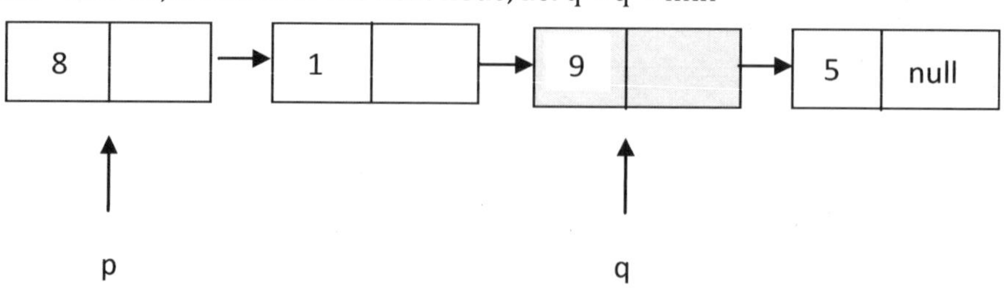

Here q-> link != null. So, it moves to the next node, i.e. q = q ->link

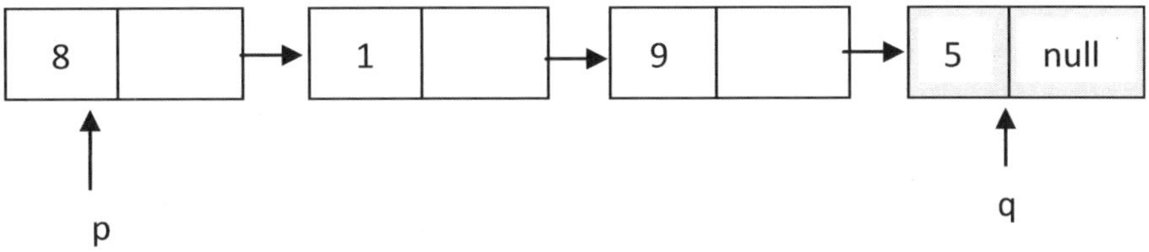

Here q-> link = null. Condition is met. So, traversing stops here and the newly created node (temp) is linked with q.

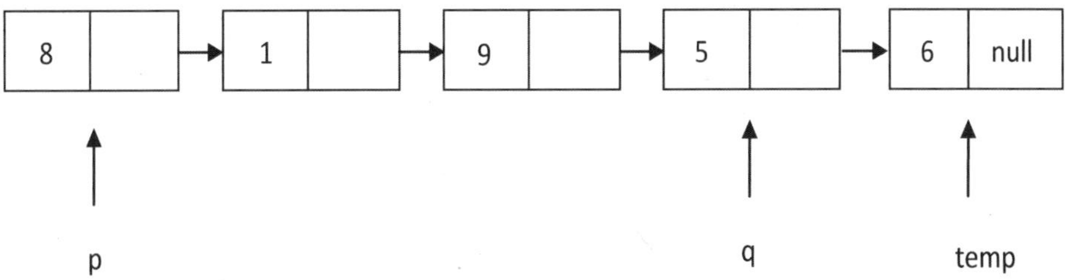

Example 5: The following program shows inserting a new node in the end of a linked list using C++ language.

```
#include <iostream>
using namespace std;

struct node {
  int data;
  node* link;
};

void insertAtEnd(node** p, int item) {
  if (*p == NULL) {
    cout << "Overflow\n";
    return;
  }

  node* temp = (node*)malloc(sizeof(node));

  if (temp == NULL) {
    cout << "Memory allocation failed\n";
    return;
```

```
    }

    temp->data = item;
    temp->link = NULL;

    node* q = *p;

    while (q->link != NULL) {
        q = q->link;
    }

    q->link = temp;
}

void printList(node* p) {
    node* q = p;
    while (q != NULL) {
        cout << q->data << " ";
        q = q->link;
    }
    cout << endl;
}

int main() {
    node* head = NULL;
    int n, data;

    cout << "Enter the number of nodes in the list: ";
    cin >> n;

    // Create the linked list
    for (int i = 1; i <= n; i++) {
        cout << "Enter data for node " << i << ": ";
        cin >> data;
```

```
    node* temp = (node*)malloc(sizeof(node));
    temp->data = data;
    temp->link = NULL;

    if (head == NULL) {
      head = temp;
    } else {
      node* last = head;
      while (last->link != NULL) {
        last = last->link;
      }
      last->link = temp;
    }
  }

  cout << "Original Linked List: ";
  printList(head);

  // Insert a new node at the end
  cout << "Enter data for the new node to insert at the end: ";
  cin >> data;
  insertAtEnd(&head, data);

  cout << "Updated Linked List after insertion: ";
  printList(head);

  return 0;
}
```

Output

Enter the number of nodes in the list: 4

Enter data for node 1: 8

Enter data for node 2: 1

Enter data for node 3: 9

Enter data for node 4: 5

Original Linked List: 8 1 9 5

Enter data for the new node to insert at the end: 6

Updated Linked List after insertion: 8 1 9 5 6

Insertion after any desired location of the list

Insertion at any desired location means to add a new node after a desired position or location of an already existing linked list.

Algorithm to insert a new node after a desired location of the linked list: Here 'p' is a pointer variable that is used to store the address of the first node of the list. 'q' is another pointer variable that is used while traversing the list. 'temp' is the newly created node. 'item' is the data to be stored in the new node. 'loc' is the location after which a new node is created.

Step 1: If p = null, then Print "Overflow"

Go to Step 9

[End of if]

Step 2: Set q = p

Step 3: Repeat Step 4 for (i = 0;i < loc;i++)

Step 4: Set q = q->link

[End of loop]

Step 5: Set temp = malloc size of struct node

Step 6: Set temp->data = item

Step 7: Set temp->link = q->link

Step 8: Set q->link = temp

Step 9: Exit

In step1, first it is checked whether there is available memory in the system or not. If there is no available memory, than an overflow message is returned. Otherwise in step2, another pointer variable q is set as p, so that the both p and q points to the first node. This is done so that the link to the first node could be saved for other purposes such as displaying the list. If the link to the first node is lost than it won't be possible to fetch the entire linked list later. So, p will be fixed and q will be used for traversing the list. In step3, for loop is used to reach to the desired location (loc). In step4 nodes are traversed till desired location is not reached. In step5 a node 'temp' is created. In step6 'item' is stored in the data part of temp. In step7 link part of temp is connected to the node next to q. In step8 the link part of q is connected to temp.

Consider the linked list shown below. Suppose we want to add a new node with data 6, after the third position (i.e. loc = 3). Then the following changes will be done in the linked list.

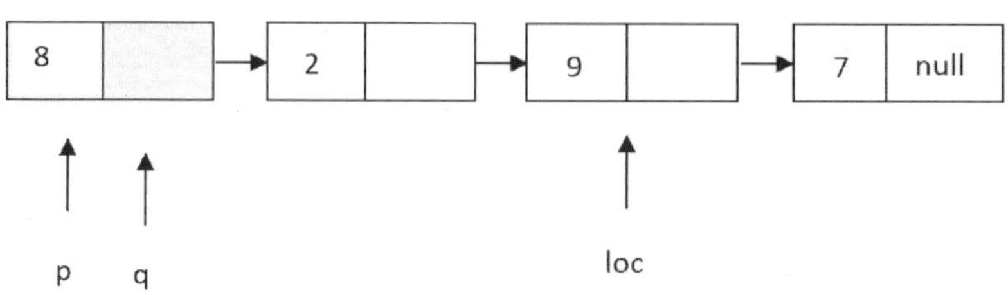

Already existing linked list.

Here i < loc. So, it moves to the next node, i.e. q = q ->link.

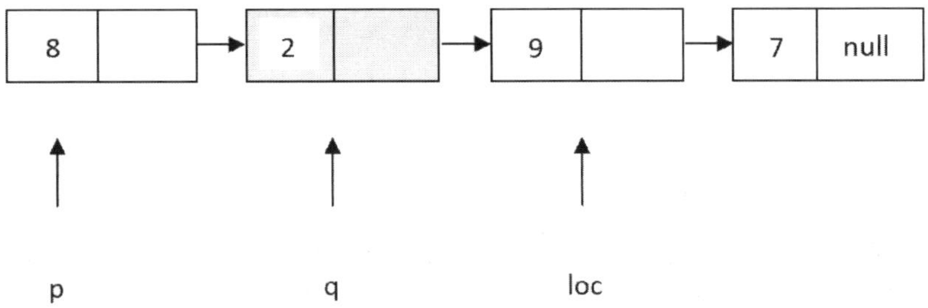

Here i < loc. So, it moves to the next node, i.e. q = q ->link

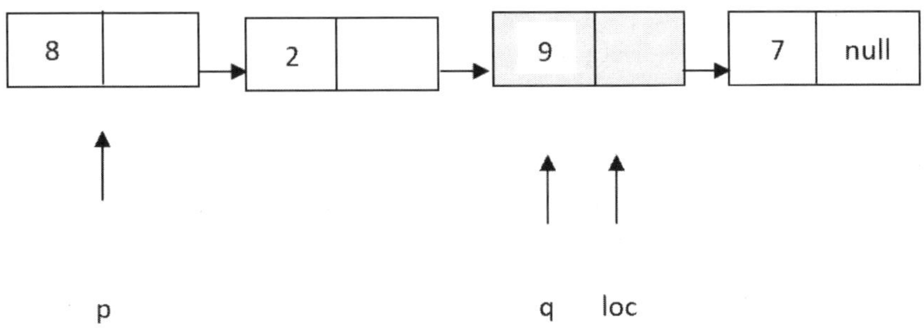

Here i ! < loc. So, it comes out of the loop and a new node temp is created.

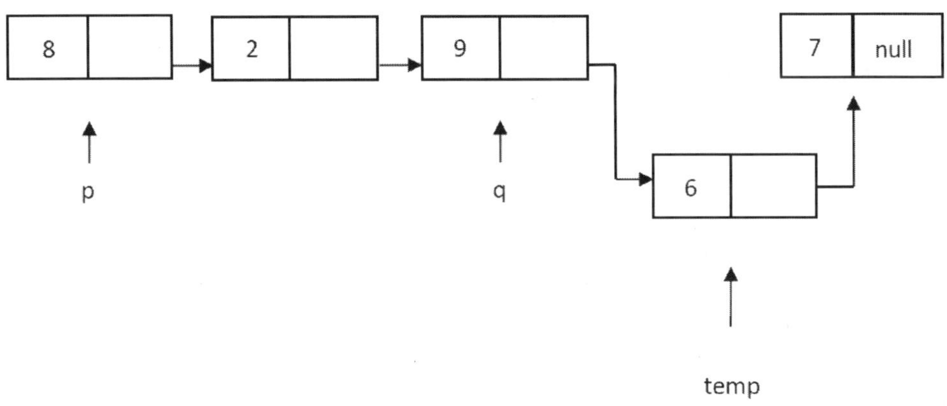

Example 6: The following program shows inserting a new node after any desired location in a linked list using C++ language.

```
#include <iostream>
using namespace std;
```

```
struct node {
  int data;
  node* link;
};

void insertAtLocation(node** p, int item, int loc) {
  if (*p == NULL) {
    cout << "Overflow\n";
    return;
  }

  node* q = *p;

  // Traverse to the location
  for (int i = 0; i < loc; i++) {
    if (q->link == NULL) {
      cout << "Location is beyond the end of the list.\n";
      return;
    }
    q = q->link;
  }

  // Create a new node
  node* temp = (node*)malloc(sizeof(node));
  temp->data = item;

  // Insert the new node
  temp->link = q->link;
  q->link = temp;
}

void printList(node* p) {
  node* q = p;
  while (q != NULL) {
    cout << q->data << " ";
```

```
    q = q->link;
  }
  cout << endl;
}

int main() {
  node* head = NULL;
  int n, data, loc;

  cout << "Enter the number of nodes in the list: ";
  cin >> n;

  // Creating the linked list
  for (int i = 1; i <= n; i++) {
    cout << "Enter data for node " << i << ": ";
    cin >> data;

    node* temp = (node*)malloc(sizeof(node));
    temp->data = data;
    temp->link = NULL;

    if (head == NULL) {
      head = temp;
    } else {
      node* last = head;
      while (last->link != NULL) {
        last = last->link;
      }
      last->link = temp;
    }
  }

  cout << "Original Linked List: ";
  printList(head);
```

```
    // Insert a new node at a specified location
    cout << "Enter the location after which we want to insert the new node: ";
    cin >> loc;
    cout << "Enter data for the new node to insert after location " << loc << ": ";
    cin >> data;
    insertAtLocation(&head, data, loc);

    cout << "Updated Linked List after insertion: ";
    printList(head);

    return 0;
}
```

Output :

```
Enter the number of nodes in the list: 4
Enter data for node 1: 8
Enter data for node 2: 2
Enter data for node 3: 9
Enter data for node 4: 7
Original Linked List: 8 2 9 7
Enter the location after which we want to insert the new node: 2
Enter data for the new node to insert after location 2 : 6
Updated Linked List after insertion: 8 2 9 6 7
```

Deleting a Node from a Linked List

In this section, we will discuss algorithms to delete a node from an already existing linked list. We will consider three instances and then see how deletion is done in each instance.

- Deleting the first node from a linked list.
- Deleting the last node from a linked list.
- Deleting a node after a desired location from a linked list.

Before we describe the algorithms in all these three cases, let us first discuss an important term called UNDERFLOW. Underflow is a condition that occurs when we try to delete a node from a linked list that is empty. This happens when START = NULL or when there are no more nodes to delete.

Note that when we delete a node from a linked list, we actually have to free the memory occupied by that node. The memory is returned to the free pool so that it can be used to store other programs and data. Whatever be the case of deletion, we always change the AVAIL pointer so that it points to the address that has been recently vacated.

Algorithm to delete the first node from a linked list: Here 'p' is a pointer variable that is used to store the address of the first node of the list. q is another pointer variable that is used for updating purpose.

Step 1: If p = null, then Print"Underflow"

Go to Step 5

[End of if]

Step 2: Set q = p

Step 3: Set p = p->link

Step 4: Delete q

Step 5: Exit

In step1, first it is checked whether there is any node present in the linked list or not. If there is no node, then an underflow message is returned. In step 2, another variable q is set to p, so that both points at the first node of the list. In step 3 p is set to point to the second node. In step 4, the first node that is pointed by q is deleted or set free, so that the deleted memory location goes to the free pool.

Consider the linked list shown below. Suppose we want to delete the first node of the list. Then the following changes will be done in the linked list.

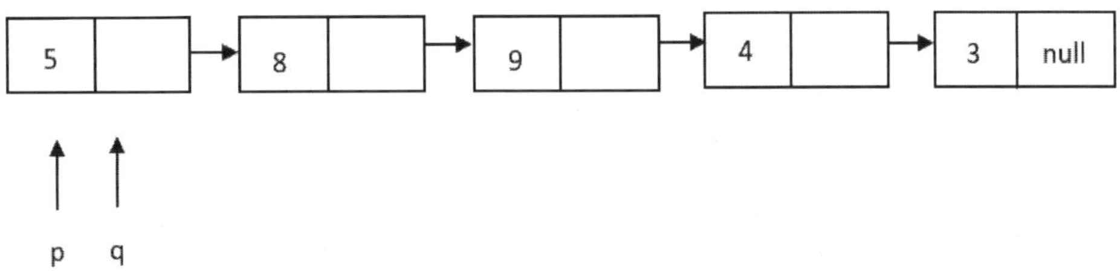

Already existing linked list where p and q points to the first node.

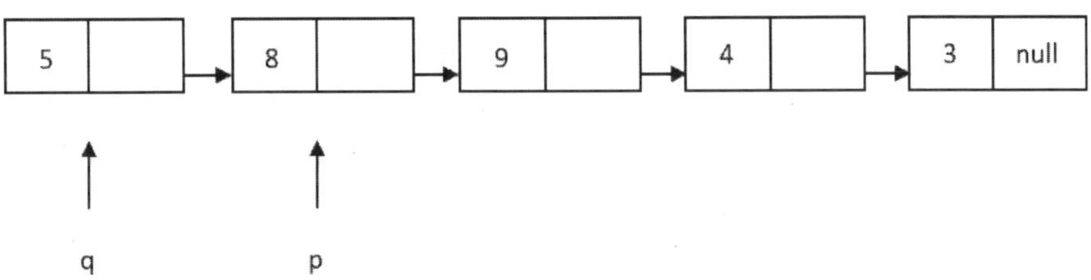

p is set to point to the second node of the list.

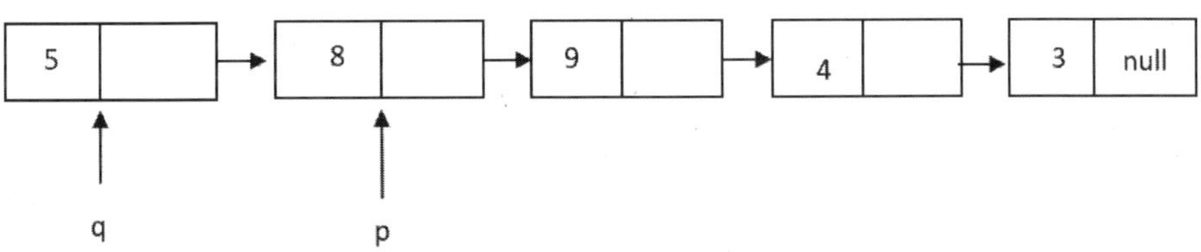

q is set free. Now the list starts from the second node.

Example 7: The following program shows deletion of first node from the beginning of a linked list using C++ language.

```
#include <iostream>
using namespace std;

struct node {
  int data;
  node* link;
};

void deleteFirstNode(node** p) {
  if (*p == NULL) {
    cout << "Underflow\n";
    return;
  }

  node* q = *p;
  *p = (*p)->link;

  delete q;
}

void printList(node* p) {
  node* q = p;
  while (q != NULL) {
    cout << q->data << " ";
    q = q->link;
  }
  cout << endl;
}

int main() {
  node* head = NULL;
  int n, data;
```

```
  cout << "Enter the number of nodes in the list: ";
  cin >> n;

  for (int i = 1; i <= n; i++) {
    cout << "Enter data for node " << i << ": ";
    cin >> data;

    node* temp = new node;
    temp->data = data;
    temp->link = NULL;

    if (head == NULL) {
      head = temp;
    } else {
      node* last = head;
      while (last->link != NULL) {
        last = last->link;
      }
      last->link = temp;
    }
  }

  cout << "Original Linked List: ";
  printList(head);

  deleteFirstNode(&head);

  cout << "Updated Linked List after deletion: ";
  printList(head);

  return 0;
}
```

Output

Enter the number of nodes in the list: 5

Enter data for node 1: 5

Enter data for node 2: 8

Enter data for node 3: 9

Enter data for node 4: 4

Enter data for node 5: 3

Original Linked List: 5 8 9 4 3

Updated Linked List after deletion: 8 9 4 3

Algorithm to delete the last node of the linked list: Here 'p' is a pointer variable that is used to store the address of the first node of the list. q is another pointer variable that is used for traversing.

Step 1: If p = null, then Print "Underflow"

Go to Step 6

[End of if]

Step 2: Set q = p

Step 3: Repeat Step 4 and 7 while q->link->link != null

Step 4: Set q= q->link

[End of loop]

Step 5: temp = q->link

Step 6: Set q->link = null

Step 7: Delete temp

Step 8: Exit

In step1, first it is checked whether there is any node present in the linked list or not. If there is no node, then an underflow message is returned. In step2, another variable q is set as p, so that both points at the first node of the list. In step3 while loop is used to traverse to the last node. Step 4, is for traversing. Step 5 stores the address of the last node in the temp pointer so that it can be freed later. Step 6 disconnects the last node from the linked list. Step 7 deallocates the memory occupied by the last node.

Consider the linked list shown below. Suppose we want to delete the last node of the list. Then the following changes will be done in the linked list.

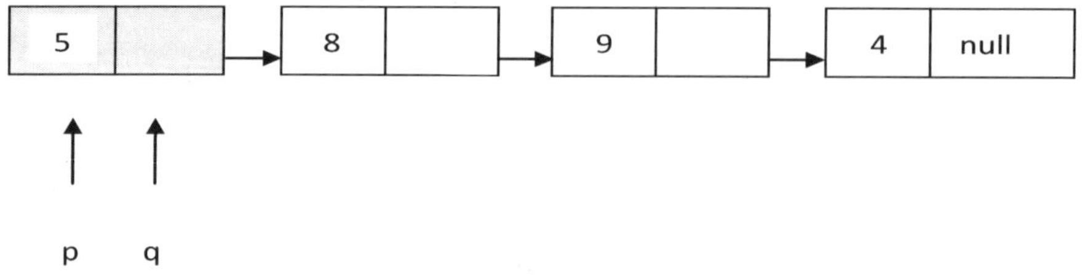

Already existing linked list where p and q points to the first node.

Here q->link ->link!= null. So, it moves to the next node, i.e. q = q ->link.

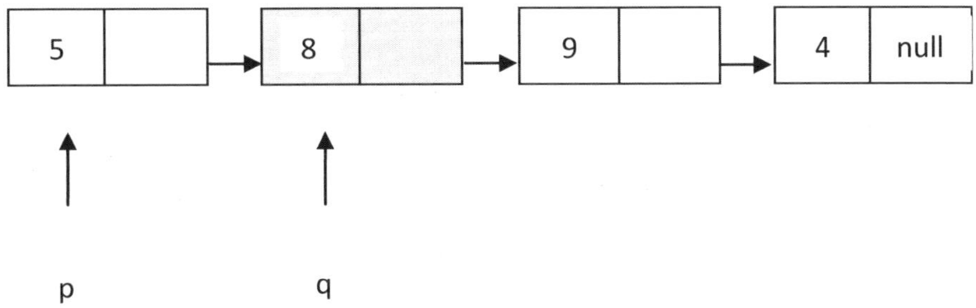

Here q->link ->link= null. So, temp is used to store the address of the second last node, i.e. temp = q->link

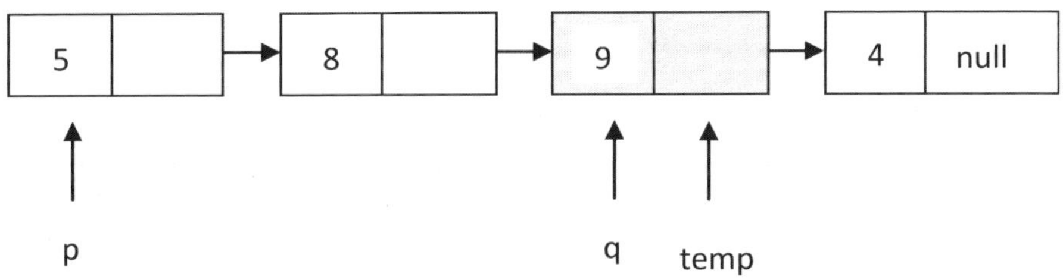

Since q is pointing to the second last node, setting q->link = NULL makes it the new last node.

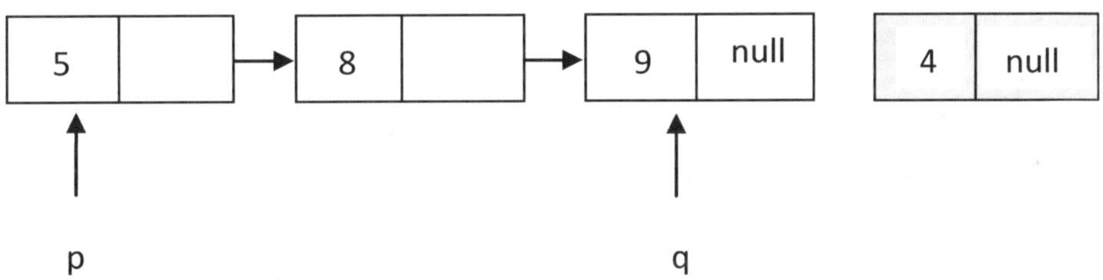

Since temp was pointing to the last node (stored in Step 5), calling free(temp) releases the memory.

Example 8: The following program shows deletion of last node from the end of a linked list using C++ language.

```
#include <iostream>
using namespace std;

struct node {
  int data;
  node* link;
};

void deleteLastNode(node** p) {
  if (*p == NULL) {
```

```
        cout << "Underflow\n";
        return;
    }

    node* q = *p;

    while (q->link != NULL && q->link->link != NULL) {
        q = q->link;
    }

    node* temp = q->link;
    q->link = NULL;

    delete temp;
}

void printList(node* p) {
    node* q = p;
    while (q != NULL) {
        cout << q->data << " ";
        q = q->link;
    }
    cout << endl;
}

int main() {
    node* head = NULL;
    int n, data;

    cout << "Enter the number of nodes in the list: ";
    cin >> n;

    for (int i = 1; i <= n; i++) {
        cout << "Enter data for node " << i << ": ";
        cin >> data;
```

```
    node* temp = new node;
    temp->data = data;
    temp->link = NULL;

    if (head == NULL) {
      head = temp;
    } else {
      node* last = head;
      while (last->link != NULL) {
        last = last->link;
      }
      last->link = temp;
    }
  }

  cout << "Original Linked List: ";
  printList(head);

  deleteLastNode(&head);

  cout << "Updated Linked List after deletion: ";
  printList(head);

  return 0;
}
```

Output

Enter the number of nodes in the list: 4

Enter data for node 1: 5

Enter data for node 2: 8

Enter data for node 3: 9

Enter data for node 4: 4

Original Linked List: 5 8 9 4

Updated Linked List after deletion: 5 8 9

Algorithm to delete a node after a desired location of the linked list: Here 'p' is a pointer variable that is used to store the address of the first node of the list. q is another pointer variable that is used for traversing.

Step 1: If p == NULL, then print "Underflow" (linked list is empty) and exit.

Step 2: Set q = p.

Step 3: Repeat Step 4 for (i = 0; i < loc; i++):

Step 4: If q->link == NULL, then print "Invalid location" and exit.

Step 5: Set q = q->link.

Step 6: If q->link == NULL, print "No node exists after the given location" and exit.

Step 7: Set temp = q->link (store the node to be deleted).

Step 8: Set q->link = temp->link (bypass the node to be deleted).

Step 9:Delete temp (deallocate the memory of the deleted node).

Step 10: Exit.

Example 9: The following program shows deletion of node after a desired location of a linked list using C++ language.

```
#include <iostream>
using namespace std;

struct node {
  int data;
  node* link;
};

void deleteAtLocation(node** p, int loc) {
  if (*p == NULL) {
    cout << "Underflow\n";
    return;
  }

  node* q = *p;

  for (int i = 0; i < loc; i++) {
    if (q->link == NULL) {
      cout << "Invalid location\n";
      return;
    }
```

```
        q = q->link;
    }

    if (q->link == NULL) {
        cout << "No node exists after the given location\n";
        return;
    }

    node* temp = q->link;
    q->link = temp->link;
    delete temp;
}

void printList(node* p) {
    node* q = p;
    while (q != NULL) {
        cout << q->data << " ";
        q = q->link;
    }
    cout << endl;
}

int main() {
    node* head = NULL;
    int n, data, loc;

    cout << "Enter the number of nodes in the list: ";
    cin >> n;

    for (int i = 1; i <= n; i++) {
        cout << "Enter data for node " << i << ": ";
        cin >> data;

        node* temp = new node;
        temp->data = data;
```

```
        temp->link = NULL;

        if (head == NULL) {
            head = temp;
        } else {
            node* last = head;
            while (last->link != NULL) {
                last = last->link;
            }
            last->link = temp;
        }
    }

    cout << "Original Linked List: ";
    printList(head);

    cout << "Enter the location after which we want to delete node: ";
    cin >> loc;

    deleteAtLocation(&head, loc);

    cout << "Updated Linked List after deletion: ";
    printList(head);

    return 0;
}
```

Output :

Enter the number of nodes in the list: 4

Enter data for node 1: 2

Enter data for node 2: 4

Enter data for node 3: 5

Enter data for node 4: 7

Original Linked List: 2 4 5 7

Enter the location after which we want to delete node: 2

Updated Linked List after deletion: 2 4 5

Algorithm to print the information stored in each node of the linked list

Step 1: [INITIALIZE] SET q = p

Step 2: Repeat Steps 3 and 4 while q != NULL

Step 3: Write q->DATA

Step 4: SET q =q->NEXT

[END OF LOOP]

Step 5: EXIT

Example 10: The following program shows to print the information stored in each node of the linked list using C++ language.

```
#include <iostream>
using namespace std;

struct node {
  int data;
  node* link;
};

void printList(node* p) {
  node* q = p;
  while (q != NULL) {
    cout << q->data << " ";
    q = q->link;
  }
  cout << endl;
}

int main() {
  node* head = NULL;
  int n, data;

  cout << "Enter the number of nodes in the list: ";
  cin >> n;

  for (int i = 1; i <= n; i++) {
    cout << "Enter data for node " << i << ": ";
    cin >> data;
```

```
        node* temp = new node;
        temp->data = data;
        temp->link = NULL;

        if (head == NULL) {
            head = temp;
        } else {
            node* last = head;
            while (last->link != NULL) {
                last = last->link;
            }
            last->link = temp;
        }
    }
    cout << "Linked List: ";
    printList(head);
    return 0;
}
```

Output :

Enter the number of nodes in the list: 4

Enter data for node 1: 1

Enter data for node 2: 3

Enter data for node 3: 5

Enter data for node 4: 6

Linked List: 1 3 5 6

Algorithm to print the number of nodes in the linked list

Step 1: [INITIALIZE] SET Count = 0

Step 2: [INITIALIZE] SET q = p

Step 3: Repeat Steps 4 and 5 while q != NULL

Step 4: SET Count = Count + 1

Step 5: SET q =q->NEXT

[END OF LOOP]

Step 6: EXIT

Example 11: The following program shows to print the number of nodes of the linked list using C++ language.

```
#include <iostream>
using namespace std;

struct node {
  int data;
  node* link;
};

int countNodes(node* p) {
  int Count = 0;
  node* q = p;

  while (q != NULL) {
    Count = Count + 1;
    q = q->link;
  }

  return Count;
}

int main() {
  node* head = NULL;
  int n, data;

  cout << "Enter the number of nodes in the list: ";
  cin >> n;

  for (int i = 1; i <= n; i++) {
    cout << "Enter data for node " << i << ": ";
    cin >> data;

    node* temp = new node;
    temp->data = data;
```

```
        temp->link = NULL;

        if (head == NULL) {
            head = temp;
        } else {
            node* last = head;
            while (last->link != NULL) {
                last = last->link;
            }
            last->link = temp;
        }
    }
    cout << "Total number of nodes in the linked list: " << countNodes(head) << endl;
    return 0;
}
```

Output

Enter the number of nodes in the list: 5

Enter data for node 1: 1

Enter data for node 2: 2

Enter data for node 3: 3

Enter data for node 4: 4

Enter data for node 5: 5

Total number of nodes in the linked list: 5

3.6 CIRCULAR LINKED LIST

In a circular linked list, the last node contains a pointer to the first node of the list. We can have a circular singly listed list as well as circular doubly linked list. Thus, a circular linked list has no beginning and no ending. The link field of the last node of a circular linked list stores the address of the first node of the list.

In order to maintain the above linked list in the memory, two arrays are used namely --- DATA and LINK. The array DATA stores the data elements of the linked list and the array LINK stores the address or pointer to the next node or data. In this arrangement it is very important to recognize the first data of the list. That is, if the first data is found than the rest of the data of the list can be easily found by means of pointers. But if the first data is not found than the entire list will be lost. Therefore, in a linked list it is very important to mark the first data of the list. The first data of every list is marked by a special pointer usually termed as start or head. In our above example, this pointer is named as 'START' and it always points to the beginning data of the list. That is, the variable START is used to store the address of the first node. In this example, START = 1, so the first data is stored at address 1, which is Apple. The corresponding LINK stores the address of the next node, which is 3. So, we will look at address 3 to fetch the next data item. The second data element obtained stored at address 3 is Mango. Again, we see the corresponding LINK to go to the next node. From the entry in the LINK, we get the next address, that is 7, and fetch Banana as the data. We repeat this procedure until we reach a position where the LINK entry contains –1 or NULL value, as it denotes the end of the linked list.

START

1 → 1

	DATA	INFO
1	Apple	3
2		
3	Mango	7
4		
5	Kiwi	10
6		
7	Banana	8
8	Orange	5
9		
10	Grapes	1

Figure 3.4: A circular linked list in the memory

Inserting a new node in a Circular Linked List

Here, we will discuss how a new node is added into an already existing linked list. We will discuss about two cases of insertion.

Case 1: The new node is inserted at the beginning of the circular linked list.

Case 2: The new node is inserted at the end of the circular linked list.

Algorithm to insert a new node at the beginning of a circular the linked list: Here 'p' is a pointer variable that is used to store the address of the first node of the list. q is another pointer variable that is used for traversing. Temp is the newly created node. Item is the data element to be inserted at the data part of temp.

Step 1: If avail = null, then Print "Overflow"

Go to Step 10

[End of if]

Step 2: Set q = p

Step 3: Set temp = malloc size of struct node

Step 4: Set temp ->data = item

Step 5: Repeat Step 7 while q->link != p

Step 6: q = q->link

[End of loop]

Step 7: Set temp ->link = p

Step 8: Set q->link = temp

Step 9: Set p = temp

Step 10: Exit

In step1, first it is checked whether there is available memory in the system or not. If there is no available memory, then an overflow message is returned. In step2, another variable q is set as p, so that both points at the first node of the list. In step3, a node 'temp' is created and in step4 data 'item' is stored in the data part and the link part is connected to 'p' which is the first node of the linked list. In step5 temp is set as p, so that the new node temp is marked as the first node.

Consider the linked list shown in below. Suppose we want to add a new node with data 8 and add it as the first node of the list. Then the following changes will be done in the linked list.

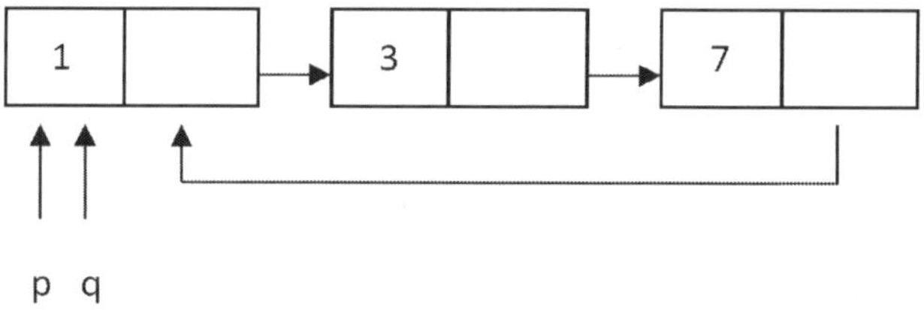

Already existing circular linked list.

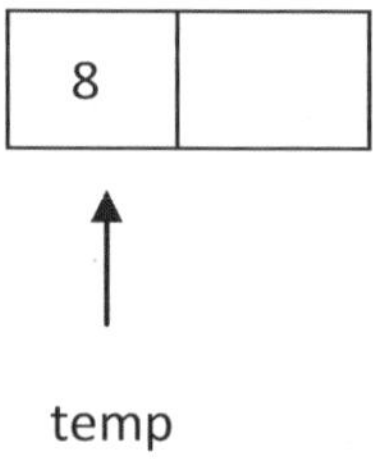

A new node temp is created and 8 is stored in its data part.

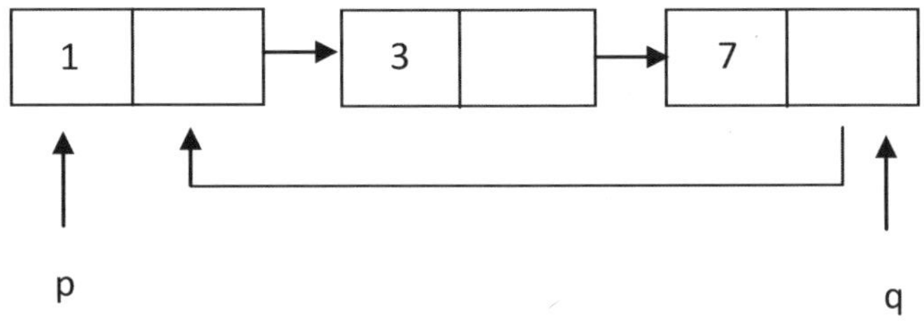

Nodes are traversed till we do not get the address of the first one in the link part of q.

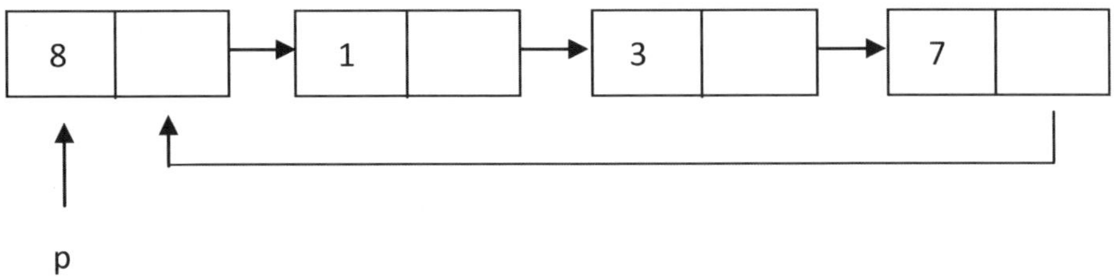

New node temp is added and p is made to point temp.

Example 12: The following program shows to insert a new node at the beginning of a circular linked list using C++ language.

```
#include <iostream>
using namespace std;

struct node {
   int data;
   node* link;
};

void insertAtFront(node **p, int item) {
   if (*p == NULL) {
      cout << "Overflow\n";
      return;
   }

   node *q = *p;

   node *temp = new node;
   if (temp == nullptr) {
      cout << "Memory allocation failed\n";
      return;
```

```
    }

    temp->data = item;

    while (q->link != *p) {
        q = q->link;
    }

    temp->link = *p;
    q->link = temp;
    *p = temp;
}

void printList(node *p) {
    if (p == nullptr) return;

    node *temp = p;
    do {
        cout << temp->data << " ";
        temp = temp->link;
    } while (temp != p);
    cout << endl;
}

int main() {
    node *head = nullptr;
    int n, data;

    cout << "Enter the number of nodes in the list: ";
    cin >> n;

    for (int i = 1; i <= n; i++) {
        cout << "Enter data for node " << i << ": ";
        cin >> data;
```

```
    node *temp = new node;
    temp->data = data;
    if (head == nullptr) {
      head = temp;
      temp->link = head;  // Points to itself, circular
    } else {
      node *last = head;
      while (last->link != head) {
        last = last->link;
      }
      last->link = temp;
      temp->link = head;  // Circular link
    }
  }

  cout << "Original Circular Linked List: ";
  printList(head);

  cout << "Enter data for the new node to insert at the front: ";
  cin >> data;
  insertAtFront(&head, data);

  cout << "Updated Circular Linked List after insertion: ";
  printList(head);

  return 0;
}
```

Output

Enter the number of nodes in the list: 3

Enter data for node 1: 1

Enter data for node 2: 3

Enter data for node 3: 7

Original Circular Linked List: 1 3 7

Enter data for the new node to insert at the front: 8

Updated Circular Linked List after insertion: 8 1 3 7

Algorithm to insert a new node at the end of a circular linked list

Here 'p' is a pointer variable that is used to store the address of the first node of the list. q is another pointer variable that is used for traversing. Temp is the newly created node. Item is the data element to be inserted at the data part of temp.

Step 1: If avail = null, then Print "Overflow"

Go to Step 9

[End of if]

Step 2: Set temp = malloc size of struct node

Step 3: Set temp ->data = item

Step 4: Set q = p

Step 5: Repeat Step 6 while q->link != p

Step 6: Set q = q ->link

[End of loop]

Step 7: Set q ->link = temp

Step 8: Set temp ->link = p

Step 9: Exit

In step1, first it is checked whether there is available memory in the system or not. If there is no available memory, then an overflow message is returned. In step2, a node 'temp' is created and in step3 data 'item' is stored in the data part of temp. In step4, another variable q is set as p, so that both points at the first node of the list. In step5 and step6, the nodes are traversed till we do not get the address of the first node in the link part of q. In step7, the link part of the last node is connected to temp, which is the newly created node. In step8, the link part of temp is connected to 'p' which is the first node of the linked list.

Consider the linked list as shown below. Suppose we want to add a new node with data 7 and add it at the end of the list. Then the following changes will be done in the linked list.

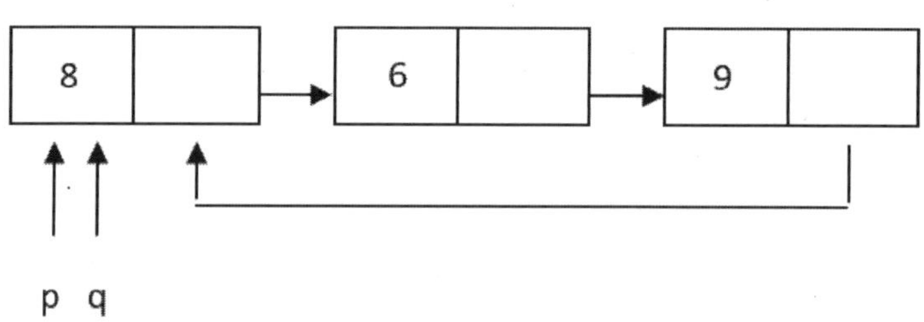

Already existing circular linked list.

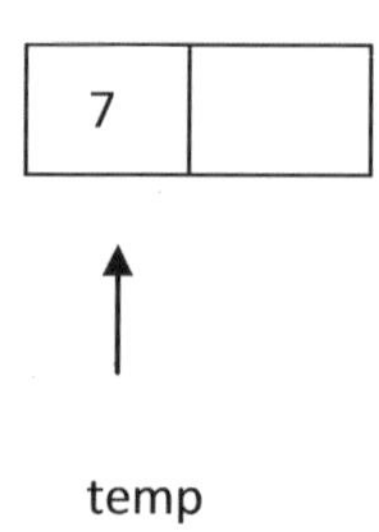

A new node temp is created and 7 is stored in its data part.

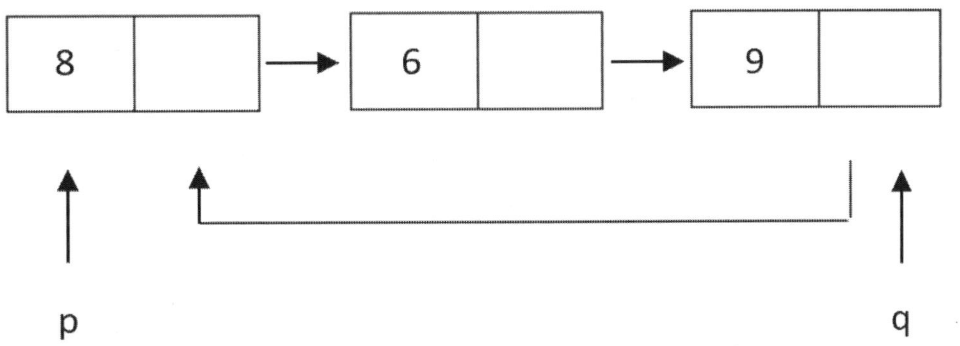

Nodes are traversed till we do not get the address of the first node in the link part of q.

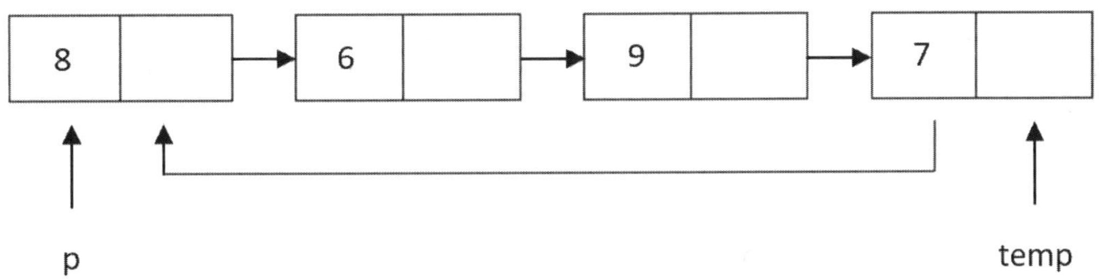

New node temp is added at the end of the list.

Example 13: The following program shows inserting a new node in end of a circular linked list using C++ language.

```
#include <iostream>
using namespace std;

struct node {
  int data;
  node* link;
};

void insertAtEnd(node **p, int item) {
  if (*p == NULL) {
    cout << "Overflow\n";
    return;
  }
```

```
    node *temp = new node;
    if (temp == NULL) {
        cout << "Memory allocation failed\n";
        return;
    }

    temp->data = item;

    node *q = *p;

    while (q->link != *p) {
        q = q->link;
    }

    q->link = temp;
    temp->link = *p;
}

void printList(node *p) {
    if (p == NULL) return;

    node *temp = p;
    do {
        cout << temp->data << " ";
        temp = temp->link;
    } while (temp != p);
    cout << endl;
}

int main() {
    node *head = NULL;
    int n, data;

    cout << "Enter the number of nodes in the list: ";
    cin >> n;
```

```
    for (int i = 1; i <= n; i++) {
        cout << "Enter data for node " << i << ": ";
        cin >> data;

        node *temp = new node;
        temp->data = data;
        if (head == NULL) {
            head = temp;
            temp->link = head;
        } else {
            node *last = head;
            while (last->link != head) {
                last = last->link;
            }
            last->link = temp;
            temp->link = head;
        }
    }

    cout << "Original Circular Linked List: ";
    printList(head);

    cout << "Enter data for the new node to insert at the end: ";
    cin >> data;
    insertAtEnd(&head, data);

    cout << "Updated Circular Linked List after insertion: ";
    printList(head);

    return 0;
}
```

Output

Enter the number of nodes in the list: 3

Enter data for node 1: 8

Enter data for node 2: 6

Enter data for node 3: 9

Original Circular Linked List: 8 6 9

Enter data for the new node to insert at the end: 7

Updated Circular Linked List after insertion: 8 6 9 7

Algorithm to insert a node after a desired location a circular linked list: Here, p is a pointer to the first node of the circular linked list. q is another pointer variable used for traversing, and ptr is used to store the node to be deleted.

Step 1: If p = null, then Print "Underflow"

Go to Step 8

[End of if]

Step 2: Set q = p

Step 3: Repeat Steps 4 and 5 while q -> link != p

Step 4: If q->data = = desired_data, exit the loop

Step 5: Set q = q -> link

[End of loop]

Step 6: If q->data != desired_data,, print "Desired node not found", and go to Step 7.

Step 7: Now, insert the new node after q:

- Create a new node ptr.
- Set ptr->data = new_data.
- Set ptr->link = q->link (new node should point to q's next node).
- Set q->link = ptr (update q's link to point to the new node).

Step 8: Exit

The algorithm starts by checking if the list is empty i.e. if p == NULL , print underflow and go to step 8. In step 2 , pointer q is initialized to p. Next, the circular linked list is traversed . Traversal continues until q -> link != p. During traversal, if q->data matches desired_data, then exit from the loop, and q is set to q->link. If the loop completes without finding the desired node, the algorithm prints "Desired node not found" in step 6. If the desired node is found, a new node ptr is created, and its data field is assigned new_data. The insertion is performed by setting ptr->link = q->link, ensuring the new node points to q's next node, and updating q->link = ptr to maintain the circular structure in step 7. Finally, the algorithm terminates after successfully inserting the node, ensuring that the circular linked list remains intact.

Consider the linked list as shown below. Suppose we want to add a new node with data 5 and add it after a desired location of the list. Then the following changes will be done in the linked list.

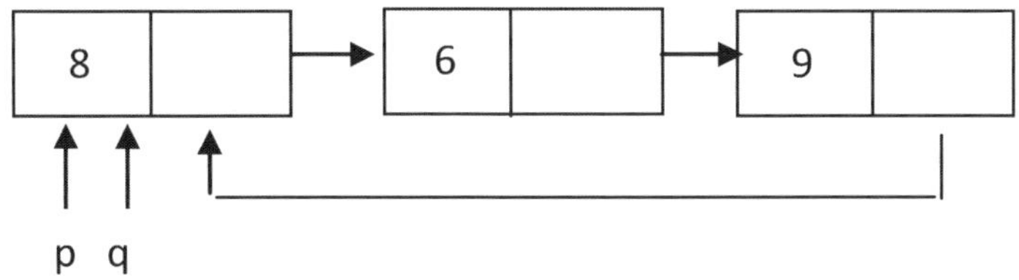

Already existing circular linked list.

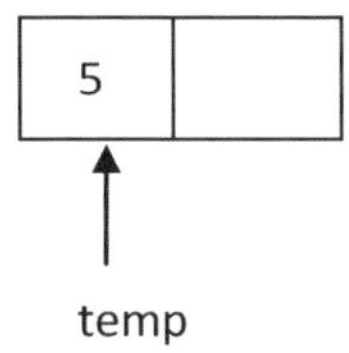

A new node temp is created and 5 is stored in its data part.

We need to add this node after node with value 6. Nodes are traversed till we find value after which we want to add the new node.

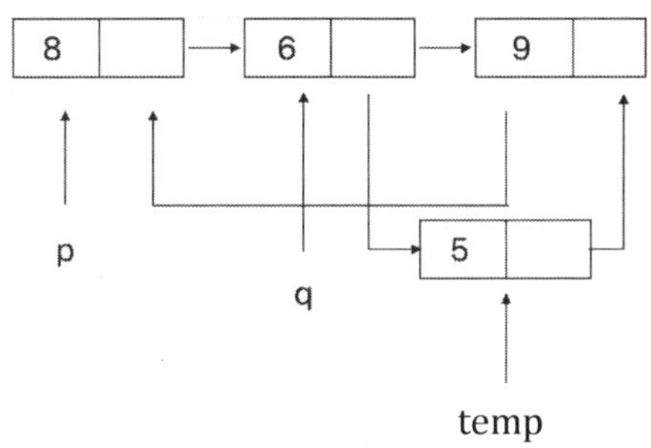

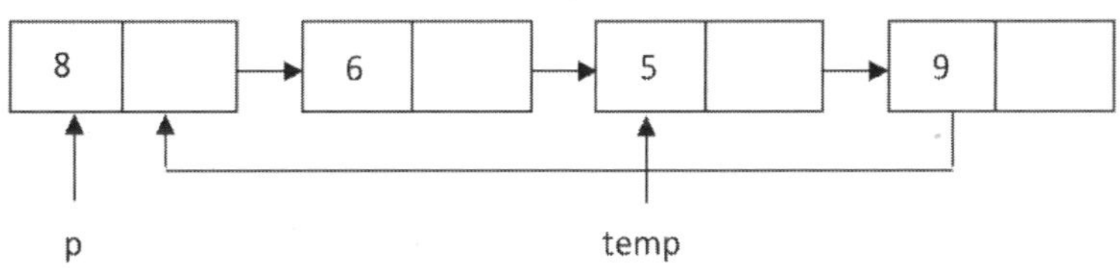

New node temp is added at the end of the list.

Example 14: The following program shows insertion of a node after a desired location of a circular linked list using C++ language.

```
#include <iostream>
using namespace std;

struct node {
   int data;
   node* link;
};
```

```
void insertAfter(node **p, int desired_data, int new_data) {
    if (*p == NULL) {
        cout << "Underflow\n";
        return;
    }

    node *q = *p;

    while (q->link != *p) {
        if (q->data == desired_data) {
            break;
        }
        q = q->link;
    }

    if (q->data != desired_data) {
        cout << "Desired node not found\n";
        return;
    }

    node *ptr = new node;
    ptr->data = new_data;
    ptr->link = q->link;
    q->link = ptr;
}

void printList(node *p) {
    if (p == NULL) return;

    node *temp = p;
    do {
        cout << temp->data << " ";
        temp = temp->link;
    } while (temp != p);
    cout << endl;
```

```
}

int main() {
   node *head = NULL;
   int n, data;

   cout << "Enter the number of nodes in the list: ";
   cin >> n;

   for (int i = 1; i <= n; i++) {
      cout << "Enter data for node " << i << ": ";
      cin >> data;

      node *temp = new node;
      temp->data = data;
      if (head == NULL) {
         head = temp;
         temp->link = head;
      } else {
         node *last = head;
         while (last->link != head) {
            last = last->link;
         }
         last->link = temp;
         temp->link = head;
      }
   }

   cout << "Original Circular Linked List: ";
   printList(head);

   int desired_data, new_data;
   cout << "Enter data for the node after which to insert a new node: ";
   cin >> desired_data;
   cout << "Enter data for the new node to insert: ";
```

```
    cin >> new_data;

    insertAfter(&head, desired_data, new_data);

    cout << "Updated Circular Linked List after insertion: ";
    printList(head);

    return 0;
}
```

Output

Enter the number of nodes in the list: 3

Enter data for node 1: 8

Enter data for node 2: 6

Enter data for node 3: 9

Original Circular Linked List: 8 6 9

Enter data for the node after which to insert a new node: 6

Enter data for the new node to insert: 5

Updated Circular Linked List after insertion: 8 6 5 9

Deleting a Node from a circular linked list

Here, we will discuss how a node is deleted from an already existing circular linked list.

We will take two cases and then see how deletion is done in each case.

Case 1: The first node is deleted.

Case 2: The last node is deleted.

Algorithm to delete the first node from a circular linked list: Here 'p' is a pointer variable that is used to store the address of the first node of the list. q is another pointer variable that is used for updating purpose.

```
Step 1: If p = null, then Print "Underflow"
                    Go to Step 9
          [End of if]
Step 2: If p->link == p  // Check if there's only one node
        Free p
        Set p = NULL
        Exit
     [End If]
```

Step 3: Set q = p

Step 4: Repeat Step 5 while q -> link! = p

Step 5: Set q = q -> link

[End of loop]

Step 6: Set q -> link = p -> link

Step 7: Delete p

Step 8: Set p = q -> link

Step 9: Exit

In step1, first it is checked whether there is any node present in the linked list or not. If there is no node, then an underflow message is returned. In step2 it is checked that if the list had only one node. In step3, another variable q is set to p, so that both points at the first node of the list. In step4 and Step5, nodes are traversed starting from the first node till we do not get the address of the first node in the link part of q. In Step6, the link part of the last node stores the address of the second node. In step7, the first node is set free, so that the deleted memory location goes to the free pool. In Step8, p is set to point to the second node.

Consider the linked list shown below. Suppose we want to delete the first node of the list. Then the following changes will be done in the linked list.

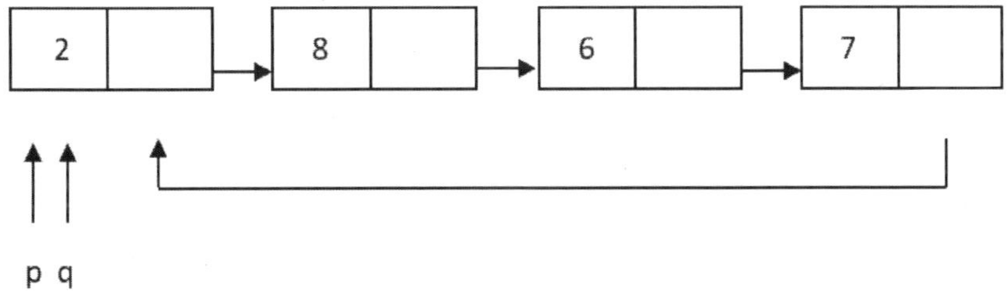

Already existing circular linked list.

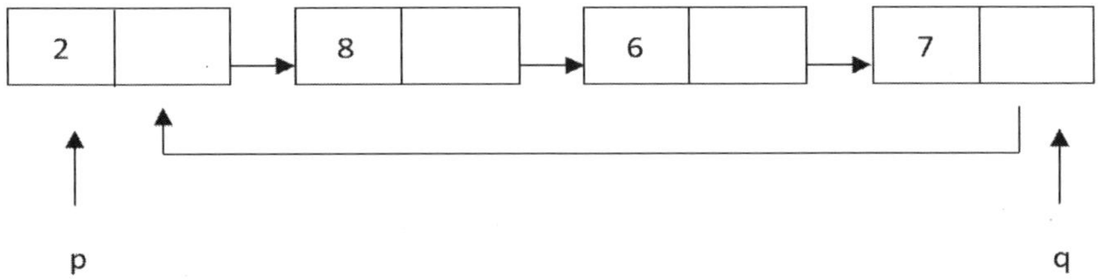

Nodes are traversed till we do not get the address of the first node in the link part of q.

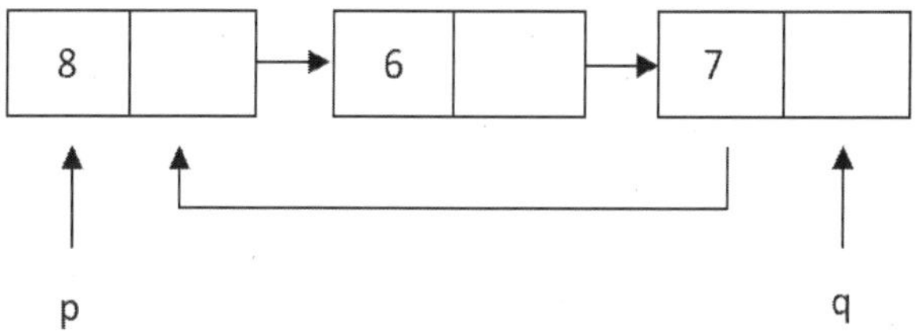

The link part of q is made to point to the second node of the list and the memory of the first node is freed. Now the second node becomes the first node of the list.

Example 15: The following program shows deleting first node of a circular linked list using C++ language.

```
#include <iostream>
using namespace std;

struct node {
   int data;
   node* link;
};

void deleteFirstNode(node **p) {
   if (*p == NULL) {
      cout << "Underflow\n";
      return;
   }

   if ((*p)->link == *p) {
      delete *p;
      *p = NULL;
      return;
   }

   node *q = *p;

   while (q->link != *p) {
      q = q->link;
```

```
    }

    q->link = (*p)->link;
    delete *p;
    *p = q->link;
}

void printList(node *p) {
    if (p == NULL) return;

    node *temp = p;
    do {
        cout << temp->data << " ";
        temp = temp->link;
    } while (temp != p);
    cout << endl;
}

int main() {
    node *head = NULL;
    int n, data;

    cout << "Enter the number of nodes in the list: ";
    cin >> n;

    for (int i = 1; i <= n; i++) {
        cout << "Enter data for node " << i << ": ";
        cin >> data;

        node *temp = new node;
        temp->data = data;
        if (head == NULL) {
            head = temp;
            temp->link = head;
        } else {
```

```
        node *last = head;
        while (last->link != head) {
          last = last->link;
        }
        last->link = temp;
        temp->link = head;
      }
   }

   cout << "Original Circular Linked List: ";
   printList(head);

   deleteFirstNode(&head);

   cout << "Updated Circular Linked List after deletion: ";
   printList(head);

   return 0;
}
```

Output :

Enter the number of nodes in the list: 4

Enter data for node 1: 2

Enter data for node 2: 8

Enter data for node 3: 6

Enter data for node 4: 7

Original Circular Linked List: 2 8 6 7

Updated Circular Linked List after deletion: 8 6 7

Algorithm to delete the last node from a circular linked list: Here 'p' is a pointer variable that is used to store the address of the first node of the list. q and ptr are two additional pointer variables that are used for updating purpose.

Step 1: If p = null, then Print "Underflow"

Go to Step 9

[End of if]

Step 2: If p->link == p   // Only one node case

Free p

Set p = NULL

[End If]

Step 3: Set q = p

Step 4: Repeat Steps 4 and 5 while q -> link! = p

Step 5: Set ptr = q

Step 6: Set q = q -> link

[End of loop]

Step 7: Set ptr -> link = p   // Second last node now points to first node

Step 8: Delete q   // Delete the last node

Step 9: Exit

In step1, first it is checked whether there is any node present in the linked list or not. If there is no node, then an underflow message is returned. In step2 the issue of single node is handled. In step3, another variable q is set as p, so that both points at the first node of the list. In step4 while loop is used to traverse to the node that stores the address of the first node in its link part (last node). Step 5, another pointer variable ptr is used to point to the same node that is being pointed by q. Step6 is for traversing. In step7, the second last node (ptr) is made to point to the first node. In Step8, the memory location of the last node is set free.

Consider the linked list shown below. Suppose we want to delete the last node of the list. Then the following changes will be done in the linked list.

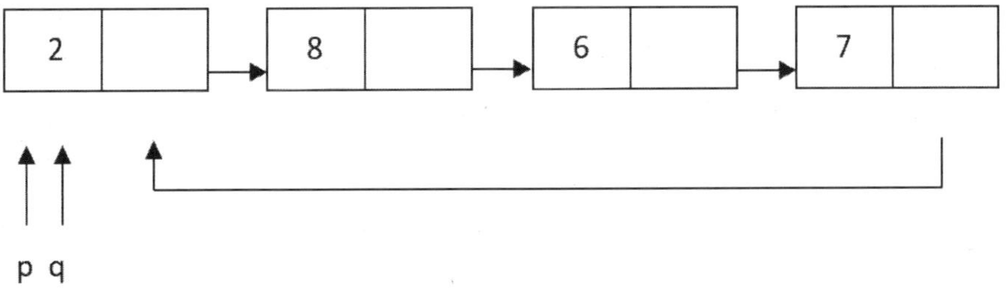

Already existing circular linked list.

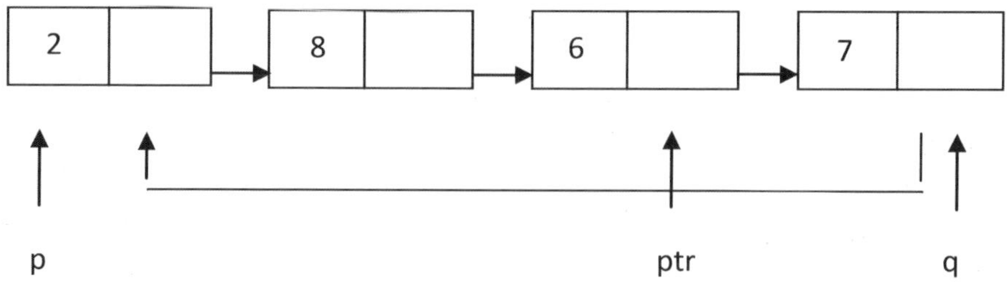

Nodes are traversed till we do not get the address of the first node in the link part of q. ptr will always point to the node preceding q.

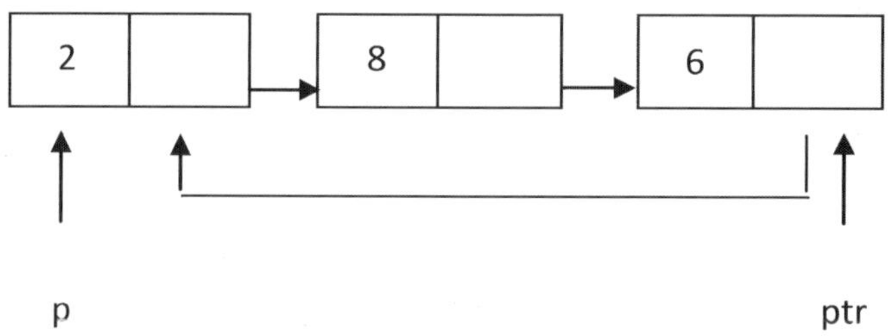

Link part of ptr is made to store the address of the first node. The memory occupied by q is set free. Now ptr is the last node of the list.

Example 16: The following program shows deleting last node of a circular linked list using C++ language.

```
#include <iostream>
using namespace std;

struct node {
  int data;
  node* link;
};

void deleteLastNode(node **p) {
  if (*p == NULL) {
    cout << "Underflow\n";
    return;
  }

  if ((*p)->link == *p) {
    delete *p;
    *p = NULL;
    return;
  }
```

```
    node* q = *p;
    node* ptr = NULL;

    while (q->link != *p) {
        ptr = q;
        q = q->link;
    }

    ptr->link = *p;
    delete q;
}

void printList(node* p) {
    if (p == NULL) return;

    node* temp = p;
    do {
        cout << temp->data << " ";
        temp = temp->link;
    } while (temp != p);
    cout << endl;
}

int main() {
    node* head = NULL;
    int n, data;

    cout << "Enter the number of nodes in the list: ";
    cin >> n;

    for (int i = 1; i <= n; i++) {
        cout << "Enter data for node " << i << ": ";
        cin >> data;
```

```
        node* temp = new node;
        temp->data = data;
        if (head == NULL) {
            head = temp;
            temp->link = head;
        } else {
            node* last = head;
            while (last->link != head) {
                last = last->link;
            }
            last->link = temp;
            temp->link = head;
        }
    }

    cout << "Original Circular Linked List: ";
    printList(head);

    deleteLastNode(&head);

    cout << "Updated Circular Linked List after deletion: ";
    printList(head);

    return 0;
}
```

Output:

Enter the number of nodes in the list: 4

Enter data for node 1: 2

Enter data for node 2: 8

Enter data for node 3: 6

Enter data for node 4: 7

Original Circular Linked List: 2 8 6 7

Updated Circular Linked List after deletion: 2 8 6

Algorithm to delete the a node after a desired location a circular linked list: Here, p is a pointer to the first node of the circular linked list. q is another pointer variable used for traversing, and ptr is used to store the node to be deleted.

Step 1: If p = null, then Print "Underflow"

Go to Step 8

[End of if]

Step 2: Set q = p

Step 3: Repeat Steps 4 and 5 while q -> link! = p

Step 4: If q->data = = desired_data, exit the loop

Step 5: Set q = q -> link

[End of loop]

Step 6: If q->data != desired_data, print "Desired node not found", and go to Step 7.

Step 7: Now, delete the node q:

- Set ptr = q->link
- If ptr = = p , print "Cannot delete, only one node after the desired node." And go to Step 8
- Set q -> link = ptr -> link
- Delete ptr.

Step 8: Exit

In step1, first it is checked whether there is any node present in the linked list or not. If the list is empty i.e. there is no node, than an underflow message is returned and exit. In step2, another variable q is initialized to point to the first node p, hence both p and q points at the first node of the list. In step3, the list is by iterating through each node, checking if the data of the current node (q->data) matches the desired_data. In step 4 , if q-> data is equal to desired_data i.e., a match is found then exit the loop. Step 5 set q to q-> link to move to the next node. In step 6, if the desired_data is not found by the time the loop completes, print "Desired node not found" and exit. In **Step 7**, the algorithm proceeds to delete the node after q. First, it sets a pointer ptr to point to the node immediately following q (i.e., ptr = q->link). The next check ensures that deletion is possible: if ptr is equal to p (meaning the node after q is the first node of the list), it prints a message saying "Cannot delete, only one node after the desired node." and exits by going to last step, as there is no node to delete beyond this. If there are multiple nodes, the algorithm then updates q->link , effectively removing it from the list by linking q to the node that follows ptr (i.e., q->link = ptr->link). Finally, memory for ptr is freed. Step 8 exits the algorithm.

Consider the linked list shown below. Suppose we want to delete a node after location 1 of the list. Then the following changes will be done in the linked list.

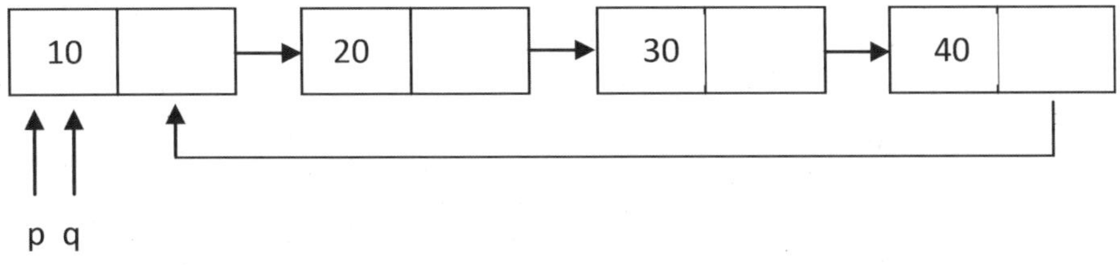

Already existing circular linked list.

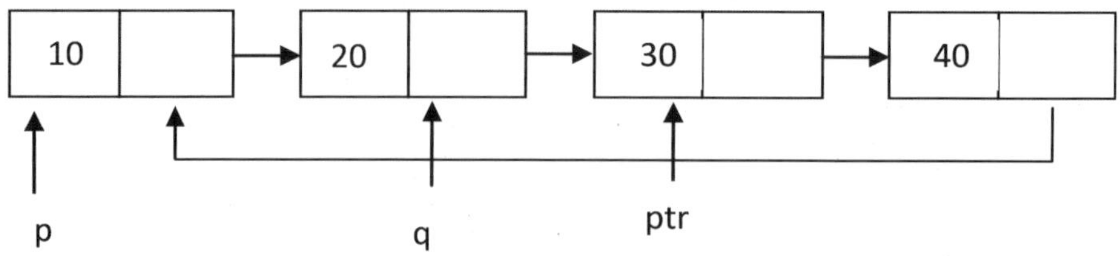

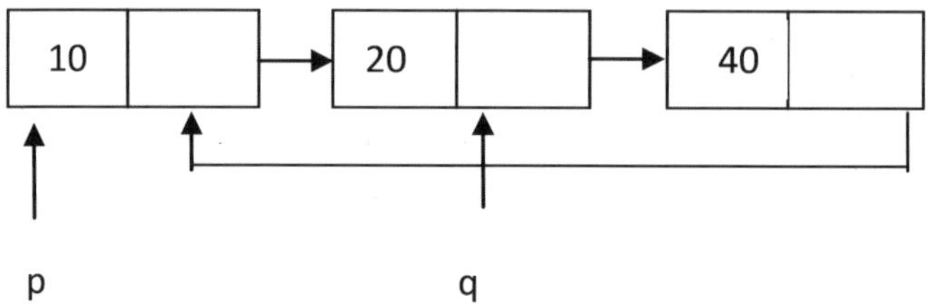

Final circular linked list after deleting a node after location 1 of the list.

Example 17: The following program shows deleting last node of a circular linked list using C++ language.

```
#include <iostream>
using namespace std;

struct node {
  int data;
  node* link;
};

void deleteAfter(node** p, int desired_data) {
  if (*p == NULL) {
    cout << "Underflow\n";
    return;
  }

  node* q = *p;

  while (q->link != *p) {
    if (q->data == desired_data) {
      break;
    }
```

```
        q = q->link;
    }

    if (q->data != desired_data) {
        cout << "Desired node not found\n";
        return;
    }

    node* ptr = q->link;

    if (ptr == *p) {
        cout << "Cannot delete, only one node after the desired node.\n";
        return;
    }

    q->link = ptr->link;
    delete ptr;
}

void printList(node* p) {
    if (p == nullptr) return;

    node* temp = p;
    do {
        cout << temp->data << " ";
        temp = temp->link;
    } while (temp != p);
    cout << endl;
}

int main() {
    node* head = nullptr;
    int n, data;

    cout << "Enter the number of nodes in the list: ";
```

```
    cin >> n;

    for (int i = 1; i <= n; i++) {
        cout << "Enter data for node " << i << ": ";
        cin >> data;

        node* temp = new node;
        temp->data = data;
        if (head == nullptr) {
            head = temp;
            temp->link = head;
        } else {
            node* last = head;
            while (last->link != head) {
                last = last->link;
            }
            last->link = temp;
            temp->link = head;
        }
    }

    cout << "Original Circular Linked List: ";
    printList(head);

    int desired_data;
    cout << "Enter the node data after which to delete the next node: ";
    cin >> desired_data;

    deleteAfter(&head, desired_data);

    cout << "Updated Circular Linked List after deletion: ";
    printList(head);

    return 0;
}
```

Output :

Enter the number of nodes in the list: 4

Enter data for node 1: 10

Enter data for node 2: 20

Enter data for node 3: 30

Enter data for node 4: 40

Original Circular Linked List: 10 20 30 40

Enter the node data after which to delete the next node: 20

Updated Circular Linked List after deletion: 10 20 40

3.7 DOUBLY LINKED LISTS

A doubly linked list is a special list where each node consists of three parts: two address parts and a data part. Two address parts are used to store two addresses: one part stores the address of the next node and the other part stores the address of the previous node. The data part stores the data element.

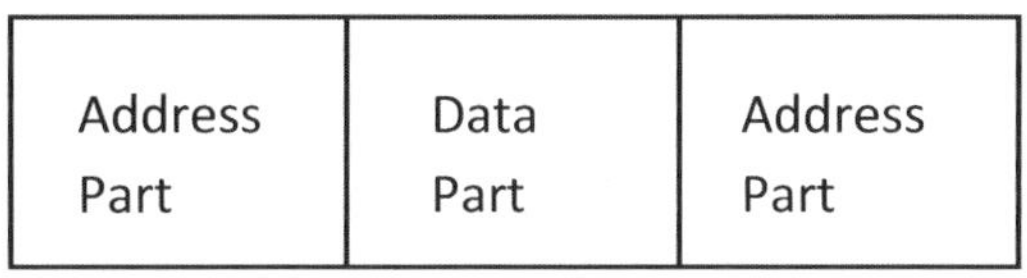

Figure 3.5: A node of doubly linked list

A doubly linked list is also known as a two-way list. In a doubly linked list, from a particular node we can travel both ways, i.e. from a particular node we can move to the last node and can also travel to the first node. It has the advantage of moving in both directions. Whereas in a singly linked list we can move in only one direction, from the first node to the last node. It is not possible to move in the opposite direction in a singly linked list.

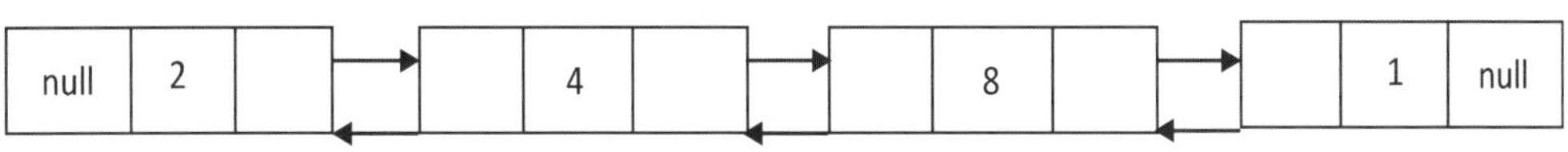

Figure 3.6: A doubly linked list

In the above figure we see that the list can be traversed in two directions. Also the list will have two null values or invalid addresses to mark the end of the list.

In C++, the structure of a doubly linked list can be given as,

```
struct Node {
int data;
Node* Next;
Node* Prev;
};
```

The prev field of the first node and the next field of the last node will contain null values or invalid addresses. The next field is used to store the address of the next node, which enables us to traverse the list in forward direction. The prev field is used to store the address of the preceding node, which enables us to traverse the list in the backward direction. In addition to the advantage of being able to move in both directions, a doubly linked list also suffers from a disadvantage. As we are going to store three fields in a node, there will be more requirement of space per node as compared to a singly linked list. However, a doubly linked list provides the ease to manipulate the elements of the list as it maintains pointers to nodes in both the directions (forward and backward). The main advantage of using a doubly linked list is that it makes searching operation very efficient.

Memory representation of doubly linked list

HEAD: 1

	PREV	DATA	NEXT
1	-1	Apple	3
2			
3	1	Mango	7
4			
5	8	Kiwi	1
6			
7	3	Banana	8
8	7	Orange	5
9			
10	5	Grapes	-1

In the figure, we see that a variable HEAD is used to store the address of the first node. Here the address of the first node is 1, i.e. HEAD = 1, so the first data is stored at address 1. Since this is the first node, it has no previous node and hence stores NULL or −1 in the PREV field. The NEXT part of the first node stores the address of the second node which is 3. We traverse to the third node. Here we find that the PREV field of the third node stores the address of the first node and the Next field of this node stores the address of the next node, i.e. 7. Similarly, we traverse list until we reach the last node where the NEXT field of the node contains NULL or -1. This denotes the end of the linked list.

Inserting a new node in a doubly linked list

A new node can be inserted into an already existing doubly linked list in three ways. These are:

- The new node is inserted at the beginning.

- The new node is inserted at the end.
- The new node is inserted after a desired location.

Algorithm to insert a new node at the beginning of a doubly linked list

Here 'p' is a pointer variable that is used to store the address of the first node of the list. 'Temp' is the newly created node. 'Item' is the data element to be inserted at the data part of temp.

Step 1: If p = null, then Print "Overflow"

Go to Step 8

[End of if]

Step 2: Set temp = malloc size of struct node

Step 3: Set temp->data = item

Step 4: Set temp->Prev = Null

Step 5: Set temp->Next = p

Step 6: Set p->Prev = temp

Step 7: Set p = temp

Step 8: Exit

In step1, first it is checked whether there is available memory in the system or not. If there is no available memory, then an overflow message is returned. Otherwise in step2, a node 'temp' is created and in step3, data 'item' is stored in the data part of the node temp. In step4, the Null is stored on the Prev part of temp. In step5, Next part of temp is connected to 'p' which is the first node of the doubly linked list. In step6, the address of temp is stored on the Prev part of the node temp. In step7, temp is set as p, so that the new node temp is marked as the first node.

Consider the linked list shown below. Suppose we want to add a new node with data 8 and add it as the first node of the list. Then the following changes will be done in the linked list.

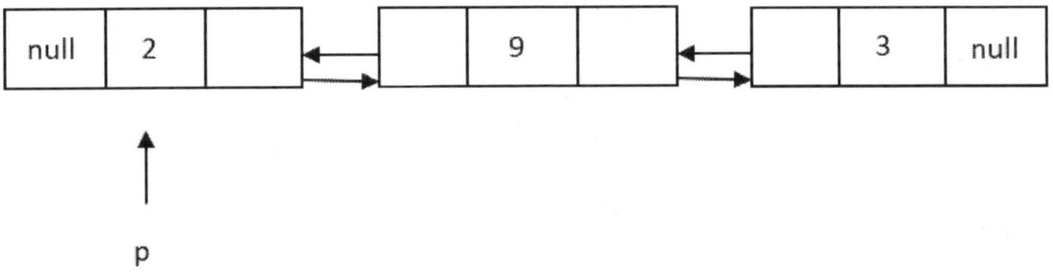

Already existing doubly linked list.

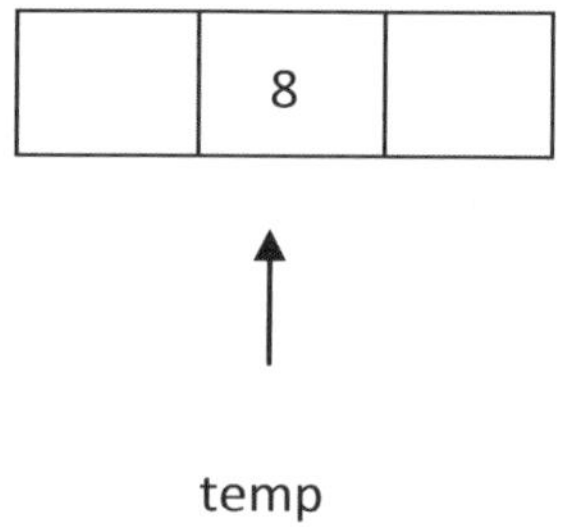

A new node temp is created and 8 is stored in its data part.

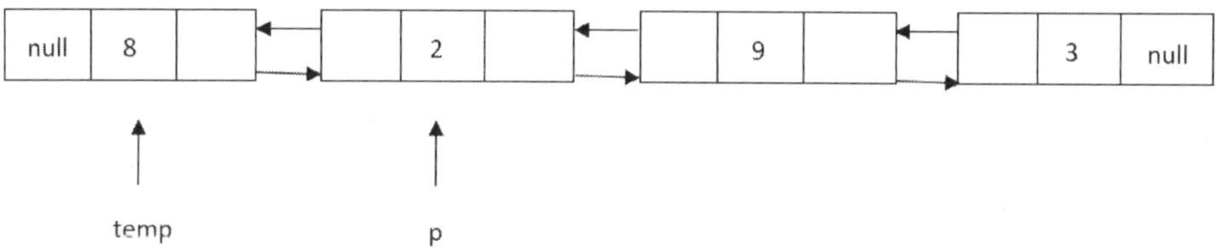

The Next part of temp is connected to p.

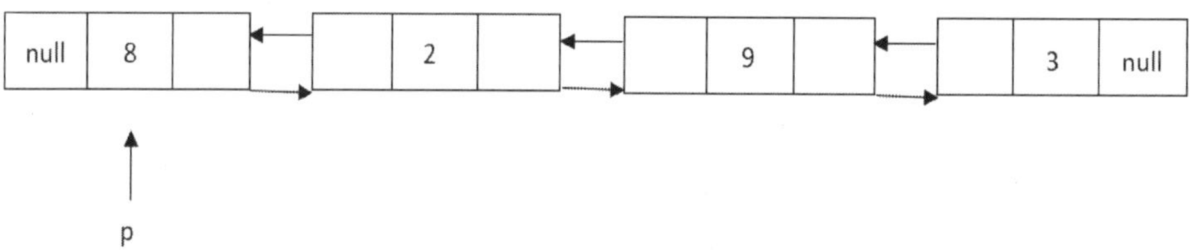

Now temp is set as p.

Example 18: The following program shows to insert a new node at the beginning of a doubly linked list using C++ language.

```
#include <iostream>
using namespace std;

struct Node {
  int data;
  Node* Next;
  Node* Prev;
};

Node* insert(Node* head, int item) {
  Node* temp = (Node*)malloc(sizeof(Node));
  if (temp == NULL) {
```

```
    cout << "Memory allocation failed" << endl;
    return head;
  }

  temp->data = item;
  temp->Next = NULL;
  temp->Prev = NULL;

  if (head == NULL) {
    return temp;
  }

  Node* last = head;
  while (last->Next != NULL) {
    last = last->Next;
  }

  last->Next = temp;
  temp->Prev = last;

  return head;
}

// Function to insert a node at the front of the list
Node* insertAtFront(Node* p, int item) {
  Node* temp = (Node*)malloc(sizeof(Node));
  if (temp == NULL) {
    cout << "Memory allocation failed" << endl;
    return p;
  }

  temp->data = item;
  temp->Prev = NULL;
  temp->Next = p;
```

```
    p->Prev = temp;
    p = temp;

    return p;
}

// Function to print the list
void printList(Node* p) {
    Node* curr = p;
    while (curr != NULL) {
        cout << curr->data << " ";
        curr = curr->Next;
    }
    cout << endl;
}

int main() {
    Node* p = NULL;
    int item, n;

    // Take input for the number of elements
    cout << "Enter the number of elements in the list: ";
    cin >> n;

    if (n <= 0) {
        cout << "List must have at least one element!" << endl;
        return 1;
    }

    // Take input for elements and insert at the end
    for (int i = 0; i < n; i++) {
        cout << "Enter element " << i + 1 << ": ";
        cin >> item;
        p = insert(p, item); // Using the renamed function
    }
```

```
  cout << "Original Doubly Linked List: ";
  printList(p);

  // Insert a new node at the front
  cout << "Enter data for the new node to insert at the front: ";
  cin >> item;

  p = insertAtFront(p, item);

  cout << "Updated Doubly Linked List after insertion: ";
  printList(p);

  return 0;
}
```

Output

Enter the number of elements in the list: 3

Enter element 1: 2

Enter element 2: 9

Enter element 3: 3

Original Doubly Linked List: 2 9 3

Enter data for the new node to insert at the front: 8

Updated Doubly Linked List after insertion: 8 2 9 3

Algorithm to insert a new node at the end of a doubly linked list: Here 'p' is a pointer variable that is used to store the address of the first node of the list. 'q' is another pointer variable that is used while traversing the list. 'Temp' is the newly created node. 'Item' is the data element to be inserted at the data part of temp.

Step 1: If p = null, then Print "Overflow"

    Go to Step 10

    [End of if]

Step 2: Set temp = malloc size of struct node

Step 3: Set temp ->data = item

Step 4: Set temp ->Next = Null

Step 5: Set q = p

Step 6: Repeat Step 7 while q -> Next != Null

Step 7: Set q = q -> next

[End of loop]

Step 8: Set q -> Next = temp

Step 9: Set temp ->Prev = q

Step 10: Exit

In step1, first it is checked whether there is available memory in the system or not. If there is no available memory, then an overflow message is returned. Otherwise in step2, a node 'temp' is created. In step3 'item' is stored in the data part and in step4 Null is stored in the Next part of temp. In step5 another pointer variable q is set as p, so that the both p and q points to the first node. This is done so that the link to the first node could be saved for other purposes such as displaying the list. If the link to the first node is lost than it won't be possible to fetch the entire linked list later. So, p will be fixed and q will be used for traversing the list. In step6 while loop is used to set the condition of traversing. Till we do not get Null value in the Next part of the node we have to traverse. Step7 is to go the next node while traversing. Once our condition is fulfilled, i.e. we get Null value in the Next part than the control will come out of the while loop and in step8 the newly created node (temp) will be connected to the last node.

Consider the linked list shown below. Suppose we want to add a new node with data 6 and add it after the last node of the list. Then the following changes will be done in the linked list.

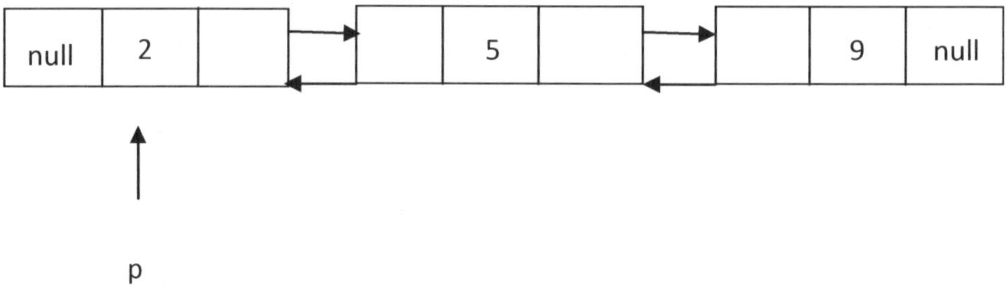

Already existing doubly linked list.

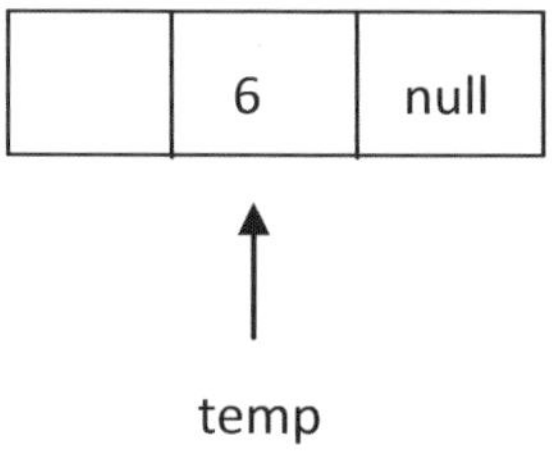

A new node temp is created and 6 is stored in its data part. Null value is stored in the Next part of temp.

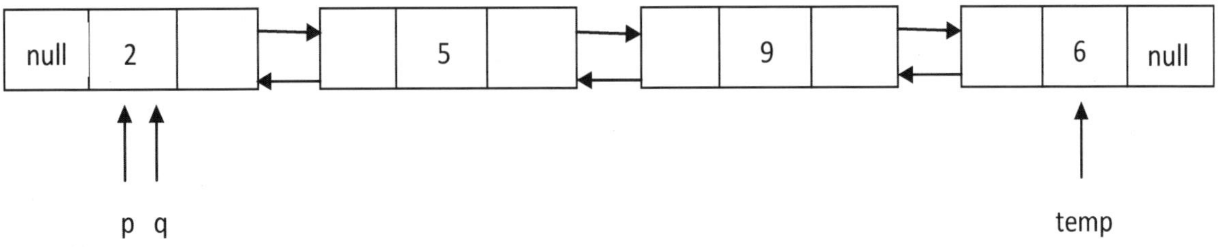

We traverse the nodes while q -> Next != Null and add temp after the last node.

Example 19: The following program shows to insert a new node at the end of a doubly linked list using C++ language.

```
#include <iostream>
using namespace std;

struct Node {
  int data;
  Node* Next;
  Node* Prev;
};

Node* createList(int n) {
  Node* p = NULL;
  int item;

  for (int i = 0; i < n; i++) {
    cout << "Enter element " << i + 1 << ": ";
    cin >> item;

    Node* newNode = (Node*)malloc(sizeof(Node));
    if (newNode == NULL) {
      cout << "Memory allocation failed" << endl;
      return p;
    }

    newNode->data = item;
```

```
        newNode->Next = NULL;
        newNode->Prev = NULL;
        if (p == NULL) {
            p = newNode;
        } else {
            Node* temp = p;
            while (temp->Next != NULL) {
                temp = temp->Next;
            }
            temp->Next = newNode;
            newNode->Prev = temp;
        }
    }

    return p;
}

Node* insertAtEnd(Node* p, int item) {
    if (p == NULL) {
        cout << "Overflow" << endl;
        return p;
    }

    Node* temp = (Node*)malloc(sizeof(Node));
    if (temp == NULL) {
        cout << "Memory allocation failed" << endl;
        return p;
    }

    temp->data = item;
    temp->Next = NULL;

    Node* q = p;
    while (q->Next != NULL) {
        q = q->Next;
```

```
    }

    q->Next = temp;
    temp->Prev = q;

    return p;
}

void printList(Node* p) {
    Node* curr = p;
    while (curr != NULL) {
        cout << curr->data << " ";
        curr = curr->Next;
    }
    cout << endl;
}

int main() {
    Node* p = NULL;
    int item, n;

    cout << "Enter the number of elements in the list: ";
    cin >> n;

    if (n <= 0) {
        cout << "List must have at least one element!" << endl;
        return 1;
    }

    p = createList(n);

    cout << "Existing Doubly Linked List: ";
    printList(p);

    cout << "Enter data for the new node to insert at the end: ";
```

```
    cin >> item;

    p = insertAtEnd(p, item);

    cout << "Updated Doubly Linked List after insertion: ";
    printList(p);

    return 0;
}
```

Output :

Enter the number of elements in the list: 3

Enter element 1: 2

Enter element 2: 5

Enter element 3: 9

Existing Doubly Linked List: 2 5 9

Enter data for the new node to insert at the end: 6

Updated Doubly Linked List after insertion: 2 5 9 6

Algorithm to insert a new node after a desired location in a doubly linked list: Here 'p' is a pointer variable that is used to store the address of the first node of the list. 'q' is another pointer variable that is used while traversing the list. 'Temp' is the newly created node. 'Item' is the data element to be inserted at the data part of temp.

Step 1: If p = null, then Print "Overflow"

Go to Step 11

[End of if]

Step 2: Set q = p

Step 3: Repeat Step 4 for (i = 0; i < loc; i++)

Step 4: Set q = q ->Next

[End of loop]

Step 5: Set temp = malloc size of struct node

Step 6: Set temp -> data = item

Step 7: Set temp -> Next = q -> Next

Step 8: Set q -> Next -> Prev = temp

Step 9: Set temp -> Prev = q

Step 10: Set q -> next = temp

Step 11: Exit

In step1, first it is checked whether there is available memory in the system or not. If there is no available memory, than an overflow message is returned. Otherwise in step2, another pointer variable q is set as p, so that the both p and q points to omit the first node. This is done so that the link to the first node could be saved for other purposes such as displaying the list. If the link to the first node is lost than it won't be possible to fetch the entire linked list later. So, p will be fixed and q will be used for traversing the list. In step3, for loop is used to reach to the desired location (loc). In step4 nodes are traversed till desired location is not reached. In step5 a node 'temp' is created. In step6 'item' is stored in the data part of temp. In step7 Next part of temp is connected to the node next to q. In step8 Prev part of q -> Next is connected to temp. In step9, the Prev part of temp is connected to the node q. In step10, the Next part of q is connected to the node temp.

Consider the linked list shown below. Suppose we want to add a new node with data 6, after the second position (i.e. loc = 2). Then the following changes will be done in the linked list.

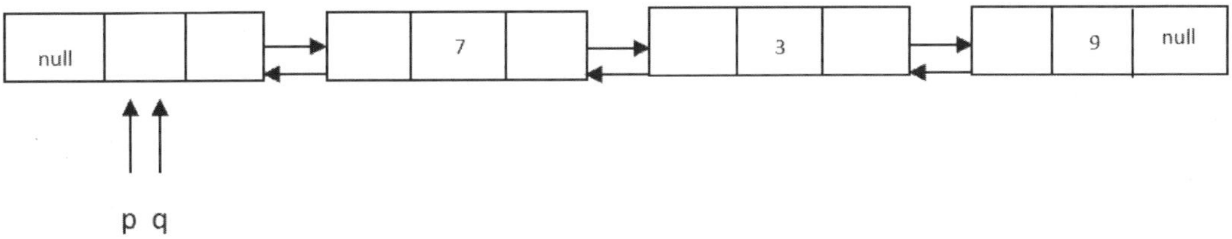

Already existing doubly linked list.

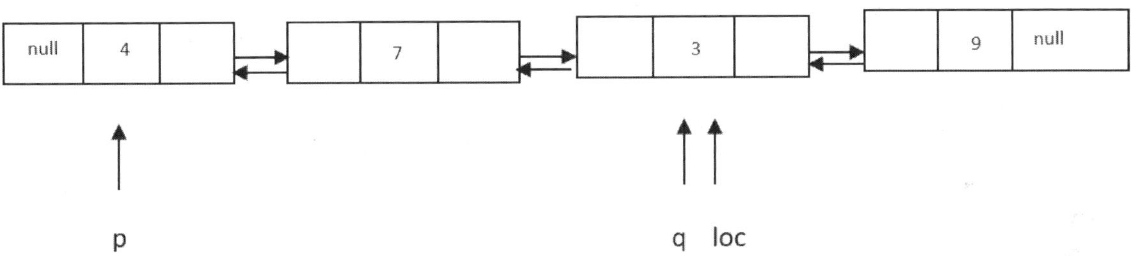

We traverse to the loc using the pointer variable q and create a node temp after the loc.

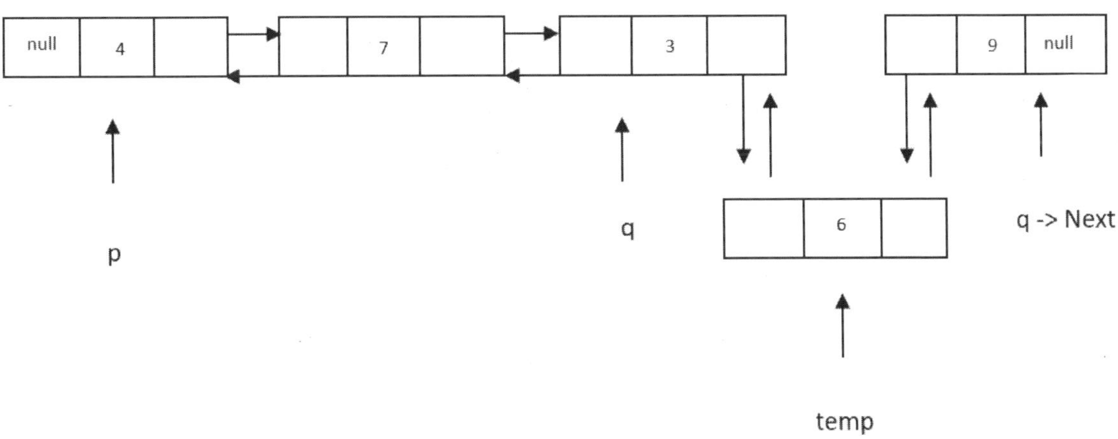

The node temp is inserted after the loc and all the links are updated.

Example 20: The following program shows to insert a new node after a desired location in a doubly linked list using C++ language.

```
#include <iostream>
#include <cstdlib>
using namespace std;

struct Node {
  int data;
  Node* Next;
  Node* Prev;
};

Node* insertatMid(Node* p, int item, int loc) {
  if (p == NULL) {
    cout << "Overflow" << endl;
    return p;
  }

  Node* q = p;
  for (int i = 0; i < loc; i++) {
    if (q == NULL) {
      cout << "Location is out of bounds!" << endl;
      return p;
    }
    q = q->Next;
  }

  Node* temp = (Node*)malloc(sizeof(Node));
  if (temp == NULL) {
    cout << "Memory allocation failed" << endl;
    return p;
  }

  temp->data = item;
  temp->Next = q->Next;
```

```
    if (q->Next != NULL) {
        q->Next->Prev = temp;
    }
    temp->Prev = q;
    q->Next = temp;

    return p;
}

Node* insert(Node* head, int item) {
    Node* temp = (Node*)malloc(sizeof(Node));
    if (temp == NULL) {
        cout << "Memory allocation failed" << endl;
        return head;
    }

    temp->data = item;
    temp->Next = NULL;
    temp->Prev = NULL;

    if (head == NULL) {
        return temp;
    }

    Node* q = head;
    while (q->Next != NULL) {
        q = q->Next;
    }

    q->Next = temp;
    temp->Prev = q;

    return head;
}
```

```
void printList(Node* p) {
  Node* curr = p;
  while (curr != NULL) {
    cout << curr->data << " ";
    curr = curr->Next;
  }
  cout << endl;
}

int main() {
  Node* p = NULL;
  int item, n, loc;

  cout << "Enter the number of elements in the list: ";
  cin >> n;

  if (n <= 0) {
    cout << "List must have at least one element!" << endl;
    return 1;
  }

  for (int i = 0; i < n; i++) {
    cout << "Enter element " << i + 1 << ": ";
    cin >> item;
    p = insert(p, item);
  }

  cout << "Original Doubly Linked List: ";
  printList(p);

  cout << "Enter location after which we want to insert the new node: ";
  cin >> loc;

  cout << "Enter data for the new node to insert: ";
  cin >> item;
```

```
  p = insertatMid(p, item, loc);

  cout << "Updated Doubly Linked List after insertion: ";
  printList(p);

  return 0;
}
```

Output :

Enter the number of elements in the list: 4

Enter element 1: 4

Enter element 2: 7

Enter element 3: 3

Enter element 4: 9

Original Doubly Linked List: 4 7 3 9

Enter location after which we want to insert the new node: 2

Enter data for the new node to insert: 6

Updated Doubly Linked List after insertion: 4 7 3 6 9

Deleting a node from a doubly linked list

Here we will discuss how to delete a node from an already existing doubly linked list. We will take three instances of deletion and see how deletion is done in each instance.

- ▶ Deleting the first node from a doubly linked list.
- ▶ Deleting the last node from a doubly linked list.
- ▶ Deleting a node after a desired location from a doubly linked list.

Algorithm to delete the first node from a doubly linked list: Here 'p' is a pointer variable that is used to store the address of the first node of the list. 'q' is another pointer variable that is used for updating purpose.

Step 1: If p = null, then Print "Underflow"

Go to Step 5

[End of if]

Step 2: Set q = p

Step 3: Set p = p-> Next

Step 4: Set p -> Prev = Null

Step 5: Free q

Step 5: Exit

In step1, first it is checked whether there is any node present in the linked list or not. If there is no node, then an underflow message is returned. In step2, another variable q is set to p, so that both points at the first node of the list. In step3 p is set to point to the second node. In step4, the first node that is pointed by q is deleted or set free, so that the deleted memory location goes to the free pool.

Consider the linked list shown below. Suppose we want to delete the first node of the list. Then the following changes will be done in the linked list.

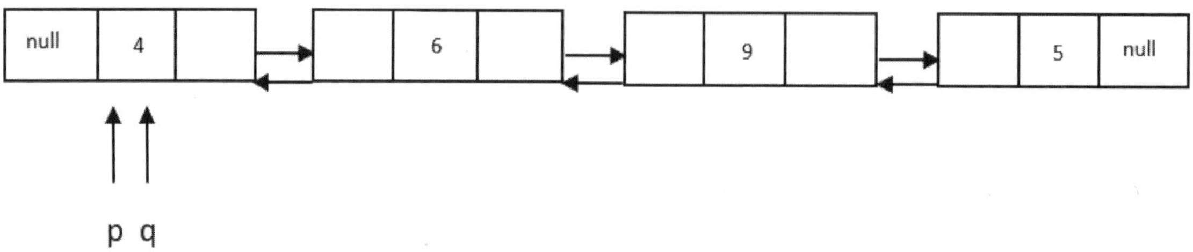

Already existing doubly linked list.

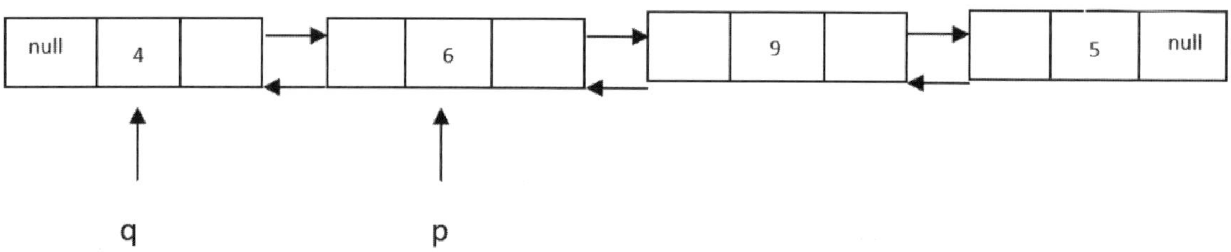

p is made to point the second node and q is made to point the first node. After that the memory location occupied by q is set free.

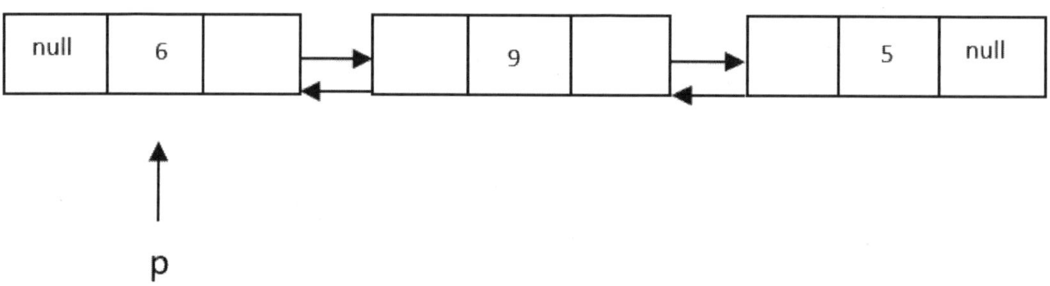

Doubly linked list after deleting the first node.

Example 21: The following program shows deletion of first node of a doubly linked list using C++ language.

```
#include <iostream>
using namespace std;

struct Node {
  int data;
```

```
    Node* next;
    Node* prev;
};

Node* createList(int n) {
    Node* head = NULL;
    Node* temp = NULL;
    Node* last = NULL;

    for (int i = 0; i < n; i++) {
        temp = (Node*)malloc(sizeof(Node));
        if (temp == NULL) {
            cout << "Memory allocation failed" << endl;
            return NULL;
        }

        cout << "Enter data for node " << i + 1 << ": ";
        cin >> temp->data;

        temp->next = NULL;
        if (head == NULL) {
            head = temp;
            temp->prev = NULL;
        } else {
            last->next = temp;
            temp->prev = last;
        }

        last = temp;
    }

    return head;
}

Node* deleteFirst(Node* p) {
```

```
    if (p == NULL) {
        cout << "Underflow" << endl;
        return NULL;
    }

    Node* q = p;
    p = p->next;
    if (p != NULL) {
        p->prev = NULL;
    }

    free(q);

    return p;
}

void printList(Node* p) {
    Node* curr = p;
    while (curr != NULL) {
        cout << curr->data << " ";
        curr = curr->next;
    }
    cout << endl;
}

int main() {
    int n;

    cout << "Enter the number of nodes in the list: ";
    cin >> n;

    Node* p = createList(n);

    cout << "Original Doubly Linked List: ";
    printList(p);
```

```
  p = deleteFirst(p);
  cout << "Doubly Linked List after deleting the first element: ";
  printList(p);

  return 0;
}
```

Output :

Enter the number of nodes in the list: 4

Enter data for node 1: 4

Enter data for node 2: 6

Enter data for node 3: 9

Enter data for node 4: 5

Original Doubly Linked List: 4 6 9 5

Doubly Linked List after deleting the first element: 6 9 5

Algorithm to delete the last node from a doubly linked list: Here 'p' is a pointer variable that is used to store the address of the first node of the list. 'q' is another pointer variable that is used for traversing.

Step 1: If p = null, then Print "Underflow"

Go to Step 7

[End of if]

Step 2: Set q = p

Step 3: Repeat while q -> Next != null

Set q= q -> Next

[End of loop]

Step 4: Set q-> Prev!= null

Set q->Prev->Next = null

Else

Set p = null [List becomes empty if only one node existed]

[End If]

Step 5: Free q

Step 6: Exit

In step1, first it is checked whether there is any node present in the linked list or not. If there is no node, then an underflow message is returned. In step2, another variable q is set as p, so that both points at the first node of the list. In step3 while loop is used to traverse to the last node. Step

4, is used to update the previous node's link. If q->Prev != NULL, it means the list has more than one node. The second-last node's Next pointer (q->Prev->Next) is set to NULL, disconnecting the last node. Otherwise, if q->Prev == NULL, it means only one node was in the list. Since this node is getting deleted, set p = NULL to indicate that the list is now empty. In step 5 memory allocated for the last node is released.

Consider the linked list shown below. Suppose we want to delete the last node of the list. Then the following changes will be done in the linked list.

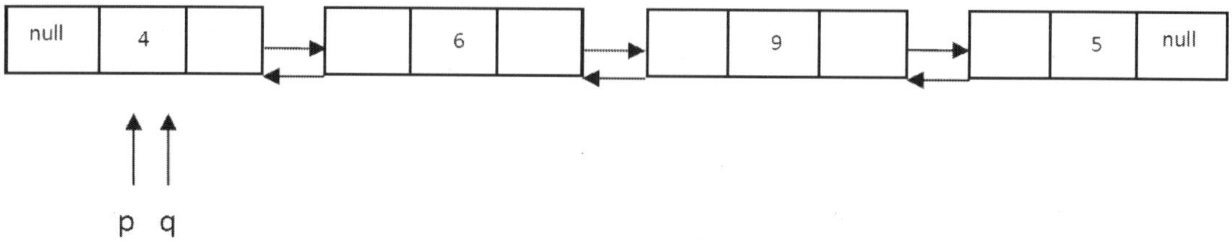

Already existing doubly linked list.

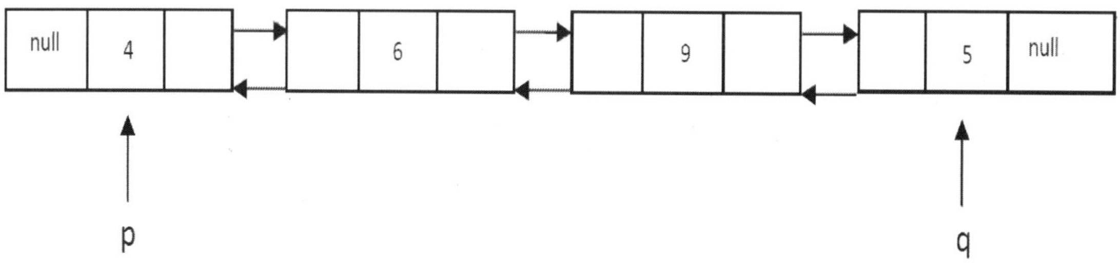

We traverse to the last node by updating the pointer q.

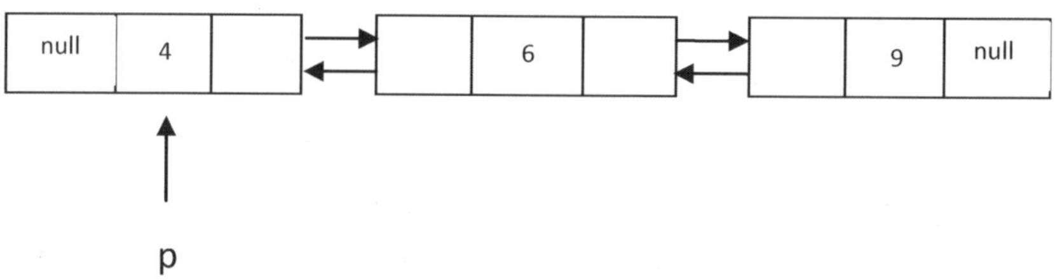

The Next part of the second last node is set as null and the memory location of the node pointed by q is set free.

Example 22: The following program shows deletion of last node of a doubly linked list using C++ language.

```
#include <iostream>

using namespace std;


struct Node {
  int data;
  Node* next;
```

```
  Node* prev;
};
Node* createList(int n) {
  Node* head = NULL;
  Node* temp = NULL;
  Node* last = NULL;

  for (int i = 0; i < n; i++) {
    temp = (Node*)malloc(sizeof(Node));
    if (temp == NULL) {
      cout << "Memory allocation failed" << endl;
      return NULL;
    }

    cout << "Enter data for node " << i + 1 << ": ";
    cin >> temp->data;

    temp->next = NULL;
    if (head == NULL) {
      head = temp;
      temp->prev = NULL;
    } else {
      last->next = temp;
      temp->prev = last;
    }

    last = temp;
  }

  return head;
}

Node* deleteLast(Node* p) {
  if (p == NULL) {
    cout << "Underflow" << endl;
```

```
        return NULL;
    }
    Node* q = p;

    while (q->next != NULL) {
        q = q->next;
    }

    if (q->prev != NULL) {
        q->prev->next = NULL;
    } else {
        p = NULL;
    }

    free(q);
    return p;
}

void printList(Node* p) {
    Node* curr = p;
    while (curr != NULL) {
        cout << curr->data << " ";
        curr = curr->next;
    }
    cout << endl;
}

int main() {
    int n;

    cout << "Enter the number of nodes in the list: ";
    cin >> n;

    Node* p = createList(n);
```

```
  cout << "Original Doubly Linked List: ";
  printList(p);
  p = deleteLast(p);

  cout << "Doubly Linked List after deleting the last element: ";
  printList(p);

  return 0;
}
```

Output :

Enter the number of nodes in the list: 4

Enter data for node 1: 4

Enter data for node 2: 5

Enter data for node 3: 9

Enter data for node 4: 5

Original Doubly Linked List: 4 5 9 5

Doubly Linked List after deleting the last element: 4 5 9

Algorithm to delete a node after a desired location of the linked list: Here 'p' is a pointer variable that is used to store the address of the first node of the list. 'q' is another pointer variable that is used for traversing.

```
Step 1: If p = null, then Print "Underflow"
                    Go to Step 9
          [End of if]
Step 2: Set q = p
Step 3: Repeat while loc > 1 and q->Next != NULL
                    Set q = q->Next
          loc = loc - 1
          [End Loop]

Step 4: If q->Next == NULL, then
                    Print "Invalid location"
Go to Step 9
          [End If]
```

Step 5: Set temp = q -> Next

Step 6: Set q -> Next = temp -> Next

Step 7: If temp->Next != NULL, then

Set temp->Next->Prev = q

[End If]

Step 8: Free temp

Step 9: Exit

Step 1 checks if the list is empty. If p == NULL, print "Underflow" and exit since there are no nodes to delete. Step 2 initialize pointer q for traversal. Set q = p, meaning q starts from the head of the list. Step 3 traverses to the desired location and a while loop is used to move q to the node before the desired location. The loop ensures that q reaches the correct position by decreasing loc in each iteration. Step 4 checks if the location is valid. If q->Next == NULL, it means there is no node after the desired location, so we print "Invalid location" and exit. Step 5 stores the node to be deleted (temp). temp = q->Next stores the reference to the node that needs to be deleted. Step 6 updates the next pointer of q. Step 7 updates the previous pointer of the next node (if it exists). If temp->Next is not NULL, update temp->Next->Prev = q to maintain the doubly linked list structure.Step 8 frees the memory occupied by temp. Step 9 exits the algorithm.

Example 23: The following program shows deletion of a node after a desired location a doubly linked list using C++ language.

```
#include <iostream>
using namespace std;

struct Node {
  int data;
  Node* next;
  Node* prev;
};

Node* createList(int n) {
  Node* head = NULL;
  Node* temp = NULL;
  Node* last = NULL;

  for (int i = 0; i < n; i++) {
```

```
        temp = (Node*)malloc(sizeof(Node));
        if (temp == NULL) {
            cout << "Memory allocation failed" << endl;
            return NULL;
        }

        cout << "Enter data for node " << i + 1 << ": ";
        cin >> temp->data;

        temp->next = NULL;
        if (head == NULL) {
            head = temp;
            temp->prev = NULL;
        } else {
            last->next = temp;
            temp->prev = last;
        }

        last = temp;
    }

    return head;
}

Node* deleteAfterLocation(Node* p, int loc) {
    if (p == NULL) {
        cout << "Underflow" << endl;
        return NULL;
    }

    Node* q = p;

    while (loc > 1 && q->next != NULL) {
        q = q->next;
        loc = loc - 1;
```

```
    }

    if (q->next == NULL) {
        cout << "Invalid location" << endl;
        return p;
    }

    Node* temp = q->next;
    q->next = temp->next;

    if (temp->next != NULL) {
        temp->next->prev = q;
    }

    free(temp);

    return p;
}

void printList(Node* p) {
    Node* curr = p;
    while (curr != NULL) {
        cout << curr->data << " ";
        curr = curr->next;
    }
    cout << endl;
}

int main() {
    int n, loc;

    cout << "Enter the number of nodes in the list: ";
    cin >> n;

    Node* p = createList(n);
```

```
    cout << "Original Doubly Linked List: ";
    printList(p);

    cout << "Enter the location you want to delete the node: ";
    cin >> loc;

    p = deleteAfterLocation(p, loc);

    cout << "Doubly Linked List after deletion: ";
    printList(p);

    return 0;
}
```

Output :

Enter the number of nodes in the list: 4

Enter data for node 1: 5

Enter data for node 2: 6

Enter data for node 3: 7

Enter data for node 4: 8

Original Doubly Linked List: 5 6 7 8

Enter the location you want to delete the node: 2

Doubly Linked List after deletion: 5 6 8

3.8 LET US SUM UP

- A linked list is a linear data structure where the data elements are stored in a special structure known as nodes.
- The nodes of a linked list are connected via the means of pointers.
- Linked list is a data structure which can be used to implement other data structures such as stacks, queues, and their variations.
- Before we insert a new node in linked lists, we need to check for overflow condition, which occurs when no free memory cell is present in the system.
- Before we delete a node from a linked list, we must first check for underflow condition which occurs when we try to delete a node from a linked list that is empty.
- When we delete a node from a linked list, we have to actually free the memory occupied by that node. The memory is returned back to the free pool so that it can be used to store other programs and data.

- In a circular linked list, the last node contains a pointer to the first node of the list.
- A doubly linked list or a two-way linked list is a linked list which contains a pointer to the next as well as the previous node in the sequence.
- The nodes of a doubly linked list consists of three parts: data part, a pointer to the next node, and a pointer to the previous node.
- The prev field of the first node and the next field of the last node contain Null. This enables to traverse the list in the backward direction as well.

3.9 CHECK YOUR PROGRESS

1. What is a node?
2. What is a linked list?
3. Differentiate between a linked list and a linear array.
4. What are the advantages of a linked list over array?
5. What are the variations of a linked list.
6. Why is a doubly linked list more useful than a singly linked list?
7. Give the advantages and uses of a circular linked list.
8. Differentiate between a circular linked list and a singly linked list.
9. How do you insert a node at the beginning of a linked list?
10. What is the difference between a singly linked list and a doubly linked list?
11. How do you insert a node at a specific position in a singly linked list?
12. How do you delete the last node from a singly linked list?
13. How do you find and delete a node with a specific value in a singly linked list?
14. How does inserting a node at the beginning of a doubly linked list differ from a singly linked list?
15. What extra pointer updates are required when inserting a node at the end of a doubly linked list?
16. How do you delete the first node in a doubly linked list?
17. How do you delete the last node in a doubly linked list?
18. How do you delete a node with a specific value in a doubly linked list?
19. What are the steps to delete the first node from a circular linked list?
20. How do you delete the last node from a circular singly linked list?
21. What is the impact of insertion and deletion operations on circular linked list traversal?
22. Write a function to traverse a doubly linked list in both forward and backward directions.

3.10 EXERCISES

Q1. A linked list contains the following elements:

$5 \rightarrow 10 \rightarrow 15 \rightarrow 20$.

Perform the following operations:

- ▶ Insert 25 at the end.
- ▶ Delete the second node.
- ▶ Insert 12 after 10.

What is the final linked list? Write a C++ program to show the implementation.

Q2. A singly linked list contains the elements:

$10 \rightarrow 20 \rightarrow 30 \rightarrow 40$

Perform the following operations:

- ▶ Insert 50 at the end.
- ▶ Delete the second node.
- ▶ Insert 25 after 20.
- ▶ Find the number of nodes.

Display the final linked list. Write a C++ program to show the implementation.

Q3. Perform the following operations on a singly linked list containing:

$10 \rightarrow 20 \rightarrow 30 \rightarrow 40 \rightarrow 50$

- ▶ Insert 25 after 20.
- ▶ Delete the node containing 40.
- ▶ Insert 60 at the end.

What is the final linked list after all operations? Write a C++ program to show the implementation.

Q4. You have the following doubly linked list:

$5 \rightleftarrows 15 \rightleftarrows 25 \rightleftarrows 35 \rightleftarrows 45$

Perform the operations:

- ▶ Insert 20 between 15 and 25.
- ▶ Delete the first node.
- ▶ Insert 50 at the end.

Show the updated doubly linked list. Write a C++ program to show the implementation.

Q6. A doubly linked list contains the following elements:

$8 \rightleftarrows 12 \rightleftarrows 18 \rightleftarrows 25$

Perform the following operations:

- ▶ Insert 30 at the end.
- ▶ Delete the first node.
- ▶ Insert15after 12.

What is the final linked list? Write a C++ program to show the implementation.

Q7. A doubly linked list contains:

$3 \rightleftarrows 6 \rightleftarrows 9 \rightleftarrows 12 \rightleftarrows 15$

Perform the following operations:

- Insert 21 at the end.
- Insert 7 before 9.
- Delete the last node.

What is the final linked list? Write a C++ program to show the implementation.

Q8. A circular linked list contains the following elements:

5 → 10 → 15 → 20 → (back to 5)

Perform the following operations:

- Insert 25 at the end.
- Delete the second node.
- Insert 12 after 10.

What is the final circular linked list? Write a C++ program to show the implementation.

Q9. A circular linked list contains the elements:

10 → 20 → 30 → 40 → 50 → (back to 10)

Perform the following operations:

- Delete the node at position 3 (1-based index).
- Insert 35 before 40.
- Insert 60 at the end.

What is the final circular linked list?Write a C++ program to show the implementation.

Q10. A circular linked list has the following nodes:

50 → 100 → 150 → 200 → (back to 50)

Perform the following operations:

- Insert 125 after 100.
- Delete the first node.
- Insert 175 before 200.

What is the final circular linked list? Write a C++ program to show the implementation.

Q11. A linked list stores student IDs in ascending order. The list currently contains:

101 → 104 → 108 → 115 → 120

Write CPP functions to:

- Insert 110 in its correct position.
- Delete 104.
- Find if 115 is present in the list.
- Reverse the linked list.

What is the final list after performing all operations? Write a C++ program to show the implementation.

Q12. A singly linked list stores student IDs in ascending order:

101 → 105 → 110 → 115 → 120

Perform the following operations:

- Insert 108 at the correct position.
- Delete 115.
- Search for 110.

What is the final linked list? Write a C++ program to show the implementation.

Q13. Given two sorted linked lists:

- List A: 1 → 3 → 5 → 7 → 9
- List B: 2 → 4 → 6 → 8 → 10

Merge them into a single sorted linked list. Write a C++ program to show the implementation.

Q14. Given a linked list:

3 → 5 → 8 → 10 → 12 → 15

Write an algorithm to reorder the list such that all even numbers appear before odd numbers while maintaining relative order.

Q15. Given a linked list, write an algorithm to detect if it is a palindrome.

4

STACK AND QUEUE

4.1 INTRODUCTION

In this chapter we will introduce two very important data structures. These are **stack** and **queue**. In the previous chapter, while studying array, we have seen that array can be used to insert and delete data – at the beginning, at the end or at any desired location. But there may be certain situations or operations where we want to restrict such insertion and deletion and may like to offer insertion and deletion only at one place i.e. in the beginning or in the end positions. Stacks and queues are two data structures which are suitable for such tasks.

In this section we will mainly concentrate on stack and its operations. We will discuss queue in the later half of this chapter.

4.1.1 STACK

A stack is basically a non-primitive, linear data structure. The data structure stack can be resembled with several real life objects, such as – a stack or pile of books, plates, coins, etc.

Figure 4.1: **Stack of books** **Stack of plates** **Stack of coins**

The operations performed in all the above-mentioned examples, resembles the operations performed by the data structure 'stack'.

Let us take the example of a stack of plates. Suppose you have a large stack of plates in front of you and you want to add one more plate to it. What will you do? Where will you place the new plate? The answer is very simple, you don't want to break any plates from the stack, so you will simply place the new plate at the top. Now if you are asked to remove one plate from the stack, which plate will you remove first? The answer is again very simple, you are going to remove one plate from the top. The data structure 'stack' behaves in a similar way.

4.1.2 STACK DEFINITION

From the above discussions we can define stack as:

A stack is a non-primitive, linear and homogeneous data structure, where insertion and deletion take place at only one end, called the top of the stack. Since all the insertion and deletion operations in a stack takes place only at one end, i.e., from the top of the stack, so the last element to be inserted, will be the first element to be removed from the stack. Therefore, stacks are also called last-in-first-out (LIFO) lists.

Following is the diagrammatic illustration of insertion onto a stack:

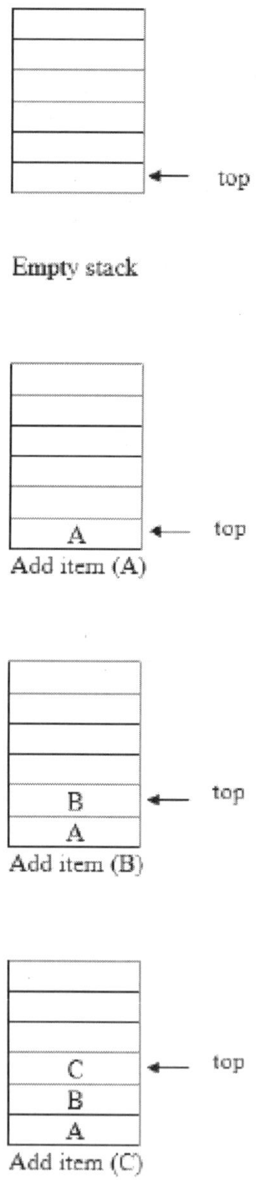

Figure 4.2: Illustration of insertion in a stack

Initially the stack was empty and we gradually started inserting data into it. While we insert new data, the top is incremented by one. Gradually the top also increases and it may have a situation where the top reaches the last location allocated to the list. When the top reaches the last location (there is no empty space) and we want to add more data, such a situation is known as overflow.

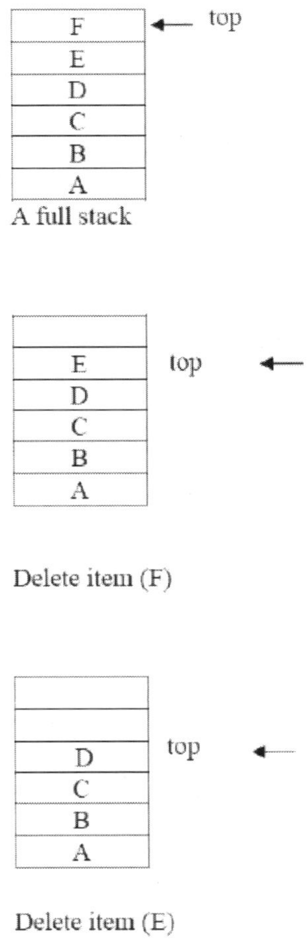

Figure 4.3: Illustration of deletion in a stack

From the figure 4.3 it is clear that, each delete operation will decrease the top by one position. A situation may come when the stack gets fully exhausted by the delete operation and there is no element left. Now if we try to delete elements, this situation will be known as underflow.

4.2 BASIC STACK OPERATIONS

The basic operations that can be performed on a stack are: **Push** and **Pop** operations.

Push Operation: Push operation means adding a new item onto the stack. While adding a new item into an existing stack, the item will be added at the top of the stack. However, before inserting or adding a new value on an existing stack, we must check the overflow condition first. Because if the stack is full, i.e., the present top is the last location of the stack, then there is no more space to add a new item. Otherwise, we can add a new value by simply incrementing the value of top by one position.

Consider a stack as shown below:

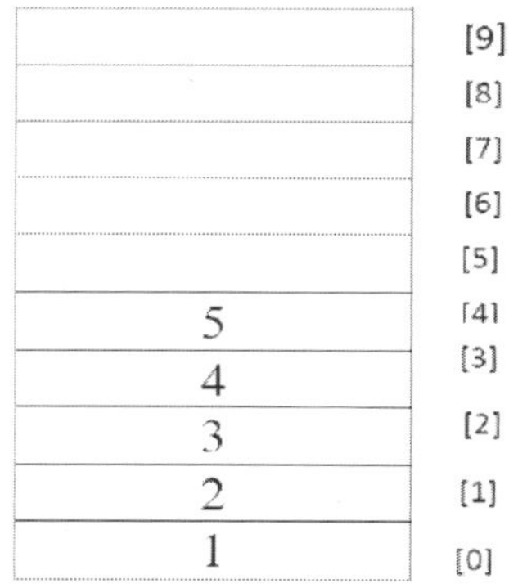

Figure 4.4: A stack

The given stack has total 10 locations out of which 5 locations are full. Since the top has not reached the last location i.e. (Max - 1), therefore we can add a new item onto the stack.

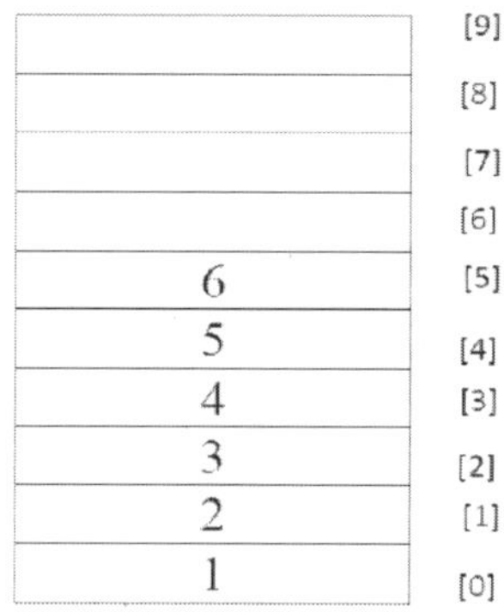

Figure 4.5: A stack after insertion or Push operation

Pop Operation: Pop operation means deleting an element from the stack. While performing pop operation the element at the top position is deleted first. However, before deleting the topmost element from a stack, we should first check the underflow condition. Because, if there is no element in the stack, we cannot delete from an empty stack. Otherwise, we can delete an item from the stack by just decrementing the top by one position.

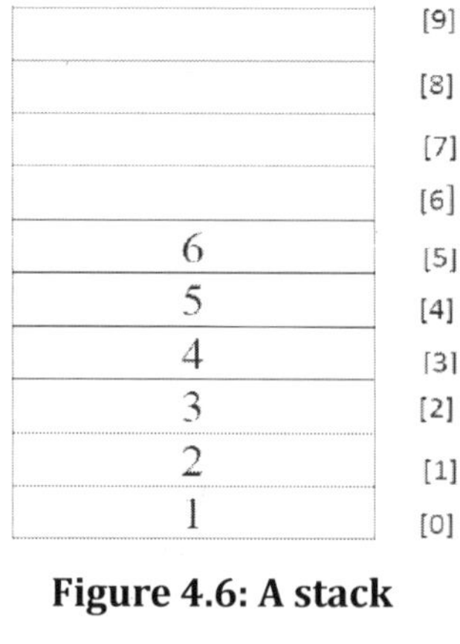

Figure 4.6: A stack

In the above stack, six locations are filled, so it is not an empty stack. Deletion can be done at location 5 i.e. the top of the stack. We decrement the top by one position, so the updated stack is:

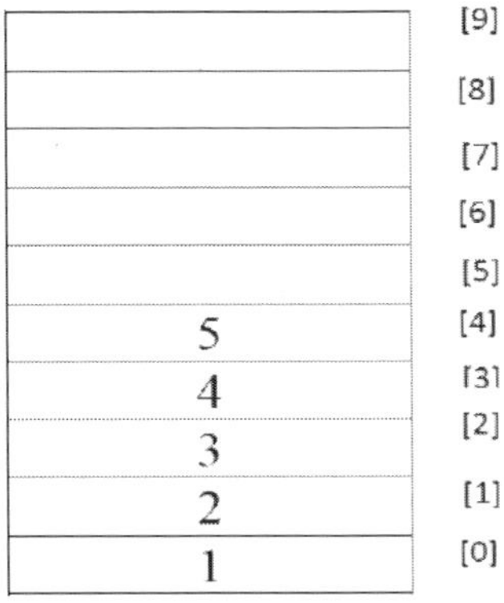

Figure 4.7: A stack after deletion or Pop operation

4.3 IMPLEMENTATION OF STACK

Stack can be implemented in two ways. These are:

- Static implementation
- Dynamic implementation

We will discuss both the implementations one by one.

4.3.1 Static implementation of stack

Stacks can be easily implemented with the help of arrays.

Every stack has a variable called 'top' associated with it. This variable is used to store the address of the topmost element of the stack. In a stack 'top' is the only position where insertion and deletion takes place. A stack also maintains a variable called 'max' which stores the value of maximum number of elements the stack can hold. The condition top = null or top = -1, shows that the stack is empty. The condition top = max – 1, shows that the stack is full.

Algorithm for Push operation: This algorithm pushes an element called 'item' onto the 'stack' at the 'top' position. 'Max' is the last location of the stack.

Step 1: If top = Max – 1, then print "Overflow".

Go to Step 4

[End of if]

Step 2: Set top = top + 1

Step 3: Set stack [top] = item

Step 4: End

In the above algorithm, in step 1, the overflow condition is checked. If there is overflow, then overflow message is returned. In step 2, the top is incremented by one position, to point to the next location. In step 3, item is inserted at the top position.

Example 1: The following program shows push operation in static implementation of stack in C++ language.

```
#include <iostream>
using namespace std;
#define MAX 5

// Stack class
class Stack {
private:
  int stack[MAX];
  int top;

public:
Stack() {
    top = -1;
  }

  // Function to push an element onto the stack
  void push(int item) {
    if (top == MAX - 1) {
      cout << "Overflow! Stack is full." << endl;
      return;
    }

    top = top + 1;
    stack[top] = item;
    cout << item << " pushed onto stack." << endl;
  }

  // Function to display the stack
  void display() {
    if (top == -1) {
      cout << "Stack is empty!" << endl;
      return;
    }
```

```
        cout << "Stack elements: ";
        for (int i = top; i >= 0; i--) {
            cout << stack[i] << " ";
        }
        cout << endl;
    }
};

int main() {
    Stack s;
    int value;

    for (int i = 0; i < MAX; i++) {
        cout << "Enter value to push: ";
        cin >> value;
        s.push(value);
    }

cout << "Attempting to push an extra element (this will cause overflow)" << endl;
s.push(0);
s.display();

return 0;
}
```

Output

Enter value to push: 10

10 pushed onto stack.

Enter value to push: 20

20 pushed onto stack.

Enter value to push: 30

30 pushed onto stack.

Enter value to push: 40

40 pushed onto stack.

Enter value to push: 50

50 pushed onto stack.

Attempting to push an extra element (this will cause overflow)

Overflow! Stack is full.

Stack elements: 50 40 30 20 10

Algorithm for Pop operation: This algorithm deletes an element from 'top' of the 'stack' and assigns it to the variable 'item'.

Step 1: If top = – 1 or top = null, then print "Underflow".

Go to Step 4

[End of If]

Step 2: Set item = stack [top]

Step 3: Set top = top - 1

Step 4: End

In the above algorithm, in step1, the underflow condition is checked. If there is underflow, a message is returned. In step2 the top of the stack is assigned to a variable 'item'. In step3 the top is decremented by one position, so that it points to the new top.

Example 2: The following program shows pop operation in static implementation of stack in C++ language.

```
#include <iostream>
using namespace std;

#define MAX 5

class Stack {
private:
  int stack[MAX];
  int top;

public:
Stack() {
    top = -1;
  }

  void push(int item) {
    if (top == MAX - 1) {
      cout << "Overflow! Stack is full." << endl;
      return;
```

```
    }
    top = top + 1;
    stack[top] = item;
    cout << item << " pushed onto stack." << endl;
  }

  void pop() {
    if (top == -1) {
      cout << "Underflow! Stack is empty." << endl;
      return;
    }
    int item = stack[top];
    top = top - 1;
    cout << item << " popped from stack." << endl;
  }

  void display() {
    if (top == -1) {
      cout << "Stack is empty!" << endl;
      return;
    }
    cout << "Stack elements: ";
    for (int i = top; i >= 0; i--) {
      cout << stack[i] << " ";
    }
    cout << endl;
  }
};

int main() {
  Stack s;
  int value;

  for (int i = 0; i < MAX; i++) {
    cout << "Enter value to push: ";
```

```
        cin >> value;
        s.push(value);
    }

    cout << "Attempting to pop 6 elements (this will cause underflow after 5 pops): " << endl;
    for (int i = 0; i < MAX; i++) {
                    s.pop();
    }

    s.pop();

    s.display();

    return 0;
}
```

Output

Enter value to push: 10
10 pushed onto stack.
Enter value to push: 20
20 pushed onto stack.
Enter value to push: 30
30 pushed onto stack.
Enter value to push: 40
40 pushed onto stack.
Enter value to push: 50
50 pushed onto stack.
Attempting to pop 6 elements (this will cause underflow after 5 pops):
50 popped from stack.
40 popped from stack.
30 popped from stack.
20 popped from stack.
10 popped from stack.
Underflow! Stack is empty.
Stack is empty!

4.3.2 Dynamic implementation of stack

In the previous section we have seen how a stack can be represented using an array. We can use linked list also to represent a stack. Implementing a stack using linked list is known as dynamic representation. Representing a stack using linked list is very efficient and has several advantages over representing a stack using array.

One of the major advantages of using dynamic representation will be in handling overflow scenario. In this case the overflow condition will never arise, as the stack is never reported as full, as long as there is enough space for dynamic memory allocation in the system. Thus, dynamic implementation provides proper memory utilization.

In a dynamic stack each element is stored in a structure called node. Each node is divided into two parts ---

- Data part
- Address part

The data part stores the data or information and the address part stores the address of the next location. The 'start' pointer of the linked list is used as the top. All insertions and deletions take place at the top position.

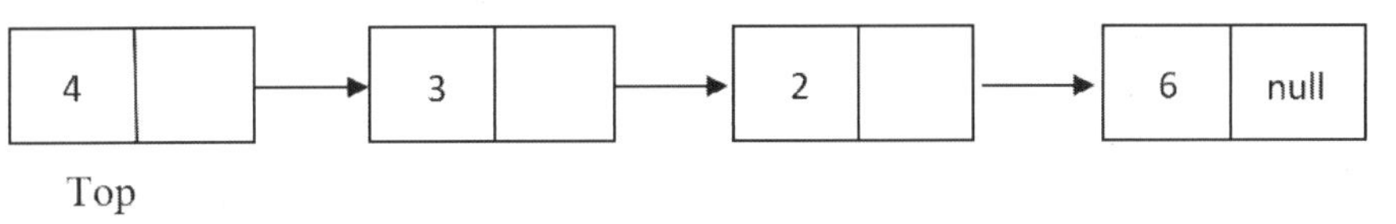

Figure 4.8: Linked list representation of stack

Now let us discuss how push and pop operations are handled in a dynamic structure.

Push Operation: The push operation is used to insert a new element into the stack. The new element will be added only at one location i.e. the top of the stack. Let us consider the following dynamic stack:

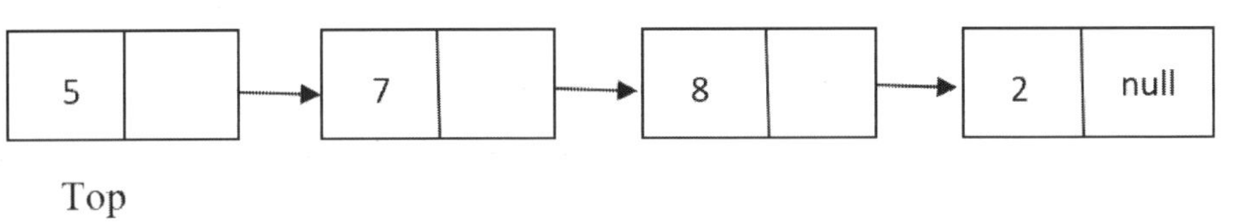

Figure 4.9: A dynamic stack

In the above stack, if we want to insert a new element, then it will be inserted at the 'top'. Suppose we want to insert a new element 6 in the above stack. For this purpose, first a new node will be created. In the data part of the new node element 6 will be stored. Now the next task is to connect the address part of the new node to the previous 'top'. At this stage we have to check, whether the new node created is the first node of the stack or the stack already exist. If top = null, this means the new node created is the first node of the stack. So, we can put a null value in the address part of the new node. If top != null, that means a stack already exist. So, we can connect the new node with the existing stack by placing the address of the previous 'top' in the address part of the new node. Now the new node is declared as 'top'.

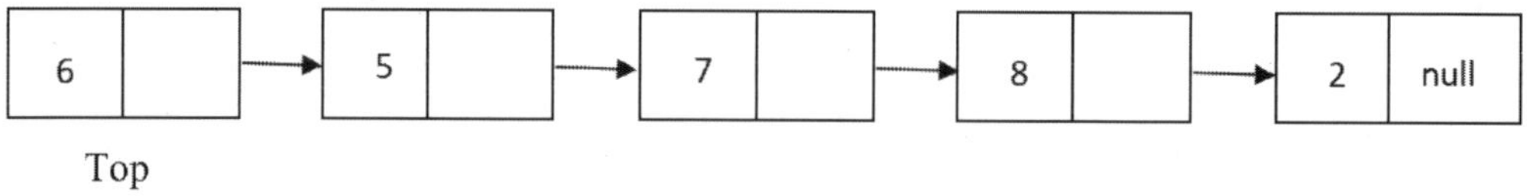

Figure 4.10: Dynamic stack after push operation.

Algorithm for Push operation: This algorithm pushes an element called 'item' onto the 'stack' at the 'top' position. 'New_node' is a temporary node where memory is allocated.

Step 1: Set new_node = avail

Step 2: Set new_node ->data = item

Step 3: If top = null

Set new_node -> link = null

Set top = new_node

Else

Set new_node -> link = top

Set top = new_node

[End of If]

Step 4: End

Example 3: The following program shows push operation in dynamic implementation of stack in C++ language.

```
#include <iostream>
using namespace std;

class Node {
public:
  int data;
  Node* link;
};

Node* top = NULL;

void push(int item) {
  Node* new_node = new Node();

  if (!new_node) {
```

```
        cout << "Stack Overflow! Memory allocation failed.\n";
        return;
    }

    new_node->data = item;

    if (top == NULL) {
        new_node->link = NULL;
        top = new_node;
    }
    else {
        new_node->link = top;
        top = new_node;
    }

    cout << item << " pushed onto stack.\n";
}

void display() {
    if (top == NULL) {
        cout << "Stack is empty!\n";
        return;
    }

    Node* temp = top;
    cout << "Stack elements: ";
    while (temp != NULL) {
        cout << temp->data << " ";
        temp = temp->link;
    }
    cout << endl;
}

int main() {
    int n, item;
```

```
    cout << "Enter the number of elements to push onto the stack: ";
    cin >> n;

    for (int i = 0; i < n; i++) {
        cout << "Enter value to push: ";
        cin >> item;
        push(item);
    }

    display();

    return 0;
}
```

Output

```
Enter the number of elements to push onto the stack: 5
Enter value to push: 1
1 pushed onto stack.
Enter value to push: 2
2 pushed onto stack.
Enter value to push: 3
3 pushed onto stack.
Enter value to push: 4
4 pushed onto stack.
Enter value to push: 5
5 pushed onto stack.
Stack elements: 5 4 3 2 1
```

In the above algorithm, in step 1, a new node is created. In step 2, the data part of the node is assigned a value 'item'. In step 3, it is checked that whether the node created is the first node or not. The address part of the new node is updated accordingly.

Pop Operation: The pop operation is used to delete an element from the top of the stack. If we want to delete an element from the stack, then we have to delete the element present at the topmost position of the stack. Here, the condition of underflow is similar to that of array representation. Before deleting the topmost element, first it has to be checked that whether the stack is empty (if top = null) or not. If the stack is empty then deletion will not be possible. In such a case, a underflow message will be displayed. In case top != null or the stack is not empty, then the element or the node pointed by the top is deleted first. After that the top is made to point to the next element or node in the stack.

Let us consider the following dynamic stack:

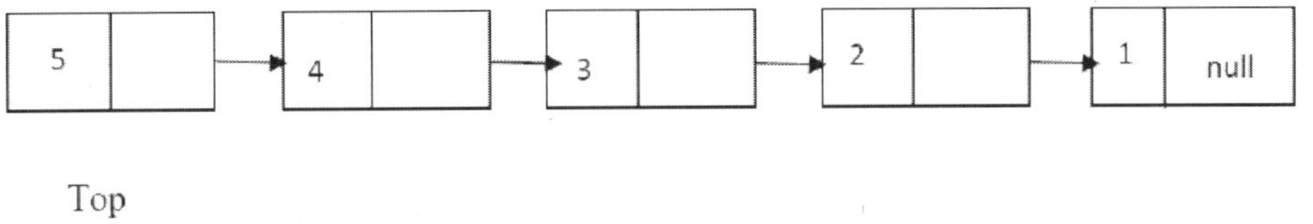

Figure 4.11: A dynamic stack.

In the above stack, the underflow condition is false, i.e. top != null. So, the topmost element or node will be deleted first. After the element 5 is deleted the top is adjusted to point to the next element or node in the list.

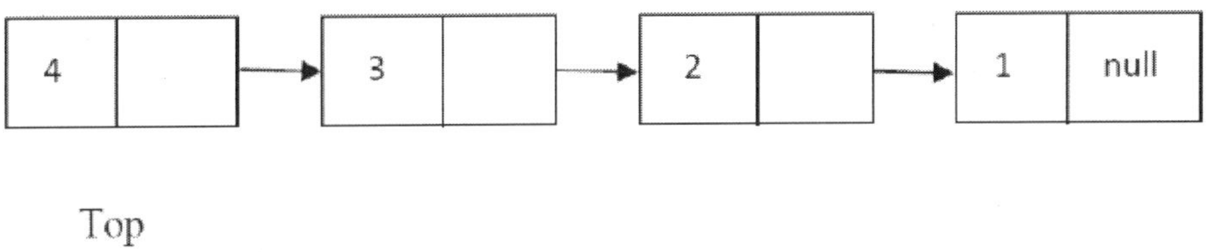

Figure 4.12: Dynamic stack after pop operation.

Algorithm for Pop operation: This algorithm deletes an element from the 'top' position of the 'stack'. 'Item' is a temporary variable where the data to be deleted is stored.

Step 1: If top = null, then print "Underflow".

Go to Step 5

[End of If]

Step 2: Set item = top

Step 3: Set top = top -> link

Step 4: Delete item

Step 5: End

Example 4: The following program shows pop operation in dynamic implementation of stack in C++language.

```
#include <iostream>

using namespace std;

class Node {
public:
   int data;
   Node* link;
```

```
};

Node* top = NULL;

void push(int item) {
    Node* new_node = new Node();

    if (!new_node) {
        cout << "Stack Overflow! Memory allocation failed.\n";
        return;
    }

    new_node->data = item;
    new_node->link = top;
    top = new_node;
    cout << item << " pushed onto stack.\n";
}

void pop() {
    if (top == NULL) {
        cout << "Underflow." << endl;
        return;
    }

    Node* item = top;
    top = top->link;

    cout << item->data << " popped from stack." << endl;
    delete item;
}

void display() {
    if (top == NULL) {
        cout << "Stack is empty!\n";
        return;
```

```
  }

  Node* temp = top;
  cout << "Stack elements: ";
  while (temp != NULL) {
    cout << temp->data << " ";
    temp = temp->link;
  }
  cout << endl;
}
int main() {
  int n, item;
  cout << "Enter the number of elements to push onto the stack: ";
  cin >> n;
  for (int i = 0;'i < n; i++) {
    cout << "Enter value to push: ";
    cin >> item;
    push(item);
  }
display();
  cout << "Attempting to pop elements from the stack...\n";
  for (int i = 0; i < n; i++) {
 pop();
  }
  pop();
  display();
  return 0;
}
```

Output

Enter the number of elements to push onto the stack: 5

Enter value to push: 10

10 pushed onto stack.

Enter value to push: 20

20 pushed onto stack.

Enter value to push: 30

30 pushed onto stack.

Enter value to push: 40

40 pushed onto stack.

Enter value to push: 50

50 pushed onto stack.

Stack elements: 50 40 30 20 10

Attempting to pop elements from the stack...

50 popped from stack.

40 popped from stack.

30 popped from stack.

20 popped from stack.

10 popped from stack.

Underflow.

Stack is empty!

In the above algorithm, in step 1, it is checked that whether the stack is empty or not. If the stack is empty, then it won't be possible to delete from empty stack. So, the program control has to go to step 5 to exit. If the stack is not empty,in step 2 the top of the stack is assigned to a variable 'item'. In step 3, the top is made to point the next node in the list. In step 4, the memory occupied by the variable 'item' is released and the memory location is given back to the free pool.

4.4 APPLICATIONS OF STACK

In this section we will discuss various applications of stack. The data structure stack is used in a number of applications. Some of them are the following:

1. Notation Conversions

- Infix to Postfix
- Infix to Prefix

2. Expression Evaluation

- Evaluating Postfix Expressions
- Evaluating Prefix Expressions

One of the major areas where stacks are frequently used are - Notation Conversion and Expression Evaluation.

Before going into the details of notation conversion and expression evaluation, it is very important to understand about the composition of an arithmetic expression.

An arithmetic expression consists of operands, operators and delimiters. It is very difficult to evaluate an arithmetic expression because an expression may be interpreted in several ways. For instance, let us consider the following expression:

X = a / b * c + d

Let a = 1, b = 2, c = 3 and d = 4

One way of interpreting the above expression could be

X = (1 / 2) * (3 + 4)

= 1 / 7

Another way of interpreting the same expression could be

X = (1 / (2 * 3)) + 4

= 25 / 6

In order to avoid the confusion of how an expression should be evaluated, we have to specify the order of operation by using parenthesis. For better interpretation the above expression could be written as follows:

X = (a / b) * (c – d)

Once the delimiters are set by using parenthesis, confusion still remains as which operation to perform first. Whether (a / b) should be solved first or (c – d) should be solved first? In order to determine which operator should be solved first, we should follow the rules of operator precedence. The operator precedence rules are as follows:

1. Any operation enclosed in parenthesis is performed first.
2. Any exponentiation operations are performed next.
3. Any multiplication or division operations are performed next.
4. Any addition and subtraction operations are performed next.

Operator	Symbol	Order of precedence
Exponentiation	^	Highest Precedence
Multiplication / Division	*, /	Next Highest Precedence
Addition / Subtraction	+ , –	Least Precedence

Table 4.1: Operator Precedence

Suppose we want to evaluate the following parenthesis free arithmetic expression:

3 ^ 2 + 4 * 2 ^ 3 – 24 / 6

Here, we first evaluate the exponentiations to obtain

9 + 4 * 8 – 24 / 6

Now, we evaluate multiplication and division to obtain

9 + 32 – 4

Lastly, we evaluate addition and subtraction to obtain

37

In the above example the expression was solved in three steps following the operator precedence rules. Once the user knows which operator to evaluate first, interpretations becomes easy and it avoids multiple result generation.

4.4.1 Notation Conversions

There are three ways available for writing an arithmetic expression. These are:

- Infix notation

- Prefix notation
- Postfix notation

Infix notation: It is the most common form of notation. In general mathematics, we everyday come across infix notation. The notation where operator is written in-between the operands is known as infix notation.

For example: A + B, C – D, E / F, G * H

Prefix notation: Prefix notation is also known as polish notation. This form of writing notations was suggested by an Polish mathematician named Han Lukasiewicz. After his name prefix notation is also known as Polish notation. In Infix notation the operator precedes the operands. That means in Prefix or Polish notation, the operator is written before the operands.

For example: + AB, - CD, / EF, * GH

One of the fundamental advantages of Polish notation is that, it does not need parenthesis to write an expression. In this notation, the order of evaluation depends on the position of the operator and operands in the expression and not on priority.

Postfix notation: Postfix notation is also known as reverse polish notation. In this notation the operator is written after the operands.

For example: AB + , CD - , EF / , GH *

Any expression written in reverse polish notation also does not need parenthesis to determine the order of operations.

When high level programming languages were developed, then at that time one of the main concerns was, how to generate machine language instructions that could properly evaluate any arithmetic expression. When we program using any high level language, we usually write our arithmetic expressions in infix notation. The computer evaluates an arithmetic expression written in infix notation in two steps. First the infix notation is converted to its equivalent postfix notation and then the postfix expression is evaluated. Here stack is used as the main tool for conversion of an infix notation to postfix and also to evaluate a postfix expression. In this section we will first discuss notation conversion and after that we will deal with evaluation of arithmetic expression.

Rules for converting infix expression to postfix

i. Parenthesize the expression starting from left to right.

ii. During parenthesizing the expression, the operands associated with operator having higher precedence are first parenthesized.

iii. The part of the expression which have been converted into postfix form is treated as a single operand.

iv. Once the expression is converted to postfix form, remove the parenthesis.

Let us now consider one example to explain the above mentioned rules better.

[It should be noted that same rules are applicable for infix to prefix conversion.]

Infix to postfix conversion

A + B * C	Infix notation
A + (B * C)	Parenthesize higher precedence operator first

A + (B C *)	Convert the multiplication
A (B C *) +	Already converted portion is treated as single operand. Convert the addition
A B C * +	Remove parenthesis. The result is postfix form.

Algorithm to convert Infix to Postfix

Let, X is an arithmetic expression written in infix notation. This algorithm finds the equivalent postfix expression Y.

Step 1: Push "("onto Stack, and add ")" to the end of X.

Step 2: Scan X from left to right and repeat Step 3 to 6 for each element of X until the Stack is empty.

Step 3: If an operand is encountered, add it to Y.

Step 4: If a left parenthesis is encountered, push it onto Stack.

Step 5: If an operator is encountered ,then:

a. Repeatedly pop from Stack and add to Y each operator (on the top of Stack) which has the same precedence as or higher precedence than operator.

b. Add operator to Stack.

[End of If]

Step 6: If a right parenthesis is encountered ,then:

a. Repeatedly pop from Stack and add to Y each operator (on the top of Stack) until a left parenthesis is encountered.

b. Remove the left Parenthesis.

[End of If]

[End of If]

Step 7: End.

Example 5: This is a program showing conversion of infix expression to postfix expression in C++ language.

```
#include <iostream>
#include <stack>
#include <cctype>
#include <string>

using namespace std;

// Function to determine precedence of operators
int precedence(char op) {
  switch (op) {
    case '+':
```

```
        case '-': return 1;
        case '*':
        case '/': return 2;
        case '^': return 3;
        default: return 0;
    }
}

// Function to convert infix to postfix
void infixToPostfix(const string &infix, string &postfix) {
    stack<char> s;
    s.push('('); // Step 1: Push '(' onto the stack
    string infix_expr = infix + ')'; // Add ')' to the end of infix expression

    int i = 0, j = 0;
    while (!s.empty()) { // Step 2: Process each element in infix
        char symbol = infix_expr[i++];

        // Step 3: If an operand is encountered, add it to postfix
        if (isalnum(symbol)) {
            postfix += symbol;
        }
        // Step 4: If a left parenthesis is encountered, push it onto the stack
        else if (symbol == '(') {
         s.push(symbol);
        }
        // Step 5: If an operator is encountered
        else if (symbol == '+' || symbol == '-' || symbol == '*' || symbol == '/' || symbol == '^') {
            while (!s.empty() && precedence(s.top()) >= precedence(symbol)) {
             postfix += s.top();
             s.pop();
            }
            s.push(symbol);
        }
        // Step 6: If a right parenthesis is encountered
```

```
        else if (symbol == ')') {
            while (!s.empty() && s.top() != '(') {
                postfix += s.top();
                s.pop();
            }
            s.pop(); // Remove '(' from stack
        }
    }
}

// Main function to test infix to postfix conversion
int main() {
    string infix, postfix;

    cout << "Enter an infix expression: ";
    cin >> infix;

    infixToPostfix(infix, postfix);

    cout << "Postfix expression: " << postfix << endl;

    return 0;
}
```

Output

Enter an infix expression: (A+B)*C-D

Postfix expression: AB+C*D-

Algorithm to convert Infix to prefix

While we use infix expressions in our day to day lives. Computers have trouble understanding this format because they need to keep in mind rules of operator precedence and also brackets. Prefix and Postfix expressions are easier for a computer to understand and evaluate.

Given two operands A and B and an operator , the infix notation implies that operator will be placed in between A and B. When the operator is placed after both operands, it is called postfix notation. And when the operator is placed before the operands, the expression issaid to be in prefix notation. Given any infix expression we can obtain the equivalent prefix and postfix format.

Step 1: Push ")" onto STACK, and add "(" to end of the A.

Step 2: Scan A from right to left and repeat step 3 to 6 for each element of A until the STACK is empty.

Step 3: If an operand is encountered add it to B.

Step 4: If a right parenthesis is encountered push it onto STACK

Step 5: If an operator is encountered then:

a. Repeatedly pop from STACK and add to B each operator (on the top of STACK) which has same or higher precedence than the operator.

b. Add operator to STACK.

Step 6: If left parenthesis is encontered then

a. Repeatedly pop from the STACK and add to B (each operator on top of stack until a left parenthesis is encounterd.

b. Remove the left parenthesis.

Step 7: Exit

Example 6: This is a program showing conversion of infix expression to prefix expression in C++ language.

```
#include <iostream>
#include <stack>
#include <cctype>
#include <string>
#include <algorithm> // for reverse()

using namespace std;

// Function to determine precedence of operators
int precedence(char op) {
  switch (op) {
    case '+':
    case '-': return 1;
    case '*':
    case '/': return 2;
    case '^': return 3;
    default: return 0;
  }
}
```

```
// Function to reverse a string
string reverseString(const string &s) {
  string reversed = s;
  reverse(reversed.begin(), reversed.end());
  return reversed;
}

// Function to convert infix to postfix
void infixToPostfix(const string &infix, string &postfix) {
  stack<char> s;
  s.push('('); // Step 1: Push '(' onto the stack
  string infix_expr = infix + ')';  // Add ')' to the end of infix expression

  int i = 0, j = 0;
  while (!s.empty()) {  // Step 2: Process each element in infix
    char symbol = infix_expr[i++];

    // Step 3: If an operand is encountered, add it to postfix
    if (isalnum(symbol)) {
      postfix += symbol;
    }
    // Step 4: If a left parenthesis is encountered, push it onto the stack
    else if (symbol == '(') {
     s.push(symbol);
    }
    // Step 5: If an operator is encountered
    else if (symbol == '+' || symbol == '-' || symbol == '*' || symbol == '/' || symbol == '^') {
      while (!s.empty() && precedence(s.top()) >= precedence(symbol)) {
        postfix += s.top();
        s.pop();
      }
      s.push(symbol);
    }
    // Step 6: If a right parenthesis is encountered
    else if (symbol == ')') {
```

```
            while (!s.empty() && s.top() != '(') {
                postfix += s.top();
                s.pop();
            }
            s.pop();  // Remove '(' from stack
        }
    }
}

// Function to convert infix to prefix
void infixToPrefix(const string &infix, string &prefix) {
    // Step 1: Reverse the infix expression
    string reversedInfix = reverseString(infix);

    // Step 2: Replace '(' with ')' and vice versa
    for (char &ch : reversedInfix) {
        if (ch == '(') {
            ch = ')';
        } else if (ch == ')') {
            ch = '(';
        }
    }

    // Step 3: Convert the modified infix expression to postfix
    string postfix = "";
    infixToPostfix(reversedInfix, postfix);

    // Step 4: Reverse the postfix expression to get the prefix expression
    prefix = reverseString(postfix);
}

// Main function to test infix to prefix conversion
int main() {
    string infix, prefix;
```

```
  cout << "Enter an infix expression: ";
  cin >> infix;

  infixToPrefix(infix, prefix);

  cout << "Prefix expression: " << prefix << endl;

  return 0;
}
```

Output

Enter an infix expression: (A+B)*C-D

Prefix expression: -*+ABCD

Infix to prefix conversion

A + B * C	Infix notation
A + (B * C)	Parenthesize higher precedence operator first
A + (* B C)	Convert the multiplication
+ A (* B C)	Already converted portion is treated as single operand. Convert the addition
+ A * B C	Remove parenthesis. The result is prefix form.

For example: The following infix expression is converted to postfix using a stack.

A+(B*C-(D/E-F)*G)*H

Expression	Stack	Output	Comment
5^E+D*(C^B+A)	Empty	-	Initial
^E+D*(C^B+A)	Empty	5	Print
E+D*(C^B+A)	^	5	Push
+D*(C^B+A)	^	5E	Push
D*(C^B+A)	+	5E^	Pop And Push
*(C^B+A)	+	5E^D	Print
(C^B+A)	+*	5E^D	Push
C^B+A)	+*(	5E^D	Push
^B+A)	+*(	5E^DC	Print
B+A)	+*(^	5E^DC	Push
+A)	+*(^	5E^DCB	Print

A)	+*(+	5E^DCB^	Pop And Push
)	+*(+	5E^DCB^A	Print
End	+*	5E^DCB^A+	Pop Until '('
End	Empty	5E^DCB^A+*+	Pop Every element

4.4.2 Expression Evaluation

Evaluating Postfix Expressions

The compiler finds it convenient to evaluate an expression written in its postfix form. This is because postfix form eliminates the need of parenthesizing an arithmetic expression which signifies priority of evaluation and also eliminates the need to observe rules of hierarchy, precedence and associativity during evaluation of an expression.

As a postfix expression can be written without parenthesis and can be evaluated as two operands and an operator at a time, this makes tasks easier for the compiler to handle.

Evaluation rule of a Postfix Expression:

- While reading the expression from left to right, push the element in the stack if it is an operand.
- Pop the two operands from the stack, if the element is an operator and then evaluate it.
- Push back the result of the evaluation. Repeat it till the end of the expression.

Algorithm for evaluation of Postfix Expression: Here 'P' is an arithmetic expression written in postfix notation. 'Stack' is used to hold the scanned elements.

Step 1: Add a right parenthesis ")" at the end of the postfix expression 'P'.

Step 2: Read the postfix expression P from left to right until ")" encountered.

Step 3: If operand is encountered, push it onto Stack.

[End If]

Step 4: If operator is encountered, then:

a. Pop two elements of the Stack, A and B, where A is the top element and B is the next to Top element

b. Evaluate B operator A

c. Push the result of B operator A onto Stack

[End If]

[End of step 2 loop]

Step 5: Set result equal to the top element on Stack.

Step 6: END

To explain the algorithm better, let us solve an example. Consider the following postfix notation: 6 5 4 * + 9 3 / -

P: 6 5 4 * + 9 3 / -) After adding a right parenthesis at the end of P. Now we scan the elements of P from left to right and place them onto the Stack accordingly.

Symbol scanned	Stack
6	6
5	6, 5
4	6, 5, 4
*	6, 20
+	26
9	26, 9
3	26, 9, 3
/	26, 3
-	23
)	

The result after evaluation is 23.

Example 7: This program shows the evaluation of postfix expression using C++ language.

```
#include <iostream>
#include <stack>
#include <cctype> // For isdigit function
#include <string>
#include <sstream> // For stringstream to handle space-separated input

using namespace std;

// Function to evaluate the postfix expression
int evaluatePostfix(const string &expr) {
  stack<int> s;
  stringstream ss(expr);
  string token;

  // Process each token separated by space
  while (ss >> token) {
    if (isdigit(token[0])) {
      // If token is a number, push it onto the stack
      s.push(stoi(token)); // Convert string to integer
    } else if (token == "+" || token == "-" || token == "*" || token == "/") {
      // If the token is an operator, pop two operands and perform the operation
      int b = s.top(); s.pop();
      int a = s.top(); s.pop();
```

```
            int result;
            if (token == "+") result = a + b;
            else if (token == "-") result = a - b;
            else if (token == "*") result = a * b;
            else if (token == "/") result = a / b;
            s.push(result); // Push the result back onto the stack
        }
    }

    // The result is the only element left in the stack
    return s.top();
}

int main() {
    string postfixExpression;

    // Input Postfix expression (space-separated)
    cout << "Enter postfix expression: ";
    getline(cin, postfixExpression); // Read entire line for expression

    // Call function to evaluate postfix expression
    int result = evaluatePostfix(postfixExpression);

    // Display the result
    cout << "Result of postfix evaluation: " << result << endl;

    return 0;
}
```

Output

Enter postfix expression: 6 5 4 * + 9 3 / -

Result of postfix evaluation: 23

Evaluating Prefix Expressions

An infix expression is difficult for the machine to know and keep track of precedence of operators. On the other hand, a postfix as well as prefix expression itself determines the precedence of operators (as the placement of operators in a postfix and prefix expression depends upon its precedence).Therefore, for the machine it is easier to carry out an expression written in postfix or prefix notations rather than an infix notation.

Algorithm for evaluation of Prefix Expression: Here 'P' is an arithmetic expression written in prefix notation. 'Stack' is used to hold the scanned elements.

Step 1: Add a left parenthesis "(" at the beginning of the prefix expression 'P'.

Step 2: Read the prefix expression P from right to left until "(" encountered.

Step 3: If operand is encountered, push it onto Stack

[End If]

Step 4: If operator is encountered, then:

a. Pop two elements of the Stack, A and B, where A is the top element and B is the next to Top element

b. Evaluate B operator A

c. Push the result of B operator A onto Stack

[End If]

[End of step 2 loop]

Step 5: Set result equal to the top element on Stack.

Step 6: END

To explain the algorithm better, let us solve an example. Consider the following postfix notation: / + 5 4 * 7

P: (/+ 5 4 * 7 3 After adding a right parenthesis at the end of P. Now we scan the elements of P from right to left and place them onto the Stack accordingly.

Symbol scanned	Stack
7	7
3	7, 3
*	21
4	21, 4
5	21, 4, 5
+	21, 9
/	2
)	

The result after evaluation is 2.

Example 8: This program shows the evaluation of prefix expression using C++ language.

```
#include <iostream>
#include <stack>
#include <cctype> // For isdigit function
#include <string>
#include <sstream> // For stringstream to handle space-separated input
```

```
using namespace std;

// Function to evaluate the prefix expression
int evaluatePrefix(const string &expr) {
  stack<int> s;

  // Read the expression from right to left
  for (int i = expr.length() - 1; i >= 0; i--) {
    if (expr[i] == ' ') {
      continue; // Ignore spaces
    }

    // If the character is a digit (operand), push it onto the stack
    if (isdigit(expr[i])) {
      s.push(expr[i] - '0'); // Convert character to integer and push
    } else if (expr[i] == '+' || expr[i] == '-' || expr[i] == '*' || expr[i] == '/') {
      // Ensure there are at least two operands in the stack
      if (s.size() < 2) {
        cout << "Invalid prefix expression!" << endl;
      exit(1);
      }
      int a = s.top(); s.pop();
      int b = s.top(); s.pop();
      int result;

      // Perform the operation based on the operator
      switch (expr[i]) {
        case '+': result = b + a; break;
        case '-': result = b - a; break;
        case '*': result = b * a; break;
        case '/':
          if (a == 0) {
            cout << "Division by zero error!" << endl;
          exit(1);
```

```
            }
            result = b / a; break;
        }
        // Push the result back onto the stack
        s.push(result);
      } else {
        cout << "Invalid character in expression!" << endl;
        exit(1);
      }
    }

    // The result should be the only element left in the stack
    if (s.size() != 1) {
      cout << "Invalid prefix expression!" << endl;
      exit(1);
    }

    return s.top();  // Return the final result
}

int main() {
    string expr;
    cout << "Enter a prefix expression: ";
    getline(cin, expr);  // Read the prefix expression from user

    int result = evaluatePrefix(expr);

    cout << "Result: " << result << endl;

    return 0;
}
```

Output

Enter a prefix expression: / + 5 4 * 7 3

Result: 2

4.5 QUEUE

In the above section we have elaborated about the data structure stack. In this section we will mainly focus on another data structure called 'queue'.

Just like stack, queue is also a non-primitive, linear data structure. The data structure queue can also be resembled with several real life examples, such as – a queue of people waiting for a bus, a queue of people waiting to purchase movie tickets or a queue of people waiting for any resource.

Figure 4.13: Various real time examples of queue.

The operations performed in all the above mentioned examples, resembles the operations performed by the data structure 'queue'.

Let us take the example of a queue of people waiting for a bus. Suppose we have a queue of some people waiting for a bus in the bus stop. Now when the bus arrives, the person who was first on the queue will board the bus first, followed by the next person in the queue and so on. The person who was at the end of the queue will be the last one to board the bus. If a new person wants to board the bus, he or she will enter the queue after the existing last person. This means the first person in the queue will be moved first, followed by other people in the sequence. And if a new person is inserted in the queue, he/she will be inserted only at the last location and not any other location. The data structure 'queue' behaves in a similar way.

4.5.1 QUEUE DEFINITION

From the above discussions we can define queue as:

A queue is a non-primitive, linear and homogeneous data structure, where insertion and deletion takes place at two ends, called rear and front. Rear is the position through which insertion takes place and front is the position through which deletion takes place.

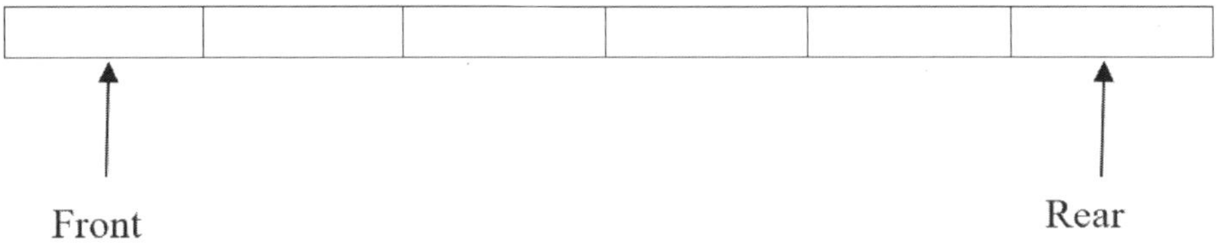

Figure 4.14: A Queue

The queue is also called a first-in-first-out (FIFO) list since the element that enters the queue first is deleted or processed first. That is, the first element that moves in a queue is also the first element to move out of the queue. The functioning of a queue is totally contradictory to the functioning of a stack. Stack is a LIFO list and queue is a FIFO list.

4.6 BASIC OPERATIONS OF QUEUE

The basic operations that can be performed on a queue are: **Insertion** and **Deletion** operations.

Insertion operation: Insertion means to add a new item or element in the queue. To better understand how the insertion operation is handled in a queue, let us take the following graphical example of a queue.

0	1	2	3	4	5

Rear = -1

Front = -1

Empty queue

The queue shown above is an empty queue. Therefore front and rear will not point to any location, rather they will hold null or some invalid value. When the first element is inserted both front and rear will point to the first location as shown below.

12					
0	1	2	3	4	5
↑	↑				
Front	Rear				

After inserting an item (12)

As we go on adding more elements to the queue, the rear goes on increasing.

12	23				
0	1	2	3	4	6
↑	↑				
Front	Rear				

After inserting second item (23)

12	23	8			
0	1	2	3	4	6
↑		↑			
Front		Rear			

After inserting third item (8)

Figure 4.15: Illustration of insertion operation

From the graphical representations shown above, it is clear that, every time we insert a new item in the queue, the rear is incremented by one position and the new item is inserted in the new updated rear.

Deletion operations: Deletion means to remove an item or element from an existing queue. To better understand how the deletion operation is handled in a queue, let us take the following graphical example of a queue.

12	23	8	10	32	
0	1	2	3	4	6
↑				↑	
Front				Rear	

We know that in a queue, deletion takes place at the front end and not at the rear end. Now from the above queue, if we want to delete than the item 12 will be deleted first, as it is pointed by the front pointer.

	23	8	10	32	
0	1	2	3	4	6
	↑			↑	
	Front			Rear	

After deleting the first item (12)

		8	10	32	
0	1	2	3	4	6
		↑		↑	
		Front		Rear	

After deleting the first item (23)

Figure 4.16: Illustration of deletion operation

From the graphical representations shown above, it is clear that, in a queue deletion takes place at the front end. Every time we delete an item the front is incremented by one position.

4.7 REPRESENTATION OF QUEUE

Like any other list queue can also be represented in 2 ways. These are:

- Static representation
- Dynamic representation

We will discuss both the representations one by one.

4.7.1 Static representation of queue

Queues can be easily implemented using arrays. This type of implementation is also called static implementation. In static implementation the capacity or limit of maximum elements the queue can hold has to be declared beforehand as the required memory blocks will be reserved during compilation of the program itself. In static implementation it is also possible to know the exact number of elements stored in the queue by using the following formula:

Total number of elements = Rear – Front + 1

Now we will discuss the algorithms for insertion and deletion operations using array representation.

Algorithm for Insertion operation

This algorithm inserts an element called 'item' in the list 'queue' at the 'rear' position. 'Front' is the location through which deletion takes place and 'rear' is the location through which insertion takes place. 'Max' is the last location of the queue.

Step 1: If front = 0 and rear = max – 1, then print "Overflow".

Go to Step 4

[End of if]

Step 2: If front = -1 and rear = -1 (Empty queue)

Set front = 0 and rear = 0

Else

Set rear = rear + 1

[End of if]

Step 3: Set queue [rear] = item

Step 4: End

Example 9: The following program shows insertion operation in static implementation of stack in C++ language.

```
#include <iostream>
#include <iostream>
using namespace std;
#define MAX 5

class Queue {
private:
  int queue[MAX];
  int front, rear;

public:
Queue() {
    front = -1;
    rear = -1;
  }

  void insert(int item) {
    if (front == 0 && rear == MAX - 1) {
      cout << "Overflow! Queue is full." << endl;
      return;
```

```
    }

    if (front == -1 && rear == -1) {
      front = 0;
      rear = 0;
    } else {
      rear = rear + 1;
    }

    queue[rear] = item;
    cout << "Inserted " << item << " into the queue." << endl;
  }

  void display() {
    if (front == -1) {
      cout << "Queue is empty." << endl;
      return;
    }

    cout << "Queue elements are: ";
    for (int i = front; i <= rear; i++) {
      cout << queue[i] << " ";
    }
    cout << endl;
  }
};

int main() {
  Queue q;
  int item;

  for (int i = 0; i < MAX; i++) {
    cout << "Enter element " << i + 1 << ": ";
    cin >> item;
    q.insert(item);
```

```
    }
    q.display();
    cout << "Enter another element (attempt to insert into full queue): ";
    cin >> item;
    q.insert(item);

    return 0;
}
```

Output

Enter element 1: 10

Inserted 10 into the queue.

Enter element 2: 20

Inserted 20 into the queue.

Enter element 3: 30

Inserted 30 into the queue.

Enter element 4: 40

Inserted 40 into the queue.

Enter element 5: 50

Inserted 50 into the queue.

Queue elements are: 10 20 30 40 50

Enter another element (attempt to insert into full queue): 12

Overflow! Queue is full.

In the above algorithm, in step 1, the overflow condition is checked. If there is overflow, then overflow message is returned. In step 2, queue empty condition is checked. If the queue is empty, then both front and rear are made to point to the first location of the queue. If both the overflow and queue empty conditions are false then the rear is incremented by one position to point to the next location, so that a new element can be inserted. In step 3, item is inserted at the updated rear position.

Algorithm for Deletion operation

This algorithm deletes an element called 'item' from the 'front' position of the list 'queue'. 'Front' is the location through which deletion takes place.

Step 1: If front = -1, then print "Underflow".

    Go to Step 4

    [End of if]

Step 2: Set item = queue [front]

Step 3: Set front = front + 1

Step 4: if (front> rear) {front = -1, rear = -1}

Step 5: End

Example 10: The following program shows deletion operation in static implementation of stack in C++ language.

```
#include <iostream>
using namespace std;
#define MAX 5

class Queue {
private:
  int queue[MAX];
  int front, rear;

public:
Queue() {
    front = -1;
    rear = -1;
  }

  void insert(int item) {
    if (rear == MAX - 1) {
      cout << "Overflow!" << endl;
      return;
    }

    if (front == -1 && rear == -1) {
      front = 0;
      rear = 0;
    } else {
      rear = rear + 1;
    }

    queue[rear] = item;
    cout << "Inserted " << item << " into the queue." << endl;
  }
```

```
  void dequeue() {
    if (front == -1) {
      cout << "Underflow!" << endl;
      return;
    }

    int item = queue[front];
    front = front + 1;

    if (front > rear) {
      front = -1;
      rear = -1;
    }
  }

  void display() {
    if (front == -1) {
      cout << "Queue is empty." << endl;
      return;
    }

    cout << "Queue elements are: ";
    for (int i = front; i <= rear; i++) {
      cout << queue[i] << " ";
    }
    cout << endl;
  }
};

int main() {
  Queue q;
  int item;

  for (int i = 0; i < MAX; i++) {
    cout << "Enter element " << i + 1 << ": ";
```

```
        cin >> item;
        q.insert(item);
    }

q.display();

q.dequeue();
q.display();

q.dequeue();
q.display();

q.dequeue();
q.display();

q.dequeue();
q.display();

q.dequeue();
q.display();

q.dequeue();

return 0;
}
```

Output :

```
Enter element 1: 10
Inserted 10 into the queue.
Enter element 2: 20
Inserted 20 into the queue.
Enter element 3: 30
Inserted 30 into the queue.
Enter element 4: 40
Inserted 40 into the queue.
Enter element 5: 50
```

Inserted 50 into the queue.

Queue elements are: 10 20 30 40 50

Queue elements are: 20 30 40 50

Queue elements are: 30 40 50

Queue elements are: 40 50

Queue elements are: 50

Queue is empty.

Underflow!

In the above algorithm, in step 1, the underflow condition is checked. If there is underflow, then underflow message is returned. In step 2, the value of the queue at the location pointed by the front is stored in a variable "item". In step 3, front is incremented so that it points to the next element in the queue.

4.7.2 Dynamic representation of queue

In the previous section we have seen how a queue can be represented using an array. We can use linked list also to represent a queue. Implementing a queue using linked list is known as dynamic representation. Representing a queue using linked list is very efficient and has several advantages over representing a queue using array.

One of the major advantages of using dynamic representation is that, it helps in effective utilization of memory. Usually we see that, while dealing with static representation, the utilization of the memory is not at all proper. There are usually instances of memory overflow and underflow. Suppose we have allocated space for 100 elements and we are storing only say 50 elements, then half of the memory space is wasted. Similarly, if we have allocated 100 memory locations and we want to store 200 elements, than again there is an issue of memory overflow. Dynamic representation offers a better solution for memory utilization. It is possible to allocate memory as per the requirement, as dynamic memory allocation is done during program run time and not during program compilation. As long as there is available space in the computer's memory, there is no issue of memory overflow.

When we implement queue using linked list, the data will be stored in a structure called node.Each node is divided into two parts ---

- Data part
- Address part

The data part stores the data or information and the address part stores the address of the next location. The 'start' pointer of the linked list is used to designate the front. Rear is used to store the address of the last element of the queue.

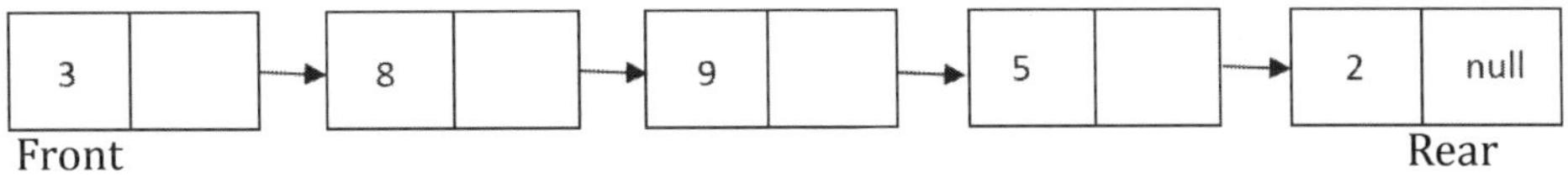

Figure 4.17: A dynamic queue.

If we want to add or insert a new element in the above linked queue, than it will be added at the rear end. Suppose we want to add a new element 6 in the above linked queue. For this purpose a new node has to be created first. But before creating a new node, the condition front = null is checked. If this condition holds true, then a new node is created, then front and rear are made to point to the new node (front = rear). In the data part of the new node 6 will be stored and in the link part null will be stored.

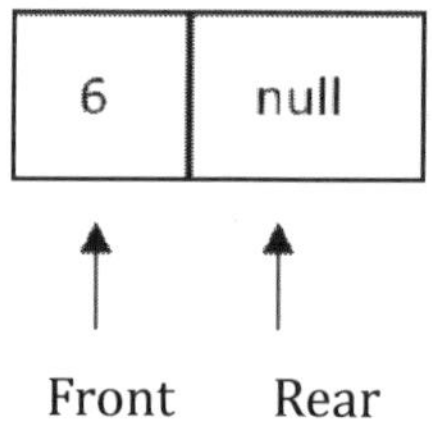

Figure 4.18: Single node in a dynamic queue.

But if we already have a linked queue as given in the above figure, then the new node will be simply added at the rear end.

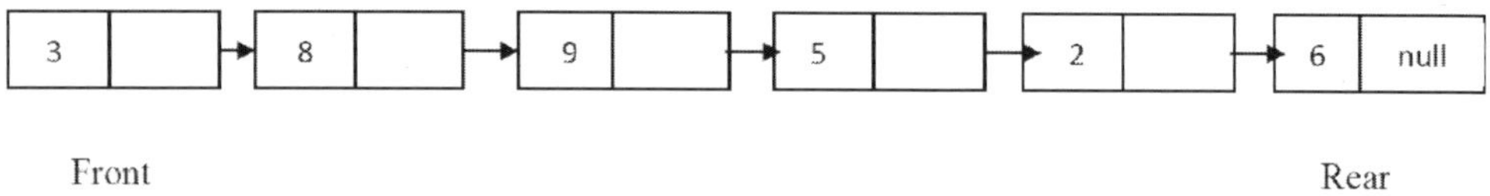

Figure 4.19: After adding a new node

If we want to delete an element from the above list, then element 3 will be deleted first. Because in a queue deletion takes place at the front end. So the first element or node that is pointed by the front is deleted first.

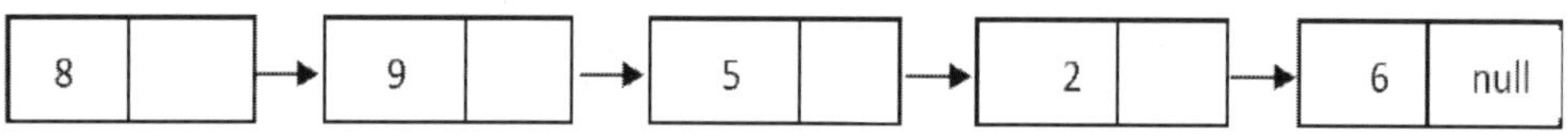

Figure 4.20: After deleting a node

Now we will discuss the algorithms for insertion and deletion operations using dynamic representation.

Algorithm for Insertion operation

This algorithm inserts an element called 'item' in the 'queue' at the 'rear' position. 'New_node' is a temporary node where memory is allocated.

Step 1: Set new_node = avail

Step 2: Set new_node -> data = item

Set new_node -> link = null

Step 3: If front = null

Set front = rear = new_node

Else

Set rear -> link = new_node

Set rear = new_node

[End of If]

Step 5: End

In the above algorithm, in step 1, a new node is created. In step 2, the data part of the node is assigned a value 'item' and the address part is assigned a null value. In step 3, it is checked that whether the node created is the first node or not. If it is the first node, then front and rear both are made to point to the first node. If this condition is not true, that means a queue already exist, then control will traverse to the last node, which is pointed by the rear and has null value in the address part. The new node will be added after the last node. In step 4, the new node is updated as rear.

Example 11: The following program shows insertion operation in dynamic implementation of stack in C++ language.

```
#include <iostream>
using namespace std;

struct Node {
   int data;
   Node* link;
};

Node* front = NULL;
Node* rear = NULL;

void insert(int item) {
   Node* new_node = new Node;
   new_node->data = item;
   new_node->link = NULL;

   if (front == NULL) {
      front = rear = new_node;
   } else {
      rear->link = new_node;
      rear = new_node;
   }

   cout << "Inserted " << item << " into the queue." << endl;
}

void display() {
```

```
    if (front == NULL) {
        cout << "Queue is empty." << endl;
        return;
    }

    Node* temp = front;
    cout << "Queue elements are: ";
    while (temp != NULL) {
        cout << temp->data << " ";
        temp = temp->link;
    }
    cout << endl;
}

int main() {
    int item, n;

    cout << "Enter the number of elements to insert: ";
    cin >> n;

    for (int i = 1; i <= n; ++i) {
        cout << "Enter element " << i << ": ";
        cin >> item;
        insert(item);
    }
    display();
    return 0;
}
```

Output:

Enter the number of elements to insert: 4

Enter element 1: 10

Inserted 10 into the queue.

Enter element 2: 20

Inserted 20 into the queue.

Enter element 3: 30

Inserted 30 into the queue.

Enter element 4: 40

Inserted 40 into the queue.

Queue elements are: 10 20 30 40

Algorithm for Deletion operation

This algorithm deletes an element from the 'front' position of the 'queue'. 'Item' is a temporary variable where the data to be deleted is stored.

Step 1: If front = null, then print "Underflow".

Go to Step 5

[End of If]

Step 2: Set item = front

Step 3: Set front = front -> link

Step 4: Delete item

Step 5: End

In the above algorithm, in step 1, it is checked that whether the queue is empty or not. If the queue is empty, then an underflow message will be returned. And, the program control will go to step 5 to exit. If the queue is not empty, in step 2 the front of the queue is assigned to a variable 'item'. In step 3, the front is made to point the next node in the list, i.e. front is updated. In step 4, the memory occupied by the variable 'item' is released and the memory location is given back to the free pool.

Example 12: The following program shows insertion operation in dynamic implementation of stack in C++ language.

```
#include <iostream>
using namespace std;

struct Node {
   int data;
   Node* link;
};

Node* front = NULL;
Node* rear = NULL;

void insert(int item) {
   Node* new_node = new Node;
   new_node->data = item;
```

```
    new_node->link = NULL;

    if (front == NULL) {
        front = rear = new_node;
    } else {
        rear->link = new_node;
        rear = new_node;
    }

    cout << "Inserted " << item << " into the queue." << endl;
}

void dequeue() {
    if (front == NULL) {
        cout << "Underflow! Queue is empty." << endl;
        return;
    }

    Node* item = front;
    front = front->link;
    delete item;
}

void display() {
    if (front == NULL) {
        cout << "Queue is empty." << endl;
        return;
    }

    Node* temp = front;
    cout << "Queue elements are: ";
    while (temp != NULL) {
        cout << temp->data << " ";
        temp = temp->link;
    }
```

```
  cout << endl;
}

int main() {
  int item, n;

  cout << "Enter the number of elements to insert: ";
  cin >> n;

  for (int i = 1; i <= n; ++i) {
    cout << "Enter element " << i << ": ";
    cin >> item;
    insert(item);
  }

display();

while (front != NULL) {
dequeue();
display();
  }

  dequeue();
  dequeue();

  return 0;
}
```

Output

Enter the number of elements to insert: 4

Enter element 1: 10

Inserted 10 into the queue.

Enter element 2: 20

Inserted 20 into the queue.

Enter element 3: 30

Inserted 30 into the queue.

Enter element 4: 40

Inserted 40 into the queue.

Queue elements are: 10 20 30 40

Queue elements are: 20 30 40

Queue elements are: 30 40

Queue elements are: 40

Queue is empty.

Underflow! Queue is empty.

Underflow! Queue is empty.

4.8 DISADVANTAGES OF LINEAR QUEUE

There are several variations of a queue (we will discuss in the next section). The queue that we have discussed in the above section is known as normal queue or simply queue. This queue has several limitations. One of the major limitations is inefficient memory allocation. To explain this better let

12	23	8	10	32	
0	1	2	3	4	6
↑				↑	
Front				Rear	

us consider an example of queue using static representation.

A static queue

12	23	8	10	32	16
0	1	2	3	4	6
↑					↑
Front					Rear

The rear has grown by one position after inserting element 16.

	23	8	10	32	16
0	1	2	3	4	6
↑					↑
Front					Rear

The element 12 is deleted and the front is updated.

		8	10	32	16
0	1	2	3	4	6
		↑			↑
		Front			Rear

The element 23 is deleted and the front is updated.

Now in this situation, the rear has reached the last position i.e. 6th location and after deleting two elements (12 and 23) the front has reached 2nd location. In this scenario is it possible to add a new element to the queue? The answer is no, because the queue will be reported as full. In a queue insertion takes place in the rear end and rear already has reached the last location, so the queue will be reported as full. In reality we could see that there are two vacant locations in the queue (0 and 1 locations). But it is not possible to add elements in these locations. We cannot insert new elements in the vacant positions created as a result of deletion operations in a queue. The queue will be reported as full once the rear reaches the last location, even if there are empty locations in reality. This is one of the major limitations of a normal queue.

4.9 TYPES OF QUEUES

In the previous section we have seen that there are various limitations of a normal queue. To meet our various requirements we use different variations of a queue. Some of the major variations of a queue are:

- Circular Queue
- Deque
- Priority Queue

We will discuss all these variations one by one.

4.9.1 Circular Queue

In the previous section we have seen that the normal queue suffers from a serious limitation, i.e. inefficient use of memory. Once the rear reaches the last location, the queue will be reported as full, even if there are free spaces at the beginning of the queue. Circular queue overcomes this limitation.

In a circular queue the front and rear ends are joined together to form a circular loop as shown below:

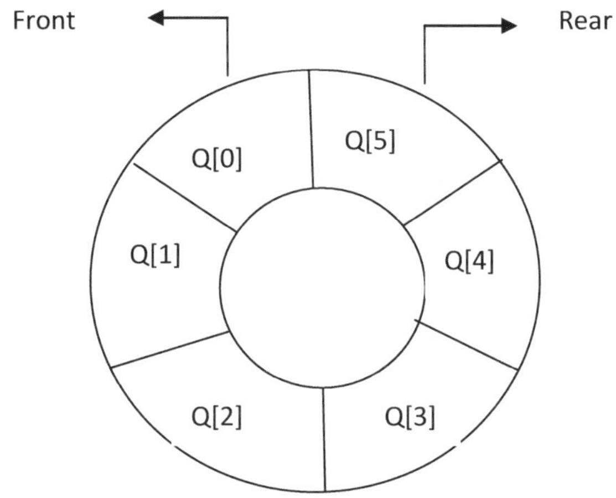

Figure 4.21: Circular Queue

The two ends of a circular queue are joined together to facilitate insertion, even if the rear reaches the last location. Once the rear reaches the last location, the front position is checked. If front != 0, that means some locations at the beginning are empty and insertion can be done. Circular queue utilizes memory very efficiently. The queue will be reported as full when it is actually full.

While working with circular queue, the following assumptions are considered:

- If front = -1, the queue is empty.
- If front = rear, the queue as single element.
- If front = 0 and rear = max – 1, then the queue is full.
- If front != 0 and rear = max – 1, then the queue is not full. Set rear = 0 to insert new element in that position.
- If rear != max -1, then rear will be incremented and new element will be inserted.

Now let us discuss the algorithms for insertion and deletion operations in a circular queue.

Algorithm for Insertion operation: This algorithm inserts an element called 'item' in the list 'queue' at the 'rear' position. 'Front' is the location through which deletion takes place and 'rear' is the location through which insertion takes place. 'Max' is the last location of the queue.

Step 1: If front = 0 and rear = max – 1, then print "Overflow".

    Go to Step 4

    [End of if]

Step 2: If front = -1 and rear = -1 (Empty queue)

        Set front = 0 and rear = 0

    Else

        If front! = 0 and rear = max – 1

            Set rear =0

        Else

            Set rear = rear + 1

        [End of if]

    [End of if]

Step 3: Set queue [rear] = item

Step 4: End

In the above algorithm, in step 1, the overflow condition is checked. If there is overflow, then overflow message is returned. In step 2, queue empty condition is checked. If the queue is empty, then both front and rear are made to point to the first location of the queue. If front! = 0 and rear = max – 1, then the queue is not full. Set rear = 0 to insert new element in that position. If all the three conditions in step 2 are false then the rear is incremented by one position to point to the next location, so that a new element can be inserted. In step 3, item is inserted at the updated rear position.

Example 13: The following program shows insertion operation in circular queue in C++ language.

```
#include <iostream>
using namespace std;
#define MAX 5
```

```
int queue[MAX];
int front = -1, rear = -1;

void insert(int item) {
  if (front == 0 && rear == MAX - 1) {
    cout << "Overflow! Queue is full." << endl;
    return;
  }

  if (front == -1 && rear == -1) {
    front = 0;
    rear = 0;
  } else if (front != 0 && rear == MAX - 1) {
    rear = 0;
  } else {
    rear = rear + 1;
  }

  queue[rear] = item;
  cout << "Inserted " << item << " into the queue." << endl;
}

void display() {
  if (front == -1) {
    cout << "Queue is empty." << endl;
    return;
  }

  cout << "Queue elements are: ";

  if (rear >= front) {
    for (int i = front; i <= rear; i++) {
      cout << queue[i] << " ";
    }
  } else {
```

```
        for (int i = front; i < MAX; i++) {
            cout << queue[i] << " ";
        }
        for (int i = 0; i <= rear; i++) {
            cout << queue[i] << " ";
        }
    }
    cout << endl;
}

int main() {
    int item, n;

    for (int i = 1; i <= MAX + 1; ++i) {
        cout << "Enter element " << i << ": ";
        cin >> item;
        insert(item);
    }

    display();

    return 0;
}
```

Output

```
Enter element 1: 10
Inserted 10 into the queue.
Enter element 2: 20
Inserted 20 into the queue.
Enter element 3: 30
Inserted 30 into the queue.
Enter element 4: 40
Inserted 40 into the queue.
Enter element 5: 50
Inserted 50 into the queue.
```

Enter element 6: 60

Overflow! Queue is full.

Queue elements are: 10 20 30 40 50

Algorithm for Deletion operation: This algorithm deletes an element called 'item' from the 'front' position of the list 'queue'. 'Front' is the location through which deletion takes place.

Step 1: If front = -1, then print "Underflow".

Go to Step 4

[End of if]

Step 2: Set item = queue [front]

Step 3: If front == rear

Set front = rear = -1

Else

If front = max – 1

Set front = 0

Else

Set front = front + 1

[End of if]

[End of if]

Step 4: End

In the above algorithm, in step 1, the underflow condition is checked. If there is underflow, then underflow message is returned. In step 2, the value of the queue at the location pointed by the front is stored in a variable "item". In step 3, two checks are done. First check is to see whether the queue has become empty after deletion and second check is to see whether front has reached the last location. The value of the front is updated accordingly.

Example 14: The following program shows deletion operation in circular queue in C++ language.

```
#include <iostream>
using namespace std;
#define MAX 5
int queue[MAX];
int front = -1, rear = -1;

void insert(int item) {
  if ((front == 0 && rear == MAX - 1) || (rear + 1) % MAX == front) {
    cout << "Overflow! Queue is full." << endl;
    return;
  }
```

```
    if (front == -1 && rear == -1) {
        front = rear = 0;
    }
    else if (rear == MAX - 1) {
        rear = 0;
    }
    else {
        rear = rear + 1;
    }

    queue[rear] = item;
    cout << "Inserted " << item << " into the queue." << endl;
}

void dequeue() {
    if (front == -1) {
        cout << "Underflow! Queue is empty." << endl;
        return;
    }

    int item = queue[front];
    cout << "Dequeued " << item << " from the queue." << endl;

    if (front == rear) {
        front = rear = -1;
    }
    else if (front == MAX - 1) {
        front = 0;
    }
    else {
        front = front + 1;
    }
}
```

```
void display() {
  if (front == -1) {
    cout << "Queue is empty." << endl;
    return;
  }

  cout << "Queue elements are: ";
  if (rear >= front) {
    for (int i = front; i <= rear; i++) {
      cout << queue[i] << " ";
    }
  } else {
    for (int i = front; i < MAX; i++) {
      cout << queue[i] << " ";
    }
    for (int i = 0; i <= rear; i++) {
      cout << queue[i] << " ";
    }
  }
  cout << endl;
}

int main() {
  int n, item;

  cout << "Enter the number of elements to insert (max " << MAX << "): ";
  cin >> n;

  for (int i = 1; i <= n; ++i) {
    cout << "Enter element " << i << ": ";
    cin >> item;
    insert(item);
  }

  display();
```

```
    while (front != -1) {
dequeue();
display();
    }
    dequeue();
    return 0;
}
```

Output :

```
Enter the number of elements to insert (max 5): 5
Enter element 1: 10
Inserted 10 into the queue.
Enter element 2: 20
Inserted 20 into the queue.
Enter element 3: 30
Inserted 30 into the queue.
Enter element 4: 40
Inserted 40 into the queue.
Enter element 5: 50
Inserted 50 into the queue.
Queue elements are: 10 20 30 40 50
Dequeued 10 from the queue.
Queue elements are: 20 30 40 50
Dequeued 20 from the queue.
Queue elements are: 30 40 50
Dequeued 30 from the queue.
Queue elements are: 40 50
Dequeued 40 from the queue.
Queue elements are: 50
Dequeued 50 from the queue.
Queue is empty.
Underflow! Queue is empty.
```

4.9.2 Deque

It is another variation of a queue. A deque is also known as double-ended queue. A deque is a linear list in which elements can be inserted as well as deleted at both ends. That is, we can insert as well as delete elements from both front and rear ends. However, we cannot add or delete elements from the middle.

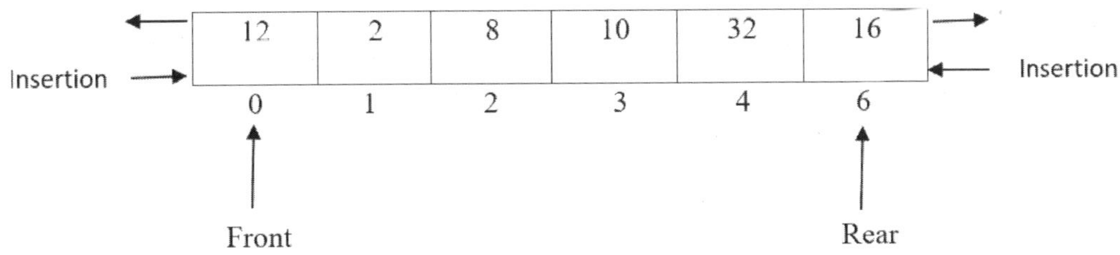

There are two types of deques. These are:

- Input restricted deque
- Output restricted deque

An **input restricted deque** is a deque where input is restricted to only one ends. In an input restricted deque insertions can be done only at one of the ends whereas deletions can be done from both the ends.

An **output restricted deque** is a deque where output or deletion is restricted to only one ends. In an output restricted deque deletions can be done only at one of the ends whereas insertions can be done from both the ends.

A Deque can be implemented either using a doubly linked list or circular array. In both implementation, we can implement all operations in O(1) time.

4.9.3 Priority Queue

In a Priority queue every item is associated with a priority value. This priority value determines the order in which they exit the queue. The elements with highest priority are processed (deleted) first.

Priority Queue is another variation of queue with following properties:

1. Every element has a priority value associated with it.

2. An element with high priority is processed or removed before an element with low priority.

3. If two elements have the same priority, they are served according to their order in the queue.

A priority queue can be implemented with help of an array with the following structure:

```
struct p_queue
{
        int item;
        int priority;
}
```

We can also use Linked List to implement priority queue. Time complexity of all operations with linked list remains same as array. But heap is generally preferred for priority queue implementation because heaps provide better performance compared to arrays or linked list.

Algorithm for priority Queue Insertion: This algorithm inserts 'item' into 'queue' based on priority. 'Size' tracks the number of elements, and if the queue is full (size = max), an overflow message is displayed. If the queue is empty, 'item' is placed at the first position. Otherwise, the correct 'pos' is found based on priority. Elements are shifted right to maintain order, and 'item' is inserted at 'pos'. Finally, 'size' is incremented.

Step 1: If size = max, then print "Overflow".

Go to Step 4.

[End of if]

Step 2: If size = 0 (Empty priority queue)

    Set queue[0] = item and increase size by 1.

Else

    If priority of item is higher than all elements in the queue

        Shift all elements right and insert item at front.

    Else

        Find correct position pos for item based on priority.

        Shift all elements from pos to size - 1 one position right.

        Insert item at pos.

    Increase size by 1.

    [End of if]

Step 3: Print "Insertion successful".

Step 4: End.

In the above algorithm, step 1 overflow condition is checked. First, if the queue is full (size == MAX), it prints "Overflow" and terminates the process. Otherwise, if the queue is empty (size == 0), the new item is placed at the first position, and the size is increased. If the queue is not empty, the algorithm checks whether the new item has the highest priority. If so, all elements are shifted right, and the item is inserted at the front. Otherwise, the correct position (pos) is determined by comparing the new item's priority with existing elements. Once pos is found, all elements from pos to size - 1 are shifted right, making space for the new item at pos in step 2. After insertion, the size is incremented, and "Insertion successful" is printed to confirm completion. This ensures that the queue remains ordered with the highest-priority elements at the front.

Example 15: The following program shows insertion operation in priority queue in C++ language.

```
#include <iostream>
using namespace std;
#define MAX 5
int queue[MAX];
int queueSize = 0; // Tracks the number of elements in the queue

void insert(int item) {
  if (queueSize == MAX) {
```

```
        cout << "Overflow! Queue is full." << endl;
        return;
    }

    int pos;
    if (queueSize == 0) {
        queue[0] = item;
    }
    else {
        for (pos = queueSize - 1; pos >= 0 && queue[pos] < item; pos--) {
            queue[pos + 1] = queue[pos];
        }
        queue[pos + 1] = item;
    }

    queueSize++;
    cout << "Insertion successful." << endl;
}

void display() {
    if (queueSize == 0) {
        cout << "Queue is empty." << endl;
        return;
    }
    cout << "Priority Queue elements: ";
    for (int i = 0; i < queueSize; i++) {
        cout << queue[i] << " ";
    }
    cout << endl;
}
int main() {
    int item, n;
    cout << "Enter the number of elements to insert: ";
    cin >> n;
    for (int i = 0; i < n; ++i) {
```

```
        cout << "Enter element " << i + 1 << ": ";
        cin >> item;
        insert(item);
    }
display();
    return 0;
}
```

Output :

Enter the number of elements to insert: 5

Enter element 1: 10

Insertion successful.

Enter element 2: 20

Insertion successful.

Enter element 3: 30

Insertion successful.

Enter element 4: 40

Insertion successful.

Enter element 5: 50

Insertion successful.

Priority Queue elements: 50 40 30 20 10

Algorithm for Priority Queue Deletion: This algorithm removes an element from the priority queue based on priority. The queue follows the rule that the highest-priority element is always removed first. The variable size tracks the number of elements in the queue. If the queue is empty (size == 0), an underflow message is displayed. Otherwise, the front element (highest-priority item) is removed, and all remaining elements are shifted left to maintain order. Finally, size is decremented.

Step 1: If size == 0 (Empty priority queue), print "Underflow" and go to Step 4.

[End of if]

Step 2: Store queue[0] (the highest-priority element) in a variable item.

Step 3: Shift all elements from index 1 to size - 1 one position left to fill the gap left by the deleted element.

Step 4: Decrease size by 1.

Step 5: Print "Deletion successful".

Step 6: End.

In the above algorithm, in Step 1, the underflow condition is checked. If the queue is empty (size == 0), it prints "Underflow" and terminates the process. Otherwise, Step 2 stores the front element in item before deletion. In Step 3, all elements from index 1 to size - 1 are shifted left by one position to maintain order. In Step 4, size is decremented to reflect the removal of an element. Finally, Step 5 prints "Deletion successful" to confirm completion, ensuring that the queue remains properly ordered with the highest-priority elements at the front.

Example 16: The following program shows deletion operation in priority queue in C++ language.

```
#include <iostream>
using namespace std;
#define MAX 5
int queue[MAX];
int queueSize = 0;

void insert(int item) {
  if (queueSize == MAX) {
    cout << "Overflow! Queue is full." << endl;
    return;
  }

  int pos;
  if (queueSize == 0) {
    queue[0] = item;
  } else {
    for (pos = queueSize - 1; pos >= 0 && queue[pos] < item; pos--) {
      queue[pos + 1] = queue[pos];
    }
    queue[pos + 1] = item;
  }

  queueSize++;
  cout << "Insertion successful." << endl;
}

void deleteHighestPriority() {
  if (queueSize == 0) {
    cout << "Underflow! Queue is empty." << endl;
    return;
  }
```

```
    int item = queue[0];

    for (int i = 1; i < queueSize; i++) {
        queue[i - 1] = queue[i];
    }
    queueSize--;
    cout << "Deletion successful." << endl;
}

void display() {
    if (queueSize == 0) {
        cout << "Queue is empty." << endl;
        return;
    }

    cout << "Priority Queue elements: ";
    for (int i = 0; i < queueSize; i++) {
        cout << queue[i] << " ";
    }
    cout << endl;
}

int main() {
    int item, n, choice;

    cout << "Enter the number of elements to insert: ";
    cin >> n;

    for (int i = 0; i < n; ++i) {
        cout << "Enter element " << i + 1 << ": ";
        cin >> item;
        insert(item);
    }

    display();
```

```
  cout << "Do you want to delete the highest-priority element? (1 for Yes, 0 for No): ";
  cin >> choice;

  if (choice == 1) {
    deleteHighestPriority();
    display();
  }
  return 0;
}
```

Output :

```
Enter the number of elements to insert: 5
Enter element 1: 23
Insertion successful.
Enter element 2: 12
Insertion successful.
Enter element 3: 67
Insertion successful.
Enter element 4: 45
Insertion successful.
Enter element 5: 89
Insertion successful.
Priority Queue elements: 89 67 45 23 12
Do you want to delete the highest-priority element? (1 for Yes, 0 for No): 1
Deleted highest-priority element: 89
Priority Queue elements: 67 45 23 12
```

Applications of Priority Queue:

1) CPU Scheduling

2) Graph algorithms like Dijkstra's shortest path algorithm, Prim's Minimum Spanning Tree, etc

3) All queue applications where priority is involved.

4.10 LET US SUM UP

- A stack is a non-primitive, linear and homogeneous data structure, where insertion and deletion takes place at only one end, called the top of the stack. Hence, a stack is called a LIFO (Last-In, First-Out) data structure as the element that is inserted last is the first one to be taken out.

- The basic operations that can be performed on a stack are: **Push** and **Pop** operations.
- Push operation means adding a new item onto the stack. Pop operation means deleting an element from the stack.
- A stack can be implemented using either linked lists or arrays.
- Infix, prefix, and postfix notations are three different but equivalent notations of writing algebraic expressions.
- In postfix notation, operators are placed after the operands, whereas in prefix notation, operators are placed before the operands.
- Postfix notations are evaluated using stacks. Every character of the postfix expression is scanned from left to right. If the character is an operand, it is pushed onto the stack. Else, if it is an operator, then the top two values are popped from the stack and the operator is applied on these values. The result is then pushed onto the stack.
- Some of the applications of stack are: Notation Conversions and Expression Evaluation
- A queue is a non-primitive, linear and homogeneous data structure, where insertion and deletion takes place at two ends, called rear and front. Rear is the position through which insertion takes place and front is the position through which deletion takes place.
- A queue is a FIFO data structure in which the element that is inserted first is the first one to be taken out.
- Queues can be implemented using both arrays and linked lists.
- In a circular queue, the first index comes after the last index.
- A deque is a linear list in which elements can be inserted as well as deleted at both ends.
- There are two types of deques: Input restricted deque and Output restricted deque.
- In an input restricted deque insertions can be done only at one of the ends whereas deletions can be done from both the ends.
- In an output restricted deque deletions can be done only at one of the ends whereas insertions can be done from both the ends.
- In a Priority queue the elements with highest priority are processed (deleted) first.

4.11 CHECK YOUR PROGRESS

1. What do you understand by stack overflow and underflow?
2. Differentiate between an array and a stack.
3. How does a stack implemented using a linked list differ from a stack implemented using an array?
4. What are the advantages of using a dynamically allocated stack over a statically allocated stack?
5. Describe the algorithm for pushing an element onto a static stack.
6. Describe the algorithm for popping an element from a static stack.
7. Why are parentheses not required in postfix/prefix expressions?
8. Explain the terms infix expression, prefix expression and postfix expression.

9. What are the rules for converting an infix expression to a postfix expression?
10. How does a stack help in infix to postfix conversion?
11. What are the steps involved in converting an infix expression to a prefix expression?
12. Differentiate between stack and queue.
13. What is a queue?
14. Explain the algorithm for inserting an element into a queue.
15. Explain the algorithm for deleting an element from a queue.
16. What is the condition for queue overflow and underflow?
17. Explain the concept of a circular queue? How is it better than a linear queue?
18. Explain the algorithm for inserting an element in a circular queue.
19. Explain the algorithm for deleting an element from a circular queue.
20. How is a circular queue different from a linear queue.
21. What is a priority queue? Give its applications.
22. What is a priority queue and how does it differ from a normal queue?
23. How is insertion and deletion performed in a priority queue?
24. How can a heap be used to implement a priority queue?
25. Give a real-world example where a priority queue is used.
26. What is a deque, and how is it different from a normal queue?
27. What are the advantages of a circular queue over a linear queue?

4.12 EXERCISES

Q.1 Convert the infix expression to prefix :

i. A + B * C - D / E
ii. A / B + C * D
iii. A / (B + C * D) - E
iv. (A + B * (C - D)) / (E + F)
v. (A + B) * (C - D) / (E + F)
vi. (A + (B - C)) * (D / E)
vii. ((A + B) * C) / (D - (E + F))
viii. A + B * C - D * E / F
ix. (A + B) * (C - D) + (E * F)
x. (A + B * (C + D)) / (E - F) * G

Q.2 Convert the infix expression to postfix :

i. (A + B) * (C - D)
ii. (A + B) * (C + D) / E

iii. A * B + C * D

iv. (A + B) * (C + D) - (E / F)

v. A + (B * C - D)

vi. A + (B - C) * (D + E)

vii. (A + B) * (C - D) + (E * F)

viii. A + B * C - (D / E + F)

ix. A + B * C - D * E / F

x. ((A + B) * C) - (D / E)

xi. (A + (B - C) * (D + E)) / F

xii. (A * B) + C / (D - E * F)

xiii. (A + B * (C + D)) / (E - F) * G

Q.3 Explain the last in first out principle with an example.

Q.4 How do you check if a stack is full or empty when using an array?

Q.5 Given the expression (5 + 3) * (2 - 8), evaluate it using a stack.

Q.6 Evaluate the expression (4 + 6) / (3 - 1) * (7 - 5) using a stack.

Q.7 Evaluate the postfix expression 6 2 / 3 4 + * using a stack.

Q.8 Evaluate the prefix expression + * 2 3 - 4 5 using a stack.

Q.9 Perform the following stack operations and return the stack contents after each operation: push 10, push 20, pop, push 44, push 50, push 60, pop, pop. What is the element at the top of the stack after the operations?

Q.10 Perform the following stack operations and return the stack contents after each operation: push 11, push 22, pop, pop, push 55, push 44, push 50, push 60, pop, pop. What is the element at the top of the stack after the operations?

Q.11 Given stack operations (push 2, push 5, push 7, pop, push 8, push 10, push 11, pop, pop, pop, pop) What will be contents of the stack at the end.

Q.12 Convert the infix expression ((A + B) * (C - D)) / E to postfix and evaluate it with values A = 1, B = 2, C = 5, D = 3, E = 4.

Q.13 Perform the following queue operations and return the queue contents after each operation. Also, find the element at the front of the queue after all operations. (Enqueue 10, enqueue 20, dequeue, dequeue, enqueue 56, enqueue, 67, enqueue 78, dequeue, dequeue)

Q.14 Suppose the queue contains (A,B,B,C,D). Perform the following operations (Dequeue, Enqueue E, Enqueue E, Dequeue, Enqueue S). What is the final content of the queue.

Q.15 Perform the following operations on a queue and return the final content in the queue. (Enqueue 3, 6, 9, 12, 15, dequeue{twice}, Enqueue 18, 21, dequeue{thrice}).

Q.16 A circular queue has a size of 5. If the front is at index 2 and the rear is at index 4, after inserting one more element, where will the rear be located?

Q.17 A queue is implemented using an array of size 6, and elements [1, 2, 13, 24, 35] are inserted. If two elements are dequeued and three more (9, 17, 28) are inserted, what will be the final queue state assuming a simple linear queue.

Q.18 What is the difference between a linear queue and a d circular queue.

Q.19 Consider a circular queue with a fixed size. Perform the following operations sequentially and determine the queue contents after each operation:

Enqueue 23, 45, Dequeue, Enqueue 44, 50 , 56, Dequeue, Dequeue.

After performing these operations, answer the following:

What are the elements remaining in the circular queue?

What are the front and rear elements of the queue?

Q.20 Suppose a circular queue of size 5 initially has elements {10, 20, 30, 40, 50}. If we perform two dequeue operations followed by two enqueue operations (60, 70), what will be the final queue state?

Q.21 Suppose a circular queue has size **N = 6**, and the following operations are performed:

Enqueue(5) , Enqueue(10) , Enqueue(15) , Dequeue() , Enqueue(20) , Enqueue(25), Enqueue(30) , Dequeue() , Enqueue(35) . What will be the final state of the queue?

Q.22 If front = 3 and rear = 1 in a circular queue of size 5, how many elements are present in the queue?

Q.23 Consider a circular queue implemented using an array of size **6**. Initially, the queue is empty. If the following operations occur: Enqueue(1), Enqueue(2), Enqueue(3), Dequeue(), Enqueue(4), Enqueue(5), Dequeue(), Enqueue(6), Enqueue(7), Dequeue(), What will be the new values of front and rear?

Q.24 What is a priority queue? How does it differ from a normal queue?

Q.25 A priority queue currently holds {45, 35, 25, 20}. If we insert 50, where will it be placed in the queue?

Q.26 Given an empty priority queue, insert the elements in the following order: 5, 8, 3, 12, 9, 1, 15. Show the final order of elements in the priority queue. Highest priority to the largest element.

Q.27 Perform the following priority queue insertions and return the queue contents after each operation: Insert 15, Insert 30, Insert 10, Insert 40, Insert 25. What is the final queue state?

Q.28 A priority queue has a maximum size of 4 and currently contains {50, 40, 30, 20}. Attempt to Insert 60 into the queue. What will be the output?

Q.29 Explain any three real-world applications of priority queues. How does priority-based processing help in these scenarios?

5

TREE

5.1 INTRODUCTION

So far, we have learnt basic data structures mainly linear. Array is a good data structure that can be accessed randomly making insertion, deletion and search fairly easy. However the Array data structure is static one. Linked Lists on the other hand is dynamic and is ideal for application that requires frequent operations such as add, delete, and update. Searching or sorting operations are difficult in linked list. This occurs because data access in linked list is sequential, which yields in larger access time. We also studied specialized Abstract data type (ADT) like, stacks and queues that allows us to solve complicated problems using these restricted data structures.

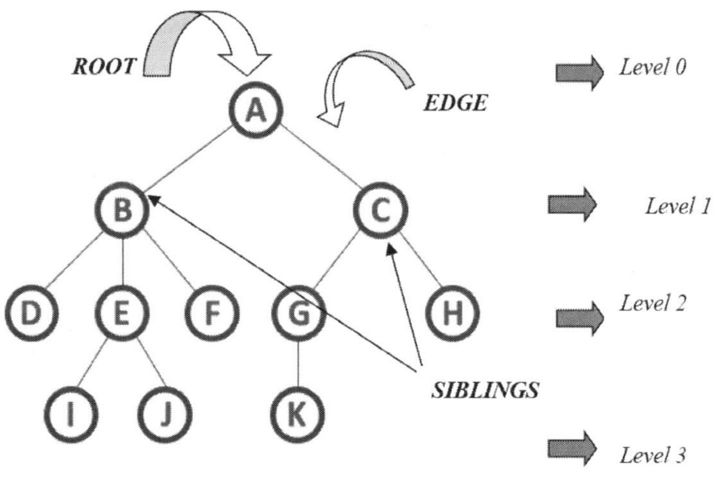

Figure 5.1: Graphical representation of a Tree

In this chapter, we are introducing a data structure that may have multiple relations among its nodes. Such a structure is called a tree. Tree is a non-linear data structure which organizes data in hierarchical structure. A tree is a collection of nodes connected by directed (or undirected) edges. In tree data structure, every individual element is called as Node. Node in a tree data structure, stores the actual data of that particular element and link to next element in hierarchical structure. Fig 5.1. shows the graphical representation of Tree data structure.

5.1.1 Terminology

a. Root

In a tree data structure, the first node is called as Root Node. We can say that root node is the origin of tree data structure. In any tree, there must be only one root node. In Fig 5.1 above, "A" is the root node.

b. Edge

The link that connects any two nodes is called an EDGE. In a tree with 'N' number of nodes there will be a maximum of 'N-1' number of edges. In Fig 5.1 above, shows an edge linking the nodes "A" and "C".

c. Parent

The node which is predecessor of any node is called as PARENT NODE. In simple words, the node which has branch from it to any other node is called as parent node. In Fig 5.1 above; A,B,C,E,G are parent nodes of their subtree.

d. Child

The node which is descendant of any node (parent) is called as CHILD Node. Basically the node which has a link from its parent node is called as child node. In a tree, any parent node can have any number of child nodes; however a child can't have more than one parent. For example, in Fig 5.1 above, "B" and "C" are the children of "A"; "D", "E" and "F" are childrens of "B".

e. Siblings

Nodes which belong to same Parent are called as SIBLINGS. For example, in Fig 5.1 above, B and C are siblings.

f. Leaf and Internal Nodes

Node which does not have a child is called as LEAF Node. In simple words, a leaf is a node with no child. They are also called External Nodes. For example, in Fig 5.1 above, "D", "I", "J", "F", "K" and "H" are leaf nodes. Nodes other than leaf nodes are called as Internal Nodes.

g. Level, Depth and Height

The root node is said to be at Level 0 and the children of root node are at Level 1 and the children of the nodes which are at Level 1 will be at Level 2 and so on as shown in Fig 5.1. Depth of a node is same as the level it belongs. Depth of a tree is the maximum value of level. The height of a node is the number of edges from the node to the deepest leaf. The height of B, C is 2. The height of a tree is a height of a root.

5.2 BINARY TREES

A tree where each node can have no more than two children is called a binary tree. We can say that a Binary tree is a special type of tree data structure in which every node can have a maximum of 2 children; left child and right child. Figure 5.2 shows a binary tree where Node A is the root. Nodes B and C are A's children. Nodes B ,E,G and D together form a subtree. Node B has two children: Its left child is D and its right child is E. Nodes A, C, and E, F are ancestors of H. Nodes D, E, and F make up level 2 of the tree; node A is at level 0. The depth of H is 3 and the height of this tree is 4

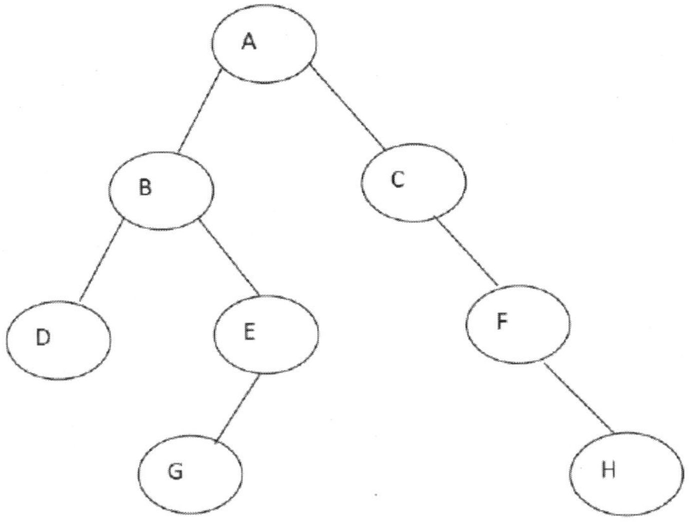

Figure 5.2: A binary tree.

A binary tree in which every node has either 2 children or no children at all is called a Full Binary Tree. Figure 5.3 (a) shows that node D has only one child F. Hence the tree is not a Full binary tree. On the other hand, Figure 5.3 (b) is an example of a Full binary tree because the nodes have either 2 children or no child at all.

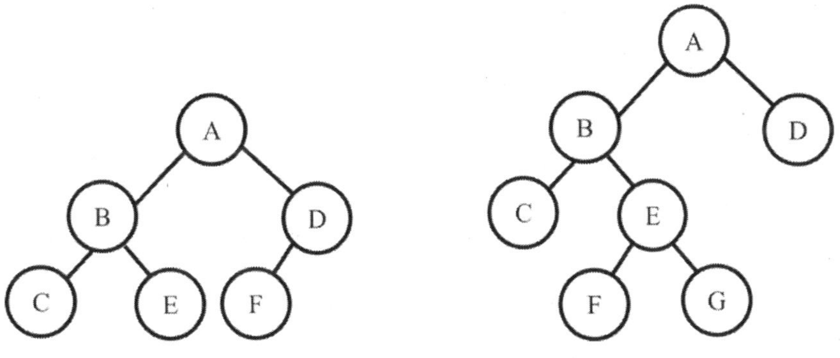

(a) (b)

Figure 5.3: Identifying a Full Binary Tree. (a) Not a Full Binary Tree (b) A Full Binary Tree.

A binary tree in which all its levels, except possibly the last have the maximum number of nodes and if all the last level nodes appear as far left as possible is called Complete Binary Tree. Figure 5.4 (a) shows that while filling the levels from up to down and left to right, the left child of node B is missing. Hence the tree is not a Complete Binary Tree. On the other hand, Figure 5. (b) is an example of a Complete Binary Tree.

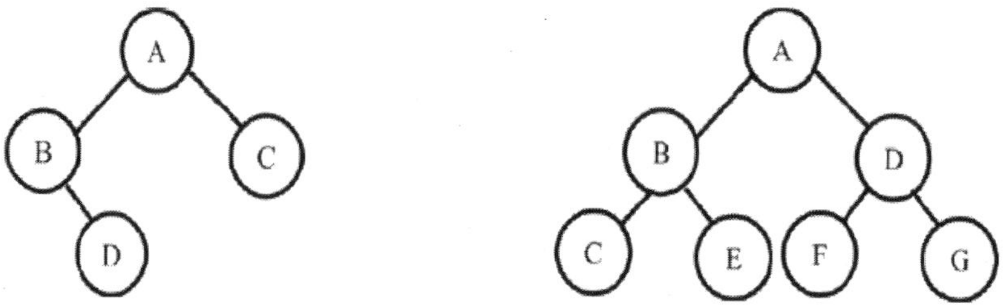

(a) (b)

Figure 5.4: Identifying a Complete Binary Tree. (a) Not a Complete Binary Tree (b) A Complete Binary Tree.

Lemma 5.1: The maximum number of nodes on level i of a binary tree is 2^{i-1}. Also maximum number of nodes in a binary tree of depth k is 2^k-1, $k \geq 0$.

A binary tree of depth k having exactly 2^k-1 nodes is called a full binary tree.

Lemma 5.2: For any non empty binary tree T, if n_t is number of terminal nodes and n_2, the number of nodes with degree 2, then $\mathbf{n_0=n_2+1}$

In a Skewed Binary Tree, all nodes except one node have one and only one child while the remaining node has no children. Figure 5.5 shows a Left Skewed Binary Tree and Right Skewed Binary Tree.

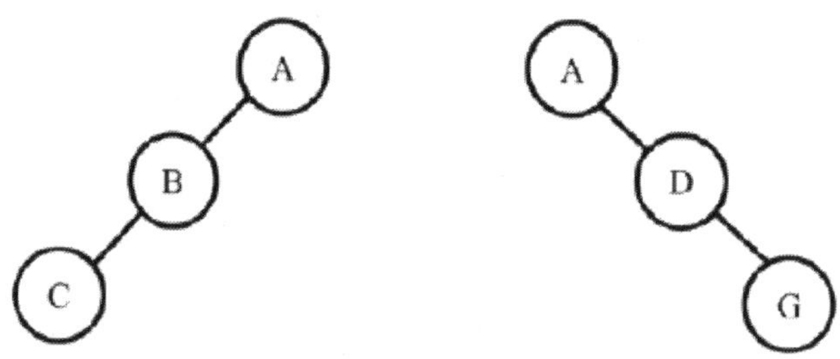

Left Skewed Binary Tree Right Skewed Binary Tree

Figure 5.5: Skewed Binary Tree.

A Binary Tree which has a root node where every node has at most two children is called as the Rooted Binary Tree. Figure 5.6 shows an example of a Rooted Binary Tree.

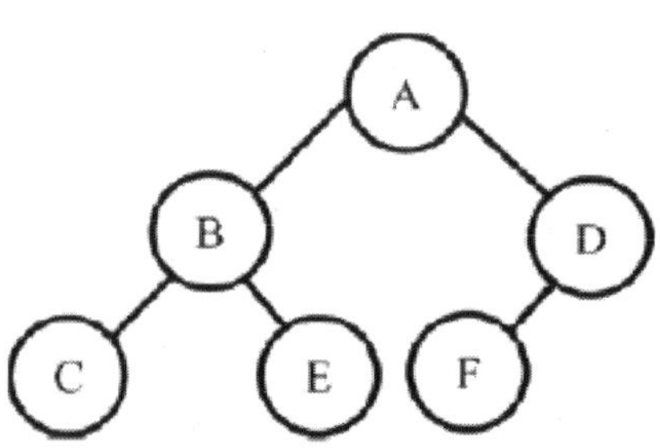

Figure 5.6: Rooted Binary Tree.

5.3 REPRESENTATION OF BINARY TREE IN MEMORY

Binary trees in memory can be represented by: Array or Linked Lists.

Let us start with the array implementation of a binary tree. Binary Trees can be represented using 1-D array in memory. For example let us store the tree in Figure 5.7 in an array T. The size of the array has to be equal to 2^n-1; where n is the height of the tree. Here, in this case it will be 2^4-1=15. So we have to take an array of size 15 i.e. [T][15]. Now the next step is to fill up the nodes in the array. The element T[0] will contain the root i.e. A. For next node is its left child i.e. B will be stored at 2x0+1=1, so T[1] will contain B. The right child of A is C, and will be stored in 2x0+2=2. So, T[2] will contain C. The child of B are D and E; so in the similar fashion they will be stored in 2x Index(B)+1=2x1+1=3 so T[3] and 2x Index(B)+2=2x1+2=4 so T[4] respectively. However, the node C does not have a Left child so the space 2x2+1=5 i.e. T[5] will contain Null. Similarly the rest of the nodes are accommodated in the array T[15] as shown in Figure 3.

The rule to store binary tree in array are:

1. The root of the tree is stored at first location i.e. at T[0].
2. The left child of tree is stored at 2i +1 and right child is stored at 2i+2 location.
3. The maximum size of the array tree is given as 2d+1-1, where d is the depth of the tree.
4. An empty tree or sub-tree is specified using NULL. If tree[0] = NULL, then it means that tree is empty.

   [T][15]

	A	B	C	D	E	Null	F	Null	Null	G	Null	Null	Null	Nul	H
	↑	↑	↑	↑	↑	↑	↑	↑	↑	↑	↑	↑	↑	↑	↑
Index	0	1	2	3	4	5	6	7	8	9	10	11	12	13	14

Figure 5.7: Array storing the tree

Now let us explore the representation of the tree through Linked List. In linked list representation,every node of the tree has three parts : the data element,the pointer to the left node and the pointer to the right node. Binary tree represented using Linked list as shown in Figure 5.8.

If any node has its left or right child empty then it will have in its respective link field, a null value. A leaf node has null value in both of its links. The structure defining a node of binary tree in C is as follows.

```
Struct node
    {
    struct node *lchild ; // points to the left child
    int DATA; // data field
    struct node *rchild; //points to the right child
    }
```

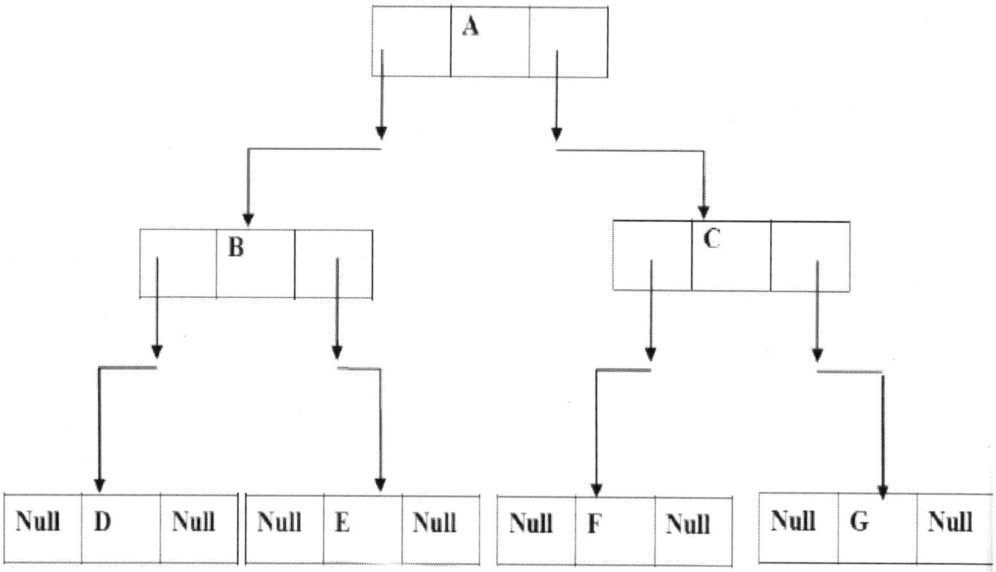

Figure 5.8: Linked List Representation

Programming Exercise 5.1

Write a program to implement a binary tree using array and linked list.

```
#include <iostream>
#include <vector>
using namespace std;

// Binary Tree using Array
class BinaryTreeArray {
private:
  vector<int> tree;
  int capacity;
public:
  BinaryTreeArray(int cap) : capacity(cap) {
    tree.resize(cap, -1);
  }
  void setRoot(int key) {
    tree[0] = key;
  }
  void setLeft(int key, int parentIndex) {
```

```
    int leftIndex = 2 * parentIndex + 1;
    if (leftIndex < capacity)
      tree[leftIndex] = key;
    else
      cout << "Left child index out of bounds.\n";
  }
  void setRight(int key, int parentIndex) {
    int rightIndex = 2 * parentIndex + 2;
    if (rightIndex < capacity)
      tree[rightIndex] = key;
    else
      cout << "Right child index out of bounds.\n";
  }
  void display() {
    cout << "Binary Tree (Array Representation): ";
    for (int val : tree)
      cout << val << " ";
    cout << endl;
  }
};

// Node structure for Linked List Implementation
struct Node {
  int data;
  Node* left;
  Node* right;
  Node(int val) : data(val), left(NULL), right(NULL) {}
};

// Binary Tree using Linked List
class BinaryTreeLinkedList {
public:
  Node* root;
  BinaryTreeLinkedList() : root(NULL) {}
  Node* insert(Node* node, int data) {
```

```
        if (node == NULL) return new Node(data);
        cout << "Insert left (L) or right (R) of " << node->data << "? ";
        char dir;
        cin >> dir;
        if (dir == 'L' || dir == 'l')
            node->left = insert(node->left, data);
        else
            node->right = insert(node->right, data);
        return node;
    }

    void inorderTraversal(Node* node) {
        if (node == NULL) return;
        inorderTraversal(node->left);
        cout << node->data << " ";
        inorderTraversal(node->right);
    }
    void display() {
        cout << "Binary Tree (Linked List Representation - Inorder Traversal): ";
        inorderTraversal(root);
        cout << endl;
    }
};

int main() {
    int n;
    cout << "Enter the number of nodes for the binary tree: ";
    cin >> n;

    if (n <= 0) {
        cout << "Invalid number of nodes!\n";
        return 1;
    }

    cout << "\n=== Binary Tree using Array ===\n";
```

```
BinaryTreeArray treeArray(n);
int value;
cout << "Enter value for root: ";
cin >> value;
treeArray.setRoot(value);

for (int i = 1; i < n; i++) {
   int key, parentIndex;
   char childType;
   cout << "Enter value for node: ";
   cin >> key;
   cout << "Enter parent index: ";
   cin >> parentIndex;
   cout << "Is this node left (L) or right (R) child? ";
   cin >> childType;

   if (childType == 'L' || childType == 'l')
      treeArray.setLeft(key, parentIndex);
   else
      treeArray.setRight(key, parentIndex);
}
treeArray.display();

cout << "\n=== Binary Tree using Linked List ===\n";
BinaryTreeLinkedList treeLinkedList;
cout << "Enter value for root: ";
cin >> value;
treeLinkedList.root = new Node(value);

for (int i = 1; i < n; i++) {
   cout << "Enter value for node: ";
   cin >> value;
   treeLinkedList.insert(treeLinkedList.root, value);
}
```

```
    treeLinkedList.display();
    return 0;
}
```

OUTPUT:

```
Enter the number of nodes for the binary tree: 7

=== Binary Tree using Array ===
Enter value for root: 1
Enter value for node: 2
Enter parent index: 0
Is this node left (L) or right (R) child? L
Enter value for node: 3
Enter parent index: 0
Is this node left (L) or right (R) child? R
Enter value for node: 4
Enter parent index: 1
Is this node left (L) or right (R) child? L
Enter value for node: 5
Enter parent index: 1
Is this node left (L) or right (R) child? R
Enter value for node: 6
Enter parent index: 2
Is this node left (L) or right (R) child? L
Enter value for node: 7
Enter parent index: 2
Is this node left (L) or right (R) child? R
Binary Tree (Array Representation): 1 2 3 4 5 6 7

=== Binary Tree using Linked List ===
Enter value for root: 1
Enter value for node: 2
Insert left (L) or right (R) of 1? L
Enter value for node: 3
Insert left (L) or right (R) of 1? R
```

Enter value for node: 4

Insert left (L) or right (R) of 1? L

Insert left (L) or right (R) of 2? L

Enter value for node: 5

Insert left (L) or right (R) of 1? L

Insert left (L) or right (R) of 2? R

Enter value for node: 6

Insert left (L) or right (R) of 1? R

Insert left (L) or right (R) of 3? L

Enter value for node: 7

Insert left (L) or right (R) of 1? R

Insert left (L) or right (R) of 3? R

Binary Tree (Linked List Representation - Inorder Traversal): 4 2 5 1 6 3 7

5.4 TRAVERSING BINARY TREES

Traversal of a binary tree means to visit each node in the tree exactly once. Unlike linear data structures like Array, Linked List, Queues, Stacks, etc which have only one logical way to traverse them, trees can be traversed in different ways. There are a number of ways to traverse a tree. All of them differ only in the order in which they visit the nodes. The three main methods of traversing a tree are:

a) Preorder Traversal b) Inorder Traversal c) Postorder Traversal

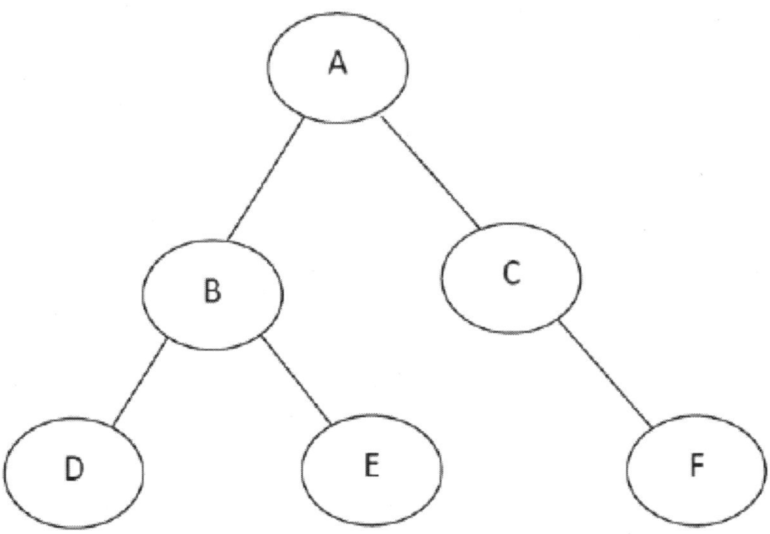

Figure 5.9: A binary tree

As a first example, consider the following binary tree in Figure 5.10:

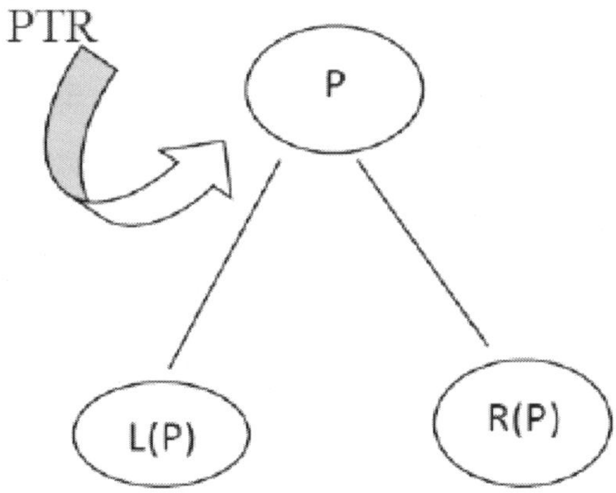

Figure 5.10: A binary tree

5.4.1 Preorder

Under preorder traversal, the root, labeled P, is visited first. Then the traversal moves to the left subtree L(P) and visits it recursively. Then preorder traversal moves to the right subtree of the root, finally visits R(P). Thus, preorder traversal visits the nodes in the order A,L(P),R(P).

Algorithm 5.1.0: Preorder(Node_type *root)

if(root)
1. Visit (root).
2. Preorder(root->left) // Traverse the left subtree
3. Preorder(root->right) // Traverse the right subtree

End if.

Preorder traversal can be implemented using a **STACK** as well. Stack is used to store address of nodes temporally. To understand it well, let us consider a pointer variable PTR, which contain the address of the node to be scanned, i.e. P. Figure 5.10 shows a binary tree with left subtree L(P) and right subtree R(P), with root P.

Algorithm 5.1.1: Preorder(Data,L,R,Root)

1. Initialize

   Top:=1

   STACK[Top]:=Null

   PTR:=Root

2. Repeat steps 3 to 5 while PTR!= Null
3. Apply Process to Data[PTR].
4. If R[PTR]!=Null, then:

   a. Top:=Top+1

   b. STACK[Top]=R[Ptr]

5. If L[PTR]!=Null, then:

    Set PTR:=L[PTR]

  Else

    Set PTR:= STACK[Top] and Top:=Top-1.

6. Exit.

5.4.2 In - Order

In In-Order traversal, the root node is visited between left child and right child. In this traversal, the left child tree is visited first, then the root node is visited and later we go for visiting right child tree. This in-order traversal is applicable for every root node of all subtrees in the tree. This is performed recursively for all nodes in the tree.

Under inorder traversal, the left child of the root, labeled L(P), is visited first recursively. Then the traversal moves to the root. The root labeled P, and it is visited second. Then inorder traversal moves to the right subtree of the root, finally visiting the subtree R (P). Thus preorder traversal visits the nodes in the order L(P),P,R(P).

Algorithm 5.2.0: Inorder(Node_type *root)

if(root)

1. Inorder(root->left) // Traverse the left subtree
2. Visit (root).
3. Inorder(root->right) // Traverse the right subtree

End if.

Inorder traversal can also be implemented using a **STACK,** which is shown in Algorithm 5.2.1.

Algorithm 5.2.1: Inorder(Data,L,R,Root)

1. Initialize

    Top:=1
    STACK[Top]:=Null
    PTR:=Root

2. while PTR!= Null

    a. Top:=Top+1 and STACK[Top]:=PTR.

    b. PTR:=:L[PTR]

    End While

3. Set PTR:= STACK[Top]
4. Set Top:=Top-1
5. While PTR!= Null repeat steps 6 to 8
6. Apply Process to Data[PTR].
7. If R[PTR]!=Null, then:

    a. PTR:=R[PTR]

    b. Go to step 3

8. Set PTR:=STACK[Top] and Top:=Top-1

9. Exit

5.4.3 Post Order

In post order traversal, the left child is visited first, then the right child is visited and then the parent node between that left and right child is visited. This process is continued recursively for all the nodes in the tree. Traversal takes place for the left subtree first, then for the right subtree and finally the root of the entire tree is visited.

Algorithm 5.3.0: Postorder(Node_type *root)

```
if(root)
1. Postorder(root->left) // Traverse the left subtree
2. Postorder(root->right) // Traverse the right subtree
3. Visit (root).
End if.
```

Postorder traversal can also be implemented using a **STACK,** which is shown in Algorithm 5.3.1.

Algorithm 5.3.1: Postorder(Data,L,R,Root)

```
1. Initialize
            Top:=1
            STACK[Top]:=Null
            PTR:=Root
2. Repeat steps 3 to 5 while PTR!= Null
3. Set Top:=Top+1 and STACK[Top]:=PTR
4. If R[PTR]!=Null, then:
            a. Top:=Top+1
            b. STACK[Top]=R[PTR]
               End if
5. Set PTR:=L[PTR]
      End While
6. Set
      a. PTR:=STACK[Top]
      b. Top:=Top-1
7. While PTR>0
         a. Apply Process to Data[PTR].
         b. Set PTR:=STACK[Top] and Top:=Top-1
8. If PTR<0 then:
      a. Set PTR:=-PTR
      b. Go to Step 2
9. Exit
```

Let us carry out all the three traversals on the tree shown in Figure 5.11.

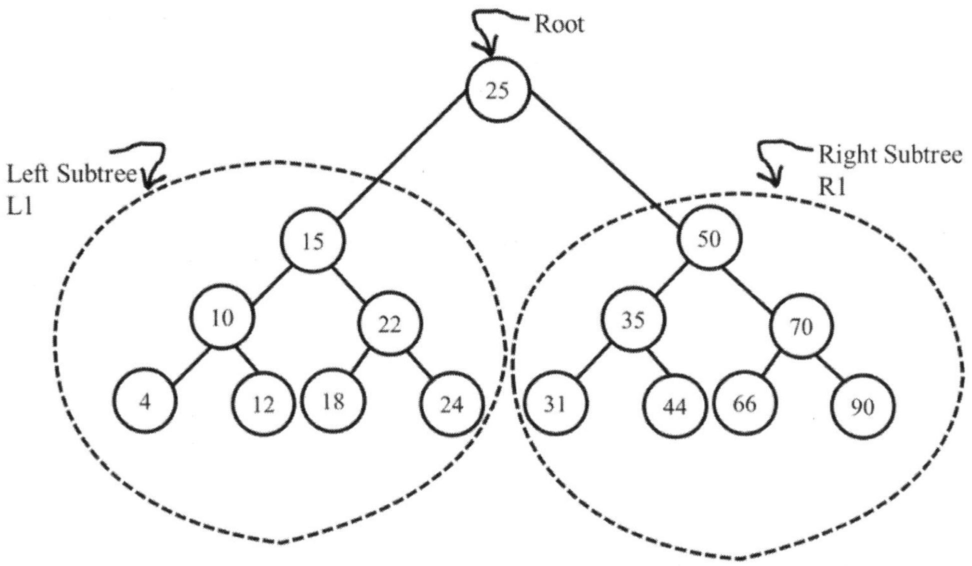

Figure 5.11: Binary Tree

Preorder Traversal

Step 1. Visit (root) node 25.

Step 2. Traverse the left subtree L1 and apply preorder on it as shown in Figure 5.12.

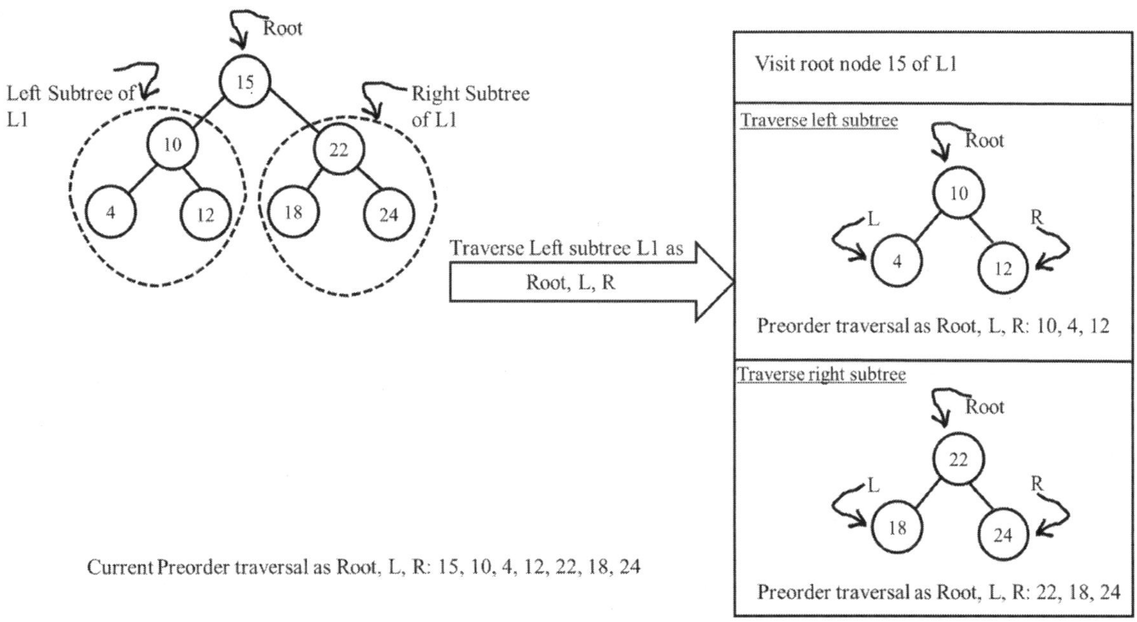

Figure 5.12: Traversing Left Subtree of the given Binary Tree.

Step 3. Traverse the right subtree R1 and apply preorder on it as shown in Figure 5.13.

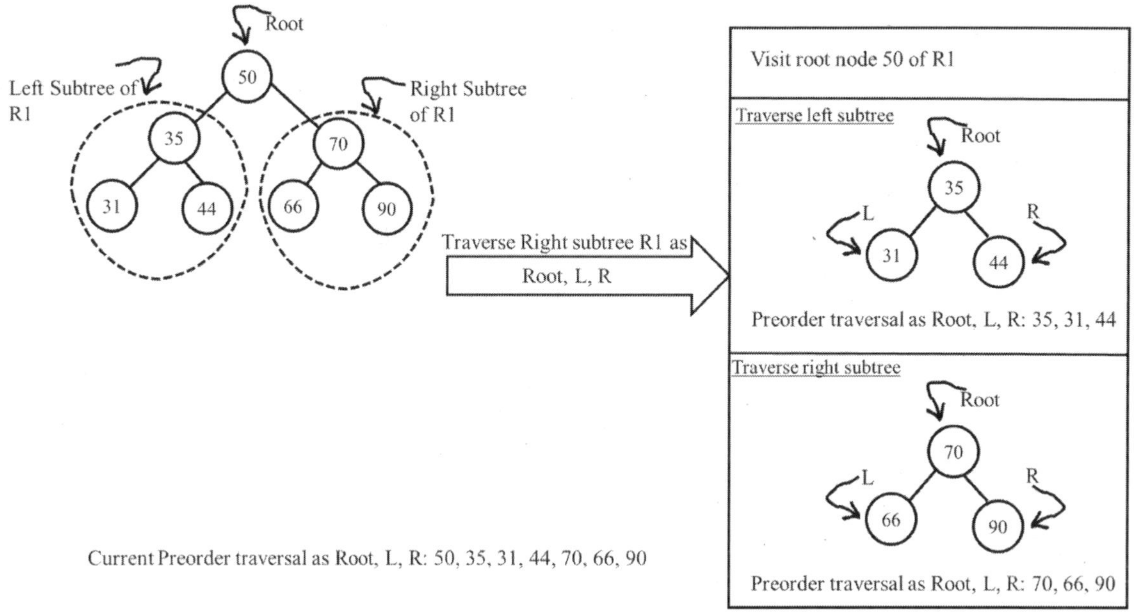

Figure 5.13: Traversing Right Subtree of the given Binary Tree.

Hence, the order of visit of nodes in Preorder will be:

25,15,10,4,12,22,18,24,50,35,31,44,70,66,90.

Preorder Traversal

Step 1. Traverse the left subtree R1 and apply inorder on it as shown in Figure 5.14.

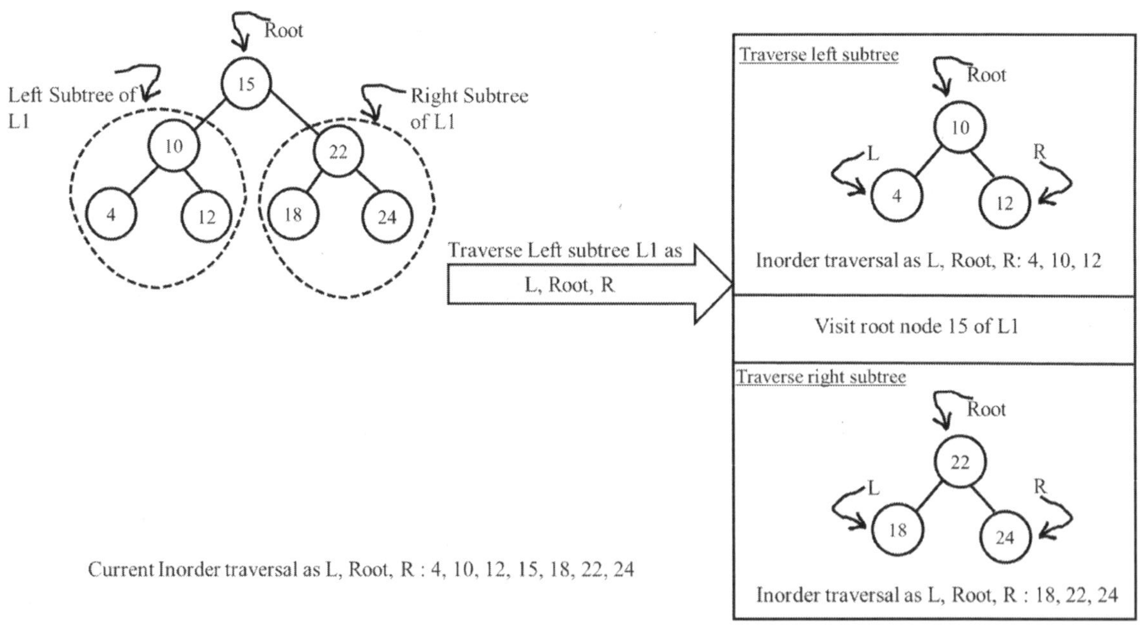

Figure 5.14: Traversing Left Subtree of the given Binary Tree.

Step 2. Visit (root) node 25.

Step 3. Traverse the right subtree R1 and apply inorder on it as shown in Figure 5.15.

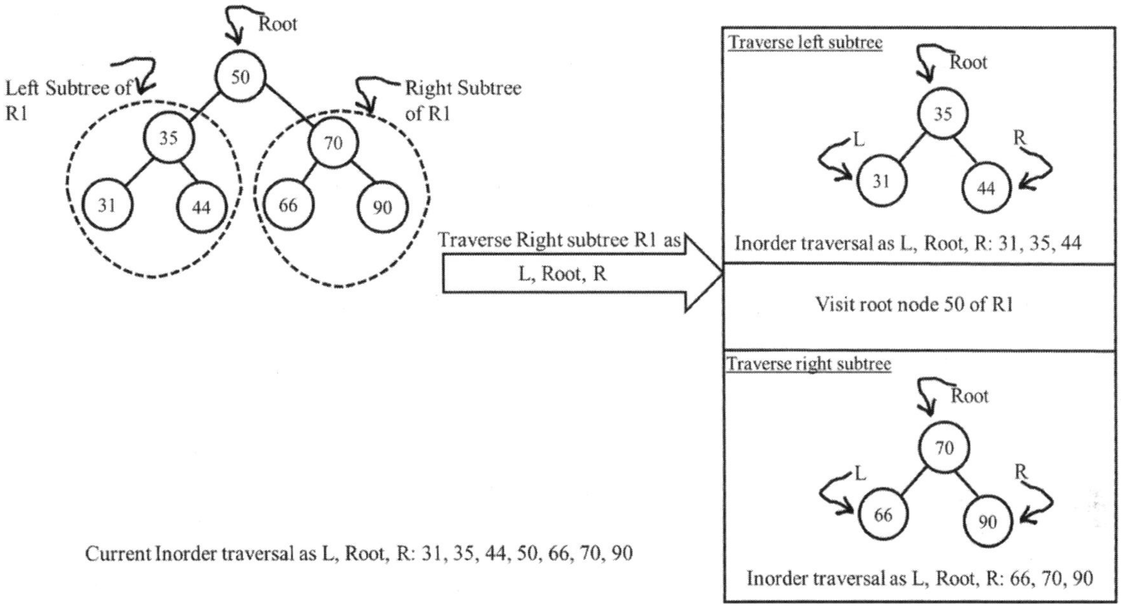

Figure 5.15: Traversing Right Subtree of the given Binary Tree.

The order of visit of nodes in Inorder will be:

4,10,12,15,18,22,24,25,31,35,44,50,66,70,90.

Postorder Traversal

Step 1. Traverse the left subtree R1 and apply postorder on it as shown in Figure 5.16.

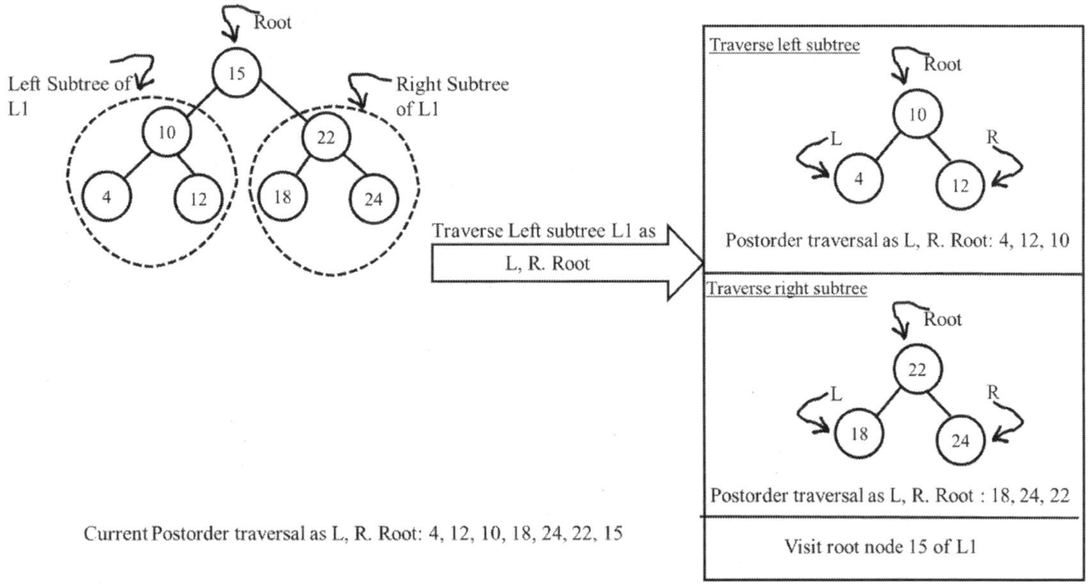

Figure 5.16: Traversing Left Subtree of the given Binary Tree.

Step 2. Traverse the right subtree R1 and apply postorder on it as shown in Figure 5.17.

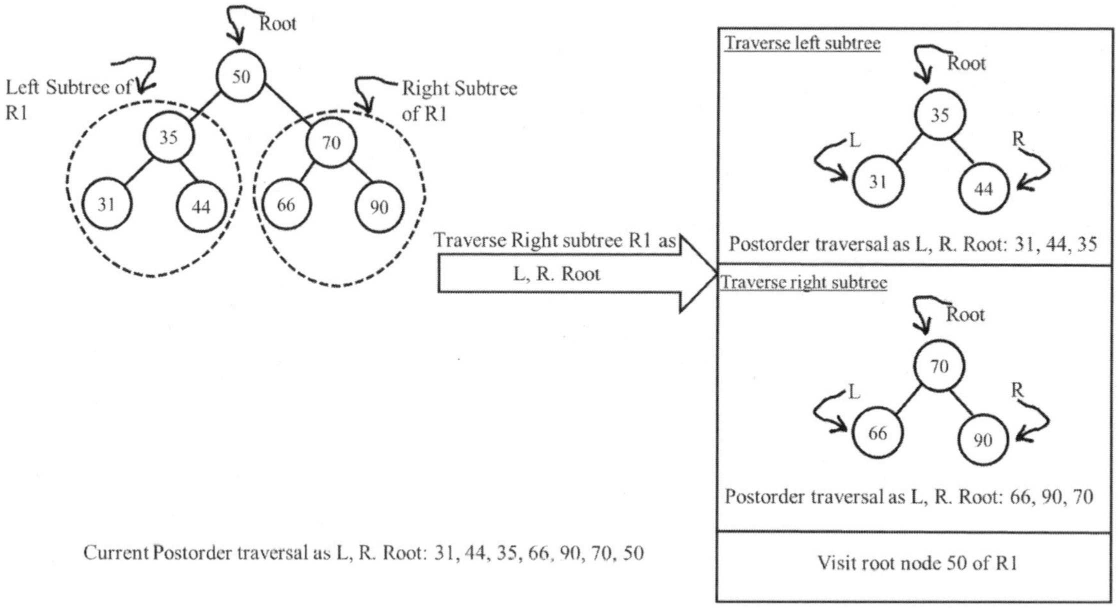

Figure 5.17: Traversing Right Subtree of the given Binary Tree.

Step 3. Visit (root) node 25.

The order of visit of nodes in Postorder will be:

4,12,10,18,24,22,15,31,44,35,66,90,70,50,25.

Programming Exercise 5.2

Write a program to perform inorder, preorder and postorder traversal in a binary tree.

```
#include <iostream>
using namespace std;

// Node structure
struct Node {
  int data;
  Node* left;
  Node* right;
  Node(int val) : data(val), left(NULL), right(NULL) {}
};

// Binary Tree class
class BinaryTree {
public:
```

```
Node* root;
BinaryTree() : root(NULL) {}

// Function to insert nodes manually
Node* insert(Node* node, int data) {
  if (node == NULL) return new Node(data);

  cout << "Insert left (L) or right (R) of " << node->data << "? ";
  char dir;
  cin >> dir;

  if (dir == 'L' || dir == 'l')
    node->left = insert(node->left, data);
  else
    node->right = insert(node->right, data);

  return node;
}

// Inorder traversal (Left - Root - Right)
void inorder(Node* node) {
  if (node == NULL) return;
  inorder(node->left);
  cout << node->data << " ";
  inorder(node->right);
}

// Preorder traversal (Root - Left - Right)
void preorder(Node* node) {
  if (node == NULL) return;
  cout << node->data << " ";
  preorder(node->left);
  preorder(node->right);
}
```

```
    // Postorder traversal (Left - Right - Root)
    void postorder(Node* node) {
        if (node == NULL) return;
        postorder(node->left);
        postorder(node->right);
        cout << node->data << " ";
    }

    void displayTraversals() {
        cout << "Inorder Traversal: ";
        inorder(root);
        cout << endl;

        cout << "Preorder Traversal: ";
        preorder(root);
        cout << endl;

        cout << "Postorder Traversal: ";
        postorder(root);
        cout << endl;
    }
};

// Main function
int main() {
    BinaryTree tree;
    int n, value;

    cout << "Enter number of nodes: ";
    cin >> n;

    if (n <= 0) {
        cout << "Invalid number of nodes!\n";
        return 1;
    }
```

```
  cout << "Enter value for root node: ";
  cin >> value;
  tree.root = new Node(value);

  for (int i = 1; i < n; i++) {
    cout << "Enter value for node: ";
    cin >> value;
    tree.insert(tree.root, value);
  }

  cout << "\nTree Traversals:\n";
  tree.displayTraversals();

  return 0;
}
```

OUTPUT:

```
Enter number of nodes: 7
Enter value for root node: 1
Enter value for node: 2
Insert left (L) or right (R) of 1? L
Enter value for node: 3
Insert left (L) or right (R) of 1? R
Enter value for node: 4
Insert left (L) or right (R) of 2? L
Enter value for node: 5
Insert left (L) or right (R) of 2? R
Enter value for node: 6
Insert left (L) or right (R) of 3? L
Enter value for node: 7
Insert left (L) or right (R) of 3? R

Tree Traversals:
Inorder Traversal: 4 2 5 1 6 3 7
```

Preorder Traversal: 1 2 4 5 3 6 7

Postorder Traversal: 4 5 2 6 7 3 1

5.5 BINARY SEARCH TREES

A binary search tree **(BST)** is a binary tree where each node has a Comparable key (and an associated value) and satisfies the restriction that the key in any node is larger than the keys in all nodes in that node's left subtree and smaller than the keys in all nodes in that node's right subtree.

Thus, BST divides all its sub-trees into two segments; the left sub-tree and the right sub-tree and can be defined as –

left_subtree (keys) ≤ node (key) ≤ right_subtree (keys)

As the name suggests BST data structure enables one to search for and find an element with an average running time of $O(\log_2 n)$. It also enables insertion and deletion with same average complexity of $O(\log_2 n)$. It overcomes the shortcomings of sorted linear array and linked list in the context of performing search, insertion and deletion. Figure 5.8 shows a pictorial representation of a Binary Search Tree. Point to observe here is that the root node key (20) has all less-valued keys on the left sub-tree and the higher valued keys on the right sub-tree.

5.5.1 SEARCHING in a BST

To search a given key in Binary Search Tree, we first compare it with root, if the key is present at root, we return root. If key is greater than root's key, we recur for right subtree of root node. Otherwise we recur for left subtree. It uses a recursive algorithm to search for a key in a BST because of its recursive structure.

Illustration to search '12' in the tree in Figure 5.18:

1. Compare with root of level 0, 20>12. The search element is smaller than root so go to left subtree with root '10'.
2. Compare with root of left subtree of level 1, 10<12. The search element is greater than root so go to right subtree with root '12'.
3. Compare with root of right subtree of level 2, 12=12. So, return element found.

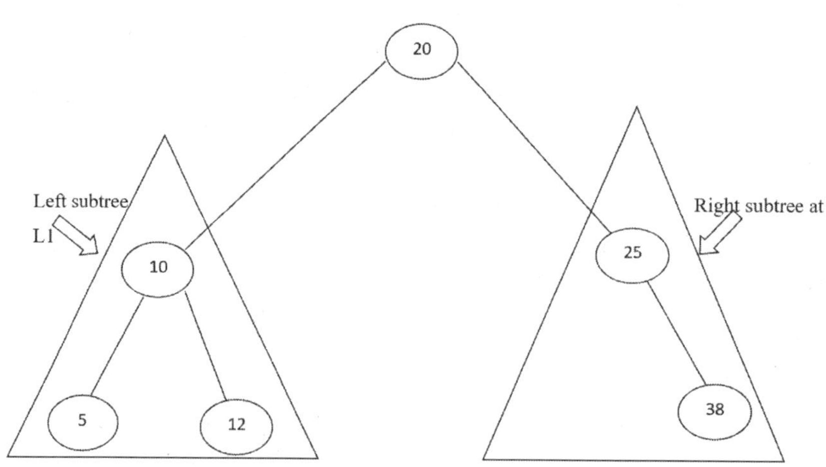

Figure 5.18: A Binary Search Tree

Let us write down the formal algorithm for searching a data in the BST. This algorithm finds the location of a given ITEM and its parent. PTR is used for traversing down the tree and SAVE is used to hold pointer to the parent node during the procedure. Here T is a BST, LOC is the location of ITEM to be found in T and PAR is the location of parent of ITEM.

Algorithm 5.4.0: SearchBST (DATA,L,R,ROOT,ITEM,LOC,PAR)

```
1. If ROOT=NULL, then                        //Empty tree
                  LOC:=Null
                  PAR:=Null
                  Exit
2. If ITEM:=DATA[ROOT], then                  //DATA is at root
                  LOC:=ROOT
                  PAR:=Null
                  Exit
3. If  ITEM<DATA[ROOT], then
                  PTR:=L[ROOT]
                  SAVE:=ROOT
   Else
                  PTR:=R[ROOT]
                  SAVE:=ROOT
4. Repeat steps 5 and 6 while PTR!= NULL  //traverse down the tree
5. If  ITEM=DATA[PTR], then
                  LOC:=PTR
                  PAR:=SAVE
                  Exit
6. If  ITEM<DATA[PTR]                         //smaller go left
                  SAVE:=PTR                                    Loop
                  PTR:=L[PTR]
                       Else

                       SAVE:=PTR   //bigger go right
                       PTR:=R[PTR]
7. LOC:=Null and PAR:=SAVE  //unsuccessful search
8. Exit
```

Complexity Analysis of the Algorithm

From the algorithm it is quite obvious that the number of comparison for carrying out a search operation is bounded by the depth of the tree which is in the order of $\log_2 n$. So the average time complexity is O($\log_2 n$). However, situation is different in case of a skewed tree, which is the worst case scenario. In that case the complexity is O(n). Recursive way of writing Search in a BST is presented in Algorithm 5.4.1.

Algorithm 5.4.1: Search BST (ROOT, ITEM)

1. if ROOT = NULL or ITEM = ROOT[DATA]

   Return ROOT

2. if ITEM < ROOT[DATA]

   Return Search BST (L[ROOT], ITEM)

3. Else

   Return Search BST (R[ROOT], ITEM)

The procedure begins its search at the root and traces a simple path downward in the tree. For each node it encounters, it compares the key ITEM with DATA[Node]. If the two keys are equal, the search terminates. If ITEM is smaller than DATA[Node], the search continues in the left subtree of Node, since the binary-search tree property implies that ITEM could not be stored in the right subtree. Symmetrically, if ITEM is larger than DATA[Node], the search continues in the right subtree.

5.5.2 INSERTION in a BST

To insert a new value into a binary search tree T, we use the procedure Insert BST. Let us write down the formal algorithm for insertion of a data in the BST. This algorithm finds the loction LOC of a given DATA in the tree or adds the DATA as a new node at location LOC.

Algorithm 5.5: Insert BST (DATA,L,R,ROOT,ITEM,LOC,PAR)

1. Function call Search BST (DATA,L,R,ROOT,ITEM,LOC,PAR)
2. If LOC!=NULL, then Exit.
3. i. if Avail=Null

   Print overflow
   Exit

   ii. else

   New:=Avail, Avail:=L[Avail] and DATA[New]:=DATA.

   Loc:=New, L[New]:=Null and R[New]:=Null.

4. If PAR=Null,then:

   Root:=New.

   Else if DATA<DATA[PAR] then

   Set L[Par]:=New.

   Else

   Set R[Par]:=New.

5. Exit

Let us construct a Binary Search Tree by inserting the following sequence of numbers:

16,22,15,4 and 20

Insert 16

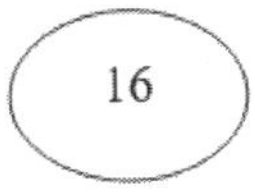

Insert 22

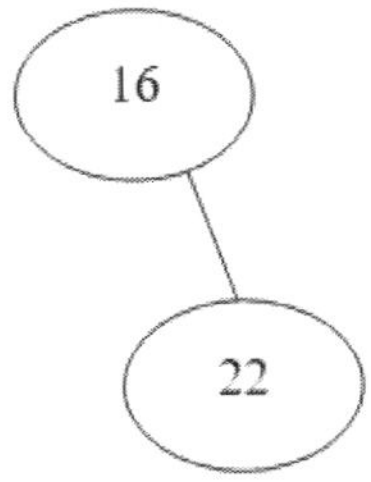

Insert 15

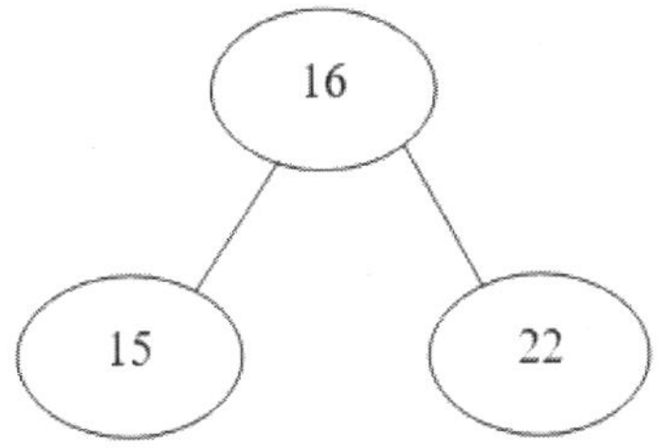

Insert 4

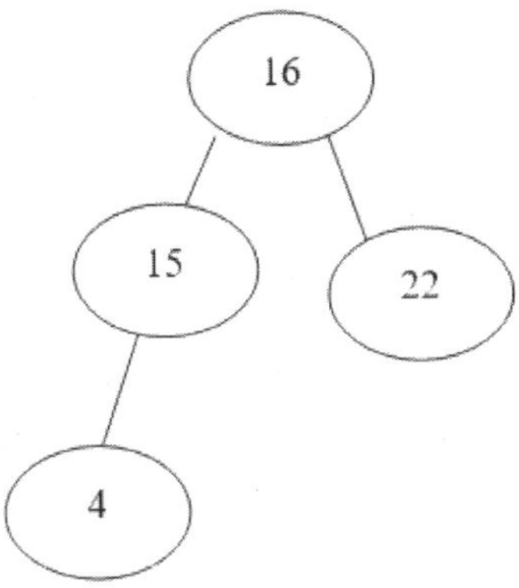

Insert 20

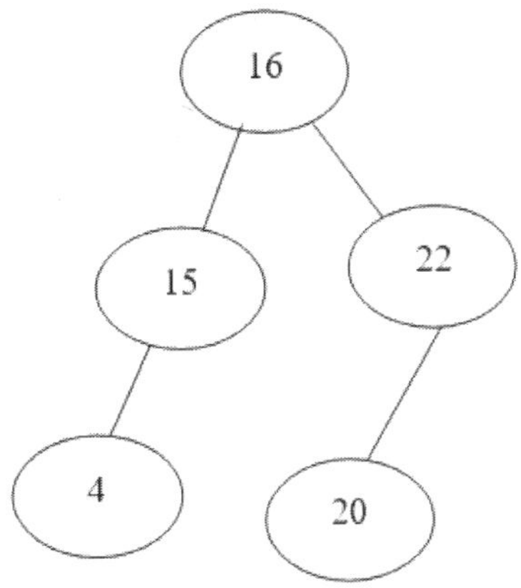

5.5.3 DELETION in a BST

Deletion is a two stage operation

- search for the node to delete
- if the node is found, run deletion algorithm.

For performing deletion of ITEM first thing is to find out the location LOC of the node that contains the ITEM whose DATA[Node]=ITEM. After finding the node 'n' to delete, three different situations may arise depending upon the number of children it has. 'n' may have no children, it may have exactly 1 children or it may have two children. The deletion procedure will be different in all these three cases, which are explained in detail now.

CASE 1. 'n' has no children:

Node 'n' is deleted by replacing location of n in the parent node 'PAR(n)' by setting a 'null' pointer.

CASE 2. 'n' has one child:

Node 'n' is deleted by replacing location of n in the parent node 'PAR(n)' by setting the location of its children L(n) or R(n).

CASE 3. 'n' has two children:

Find the inorder successor S(n) of n in the tree T. Delete S(N) (using case 1 or 2) and then replace node 'n' by S(n).

Let us understand all these cases with an example. Say we want to delete '38' from the tree in Figure 5.9. Node '38' has no children and hence it will come under **Case 1**. So deletion is performed simply assigning null pointer to its parent. Figure 5.9(a) shows the tree after deleting '38'.

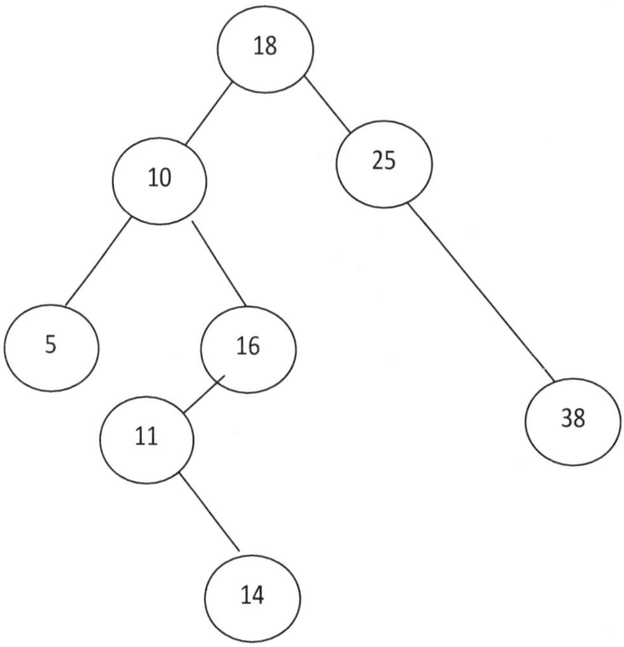

Figure 5.19: A Binary Search Tree

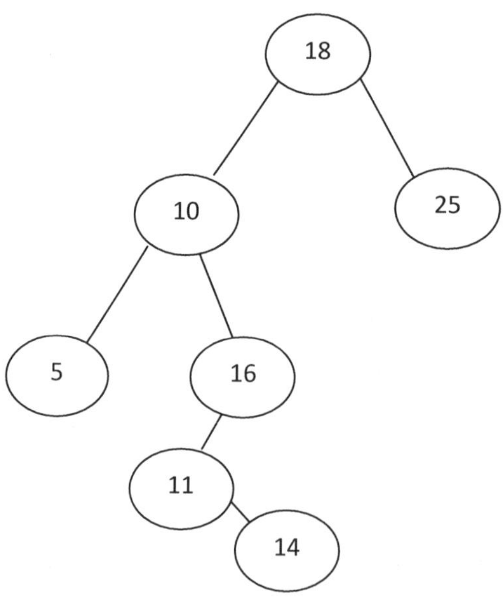

Figure 5.19 (a): after deleting '38'

Now say we want to delete '25' from the tree in Figure 5.19. The node '25' has one child and hence it will come under **Case 2.** Figure 5.19 (b) shows the tree after deletion of '25'. The deletion is accomplished by changing the right pointer of parent node '18' to only child of '25'.

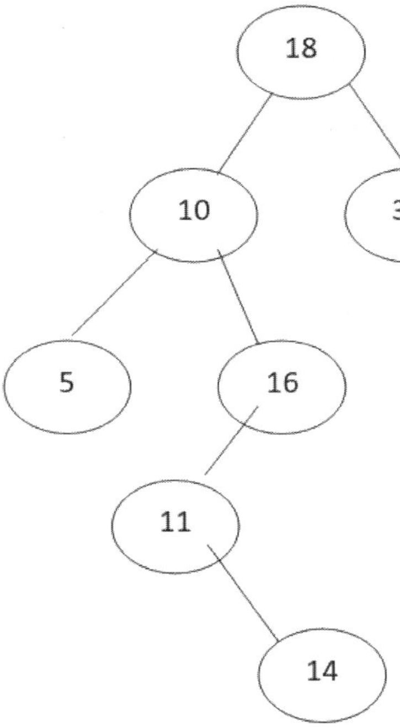

Figure 5.19 (b): after deleting '25'

Now say we want to delete '10' from the tree in Figure 5.19. The node '10' has two children and hence it will come under **Case 3.** '11' is the inorder successor of '10'. Now replacing '10' with '11' and rearranging accordingly will give Figure 5.19 (c).

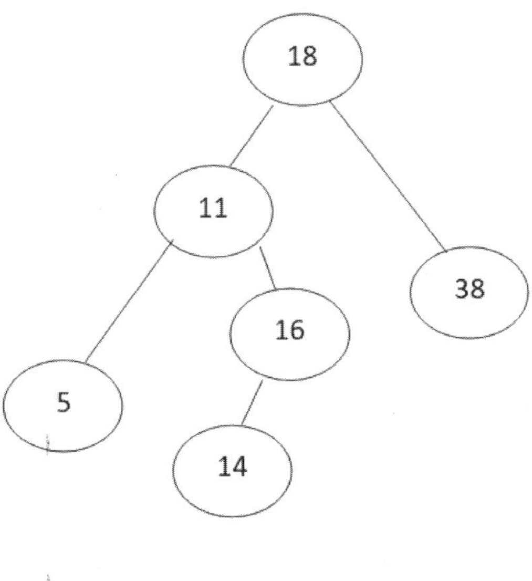

Figure 5.19 (c): after deleting '10'

Algorithm 5.6: DeleteBST (DATA,L,R,ROOT,AVAIL,ITEM)

```
1. Call SearchBST (DATA,L,R,ROOT,ITEM,LOC,PAR)
2. If LOC=Null, write ITEM not found and Exit.
3. Else if
   R[LOC]!=Null and L[LOC]!=Null then
   Call CASE3BST ( DATA,L,R,ROOT,LOC,PAR)// two children node
   Else
   Call CASE2BST ( DATA,L,R,ROOT, LOC,PAR)// one or no children node
4. L[LOC]:=Avail and Avail:=LOC
5. Exit
```

Algorithm 5.6.a: CASE2BST (DATA,L,R,ROOT, LOC,PAR)

```
1. If L[LOC]=Null and R[LOC]=Null then
                   Child:=Null
   Else if L[LOC]!=Null then
                   Child:=L[LOC]
   Else
                   Child:=R[LOC]
2. If PAR!=Null  then
           If LOC=L[PAR] then:
                   L[PAR]:=CHILD
           Else
                   R[PAR]:=CHILD
   Else
           ROOT:=CHILD
3. Exit
```

Algorithm 5.6.b: CASE3BST (DATA,L,R,ROOT, LOC,PAR)

```
1. //Find the Successor SUC
   a. P:=R[LOC] and S:=LOC
   b. Repeat while L[P]!=Null
        S:=P and P:=L[P]
   c. SUC:=P and PSUC:=S.
2. CASE2BST ( DATA,L,R,ROOT, SUC,PSUC)
3. If PAR!=Null  then
```

```
            If LOC=L[PAR] then:
                    L[PAR]:=SUC
            Else
            R[PAR]:=SUC
    Else
            ROOT:=SUC
```

4. L[SUC]:=L[LOC] and R[SUC]:=R[LOC]

5. Exit

Programming Exercise 5.3

Write a program to implement a binary search tree and perform insertion, deletion and searching in the BST.

```
#include <iostream>
using namespace std;

// Node structure for the BST
struct Node {
  int data;
  Node* left;
  Node* right;
};
// Function to create a new node
Node* createNode(int data) {
  Node* newNode = new Node();
  newNode->data = data;
  newNode->left = newNode->right = nullptr;
  return newNode;
}

// Function to insert a node in BST
Node* insert(Node* root, int data) {
  if (root == nullptr) return createNode(data);

  if (data < root->data)
    root->left = insert(root->left, data);
  else if (data > root->data)
```

```
        root->right = insert(root->right, data);

    return root;
}

// Function to search a node in BST
bool search(Node* root, int key) {
    if (root == nullptr) return false;
    if (root->data == key) return true;
    if (key < root->data)
        return search(root->left, key);
    return search(root->right, key);
}
// Function to find the minimum value node
Node* findMin(Node* root) {
    while (root->left != nullptr)
        root = root->left;
    return root;
}
// Function to delete a node from BST
Node* deleteNode(Node* root, int key) {
    if (root == nullptr) return root;
    if (key < root->data)
        root->left = deleteNode(root->left, key);
    else if (key > root->data)
        root->right = deleteNode(root->right, key);
    else {
        // Case 1 & 2: Node with one or no child
        if (root->left == nullptr) {
            Node* temp = root->right;
            delete root;
            return temp;
        } else if (root->right == nullptr) {
            Node* temp = root->left;
            delete root;
            return temp;
```

```
    }
    // Case 3: Node with two children
    Node* temp = findMin(root->right);
    root->data = temp->data;
    root->right = deleteNode(root->right, temp->data);
  }
  return root;
}

// Inorder traversal of BST
void inorder(Node* root) {
  if (root != nullptr) {
    inorder(root->left);
    cout << root->data << " ";
    inorder(root->right);
  }
}
int main() {
  Node* root = nullptr;
  int choice, val;
  do {
    cout << "\nBST Operations:\n";
    cout << "1. Insert\n2. Search\n3. Delete\n4. Display (Inorder)\n5. Exit\nEnter choice: ";
    cin >> choice;
    switch (choice) {
      case 1:
        cout << "Enter value to insert: ";
        cin >> val;
        root = insert(root, val);
        break;
      case 2:
        cout << "Enter value to search: ";
        cin >> val;
        if (search(root, val))
          cout << "Value found!\n";
```

```
            else
              cout << "Value not found!\n";
            break;
          case 3:
            cout << "Enter value to delete: ";
            cin >> val;
            root = deleteNode(root, val);
            break;
          case 4:
            cout << "Inorder traversal: ";
            inorder(root);
            cout << endl;
            break;
                  case 5:
            cout << "Exiting...\n";
            break;
          default:
            cout << "Invalid choice!\n";
        }
    } while (choice != 5);
    return 0;
}
```

OUTPUT:

BST Operations:

1. Insert
2. Search
3. Delete
4. Display (Inorder)
5. Exit

Enter choice: 4

Inorder traversal: 4 7

BST Operations:

1. Insert

2. Search

3. Delete

4. Display (Inorder)

5. Exit

Enter choice: 1

Enter value to insert: 8

5.6 AVL SEARCH TREES

As discussed in the previous section the binary search tree **(BST)** takes $O(\log_2 n)$ running time for searching an element in the tree in average case. However, a BST can be skewed sometime. To understand it more clearly let us take an example. Consider the elements 120, 110, 96,75,64,32,12,9 and perform the operation using **Algorithm 5.5.** The tree generated would look like as in Figure5.10. In a similar way if we insert 9, 12,32,64,96,110,120 the tree generated will look like as in Figure 5.11.

In such cases the worst case complexity of search is O(n), which violates the basic objective of having a binary search tree. To avoid this kind of situation a binary search tree has to be height balanced, so as to maintain searching complexity in terms of O(log n). One such popular tree was proposed by Adelson-Velskii and Landis and the tree was named after them (AVL). As the definition goes:

A non empty binary tree T is an AVL tree if given T^L and T^r to be left and right sub-trees of T are AVL trees and $|H^l - H^R| \leq 1$, where H^l and H^R to be height of left and right sub trees respectively. This $|H^l - H^R|$ is known as balance factor(BF) and for an AVL tree the balance factor can be either 0,1, or -1. An empty tree is an AVL tree.

5.6.1 INSERTION IN AN AVL SEARCH TREE

To make sure that the given tree remains AVL after every insertion, we must augment the standard BST insert operation to perform some re-balancing. Left Rotation and Right Rotation are the two basic operations that can be performed to re-balance a BST without violating the BST property. To perform these rotations we need to identify the node A whose balance factor (BF) is neither 0,1 or-1 and which is also the nearest ancestor to the inserted node on the path to the root. It also implies that all nodes from inserted node to A will have BF to be 0,1,-1.

Four rebalancing rotations possible are:

LL rotation: Inserted node is in the left subtree of left subtree of node A

RR rotation: Inserted node is in the right subtree of right subtree of node A

LR rotation: Inserted node is in the right subtree of left subtree of node A

RL rotation: Inserted node is in the left subtree of right subtree of node A

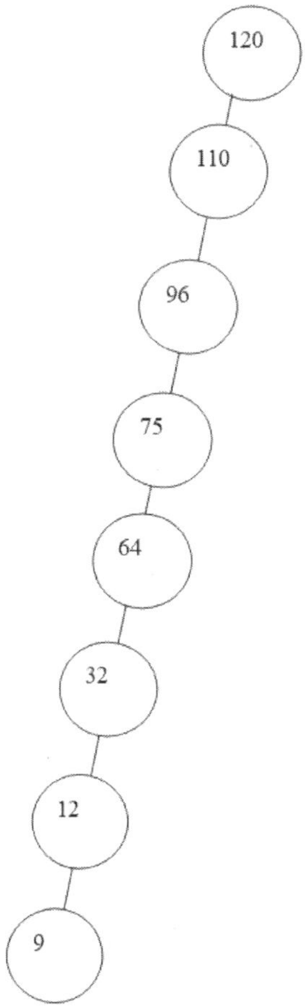

Figure 5.20: A left skewed tree

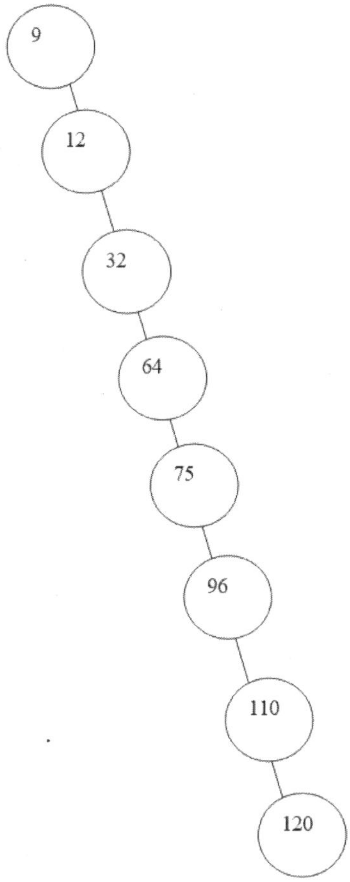

Figure 5.21: A right skewed tree

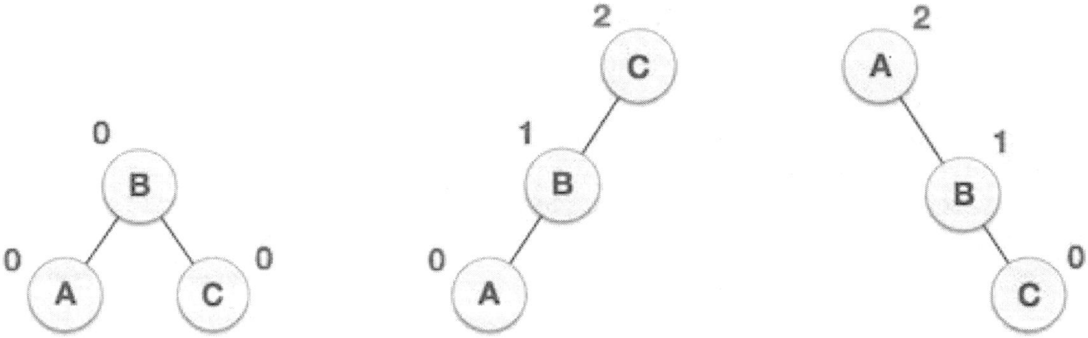

Figure 5.22: Nodes with balance factors

LL rotation

AVL tree may become unbalanced, if a node is inserted in the left subtree of the left subtree. The tree then needs a right rotation.

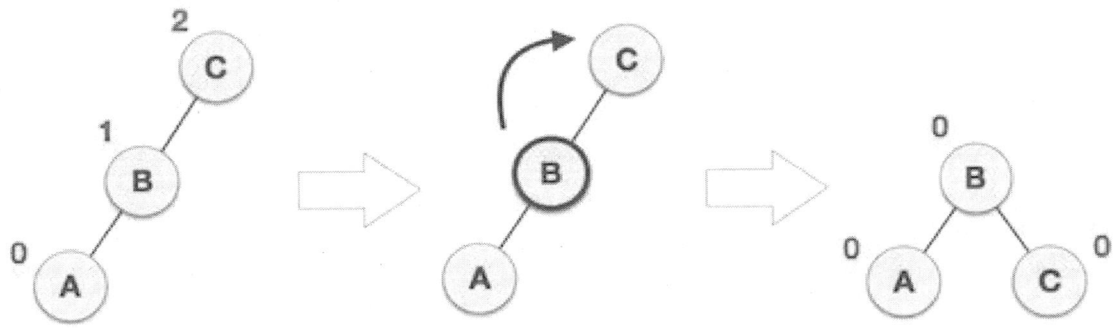

Figure 5.23: LL rotation

As depicted, the unbalanced node becomes the right child of its left child by performing a right rotation.

RR rotation

If a tree becomes unbalanced, when a node is inserted into the right subtree of the right subtree, then we perform a single left rotation –

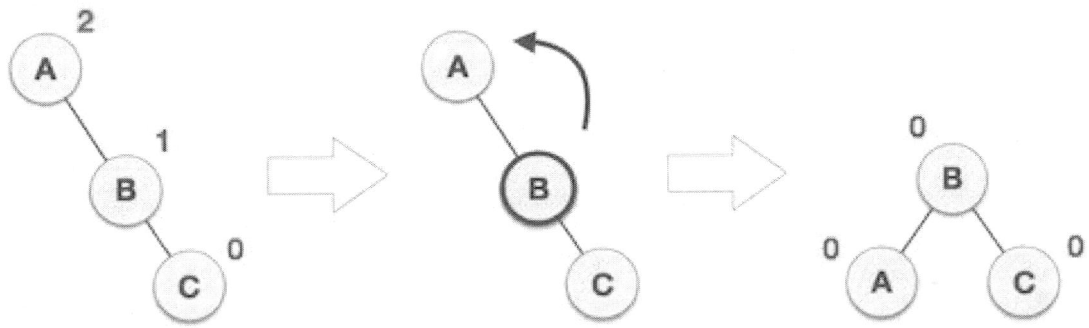

Figure 5.24: RR rotation

In our example, node **A** has become unbalanced as a node is inserted in the right subtree of A's right subtree. We perform the left rotation by making **A** the left-subtree of B.

LR Rotation

LR rotation is to be performed if the new node is inserted into the right of the left sub-tree of node A. In LR rotation, node C becomes the root node of the tree, while the node B and A becomes its left and right child respectively. T1 and T2 becomes the left and right sub-tree of Node B respectively whereas, T3 and T4 becomes the left and right sub-tree of Node A as in Figure 5.25.

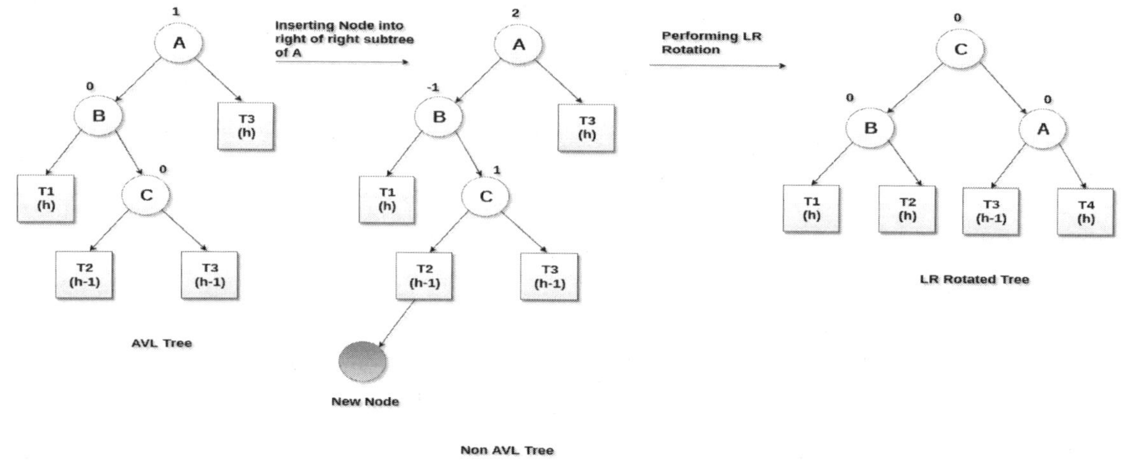

Figure 5.25: LR rotation

Let us take an example. Say we need to insert '70' into the tree shown in the Figure 5.26. According to the property of binary search tree, the node with value 70 is inserted into the right of the left sub-tree of the root of tree. As shown in the figure, the balance factor of the root node disturbed upon inserting 70 and this becomes the critical node A. To rebalance the tree, LR rotation is to be performed. Node C i.e. 75 will become the new root node of the tree with B and A as its left and right child respectively. Sub-trees T1, T2 become the left and right sub-tree of B while sub-trees T3, T4 become the left and right sub-tree of A. The procedure is shown in the Figure 5.26.

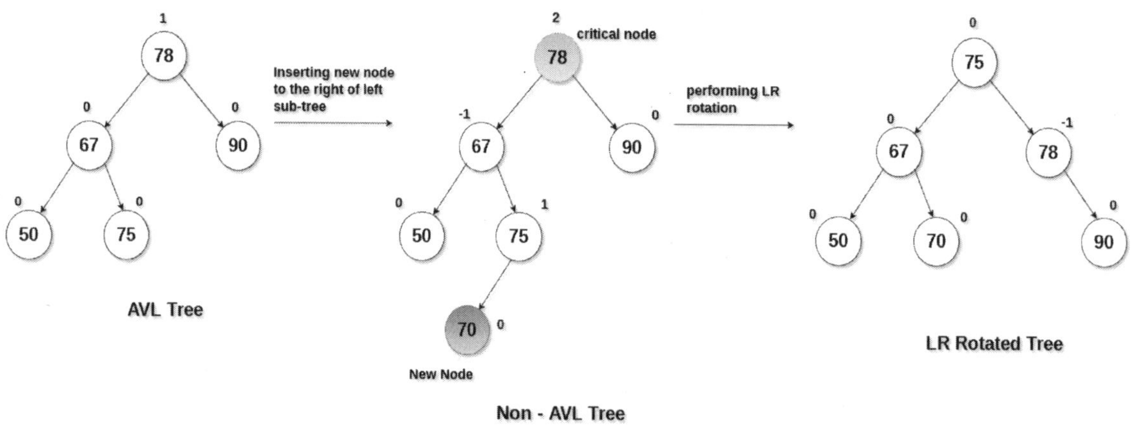

Figure 5.26: LR rotation example

RL Rotation

RL rotations is to be performed if the new node is inserted into the left of right sub-tree of the critical node A. Let us consider, Node B is the root of the right sub-tree of the critical node, Node C is the root of the sub-tree in which the new node is inserted. Let T1 be the left sub-tree of the critical node A, T2 and T3 be the left and right sub-tree of Node C respectively, sub-tree T4 be the right sub-tree of Node B.

Since, RL rotation is the mirror image of LR rotation. In this rotation, the node C becomes the root node of the tree with A and B as its left and right children respectively. Sub-trees T1 and T2 becomes the left and right sub-trees of A whereas, T3 and T4 becomes the left and right sub-trees of B.

The process of RL rotation is shown in the figure 5.27.

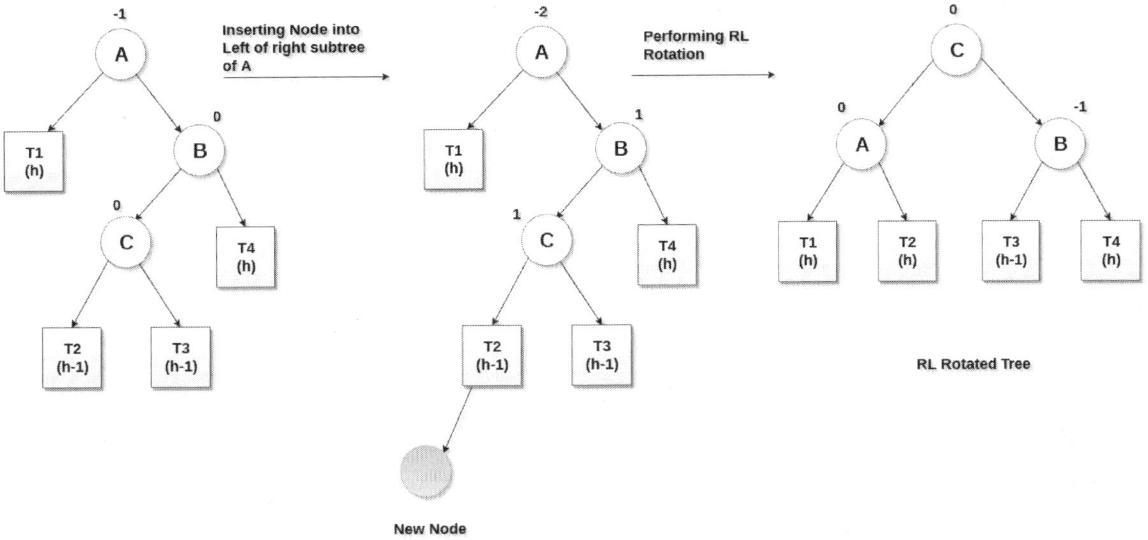

Figure 5.27: RL rotation

Let us take an example. Say we need to insert '92' into the tree shown in the following figure. Insertion of '92' disturbs the balance factor of the node '92' and it becomes the critical node A with '105' as the node B and '95' with the node C. In RL rotation, C becomes the root of the tree with node A (90) and B (105) as its left and right children respectively. The tree will be rotated as shown in the figure 5.28.

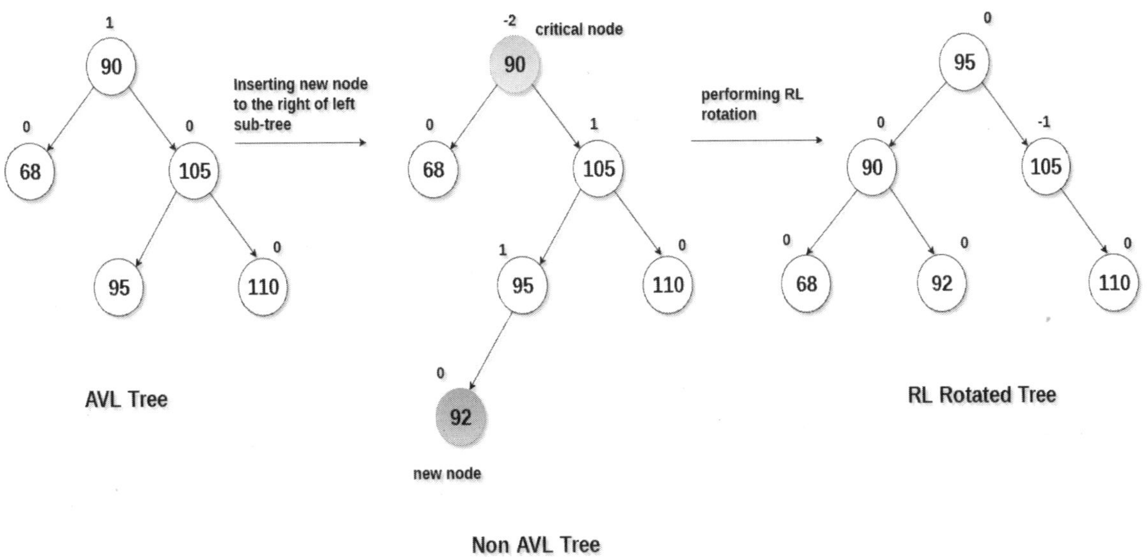

Figure 5.28: RL rotation example

Example: Perform AVL insertion for the following nodes: 21, 26, 30, 9, 4, 14, 28, 18, 15.

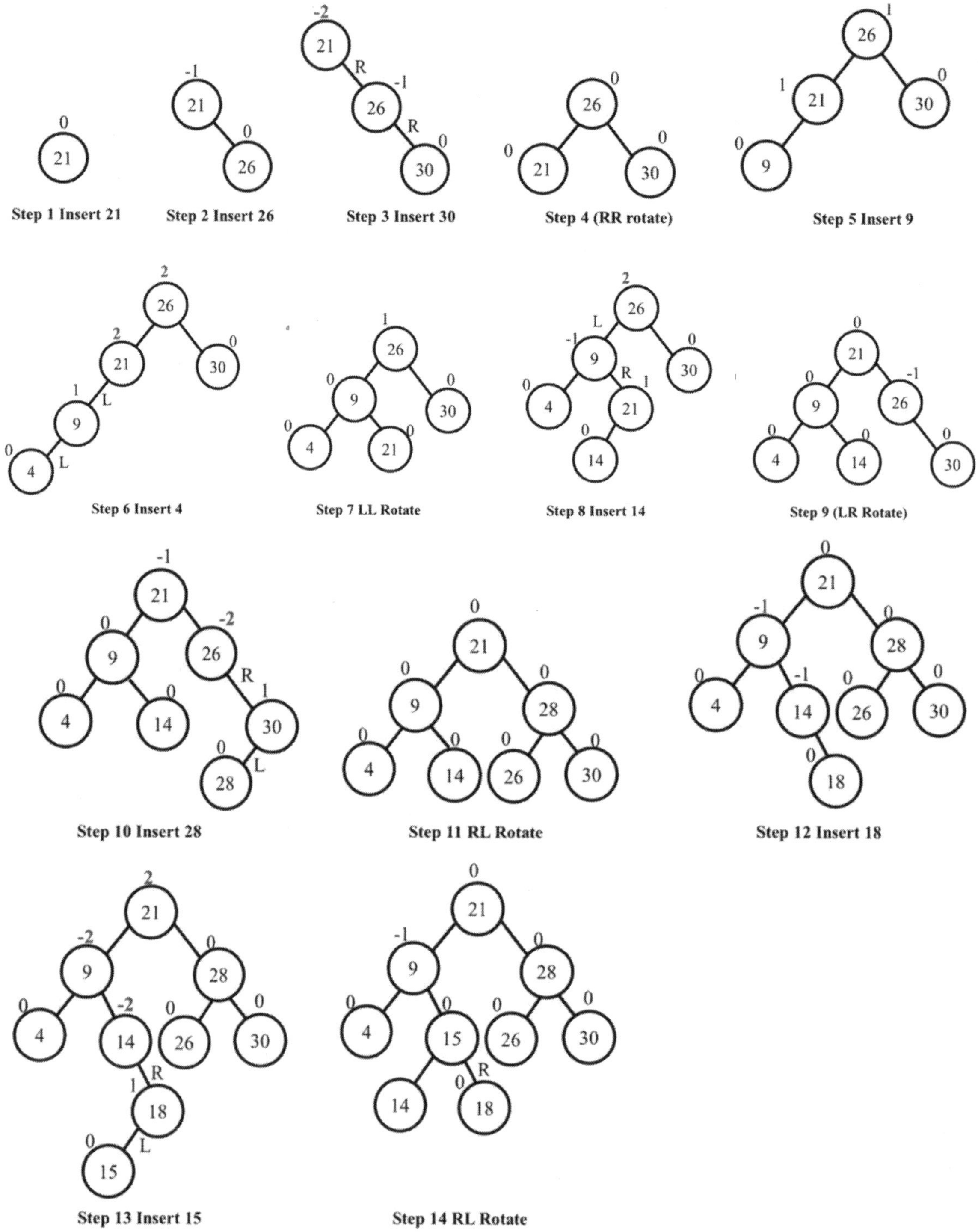

Figure 5.29: AVL Tree Insertion.

5.6.2 DELETION IN AN AVL SEARCH TREE

In order to perform deletion in an AVL tree, one must know how to:

- perform deletion in a binary search tree and
- perform rotation in an AVL tree.

Deletion may disturb balance in an AVL tree due to which R rotation and L rotation are performed. The variations of R rotation are R_0 rotation, R_1 rotation and R_{-1} rotation. Similarly, the variations of L rotation are L_0 rotation, L_1 rotation and L_{-1} rotation. This section discusses about R rotations and L rotations in detail.

R_0 Rotation

If the node which is deleted (Say d) is from the right subtree, then:

- We have to find balance factor of critical node (Say A) (closest ancestor node on the path from root node to d that does not have balance factor as 1, 0, -1).
- We have to find balance factor of root of critical node's left sub tree (Say B). R_0 rotation is applied if balance factor of B is 0.
- During this process, LL rotation must be performed.

Example: Consider the AVL tree given below and delete 40 from it.

Deletion has occurred at right subtree. Balance factor of ancestor (critical) node A=30 is 2 and balance factor of node B=10 is 0. This is a case of R_0 rotation and hence LL rotation is applied.

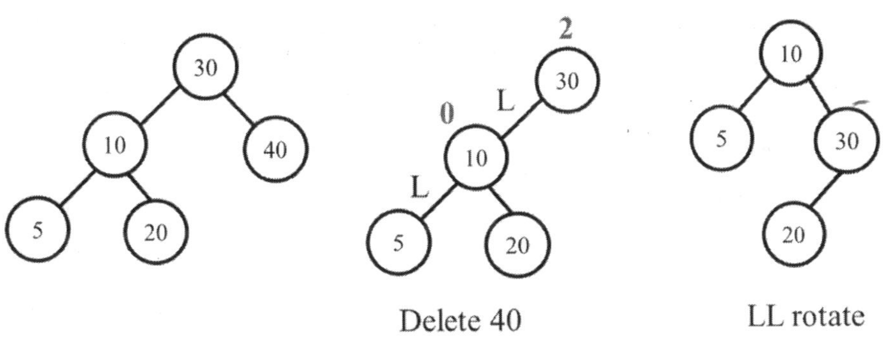

Figure 5.30: R_0 rotation in AVL tree

R_1 Rotation

If the node which is deleted (Say d) is from the right subtree, then:

- We have to find balance factor of critical node (Say A) (closest ancestor node on the path from root node to d that does not have balance factor as 1, 0, -1).
- We have to find balance factor of root of critical node's left sub tree (Say B). R_1 rotation is applied if balance factor of B is 1.
- During this process, LL rotation must be performed.

Example: Consider the AVL tree given below and delete 40 from it.

Deletion has occurred at right subtree. Balance factor of critical node A=30 is 2 and balance factor of node B=10 is 1. This is a case of R_1 rotation and hence LL rotation is applied.

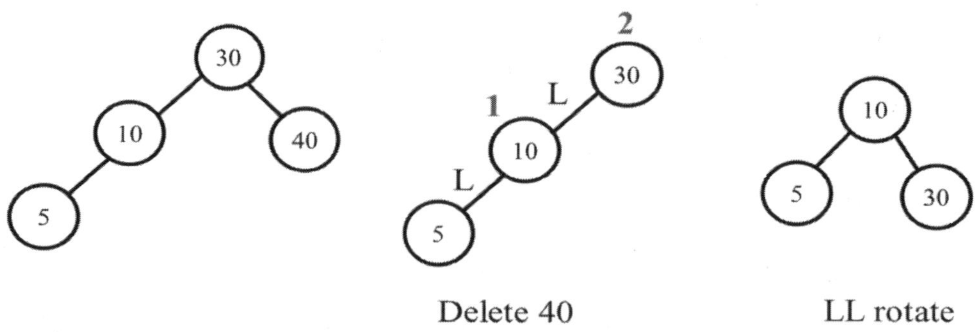

Figure 5.31: R_1 rotation in AVL tree

R_{-1} Rotation

If the node which is deleted (Say d) is from the right subtree, then:

- We have to find balance factor of critical node (Say A) (closest ancestor node on the path from root node to d that does not have balance factor as 1, 0, -1).
- We have to find balance factor of root of critical node's left sub tree (Say B). R_{-1} rotation is applied if balance factor of B is -1.
- During this process, LR rotation must be performed.

Example: Consider the AVL tree given below and delete 40 from it.

Deletion has occurred at right subtree. Balance factor of critical node A=30 is 2 and balance factor of node B=10 is -1. This is a case of R_{-1} rotation and hence LR rotation is applied.

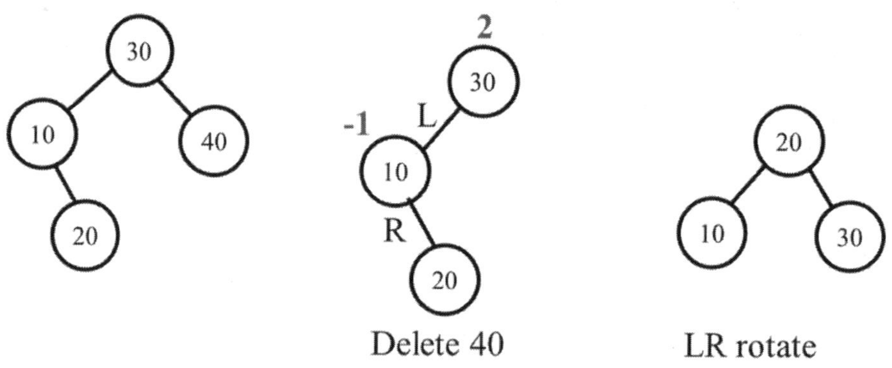

Figure 5.32: R_{-1} rotation in AVL tree

L_0 Rotation

If the node which is deleted (Say d) is from the left subtree, then:

- We have to find balance factor of critical node (Say A) (closest ancestor node on the path from root node to d that does not have balance factor as 1, 0, -1).
- We have to find balance factor of root of critical node's right sub tree (Say B). L_0 rotation is applied if balance factor of B is 0.
- During this process, RR rotation must be performed.

Example: Consider the AVL tree given below and delete 20 from it.

Deletion has occurred at right subtree. Balance factor of critical node A=30 is -2 and balance factor of node B=40 is 0. This is a case of R_0 rotation and hence RR rotation is applied.

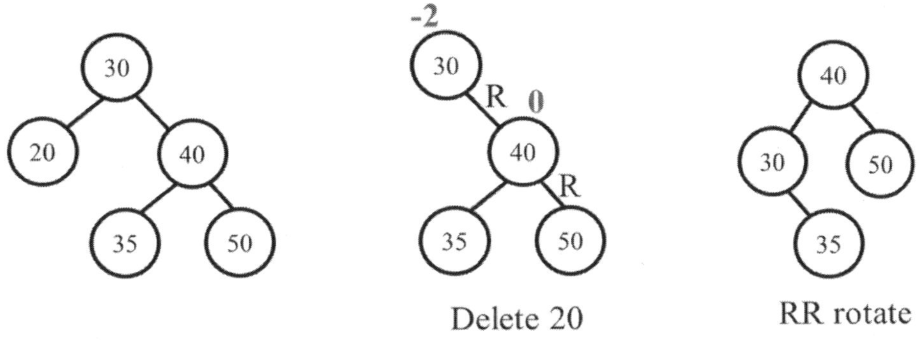

Figure 5.33: L_0 rotation in AVL tree

L_1 Rotation

If the node which is deleted (Say d) is from the left subtree, then:

- We have to find balance factor of critical node (Say A) (closest ancestor node on the path from root node to d that does not have balance factor as 1, 0, -1).
- We have to find balance factor of root of critical node's left sub tree (Say B). L_1 rotation is applied if balance factor of B is 1.
- During this process, RL rotation must be performed.

Example: Consider the AVL tree given below and delete 20 from it.

Deletion has occurred at right subtree. Balance factor of critical node A=30 is 2 and balance factor of node B=10 is 1. This is a case of R_1 rotation and hence RL rotation is applied.

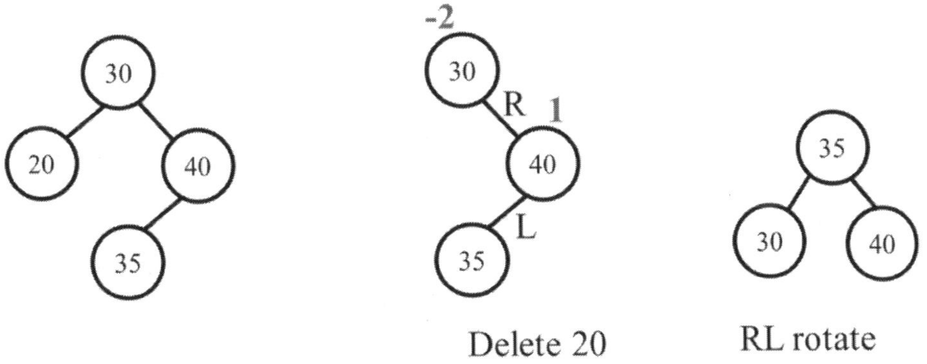

Figure 5.34: L_1 rotation in AVL tree

L_{-1} Rotation

If the node which is deleted (Say d) is from the left subtree, then:

- We have to find balance factor of critical node (Say A) (closest ancestor node on the path from root node to d that does not have balance factor as 1, 0, -1).

- We have to find balance factor of root of critical node's left sub tree (Say B). L_{-1} rotation is applied if balance factor of B is -1.
- During this process, RR rotation must be performed.

Example: Consider the AVL tree given below and delete 20 from it.

Deletion has occurred at right subtree. Balance factor of critical node A=30 is -2 and balance factor of node B=40 is -1. This is a case of L_{-1} rotation and hence RR rotation is applied.

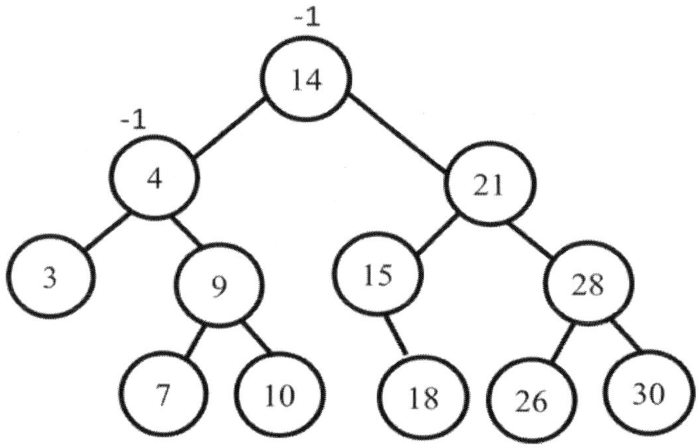

Figure 5.35: L_{-1} rotation in AVL tree

Example: Delete nodes 2, 3, 10, 18, 4, 9, 14, 7, 15 in sequence from the AVL tree given below:

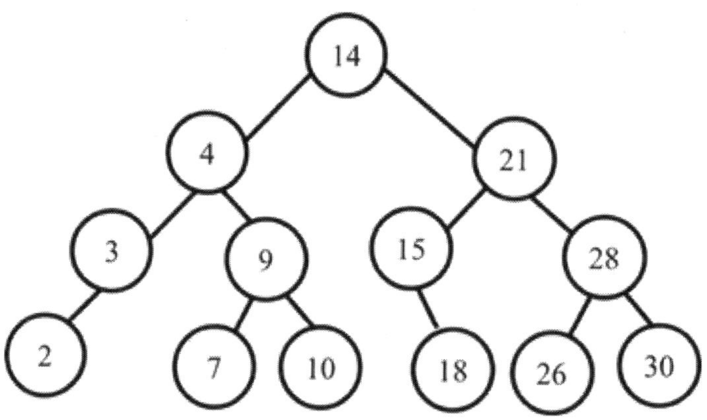

Figure 5.36: Given AVL tree

First node 2 (leaf node) is deleted directly from left subtree as shown in Figure 5.37 (a). Ancestors of node 2 are 3, 4 and 14 whose balance factors are in -1,0,1.

Next node 3 (leaf node) is deleted directly as shown in Figure 5.37 (b). Ancestor of node 3 is node 4 whose balance factor is -2. Node 3 is deleted from LHS of node 4, so it is a L type of deletion. RHS child of node 4 is 9 whose balance factor is 0. Hence, L_0 type of deletion (RR rotate) is applied on the

AVL tree which is shown in Figure 5.37 (c).

Next leaf node 10 is deleted directly [Refer to Figure 5.37 (d)]. Ancestor of node 10 is node 9. Balance factor of node 9 is 2 which makes the AVL tree unbalanced. Deletion of node 10 was done from RHS of node 9 (ancestor critical node). So, it is a R type of deletion.

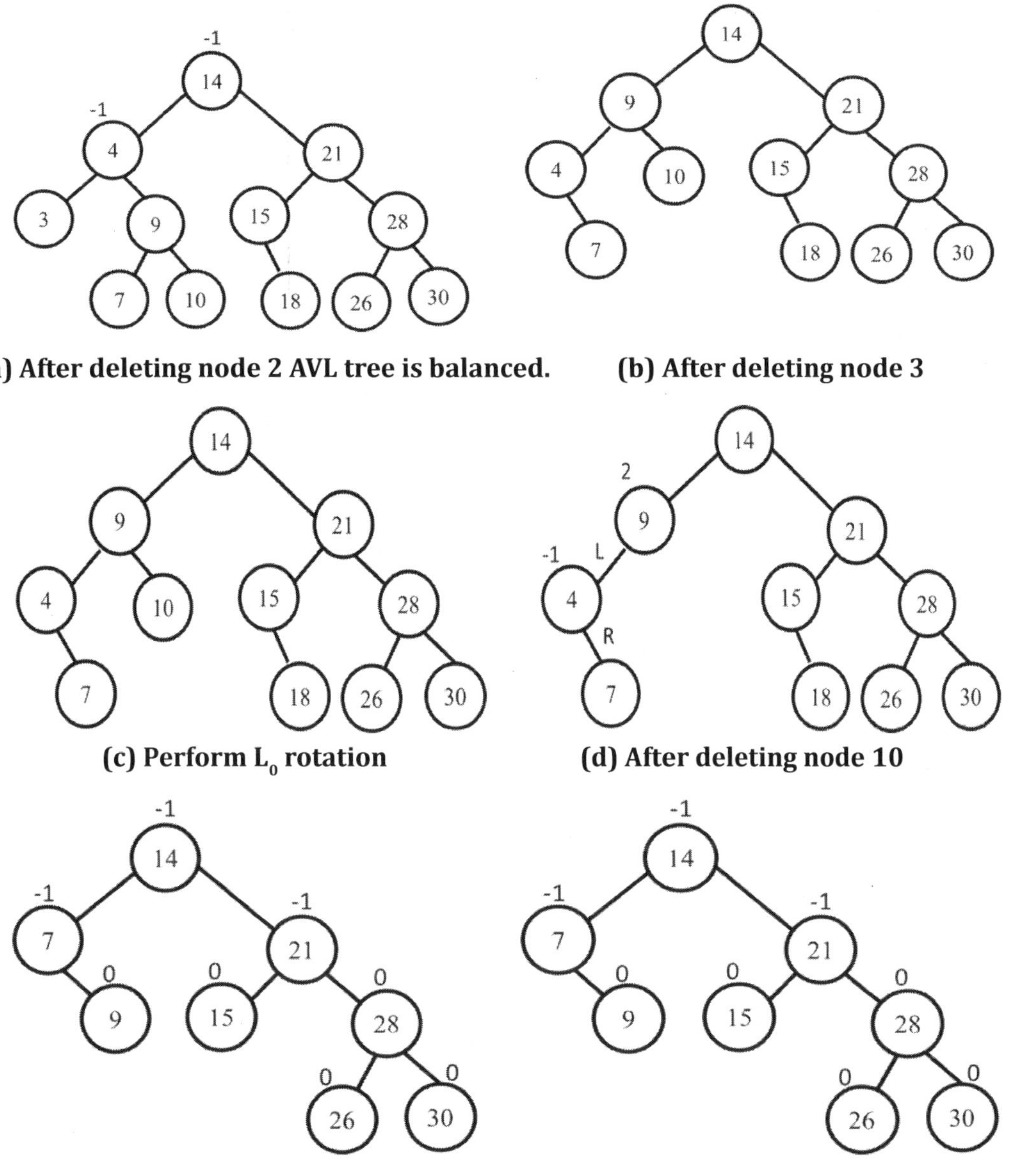

(a) After deleting node 2 AVL tree is balanced. **(b) After deleting node 3**

(c) Perform L_0 rotation **(d) After deleting node 10**

(e) Perform R_{-1} rotation **(f) After deleting nodes 18 and 4**

Figure 5.37: AVL Deletion Part 1

LHS child of node 9 is node 4 whose balance factor is -1. This is depicted in Figure 5.37 (d). Hence, R_{-1} type of deletion (LR rotate) is applied on the AVL tree which is shown in Figure 5.37 (e).

Now, node 18 is deleted. After deleting node 18, AVL tree is balanced. Similarly, the balancing remains same with the deletion of node 4 [Refer to Figure 5.36 (f)].

Next leaf node 9 is directly deleted as visualized in Figure 5.38 (a). Ancestors of node 9 are node 7 and node 14, out of which node 14 has balance factor of -2. Balance factor of RHS child of node 14 is -1. Hence, L_{-1} type of deletion (RR rotate) is applied on the AVL tree which is shown in Figure 5.38 (b).

Next internal node 14 is deleted. Child of node 14 is node 7 (inorder predecessor i.e maximum element in left subtree). Node 14 is replaced by node 7 as shown in Figure 5.38 (c). Then, internal node 7 is also deleted. Node 7 has no inorder predecessor but has closest node as node 15. So node 7 is replaced by node 15 as shown in Figure 5.38 (d).

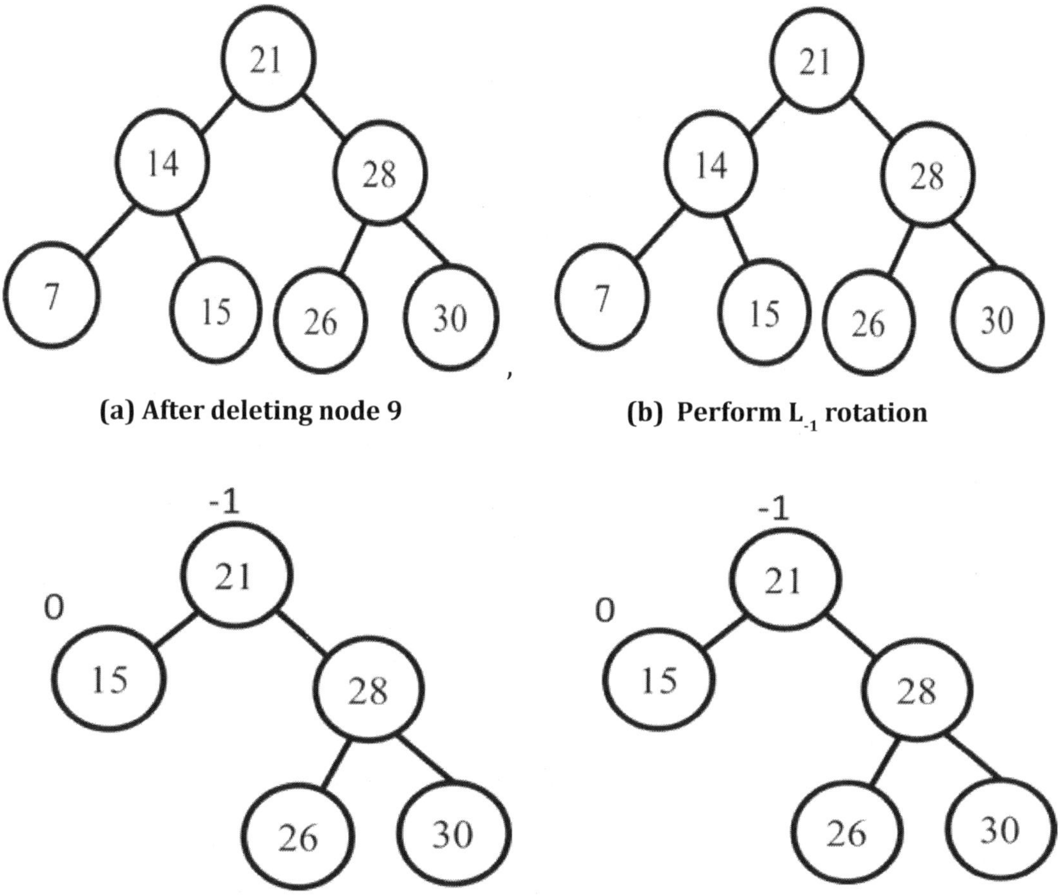

(a) After deleting node 9 **(b) Perform L_{-1} rotation**

(c) After deleting node 14 **(d) After deleting node 7**

Figure 5.38: AVL Deletion Part 2

Leaf node 15 is directly deleted. Its ancestor is node 21 whose balance factor is -2. Deletion of node 15 is from LHS of node 21. Hence, this is a L type of deletion. This is shown in Figure 5.39 (a). Balance factor of RHS child of node 21 is 0. Therefore, L_0 type of deletion (RR rotate) is applied on the tree.

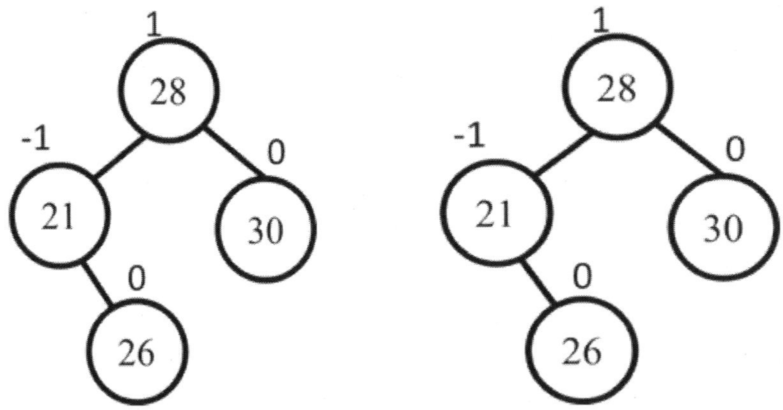

(a) After deleting node (b) Perform L_0 rotation

Figure 5.39: AVL Balanced tree after Deletion

Note: If we want to delete root node from an AVL tree, then deletion will occur in the same way nodes are deleted in binary search tree. The root node gets replaced by either of its inorder predecessor (maximum element in left subtree) or successor (minimum element in right subtree).

Programming Exercise 5.4

Write a program to implement a AVL tree and perform insertion, deletion and searching in the tree.

```
// Function to create a new node
Node* createNode(int key) {
   Node* node = new Node();
   node->key = key;
   node->left = node->right = nullptr;
   node->height = 1;
   return node;
}
// Get Balance Factor
int getBalanceFactor(Node* node) {
   return (node == nullptr) ? 0 : getHeight(node->left) - getHeight(node->right);
}
// Right Rotate
Node* rightRotate(Node* y) {
   Node* x = y->left;
   Node* T2 = x->right;
   x->right = y;
   y->left = T2;
```

```
    y->height = max(getHeight(y->left), getHeight(y->right)) + 1;
    x->height = max(getHeight(x->left), getHeight(x->right)) + 1;
    return x;
}
// Left Rotate
Node* leftRotate(Node* x) {
    Node* y = x->right;
    Node* T2 = y->left; y->left = x;
    x->right = T2;
    x->height = max(getHeight(x->left), getHeight(x->right)) + 1;
    y->height = max(getHeight(y->left), getHeight(y->right)) + 1;
    return y;
}
// Find Minimum Value Node
Node* minValueNode(Node* node) {
    Node* current = node;
    while (current->left != nullptr)
        current = current->left;
    return current;
}

// Delete a node
Node* deleteNode(Node* root, int key) {
    if (root == nullptr)
        return root;
    if (key < root->key)
        root->left = deleteNode(root->left, key);
    else if (key > root->key)
        root->right = deleteNode(root->right, key);
    else {
        if ((root->left == nullptr) || (root->right == nullptr)) {
            Node* temp = root->left ? root->left : root->right;
            if (temp == nullptr) {
                temp = root;
                root = nullptr;
```

```
            } else
                *root = *temp;
            delete temp;
        } else {
            Node* temp = minValueNode(root->right);
            root->key = temp->key;
            root->right = deleteNode(root->right, temp->key);
        }
    }
    if (root == nullptr)
        return root;
    root->height = 1 + max(getHeight(root->left), getHeight(root->right));
    int balance = getBalanceFactor(root);
    if (balance > 1 && getBalanceFactor(root->left) >= 0)
        return rightRotate(root);
    if (balance > 1 && getBalanceFactor(root->left) < 0) {
        root->left = leftRotate(root->left);
        return rightRotate(root);
    }
    if (balance < -1 && getBalanceFactor(root->right) <= 0)
        return leftRotate(root);
    if (balance < -1 && getBalanceFactor(root->right) > 0) {
        root->right = rightRotate(root->right);
        return leftRotate(root);
    }
    return root;
}
// Search for a key
bool search(Node* root, int key) {
    if (root == nullptr)
        return false;
    if (root->key == key)
        return true;
    if (key < root->key)
        return search(root->left, key);
```

```
    return search(root->right, key);
}
// Inorder Traversal
void inorder(Node* root) {
    if (root != nullptr) {
        inorder(root->left);
        cout << root->key << " ";
        inorder(root->right);
    }
}
// Menu-driven program
int main() {
    Node* root = nullptr;
    int choice, value;
    do {
        cout << "\nAVL Tree Operations:\n";
        cout << "1. Insert\n2. Delete\n3. Search\n4. Display (Inorder)\n5. Exit\n";
        cout << "Enter your choice: ";
        cin >> choice;
        switch (choice) {
            case 1:
                cout << "Enter value to insert: ";
                cin >> value;
                root = insert(root, value);
                break;
            case 2:
                cout << "Enter value to delete: ";
                cin >> value;
                root = deleteNode(root, value);
                break;
            case 3:
                cout << "Enter value to search: ";
                cin >> value;
                cout << (search(root, value) ? "Found\n" : "Not Found\n");
                break;
```

```
            case 4:
                cout << "AVL Tree (Inorder): ";
                inorder(root);
                cout << "\n";
                break;
            case 5:
                cout << "Exiting...\n";
                break;
            default:
                cout << "Invalid choice!\n";
        }
    } while (choice != 5);
    return 0;
}
```

OUTPUT:

```
AVL Tree Operations:
1. Insert
2. Delete
3. Search
4. Display (Inorder)
5. Exit
Enter your choice: 1
Enter value to insert: 5

AVL Tree Operations:
1. Insert
2. Delete
3. Search
4. Display (Inorder)
5. Exit
Enter your choice: 1
Enter value to insert: 76
```

AVL Tree Operations:
1. Insert
2. Delete
3. Search
4. Display (Inorder)
5. Exit
Enter your choice: 1
Enter value to insert: 4

AVL Tree Operations:
1. Insert
2. Delete
3. Search
4. Display (Inorder)
5. Exit
Enter your choice: 1
Enter value to insert: 8

AVL Tree Operations:
1. Insert
2. Delete
3. Search
4. Display (Inorder)
5. Exit
Enter your choice: 1
Enter value to insert: 6

AVL Tree Operations:
1. Insert
2. Delete
3. Search
4. Display (Inorder)
5. Exit
Enter your choice: 4
AVL Tree (Inorder): 4 5 6 8 76

5.7 B Tree

A B-tree is a tree data structure that keeps data sorted and allows searches, insertions, and deletions in logarithmic amortized time. Unlike self-balancing binary search trees, it is optimized for systems that read and write large blocks of data. It is most commonly used in database and file systems.

Important properties of a B-tree:

- B-tree nodes have many more than two children.
- A B-tree node may contain more than just a single element.

The set formulation of the B-tree rules: Every B-tree depends on a positive constant integer called MINIMUM, which is used to determine how many elements are held in a single node.

Rule 1: The root can have as few as one element (or even no elements if it also has no children); every other node has at least MINIMUM elements.

Rule 2: The maximum number of elements in a node is twice the value of MINIMUM.

Rule 3: The elements of each B-tree node are stored in a partially filled array, sorted from the smallest element (at index 0) to the largest element (at the final used position of the array).

Rule 4: The number of subtrees below a nonleaf node is always one more than the number of elements in the node.

- Subtree 0, subtree 1, ...

Rule 5: For any nonleaf node:

- An element at index *i* is greater than all the elements in subtree number *i* of the node, and
- An element at index *i* is less than all the elements in subtree number *i* + 1 of the node.

Rule 6: Every leaf in a B-tree has the same depth. Thus it ensures that a B-tree avoids the problem of a unbalanced tree.

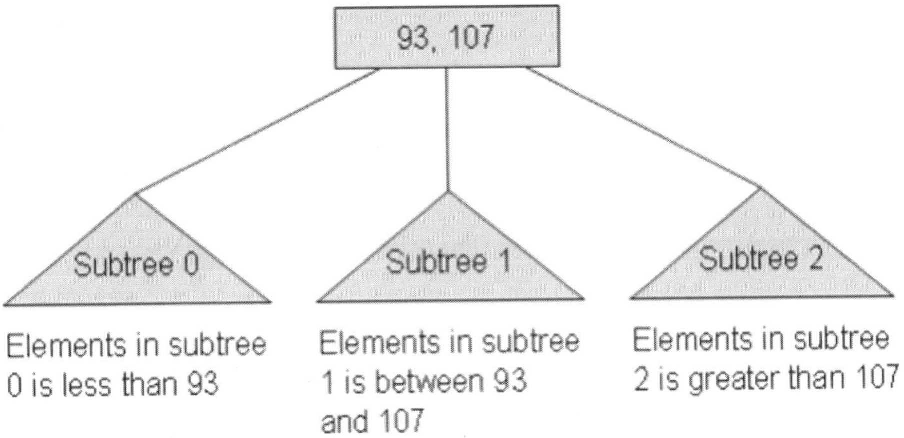

Figure 5.40: A B tree

5.7.1 Basic operations on B-trees

In this section, we present the details of the operations B-TREE-SEARCH, B-TREE-CREATE, and B-TREE-INSERT. In these procedures, we adopt two conventions:

The root of the B-tree is always in main memory, so that a DISK-READ on the root is never required; a DISK-WRITE of the root is required, however, whenever the root node is changed.

Any nodes that are passed as parameters must already have had a DISK-READ operation performed on them.

The procedures we present are all "one-pass" algorithms that proceed downward from the root of the tree, without having to back up.

5.7.2 Searching a B-tree

Searching a B-tree is much like searching a binary search tree, except that instead of making a binary, or "two-way," branching decision at each node, we make a multiway branching decision according to the number of the node's children. More precisely, at each internal node x, we make an $(n[x] + 1)$-way branching decision.

B-TREE-SEARCH is a straightforward generalization of the TREE-SEARCH procedure defined for binary search trees. B-TREE-SEARCH takes as input a pointer to the root node x of a subtree and a key k to be searched for in that subtree. The top-level call is thus of the form B-TREE-SEARCH($root[T]$, k). If k is in the B-tree, B-TREE-SEARCH returns the ordered pair (y,i) consisting of a node y and an index i such that $key_i[y] = k$. Otherwise, the value NIL is returned.

```
B-TREE-SEARCH(x, k)
1 i←1
2 while i ≤ n[x] and k ≥ key_i[x]
3    do i ← i + 1
4 if i ≤ n[x] and k = key_i[x]
5    then return (x, i)
6 if leaf [x]
7    then return NIL
8    else DISK-READ(c_i[x])
9         return B-TREE-SEARCH(c_i[x], k)
```

Using a linear-search procedure, lines 1-3 find the smallest i such that k keyi[x], or else they set i to n[x] + 1. Lines 4-5 check to see if we have now discovered the key, returning if we have. Lines 6-9 either terminate the search unsuccessfully (if x is a leaf) or recurse to search the appropriate subtree of x, after performing the necessary DISK-READ on that child.

As in the TREE-SEARCH procedure for binary search trees, the nodes encountered during the recursion form a path downward from the root of the tree. The number of disk pages accessed by B-TREE-SEARCH is therefore $\Theta(h) = \Theta(\log_t n)$, where h is the height of the B-tree and n is the number of keys in the B-tree. Since $n[x] < 2t$, the time taken by the **while** loop of lines 2-3 within each node is $O(t)$, and the total CPU time is $O(th) = O(t \log_t n)$.

5.7.3 Creating an empty B-tree

To build a B-tree T, we first use B-TREE-CREATE to create an empty root node and then call B-TREE-INSERT to add new keys. Both of these procedures use an auxiliary procedure ALLOCATE-NODE, which allocates one disk page to be used as a new node in $O(1)$ time. We can assume that a node created by ALLOCATE-NODE requires no DISK-READ, since there is as yet no useful information stored on the disk for that node.

B-TREE-CREATE(*T*)

```
x ←ALLOCATE-NODE()
leaf[x] ← TRUE
n[x] ← 0
DISK-WRITE(x)
root[T] ← x
```

B-TREE-CREATE requires $O(1)$ disk operations and $O(1)$ CPU time.

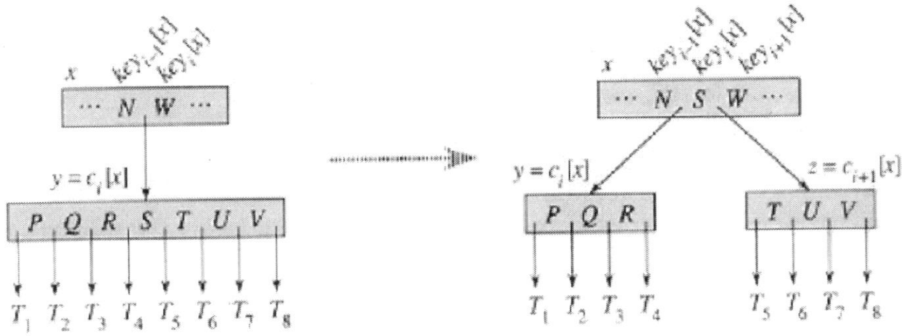

5.7.4 Splitting a node in a B-tree

Inserting a key into a B-tree is significantly more complicated than inserting a key into a binary search tree. A fundamental operation used during insertion is the ***splitting*** of a full node *y* (having $2t - 1$ keys) around its ***median key*** $key^t[y]$ into two nodes having $t - 1$ keys each. The median key moves up into *y*'s parent--which must be nonfull prior to the splitting of *y*--to identify the dividing point between the two new trees; if *y* has no parent, then the tree grows in height by one. Splitting, then, is the means by which the tree grows.

The procedure B-TREE-SPLIT-CHILD takes as input a *nonfull* internal node *x* (assumed to be in main memory), an index *i*, and a node *y* such that $y = c_i[x]$ is a *full* child of *x*. The procedure then splits this child in two and adjusts *x* so that it now has an additional child.

The full node *y* is split about its median key *S*, which is moved up into *y*'s parent node *x*. Those keys in *y* that are greater than the median key are placed in a new node *z*, which is made a new child of *x*.

B-TREE-SPLIT-CHILD(*x,i,y*)

```
z ←ALLOCATE-NODE()
leaf[z] ←leaf[y]
n[z] ← t - 1
for j ←1 to t - 1
    do key^j[z] ← key^{j+t}[y]
if not leaf [y]
```

```
7     then for j ←1 to t
8              do c_j[z] ←c_{j+t}[y]
9  n[y] ←t - 1
10 for j ← n[x] + 1 downto i + 1
11      do c_{j+1}[x] ← c_j[x]
12 c_i+1[x] ← z
13 for j ← n[x] downto i
14      do key_{j+1}[x] ← key_j[x]
15 key_i[x] ← key_t[y]
16 n[x] ← n[x] + 1
17 DISK-WRITE(y)
18 DISK-WRITE(z)
19 DISK-WRITE(x)
```

B-TREE-SPLIT-CHILD works by straightforward "cutting and pasting. " Here, *y* is the *i*th child of *x* and is the node being split. Node *y* originally has 2*t* - 1 children but is reduced to *t* - 1 children by this operation. Node *z* "adopts" the *t* - 1 largest children of *y*, and *z* becomes a new child of *x*, positioned just after y in *x*'s table of children. The median key of *y* moves up to become the key in *x* that separates *y* and *z*.

Lines 1-8 create node *z* and give it the larger *t* - 1 keys and corresponding *t* children of *y*. Line 9 adjusts the key count for *y*. Finally, lines 10-16 insert *z* as a child of *x*, move the median key from *y* up to *x* in order to separate *y* from *z*, and adjust *x*'s key count. Lines 17-19 write out all modified disk pages. The CPU time used by B-TREE-SPLIT-CHILD is $\Theta(t)$, due to the loops on lines 4-5 and 7-8.

5.7.5 Inserting a key into a B-tree

Inserting a key *k* into a B-tree *T* of height *h* is done in a single pass down the tree, requiring *O(h)* disk accesses. The CPU time required is $O(th) = O(t \log_t n)$. The B-TREE-INSERT procedure uses B-TREE-SPLIT-CHILD to guarantee that the recursion never descends to a full node.

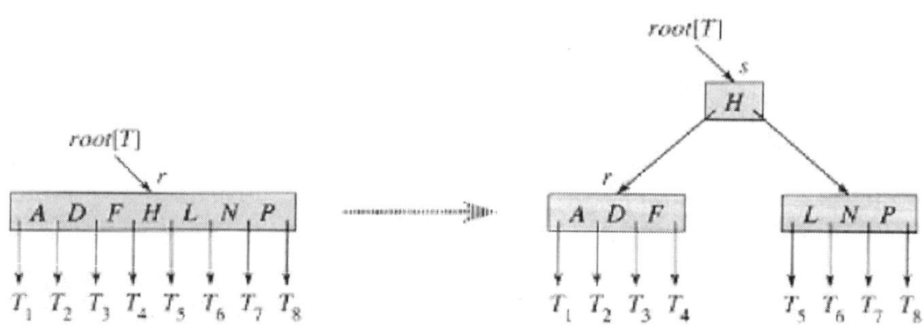

B-TREE-INSERT(*T*,*k*)

```
r ← root[T]
if n[r] = 2t - 1
```

```
3   then s ← ALLOCATE-NODE()
4        root[T] ← s
5        leaf[s] ← FALSE
6        n[s] ← 0
7        c^1[s] ← r
8        B-TREE-SPLIT-CHILD(s,1,r)
9        B-TREE-INSERT-NONFULL(s,k)
10 else B-TREE-INSERT-NONFULL(r,k)
```

Lines 3-9 handle the case in which the root node *r* is full: the root is split and a new node *s* (having two children) becomes the root. Splitting the root is the only way to increase the height of a B-tree. Unlike a binary search tree, a B-tree increases in height at the top instead of at the bottom. The procedure finishes by calling B-TREE-INSERT-NONFULL to perform the insertion of key *k* in the tree rooted at the nonfull root node. B-TREE-INSERT-NONFULL recurses as necessary down the tree, at all times guaranteeing that the node to which it recurses is not full by calling B-TREE-SPLIT-CHILD as necessary.

The auxiliary recursive procedure B-TREE-INSERT-NONFULL inserts key *k* into node x, which is assumed to be nonfull when the procedure is called. The operation of B-TREE-INSERT and the recursive operation of B-TREE-INSERT-NONFULL guarantee that this assumption is true.

B-TREE-INSERT-NONFULL(*x*,*k*)

```
1 i ← n[x]
2 if leaf[x]
3    then while i ≥1 and k < key^i[x]
4           do key_i+1 [x] ←key^i[x]
5              i ←i - 1
6         key_i+1[x] ← k
7         n[x] ← n[x] + 1
8         DISK-WRITE(x)
9 else while i ≥ 1 and k < key^i[x]
10           do i ≥ i - 1
11       i ≥i + 1
12       DISK-READ(c^i[x])
13       if n[c^i[x]] = 2t - 1
14         then B-TREE-SPLIT-CHILD(x,i,c^i[x])
15              if k > key^i[x]
16                then i ← i + 1
17       B-TREE-INSERT-NONFULL(c^i[x],k)
```

The B-TREE-INSERT-NONFULL procedure works as follows. Lines 3-8 handle the case in which *x* is a leaf node by inserting key *k* into *x*. If *x* is not a leaf node, then we must insert *k* into the appropriate leaf node in the subtree rooted at internal node *x*. In this case, lines 9-11 determine the child of *x* to which the recursion descends. Line 13 detects whether the recursion would descend to a full child, in which case line 14 uses B-TREE-SPLIT-CHILD to split that child into two nonfull children, and lines 15-16 determine which of the two children is now the correct one to descend to. (Note that there is no need for a DISK-READ($c_i[x]$) after line 16 increments *i*, since the recursion will descend in this case to a child that was just created by B-TREE-SPLIT-CHILD.) The net effect of lines 13-16 is thus to guarantee that the procedure never recurses to a full node. Line 17 then recurses to insert *k* into the appropriate subtree.

Let us understand the algorithm with an example tree of minimum degree 't' as 3 and a sequence of integers 10, 20, 30, 40, 50, 60, 70, 80 and 90 in an initially empty B-Tree.

Initially root is NULL. Let us first insert 10.

Insert 10

Let us now insert 20, 30, 40 and 50. They all will be inserted in root because maximum number of keys a node can accommodate is 2*t – 1 which is 5.

Insert 20, 30, 40 and 50

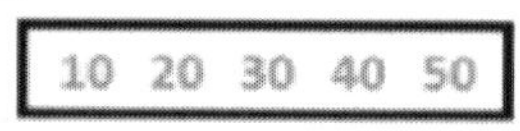

Let us now insert 60. Since root node is full, it will first split into two, then 60 will be inserted into the appropriate child.

Insert 60

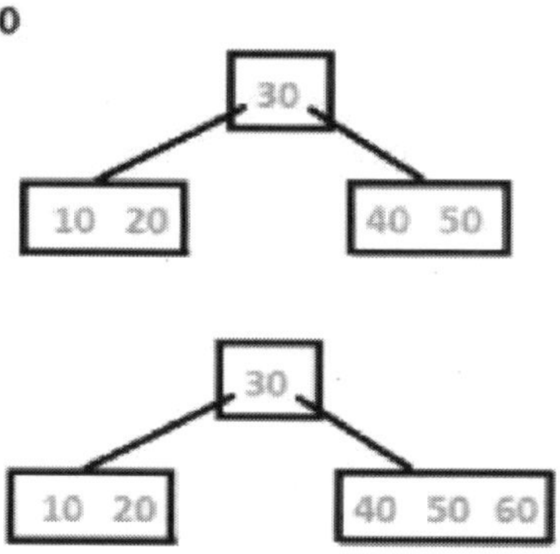

Let us now insert 70 and 80. These new keys will be inserted into the appropriate leaf without any split.

Insert 70 and 80

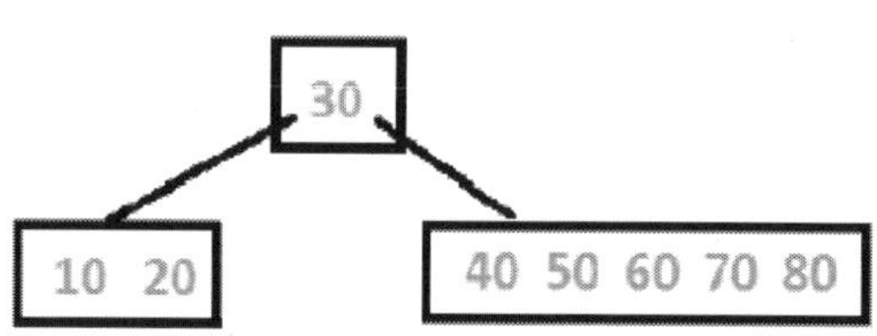

Let us now insert 90. This insertion will cause a split. The middle key will go up to the parent.

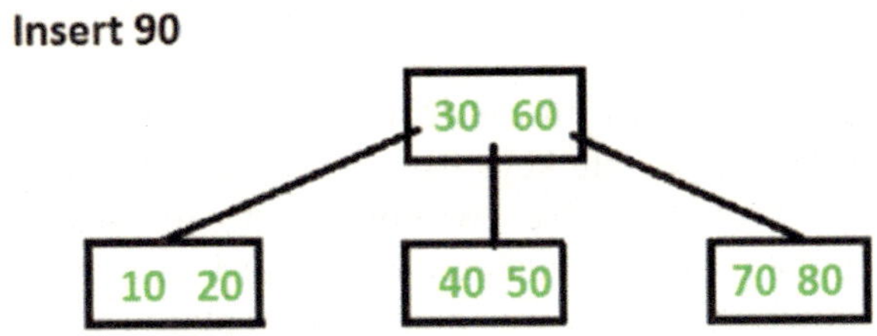

5.7.6 Deleting a key from a B-tree

Deletion from a B-tree is analogous to insertion but a little more complicated. We sketch how it works instead of presenting the complete pseudocode.

Assume that procedure B-TREE-DELETE is asked to delete the key k from the subtree rooted at x. This procedure is structured to guarantee that whenever B-TREE-DELETE is called recursively on a node x, the number of keys in x is at least the minimum degree t. Note that this condition requires one more key than the minimum required by the usual B-tree conditions, so that sometimes a key may have to be moved into a child node before recursion descends to that child. This strengthened condition allows us to delete a key from the tree in one downward pass without having to "back up" (with one exception, which we'll explain). The following specification for deletion from a B-tree should be interpreted with the understanding that if it ever happens that the root node x becomes an internal node having no keys, then x is deleted and x's only child $c_1[x]$ becomes the new root of the tree, decreasing the height of the tree by one and preserving the property that the root of the tree contains at least one key (unless the tree is empty).

Various cases of deleting keys from a B-tree:

1. If the key k is in node x and x is a leaf, delete the key k from x.
2. If the key k is in node x and x is an internal node, do the following.
   a. If the child y that precedes k in node x has at least t keys, then find the predecessor k' of k in the subtree rooted at y. Recursively delete k', and replace k by k' in x. (Finding k' and deleting it can be performed in a single downward pass.)
   b. Symmetrically, if the child z that follows k in node x has at least t keys, then find the successor k' of k in the subtree rooted at z. Recursively delete k', and replace k by k' in x. (Finding k' and deleting it can be performed in a single downward pass.)
   c. Otherwise, if both y and z have only t- 1 keys, merge k and all of z into y, so that x loses both k and the pointer to z, and y now contains $2t$ - 1 keys. Then, free z and recursively delete k from y.
3. If the key k is not present in internal node x, determine the root $c_i[x]$ of the appropriate subtree that must contain k, if k is in the tree at all. If $c_i[x]$ has only t - 1 keys, execute step 3a or 3b as necessary to guarantee that we descend to a node containing at least t keys. Then, finish by recursing on the appropriate child of x.
   a. If $c_i[x]$ has only t - 1 keys but has a sibling with t keys, give $c_i[x]$ an extra key by moving a key from x down into $c_i[x]$, moving a key from $c_i[x]$'s immediate left or right sibling up into x, and moving the appropriate child from the sibling into $c_i[x]$.

b. If $c_i[x]$ and all of $c_i[x]$'s siblings have t - 1 keys, merge c_i with one sibling, which involves moving a key from x down into the new merged node to become the median key for that node.

Since most of the keys in a B-tree are in the leaves, we may expect that in practice, deletion operations are most often used to delete keys from leaves. The B-TREE-DELETE procedure then acts in one downward pass through the tree, without having to back up. When deleting a key in an internal node, however, the procedure makes a downward pass through the tree but may have to return to the node from which the key was deleted to replace the key with its predecessor or successor (cases 2a and 2b).

Although this procedure seems complicated, it involves only $O(h)$ disk operations for a B-tree of height h, since only $O(1)$ calls to DISK-READ and DISK-WRITE are made between recursive invocations of the procedure. The CPU time required is $O(th) = O(t \log_t n)$.

The following example explains the deletion process in a B tree.

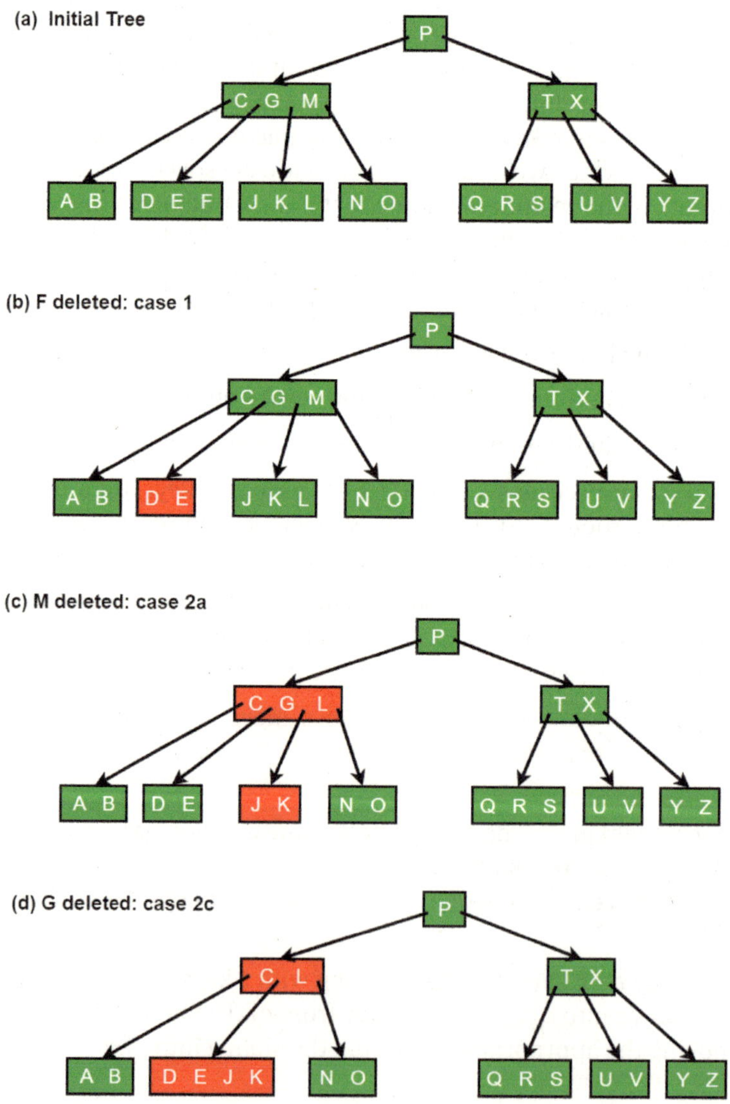

Programming Exercise 5.5

Write a program to implement a B tree.

```
#include <iostream>
using namespace std;
class BTreeNode {
public:
    int *keys;
    int t;
    BTreeNode **C;
    int n;
    bool leaf;
    BTreeNode(int t, bool leaf);
    void traverse();
    BTreeNode *search(int k);
    void insertNonFull(int k);
    void splitChild(int i, BTreeNode *y);
    int findKey(int k);
    void remove(int k);
    void removeFromLeaf(int idx);
    void removeFromNonLeaf(int idx);
    int getPred(int idx);
    int getSucc(int idx);
    void fill(int idx);
    void borrowFromPrev(int idx);
    void borrowFromNext(int idx);
    void merge(int idx);
    friend class BTree;
};
class BTree {
public:
    BTreeNode *root;
    int t;
    BTree(int t) { root = nullptr; this->t = t; }
    void traverse() { if (root) root->traverse(); }
    BTreeNode* search(int k) {return (root ==nullptr)?nullptr:root->search(k); }
```

```
    void insert(int k);
    void remove(int k);
};
BTreeNode::BTreeNode(int t1, bool leaf1) {
    t = t1;
    leaf = leaf1;
    keys = new int[2*t-1];
    C = new BTreeNode *[2*t];
    n = 0;
}
void BTree::insert(int k) {
    if (!root) {
        root = new BTreeNode(t, true);
        root->keys[0] = k;
        root->n = 1;
    } else {
        if (root->n == 2*t-1) {
            BTreeNode *s = new BTreeNode(t, false);
            s->C[0] = root;
            s->splitChild(0, root);
            int i = (s->keys[0] < k) ? 1 : 0;
            s->C[i]->insertNonFull(k);
            root = s;
        } else root->insertNonFull(k);
    }
}
void BTreeNode::insertNonFull(int k) {
    int i = n - 1;
    if (leaf) {
        while (i >= 0 && keys[i] > k) {
            keys[i+1] = keys[i];
            i--;
        }
        keys[i+1] = k;
        n++;
```

```
  } else {
    while (i >= 0 && keys[i] > k) i--;
    if (C[i+1]->n == 2*t-1) {
      splitChild(i+1, C[i+1]);
      if (keys[i+1] < k) i++;
    }
    C[i+1]->insertNonFull(k);
  }
}
void BTreeNode::splitChild(int i, BTreeNode *y) {
  BTreeNode *z = new BTreeNode(y->t, y->leaf);
  z->n = t - 1;
  for (int j = 0; j < t-1; j++)
    z->keys[j] = y->keys[j+t];
  if (!y->leaf)
    for (int j = 0; j < t; j++)
      z->C[j] = y->C[j+t];
  y->n = t - 1;
  for (int j = n; j >= i+1; j--)
    C[j+1] = C[j];
  C[i+1] = z;
  for (int j = n-1; j >= i; j--)
    keys[j+1] = keys[j];
  keys[i] = y->keys[t-1];
  n++;
}
  for (int j = n; j >= i+1; j--)
    C[j+1] = C[j];
  C[i+1] = z;
  for (int j = n-1; j >= i; j--)
    keys[j+1] = keys[j];
  keys[i] = y->keys[t-1];
  n++;
}
void BTreeNode::traverse() {
```

```
    int i;
    for (i = 0; i < n; i++) {
        if (!leaf) C[i]->traverse();
        cout << " " << keys[i];
    }
    if (!leaf) C[i]->traverse();
}
BTreeNode *BTreeNode::search(int k) {
    int i = 0;
    while (i < n && k > keys[i]) i++;
    if (keys[i] == k) return this;
    if (leaf) return nullptr;
    return C[i]->search(k);
}
void BTree::remove(int k) {
    if (!root) {
        cout << "The tree is empty\n";
        return;
    }
    root->remove(k);
    if (root->n == 0) {
        BTreeNode *tmp = root;
        root = (root->leaf) ? nullptr : root->C[0];
        delete tmp;
    }
}

void BTreeNode::remove(int k) {
    cout << "Deletion is not yet implemented!\n";
}
int main() {
    BTree t(3);
    int choice, key;
    do {
        cout << "\n1. Insert\n2. Delete\n3. Search\n4. Traverse\n5. Exit\nEnter choice: ";
```

```
        cin >> choice;
        switch(choice) {
            case 1: cout << "Enter key: "; cin >> key; t.insert(key); break;
            case 2: cout << "Enter key: "; cin >> key; t.remove(key); break;
            case 3: cout << "Enter key: "; cin >> key;
                if (t.search(key)) cout << "Key found\n";
                else cout << "Key not found\n";
                break;
            case 4: cout << "Traversal: "; t.traverse(); cout << endl; break;
            case 5: cout << "Exiting...\n"; break;
            default: cout << "Invalid choice\n";
        }
    } while(choice != 5);
    return 0;
}
```

OUTPUT:

```
1. Insert
2. Delete
3. Search
4. Traverse
5. Exit
Enter choice: 1
Enter key: 5

1. Insert
2. Delete
3. Search
4. Traverse
5. Exit
Enter choice: 1
Enter key: 7

1. Insert
2. Delete
3. Search
```

4. Traverse
5. Exit
Enter choice: 1
Enter key: 3

1. Insert
2. Delete
3. Search
4. Traverse
5. Exit
Enter choice: 1
Enter key: 9
1. Insert
2. Delete
3. Search
4. Traverse
5. Exit
Enter choice: 4
Traversal: 3 5 7 9

5.8 Heap Tree

A binary heap is a complete binary tree which satisfies the heap ordering property. The ordering can be one of two types:

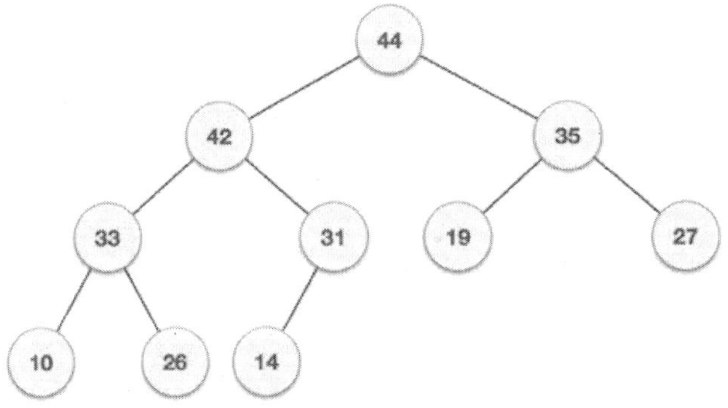

Figure 5.41: Max Heap

Max -Heap property: the value of each node is less than or equal to the value of its parent, with the maximum-value element at the root.

Figure 5.41 shows an example of max-heap

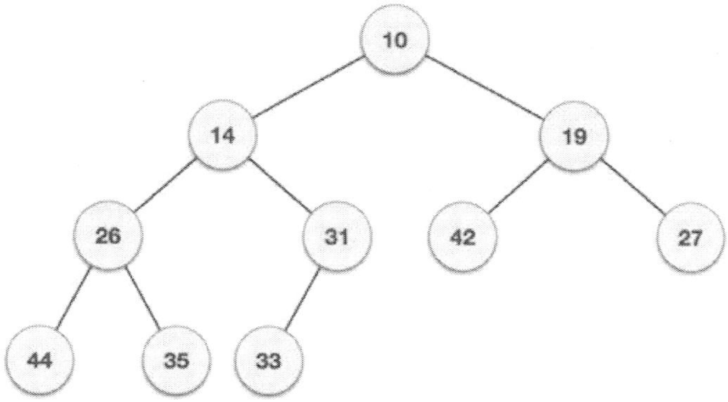

Figure 5.42 is an example of min-heap

Min-Heap property: the value of each node is greater than or equal to the value of its parent, with the minimum-value element at the root.

5.8.1 Array Implementation of Heap

A complete binary tree can be uniquely represented by storing its level order traversal in an array. Consider k-th element of the array, the

its left child is located at 2*k index

its right child is located at 2*k+1. index

its parent is located at k/2 index.

5.8.2 Operations

Insert

The new element is initially appended to the end of the heap (as the last element of the array). The heap property is repaired by comparing the added element with its parent and moving the added element up a level (swapping positions with the parent). The comparison is repeated until the parent is larger than or equal to the percolating element.

DeleteMin

The minimum element can be found at the root, which is the first element of the array. We remove the root and replace it with the last element of the heap and then restore the heap property by percolating down. Similar to insertion, the worst-case runtime is O(log n).

Algorithm : Heap Insertion (Max Heap)

Input: A max heap H and a new element x to be inserted.

Output: A valid max heap with x inserted.

1. Insert x at the last position of the heap (i.e., append it to the heap array).
2. Let i be the index of the newly inserted element.
3. Repeat until i is the root (i.e., i > 0):
   a. Find the parent index p = (i - 1) / 2 (integer division).
   b. If H[p] < H[i], swap H[p] and H[i].

c. Set i = p (move up to the parent).

d. Otherwise, stop (heap property is satisfied).

4. End.

Algorithm : Heap Insertion (Min Heap)

Input: A min heap H and a new element x to be inserted.

Output: A valid min heap with x inserted.

1. Insert x at the last position of the heap (i.e., append it to the heap array).

2. Let i be the index of the newly inserted element.

3. Repeat until i is the root (i.e., i > 0):

a. Find the parent index p = (i - 1) / 2 (integer division).

b. If H[p] > H[i], swap H[p] and H[i].

c. Set i = p (move up to the parent).

d. Otherwise, stop (heap property is satisfied).

4. End.

Example: Build a max heap from the given set of numbers: 32, 15, 20, 30, 12, 25, and 16.

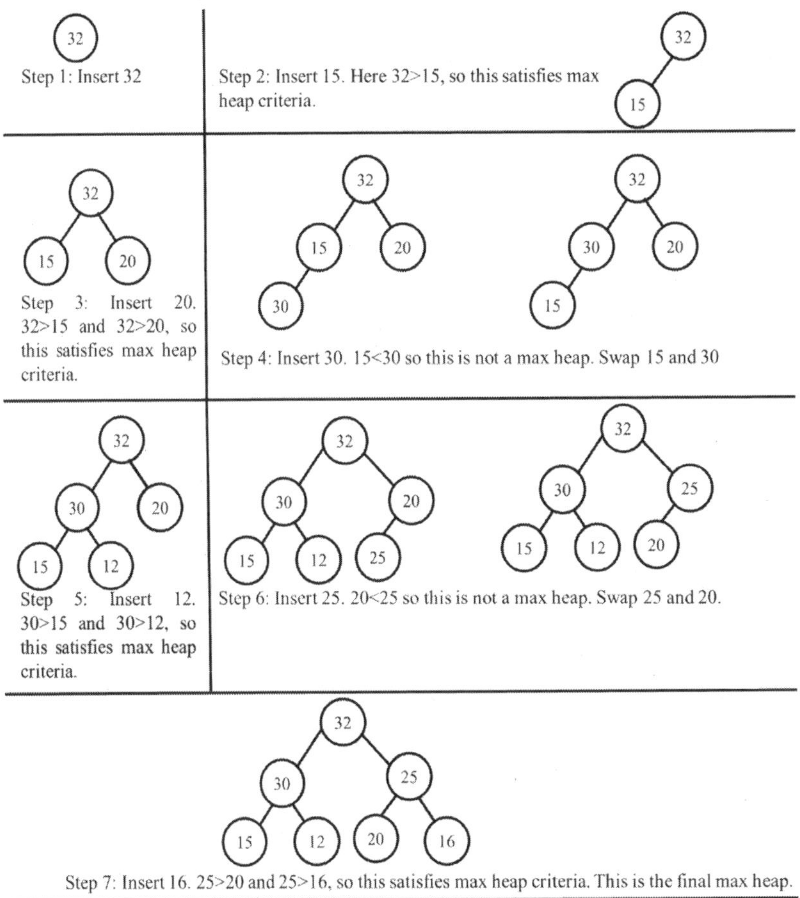

Algorithm : Heap Deletion (Max Heap)

Input: A max heap H of size n.

Output: A valid max heap after removing the maximum element (root).

1. Delete the root (first element of the heap).
2. Replace the root with the last element of the heap.
3. Remove the last element from the heap.
4. Heapify-down to restore the max heap property:
    a. Let i be the index of the root (0).
    b. Find the largest among H[i], left child H[2i + 1], and right child H[2i + 2].
    c. If the largest is not H[i], swap H[i] with the largest child.
    d. Set i to the index of the swapped child.
    e. Repeat until the heap property is satisfied or i reaches a leaf node.
5. End.

Algorithm: Heap Deletion (Min Heap)

Input: A min heap H of size n.

Output: A valid min heap after removing the minimum element (root).

1. Delete the root (first element of the heap).
2. Replace the root with the last element of the heap.
3. Remove the last element from the heap.
4. Heapify-down to restore the min heap property:
    a. Let i be the index of the root (0).
    b. Find the smallest among H[i], left child H[2i + 1], and right child H[2i + 2].
    c. If the smallest is not H[i], swap H[i] with the smallest child.
    d. Set i to the index of the swapped child.
    e. Repeat until the heap property is satisfied or i reaches a leaf node.
5. End.

Example: Consider the max heap shown below and delete nodes 25 and 16.

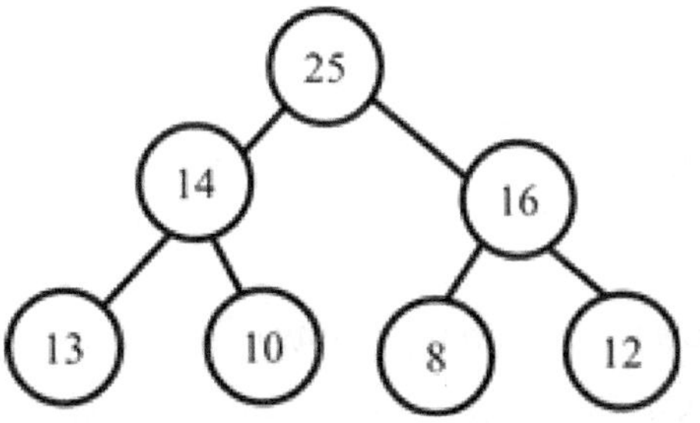

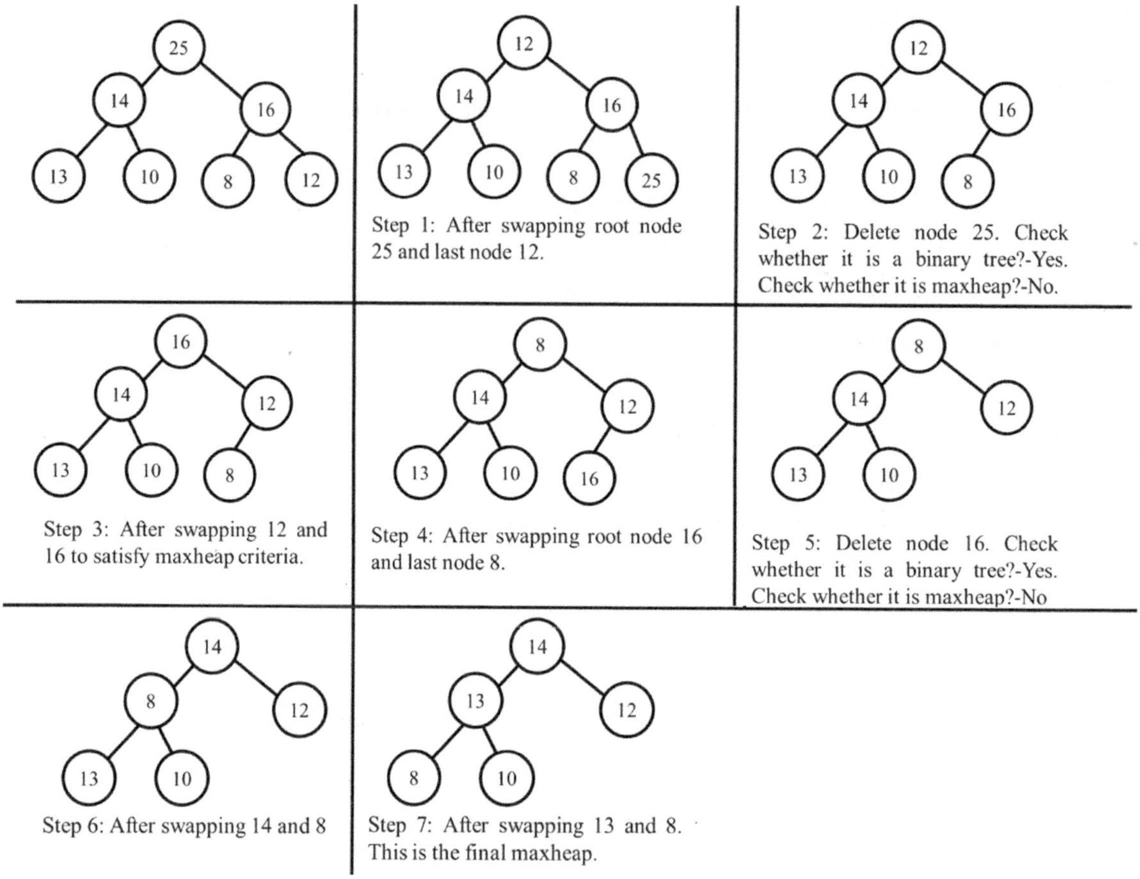

Step 1: After swapping root node 25 and last node 12.

Step 2: Delete node 25. Check whether it is a binary tree?-Yes. Check whether it is maxheap?-No.

Step 3: After swapping 12 and 16 to satisfy maxheap criteria.

Step 4: After swapping root node 16 and last node 8.

Step 5: Delete node 16. Check whether it is a binary tree?-Yes. Check whether it is maxheap?-No

Step 6: After swapping 14 and 8

Step 7: After swapping 13 and 8. This is the final maxheap.

5.8.3 Applications of Heap data structure

There are two main applications of heap data structure:

1. Priority Queue
2. Heap Sort

Priority Queue

In a priority queue, each element has a priority; when an element is removed it must be the element on the queue with the highest priority. A very efficient way to implement a priority queue is with a heap ordered by priority - each node is higher priority than everything below it. The highest priority element, then, is at the top of the heap.

Heap Sort

One major application of Heap is sorting. HeapSort uses the heap data structure to sort values in exactly the same way as Tree Sort used a binary search tree. To sort an array, or list, containing N values there are two steps:

- insert each value into a heap (initially empty).
- remove each value form the heap in ascending order (this is done by N successive calls to get_smallest).

Algorithm Heap Sort

1. Build a heap tree with the given set of data to sort the data in ascending /descending order.

2. **(a)** Delete the root node from the heap.

(b) Place the last leaf node in the root position.

(c) Rebuild the heap.

(d) Place the deleted node in the output.

3. Continue Step-2 until the heap tree is empty.

Programming Exercise 5.6

Write a program to implement a Heap tree.

```
#include <iostream>
#include <vector>

using namespace std;

class MaxHeap {
private:
  vector<int> heap;

  void heapifyUp(int index) {
    while (index > 0 && heap[index] > heap[(index - 1) / 2]) {
      swap(heap[index], heap[(index - 1) / 2]);
      index = (index - 1) / 2;
    }
  }

  void heapifyDown(int index) {
    int left = 2 * index + 1;
    int right = 2 * index + 2;
    int largest = index;

    if (left < heap.size() && heap[left] > heap[largest])
      largest = left;
    if (right < heap.size() && heap[right] > heap[largest])
      largest = right;
```

```
    if (largest != index) {
      swap(heap[index], heap[largest]);
      heapifyDown(largest);
    }
  }

public:
  void insert(int value) {
    heap.push_back(value);
    heapifyUp(heap.size() - 1);
  }

  void deleteMax() {
    if (heap.empty()) {
      cout << "Heap is empty!\n";
      return;
    }
    heap[0] = heap.back();
    heap.pop_back();
    heapifyDown(0);
  }

  void display() {
    cout << "Heap elements: ";
    for (int val : heap) {
      cout << val << " ";
    }
    cout << endl;
  }
};

int main() {
  MaxHeap heap;
  int n, value;
```

```
    cout << "Enter number of elements to insert in heap: ";
    cin >> n;

    cout << "Enter elements:\n";
    for (int i = 0; i < n; i++) {
        cin >> value;
        heap.insert(value);
    }

    cout << "Max Heap after insertion: ";
    heap.display();

    heap.deleteMax();
    cout << "Heap after deleting max element: ";
    heap.display();

    return 0;
}
```

OUTPUT:

```
Enter number of elements to insert in heap: 5
Enter elements:
10 20 5 6 1
Max Heap after insertion: 20 10 5 6 1
Heap after deleting max element: 10 6 5 1
```

Programming Exercise 5.7

Write a program to implement a Heap sort algorithm.

```
#include <iostream>
#include <vector>
using namespace std;

// Function to heapify a subtree
void heapify(vector<int>& arr, int n, int i) {
    int largest = i;
    int left = 2 * i + 1;
```

```
    int right = 2 * i + 2;

    if (left < n && arr[left] > arr[largest])
      largest = left;
    if (right < n && arr[right] > arr[largest])
      largest = right;
    if (largest != i) {
      swap(arr[i], arr[largest]);
      heapify(arr, n, largest);
    }
}

// Heap Sort function
void heapSort(vector<int>& arr) {
    int n = arr.size();
    // Build max heap
    for (int i = n / 2 - 1; i >= 0; i--)
      heapify(arr, n, i);
    // Extract elements one by one
    for (int i = n - 1; i > 0; i--) {
      swap(arr[0], arr[i]);
      heapify(arr, i, 0);
    }
}


int main() {
    int n;
    cout << "Enter number of elements: ";
    cin >> n;
    vector<int> arr(n);
    cout << "Enter elements:\n";
    for (int i = 0; i < n; i++) {
      cin >> arr[i];
    }
```

```
  heapSort(arr);
  cout << "Sorted array: ";
  for (int num : arr) {
     cout << num << " ";
  }
  cout << endl;
  return 0;
}
```

OUTPUT:

Enter number of elements: 6

Enter elements:

12 11 13 5 6 7

Sorted array: 5 6 7 11 12 13

5.9 RED-BLACK TREES

Binary search tree, in which, there is no path from the root to a leaf which is more than twice as long as any other path from the root to a leaf is called a Red Black tree (RBT). A RBT satisfies the following properties:

- Every node is either red or black.
- Root is always black.
- Every leaf which is Nil is black.
- If a node is red, then both its children are black. Hence, there must be no red-red parent-child relationship.
- Every simple path from a node to a descendent leaf contains the same number of black nodes.

Figure 5.43 shows some red-black trees that follow the above properties.

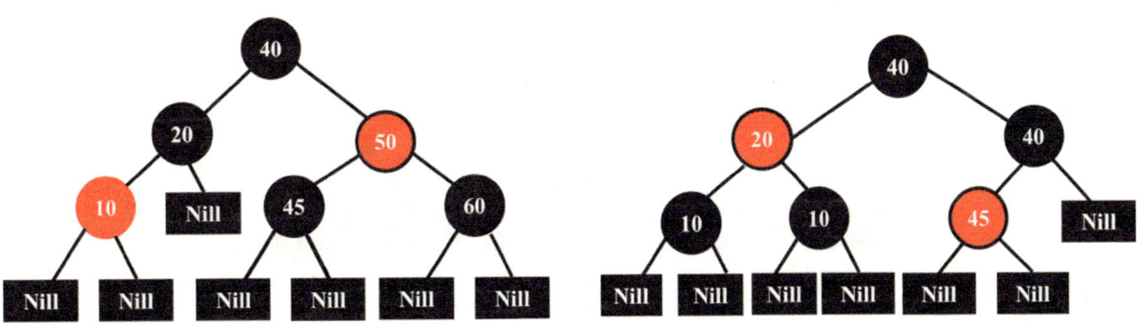

a b

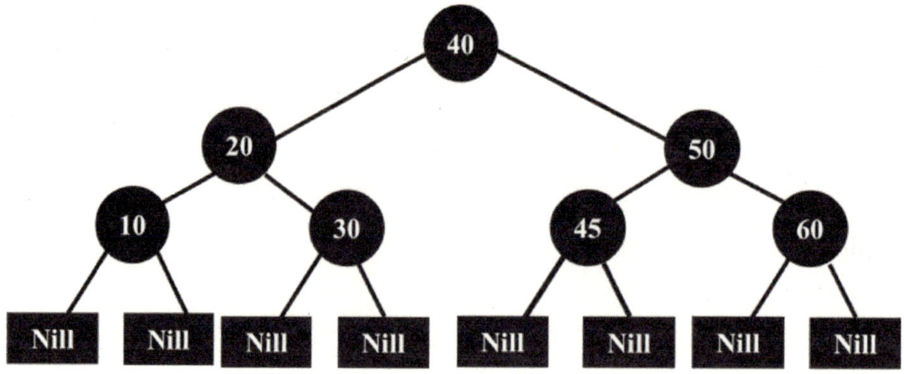

(c)

Figure 5.43: Red-black trees.

Figure 5.44 shows some binary search trees that are not red-black trees.

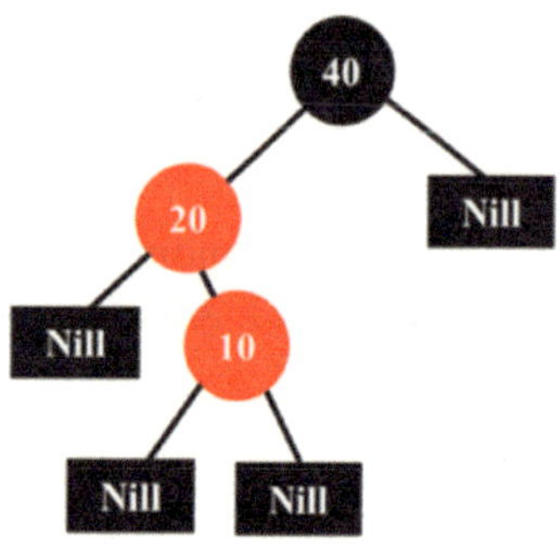

This is not a red-black tree because red-red parent-child relation exists.

(a)

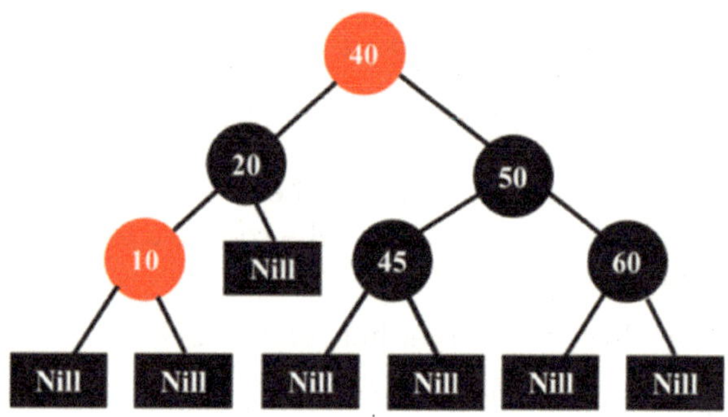

This is not a red-black tree because the root node is red.

(b)

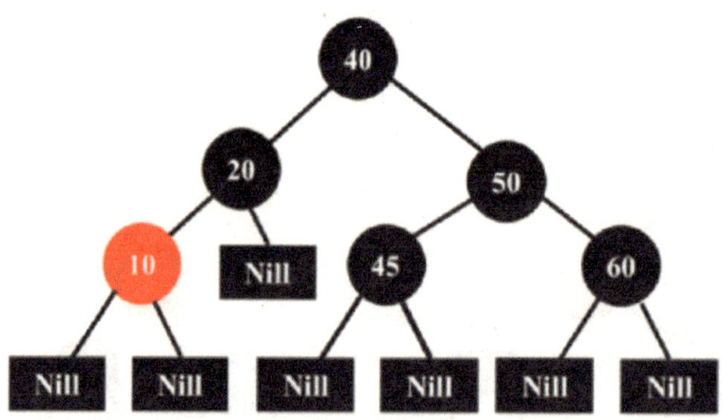

This is not a red-black tree because every path (for eg. path 40-50-60-Nil and 40-20-10-Nil) from a given node to any of its leaf nodes does not have equal number of black nodes.

(c)

Figure 5.44: Non Red-black Trees

5.9.1 Red Black Tree Insertion

In order to balance the red-black tree, recoloring (change in node's color) and rotation are performed. Recoloring is tried first, but if it does not work, then rotation must be performed.

1. If tree is empty, create new node as root node with color black.
2. If tree is not empty, create new node as leaf node with color red.
3. If parent of newnode is black then exit.
4. If parent of newnode is red, then check the color of parent's sibling of new node.
   a). If color of parent's sibling of new node is black or null then do suitable rotation and recolor.
   b). If color of parent's sibling of new node is red, then recolor and also check if parent's parent of new node is not root node then recolor it and recheck.

Example: Create a red-black tree with elements 10, 18, 5, 4, 15, 17, 25, 60, 1, 90

Insert element 10 as root node in black color. 

Insert 18 as red. 18>10, so 18 is right child of 10. Parent of 18 is node 10 which is black, so exit.

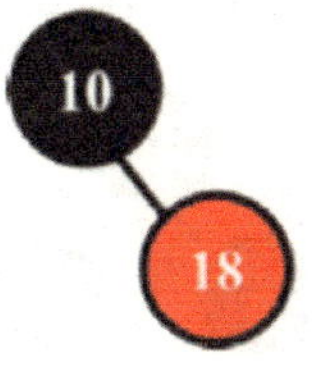

Insert 5 (red) as left child of 10. Parent of 5 is 10 (black), so exit. The tree becomes a red-black tree.

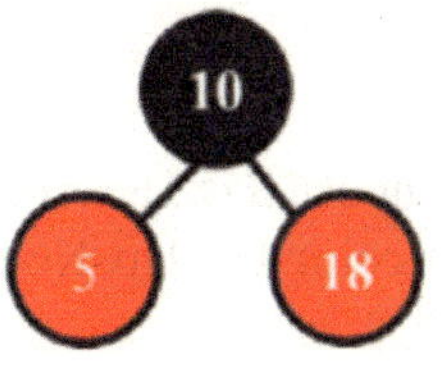

Insert 4 as red node to left of 5. Now it is not a red-black tree due to the red-red relation between nodes 4 and 5.

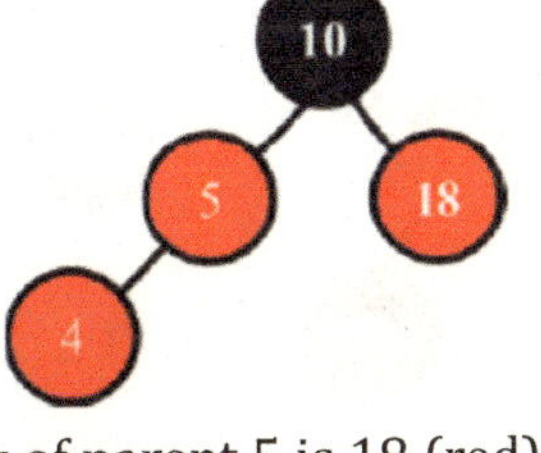

Parent of new node 4 is 5 (red). Sibling of parent 5 is 18 (red). So, recolor siblings 5 and 18. Now, it is a red-black tree. Parent of 4 is 5 and parent of 5 is 10 (black) which is a root node, so we do nothing.

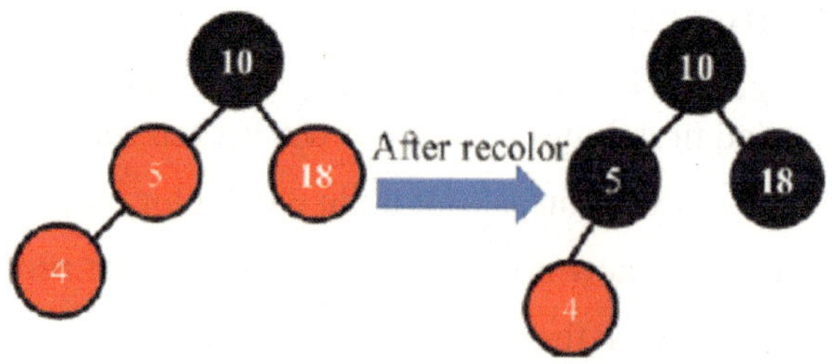

Now insert 15 as red towards left of 18. 18 (black) is parent of 15, so exit.

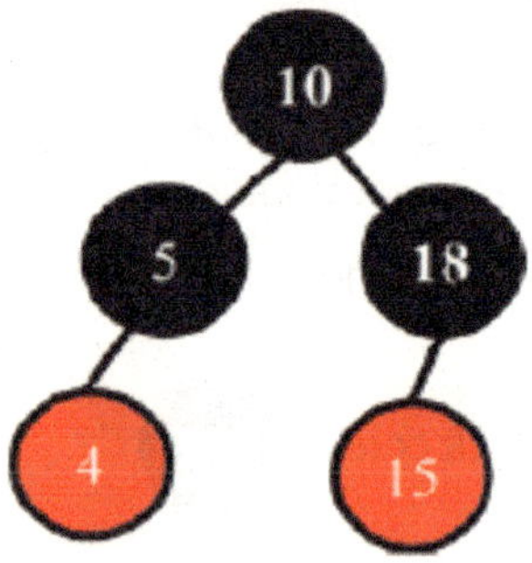

Insert 17 (red) as right child of 15. Parent of 17 is 15 which is red. Sibling of 15 is nil (black), so we rotate 15 to left first. Then rotate 18 to right. Also recolor 17 and 18.

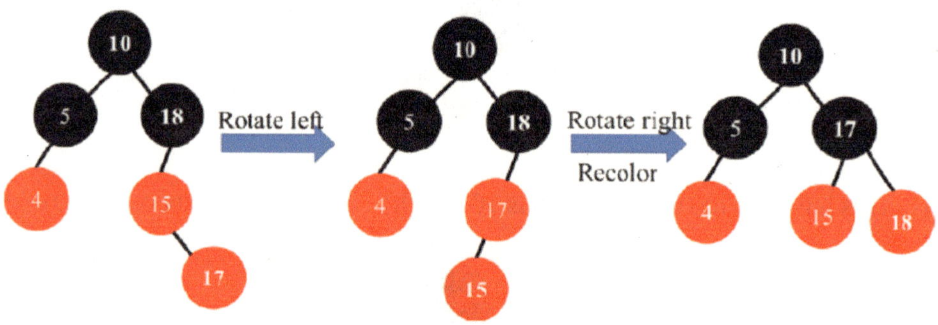

Insert 25 (red) as right child of 18. Sibling of 18 is 15 which is red. Then recolor siblings 15 and 18. Parent of 18 is 17 which is not root. So recolor 17 also. Now the tree satisfies red-black tree criteria.

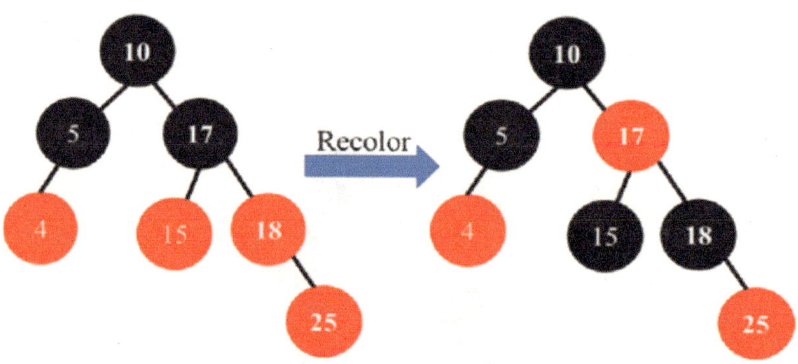

Insert 60 (red) as right child of 25. Parent of 60 is 25 (red). Color of sibling of 25 is black (nil), then we left rotate. We recolor 18 and 25 between which rotation is done.

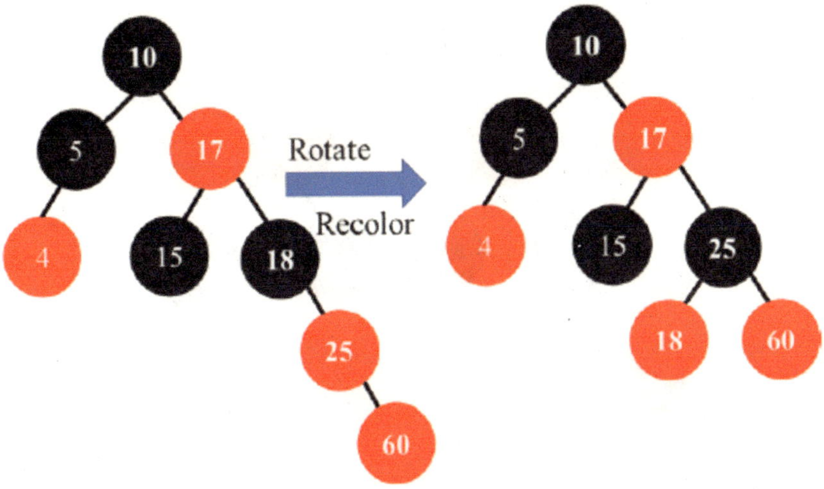

Insert element 1 (red) as left child of 4. Parent of 1 is 4 (red). Sibling of 4 is Nil (black). LL problem arises here. We right rotate 4 and 5 and recolor them.

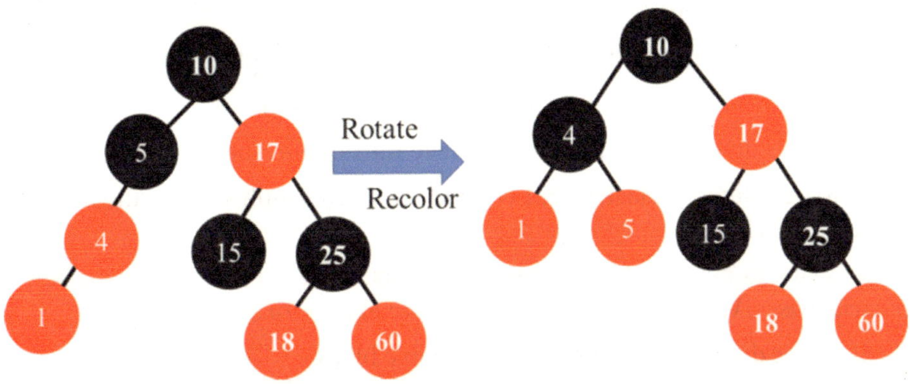

Insert 90 (red) as right child of 60 (red). The nodes 18 and 60 are siblings, so recolor them. Parent of 60 is 25 (black), which is not a root node. So, recolor node 25.

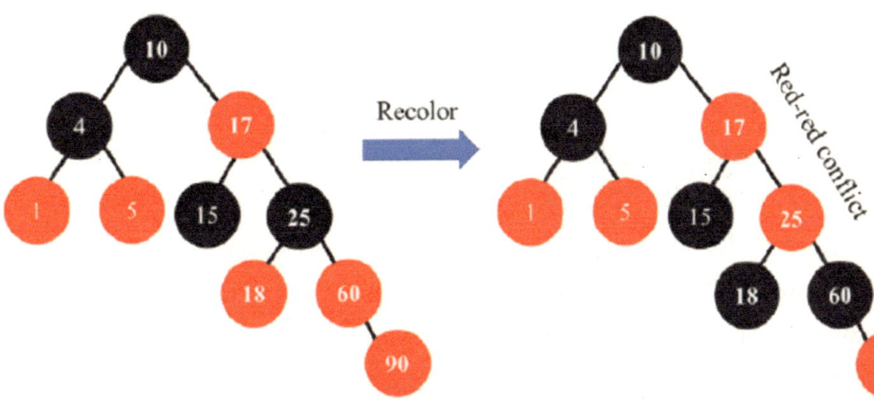

In order to solve the red-red conflict in the tree, let us consider 25 as a new node. Parent of 25 is 17 (red). Sibling of 17 is 4 (black). We left rotate 10 and 17 and recolor them. Now, the tree is a red-black tree.

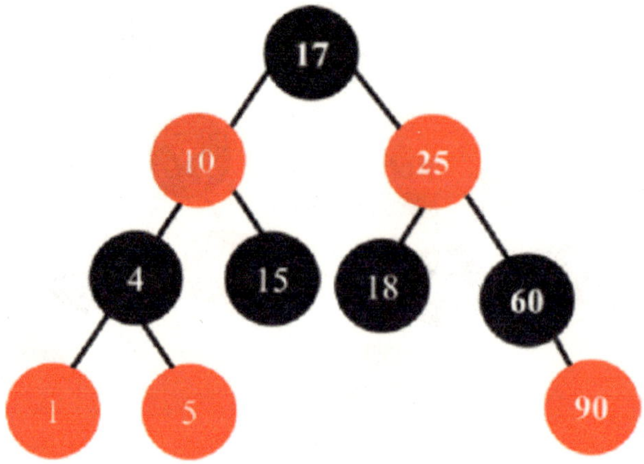

5.9.2 Red Black Tree Deletion

The cases of deletion in red black tree are mentioned below:

1. Perform BST deletion.
2. If node **to be deleted** is red and has no children, then simply delete it.
3. Internal nodes will always retain its color during deletion.
4. If root node is double black then just remove the double black.
5. If node to be deleted is black with 1 child in red, then simply replace the node with its child and delete its child.
6. Say we want to delete a black node which has black children, in this case double black scenario arises. We need to convert the double black into single black.
   - 6.1. If root is double black, just remove double black.
   - 6.2. If any node is double black, always check its siblings.
   - 6.3. If sibling of double black is black and double black's children are also black, then remove double black node and:
     - 6.3.1 Add black color from double black to its parent.
       - 6.3.3.1 If parent is red, then it becomes black.
       - 6.3.3.2 If parent is black, then it becomes double black.
     - 6.3.2 Recolor sibling to red.
     - 6.3.3 If still double black problem exists, we apply other cases.
7. If double node's sibling is red then:
   - 7.1. Swap colors of parent and its sibling.
   - 7.2. Rotate parent of double black node in double black node's direction.
   - 7.3. Reapply cases.

Example: Delete node 30 from the red-black tree.

Using Case 2, 30 is directly deleted as it is a leaf node in red.

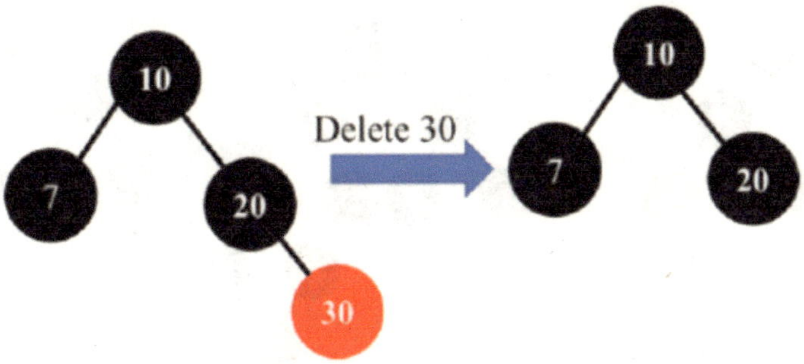

Example: Delete node 20 from the red-black tree.

Following the BST deletion technique, we replace node 20 with node 30. Now 30 (red) which has no children is deleted directly.

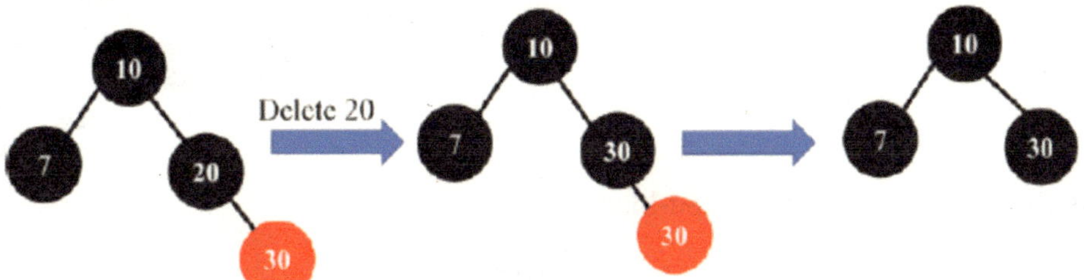

Example: Delete node 30 from the red-black tree.

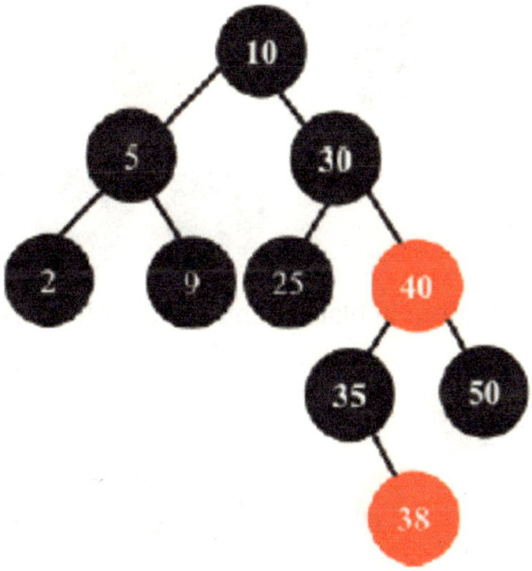

30 is an internal node, so we can't delete it directly. Instead, we have to replace it with its child. Using BST deletion rule, we replace 30 with 35 which is the smallest node from right sub-tree of 30. In order to delete 35 (black) which has 1 child in red, we simple replace 35 with the child (node 38). The leaf node 38 in red is deleted directly.

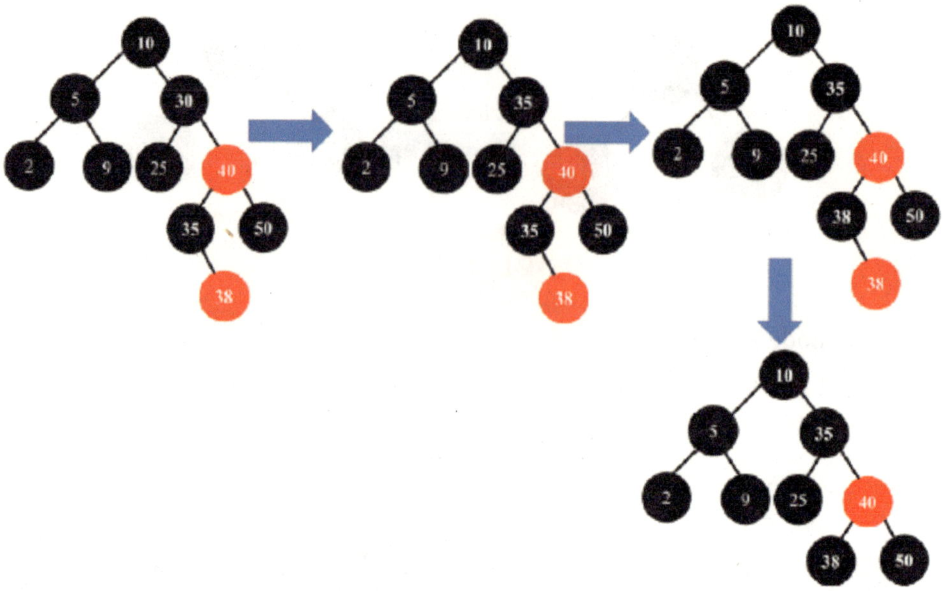

Example: Delete node 20 from the red-black tree.

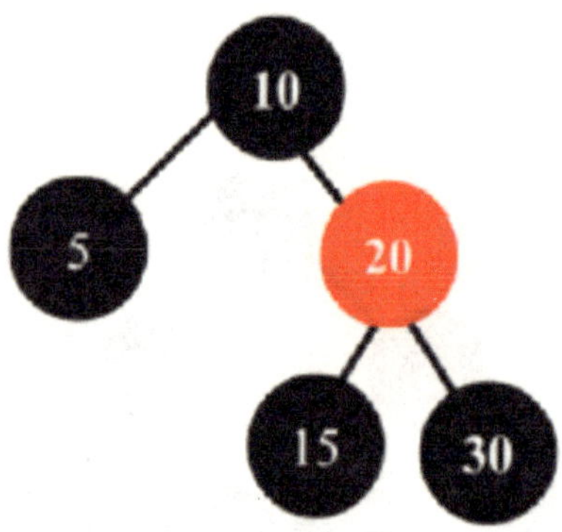

20 is internal node with two children in black. Replace 20 with 30 from right sub tree.

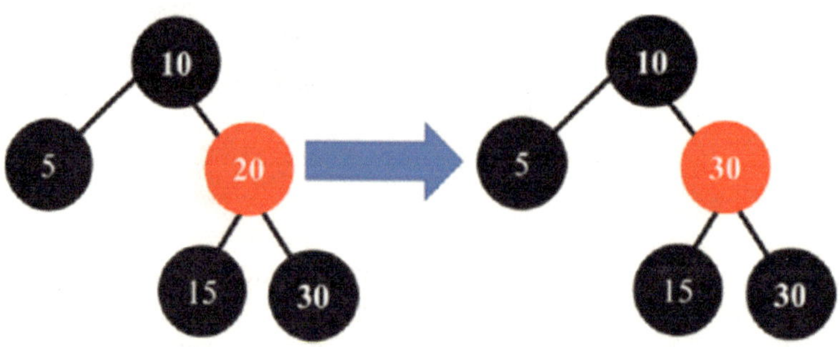

Now the leaf node 30 can not be deleted directly as it is black and has nil children in black color. This is a double black scenario.

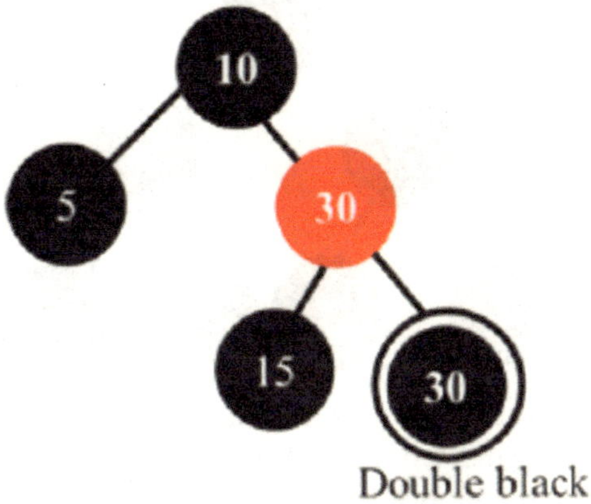

Using Step 5.2, we check the sibling of double black node. The sibling 15 is black. The children of 15 are nil (black). So, using Step 6.3.1, we remove one black color from double black to its parent 30 (red) thus removing double black node 30. We recolor sibling 15 using Step 6.3.2.

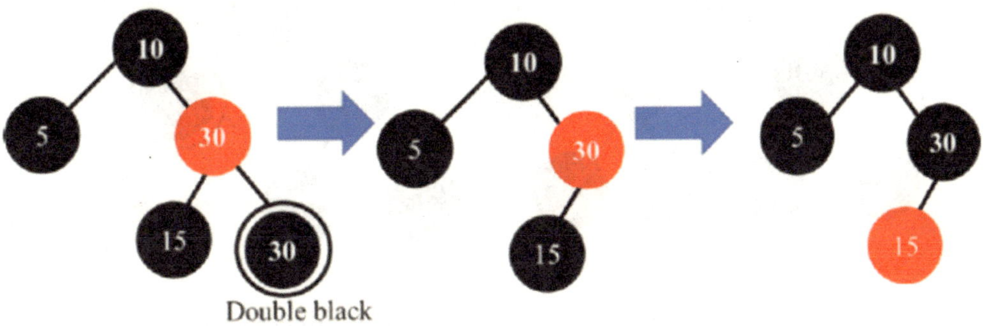

Example: Delete node 15 from the red-black tree.

The leaf node 15 cannot be deleted directly as it is black and has nil children in black color. This is a double black scenario. Using Step 6.2, we check the sibling which is 30 (black). The children of node 30 are nil (black). So, using Step 6.3.1, we remove one black color from double black to its parent 20 thus removing double black node nil. Sibling 30 is recolored using Step 6.3.2.

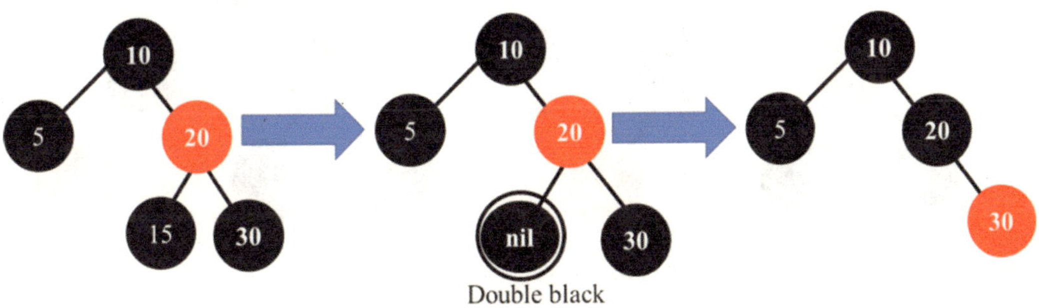

Example: Delete node 15 from the red black tree.

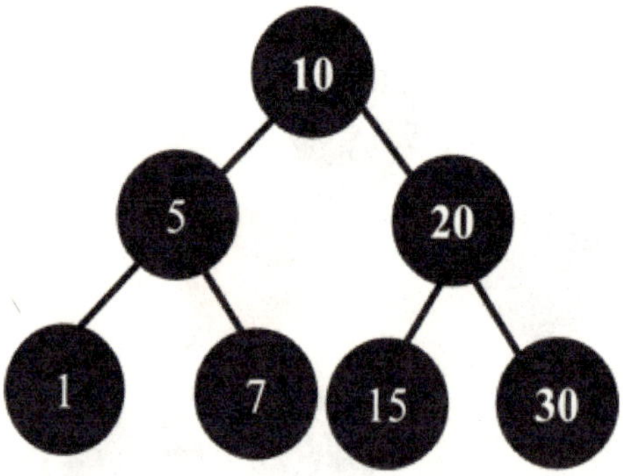

The leaf node 15 cannot be deleted directly as it is black and has nil children in black color. This is a double black scenario. Using Step 6.2, we check the sibling of 15 which is 30 (black). The children of node 30 are nil (black). So, using Step 6.3.1, we remove one black color from double black nil to its parent 20 thus removing double black node nil. Node 20 is double black now. Sibling 30 is recolored using Step 6.3.2.

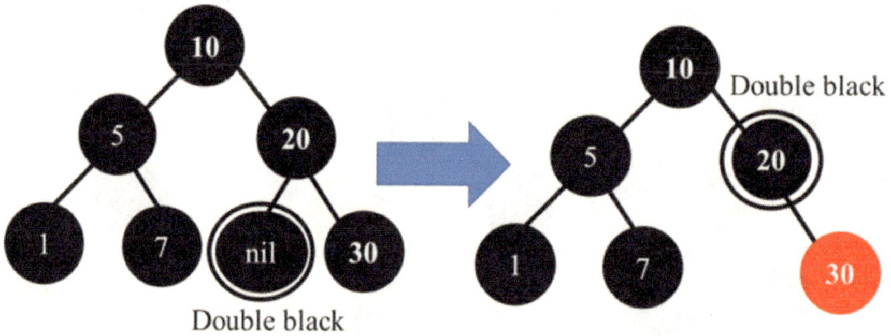

Double black scenario arises at node 20 whose sibling is node 5 (black). Children of 5 are also black. So we give one black to the parent (node 10) of node 20. Sibling node 5 becomes red and node 10 (root) becomes double node. Now we remove one black from the root.

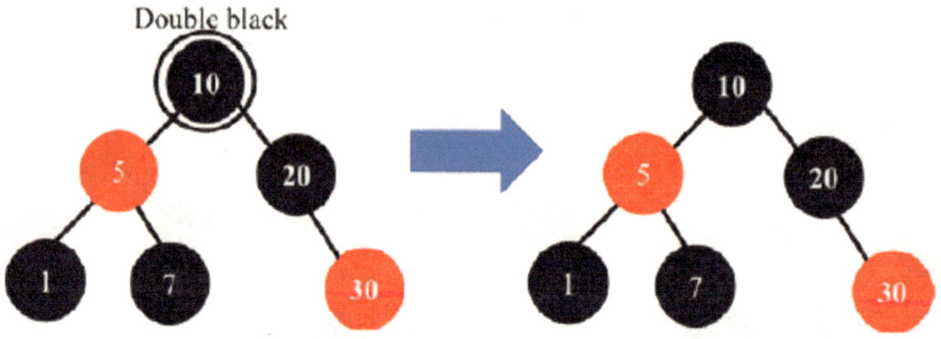

Example: Delete node 15 from the red black tree.

The leaf node 15 cannot be deleted directly as it is black and has nil children in black color. This is a double black scenario. We check the sibling of 15 which is 30 (red).

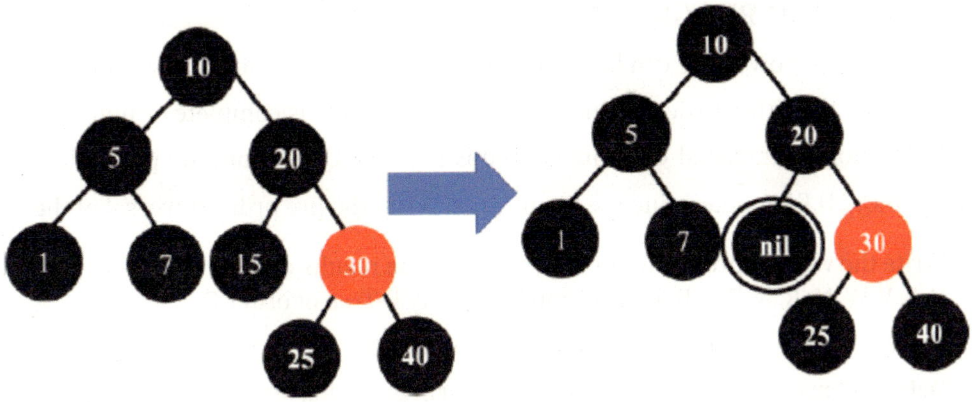

Thus, using Step 7.1, we swap colors of nodes 30 and 20. Using Step 7.2, we rotate node 20 in the double black node's direction. Sibling of double black node (nil) is 25 (black). Children of 25 are nil (black). Step 6 is applied here. We remove double node and give one black to node 20 and node 25 gets recolored to red.

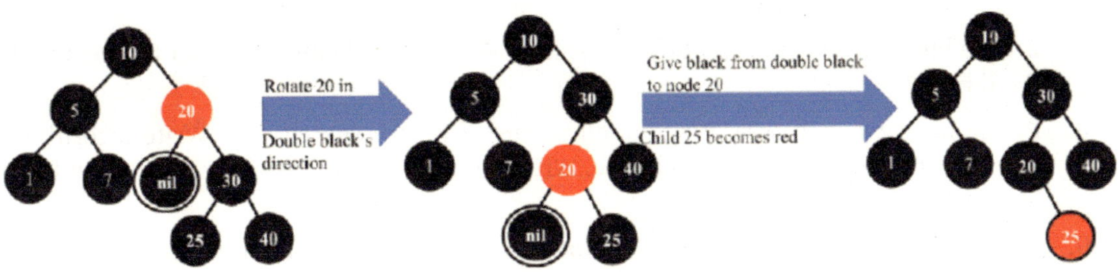

5.10 LET US SUM UP

- This chapter introduced the concept of "Tree", a nonlinear hierarchical data structure. The chapter discussed various terminology associated with tree. Binary tree, Binary search tree, AVL tree, Heap tree, B tree, red black trees are explained in detail.
- Various trees have various applications. One reason to use tree, is because of its advantage to store information that naturally forms a hierarchy.
- In BST, search for a given key in moderate time is possible.
- Self-balancing search trees like AVL and Red-Black trees guarantee an upper bound of O(logn) for search.
- Self-balancing search trees like AVL and Red-Black trees guarantee an upper bound of O(logn) for insertion and deletion.
- Heap is a tree data structure which is implemented using arrays and used to implement priority queues.
- B-Tree is used to implement indexing in databases.

5.11 CHECK YOUR PROGRESS

1. Define Tree. How a tree can be stored in memory? Explain with an example.
2. Write an algorithm to determine whether a binary tree is complete or not.

   If the inorder traversal of a binary tree is B,I,D,A,C,Q,E,H,F and its postorder traversal is II,D,B,Q,C,H,F,E,A determine the binary tree. Write the pre order traversal of the same tree.
3. Write the various properties of B- Tree. Show the results of inserting the keys F, S, Q, K, C, L, H, T, V, W, M, R, N, P, A, B in order into an empty B-Tree of order 5.
4. Discuss the different cases of rotations in AVL trees.
5. Define binary tree. Write algorithm to perform preorder, inorder and post order traversals.
6. Find the original tree from the following given traversal order :
   i. Inorder : EACKFHDBG, Preorder : FAEKCDHGB
   ii. Preorder : GBQACKFPDERH, Inorder : QBKCFAGPEDHR
   iii. Inorder : MEPAQTRCFK, Postorder : MPEQRCTKFA.
7. Draw a binary tree with Inorder traversal: B C A E G D H F I J and Preorder traversal: A B C D E G F H I J
8. Define binary search tree. Write applications of binary search tree. Write algorithm to delete a node from binary search tree. Write an algorithm to insert an element in Binary Search Tree (BST).
9. Explain binary search tree and its operations. Make a binary search tree for the following sequence of numbers and show all the steps: 45,32,90, 34,68,72,15,24, 30, 66, 11, 50, 10.
10. What is the maximum node in a binary tree of height h?
11. Consider the following AVL tree, insert 2,12,7,10 in the tree and make proper rotation to maintain AVL property.

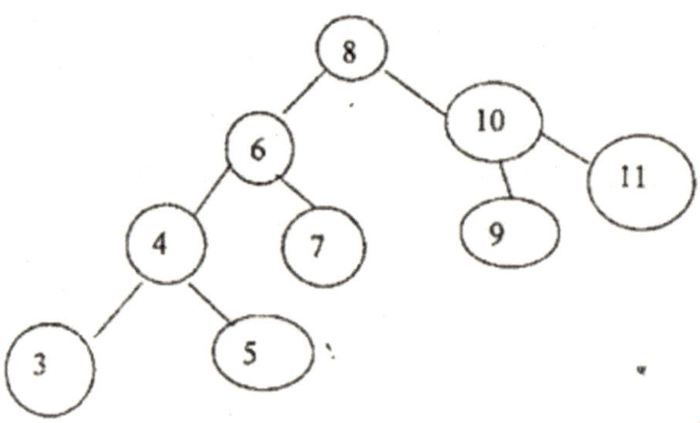

12. Draw an AVL tree on following inputs, assume that tree is initially empty : 45, 55, 65, 75, 80, 90, 100, 110, 120, 130, 40, 35, 25, 20, 15, 10, 5.
13. Describe all rotations in AVL tree. Construct AVL tree from the following nodes: B, C, G E, F, D,A.

14. Write a program to perform binary search and make its complexity analysis.
15. Define B tree. What are applications of B tree? Draw a B tree of order 4 by insertion of the following keys in order: Z,U,A,I,W,L,P,X,C,J,D,M,T,B,Q,E,H,S,K,N,R,G,Y,F,O,V.
16. Show the results of inserting the keys

    F, S, Q, K, C, L, H, T, V, W, M, R, N, P, A, B, X, Y, D, Z, E in order into an empty B-tree. Only draw the configurations of the tree just before some node must split, and also draw the final configuration.
17. Explain under what circumstances, if any, redundant DISK-READ or DISK-WRITE operations are performed during the course of executing a call to B-TREE-INSERT. (A redundant DISK-READ is a DISK-READ for a page that is already in memory. A redundant DISK-WRITE writes to disk a page of information that is identical to what is already stored there).
18. Explain how to find the minimum key stored in a B-tree and how to find the predecessor of a given key stored in a B-tree.
19. Derive a tight upper bound on the number of keys that can be stored in a B-tree of height h as a function of the minimum degree t.
20. Discuss red black tree properties.

6

GRAPH

6.1 INTRODUCTION

A graph (G) is made of a set of vertices (V) and edges (E), each one of them (e € E) connects two vertices (u, v € V). The graph can also be represented by G= (V, E). Basically a graph is a set of points (vertices) connected by lines (edge).

The basic idea of graphs was introduced in 18th century by the great Swiss mathematician Leonhard Euler. He used graphs to solve the famous Königsberg bridge problem. Figure 6.1 shows an image of the problem.

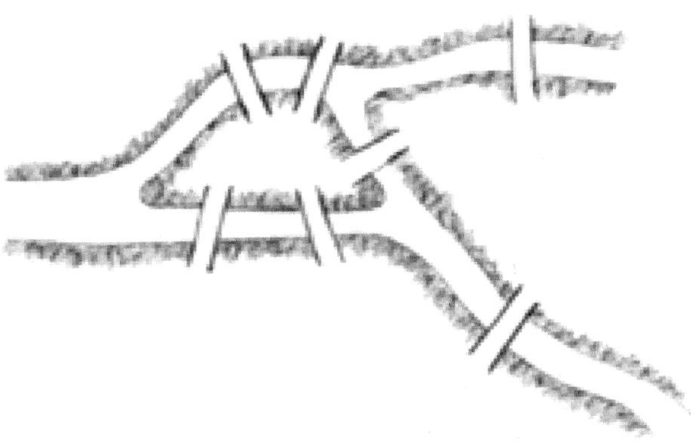

Figure 6.1: Königsberg bridge problem

The definition of the problem is such; German city of Königsberg was situated on the river Pregel. It had a park situated on the banks of the river and two islands. Mainland and islands were joined by seven bridges. A problem was whether it was possible to take a walk through the town in such a way as to cross over every bridge once, and only once. For solving the problem it needs to be modelled to a graph. Figure 6.2 shows the graph model of this problem.

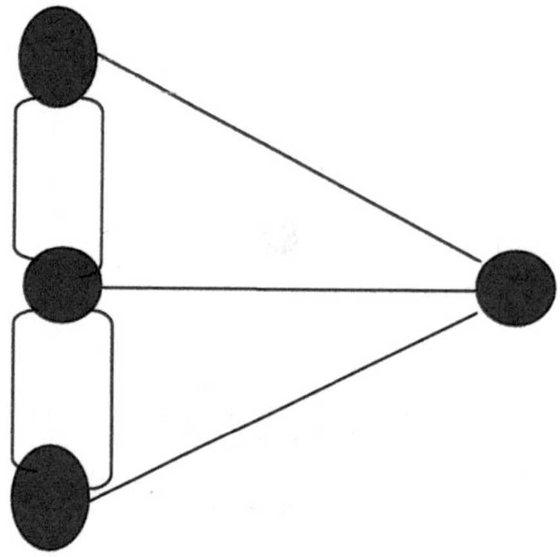

Figure 6.2: Graph model of this problem.

6.2 BASIC TERMINOLOGIES

A large number of definitions are related with graphs. Let us start with an introduction to various types of graphs.

Graph which is having nonempty set of vertices connected at most by one edge is known as simple graph, as shown in Figure 3.a. However if there are multiple edges that connects same endpoints, or there is a presence of loop, than the graph is called a multigraph as shown in Figure 6.3.b.

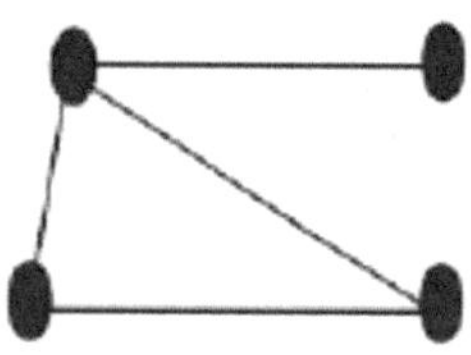

Figure 6.3.a: Simple graph

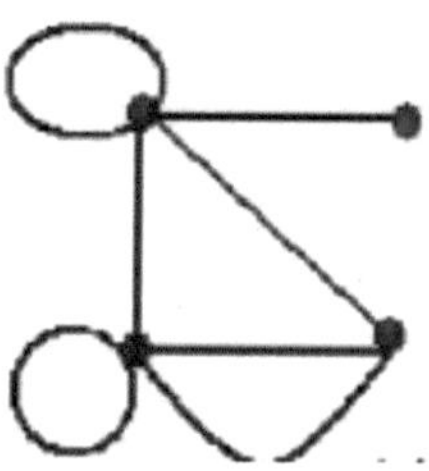

Figure 6.3.b: Multi-graph

If we pay a little attention we can find out the property that is common between these two graphs in Figure 6.3.a and Figure 6.3.b. In both these cases the set of edges are unordered, because of this these graphs are called undirected graph. A directed graph consists of vertices and ordered pairs of edges as shown in Figure 6.4.

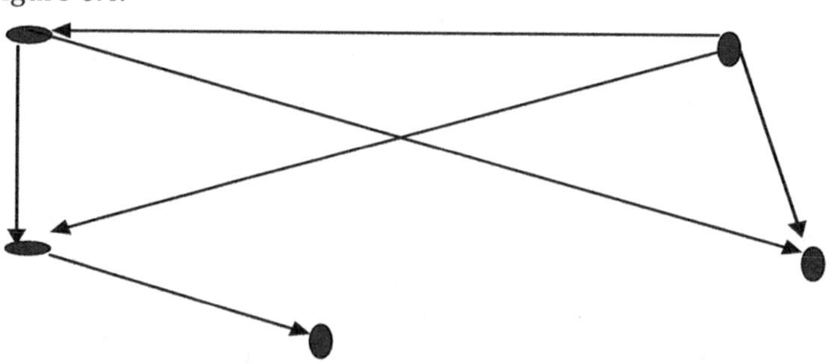

Figure 6.4: Directed graph

Finite and Infinite Graphs

A finite graph is a graph G = (V, E) such that V and E are finite sets. An infinite graph is one with an infinite set of vertices or edges or both.

Adjacent, Incidence and Degree

Adjacency of two vertices comes from their sharing of a common edge. For two vertices A and *B* to be adjacent there has to be an edge *e* joining them. Similarly, Adjacency of two edges comes from their sharing of a common vertex. For two edges $e_1$and e_2 to be adjacent there has to be a common vertex A joining them. An edge and a vertex on that edge are called incident with each another. If the vertex *A* is on edge *e*, in that case A and *e* are said to beincident on each other.

In graph theory, the degree of a vertex of a graph is the number of edges incident to the vertex. The degree of a vertex v is denoted deg(v). The important point to note is that the sum of the degrees of all the vertices in a graph is twice the number of edges.

$$\Sigma \deg v = 2e$$

Walk, Path and Circuits

A walk is defined as a finite alternating sequence of vertices and edges that starts and completes with vertices in such a way that each edge is incident with the vertices preceding and following it. An open walk no vertices appearing more than once is called a path. A closed walk in which except start and end vertex no other vertex appears more than once is called a circuit.

Connected Graph

A graph G is connected if there is at least one path between every pair of vertices in G. Otherwise G is a disconnected graph.

Euler Graph

If a graph G contains a closed walk such that the walk contains all the edges of the graph than the graph is called an Euler graph. A given graph G is Euler if only all the vertices of G are of even degree and all its edges belong to a single component.

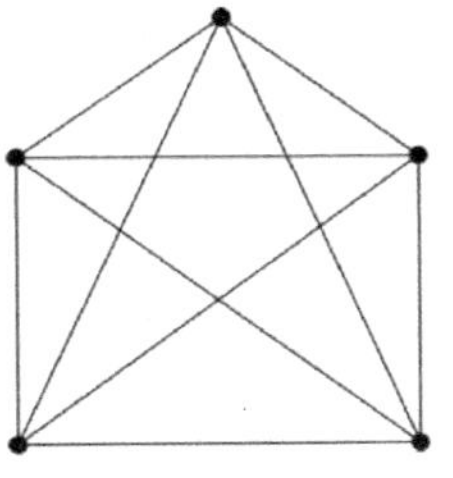

Figure 6.5: Euler Graph

6.3 APPLICATIONS OF GRAPH

Since graphs are powerful abstractions, they are of extreme significant in modelling data. In general, many problems in computer science can be mapped to known graph problems. Some of the graph applications are mentioned here.

- Social networking:

Graphs that represent who knows whom, who communicates with whom, who influences whom or other relationships in social structures. Social networking site like Facebook may use"Friend suggestion problem" with graph modelling.

- **Operating System**:

Resource Allocation to processes by Operating System may be done with graph modelling.

- **Google maps:**

Google maps uses graphs for building transportation systems.

- **Document link:**

The web can be modelled as a graph, where each web page is a vertex, and each hyperlink a directed edge.

- **Network traffic:**

The Network traffic can be modelled as a graph, where Vertices are IP addresses and edges are the packets that flow between them.

- **Compilers:**

Graphs are used extensively in compilers. They can be used for type inference, for so called data flow analysis, register allocation and many other purposes.

6.4 REPRESENTATION OF GRAPH

Adjacency matrix

Easiest possible way to represent a graph is to create a as a 2D array representing relations among the edges. In this representation a matrix of size equal to vertices size (VxV) is created. If there is an edge between two vertices then that particular location is filled with 1 otherwise 0; i.eAdjM [i] [j] = 1 when there is edge between Vertex i and Vertex j, else 0. Let us take an example of a graph in Figure 6.6.

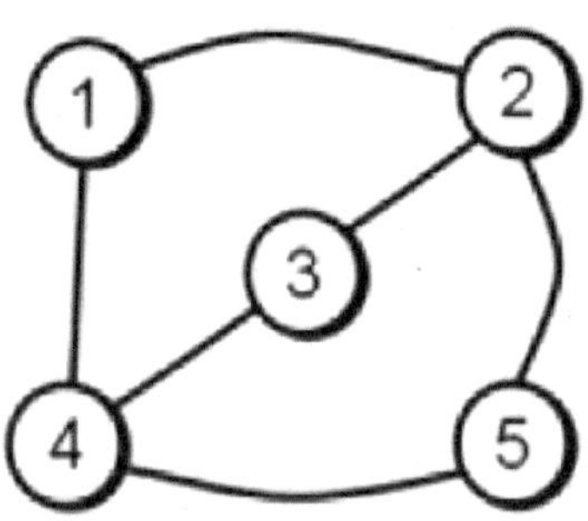

Figure 6.6.a: Graph

	1	2	3	4	5
1	0	1	0	1	0
2	1	0	1	0	1
3	0	1	0	1	0
4	1	0	1	0	1
5	0	1	0	1	0

Figure 6.6.b: Adjacency matrix

Adjacency List

Adjacency List is basically an Array of Linked List, where the size of the array is exactly same as the number of Vertices in the graph. Every Vertex of the graph has a Linked List associated with it. Each Node in this Linked list represents the reference to the other vertices which share an edge with the current vertex. The weights can also be stored in the Linked List Node.

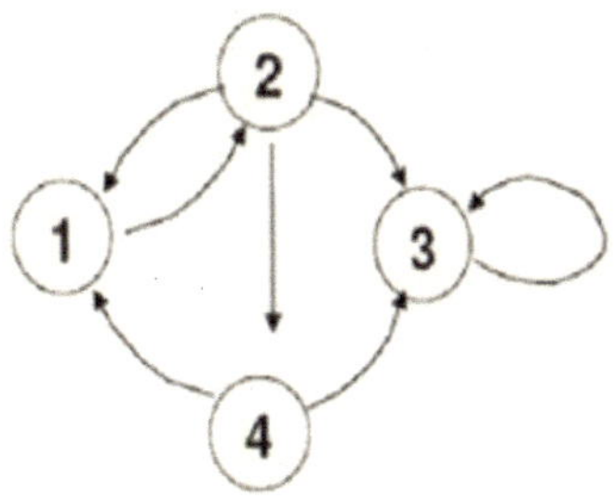

Figure 6.7.a: Graph

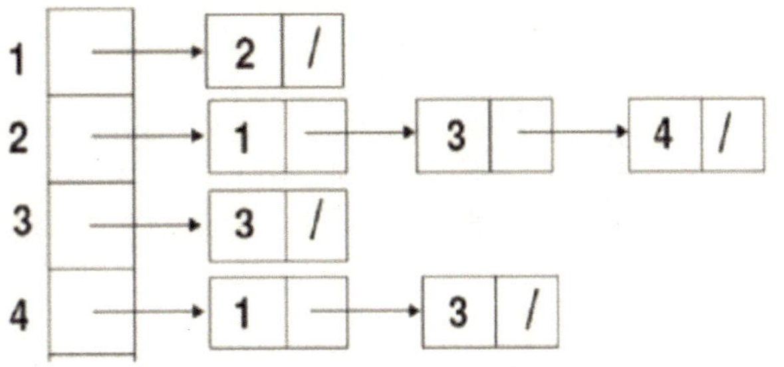

Figure 6.7.b: Adjacency List

6.5 TRAVERSAL OF A GRAPH

Graph traversal happens in two standard ways: depth first search or breath first search. Only difference in these two approaches is in the data structure to hold data during processing. Breath first search uses a queue while depth first uses a stack for holding data during the operation

The DFS algorithm works as follows:

- Start by putting any one of the graph's vertices on top of a stack.
- Take the top item of the stack and add it to the visited list.
- Create a list of that vertex's adjacent nodes. Add the ones which aren't in the visited list to the top of stack.
- Keep repeating steps 2 and 3 until the stack is empty.

To understand it better let us take an example.

1.

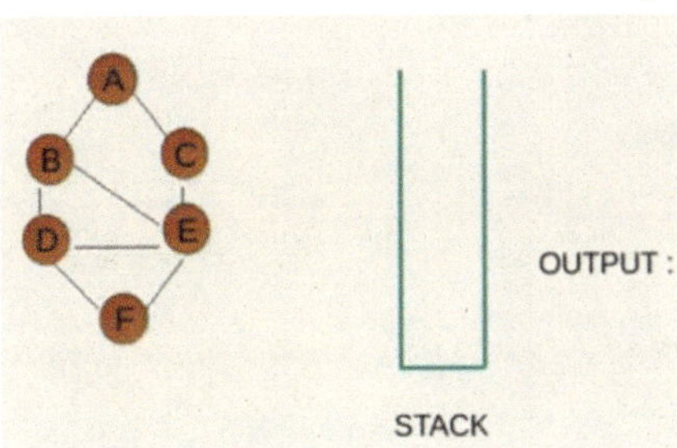

2.

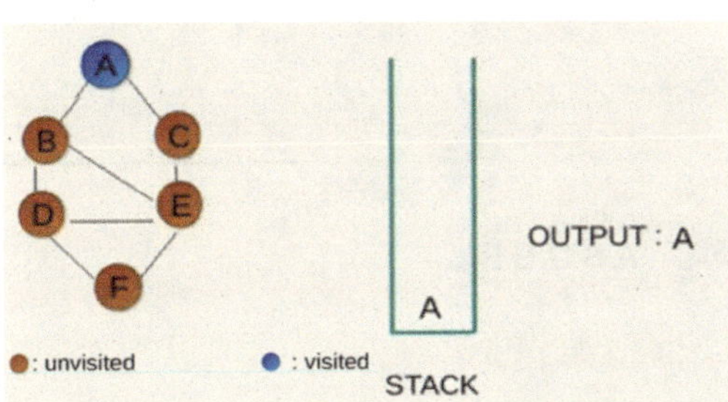

3.

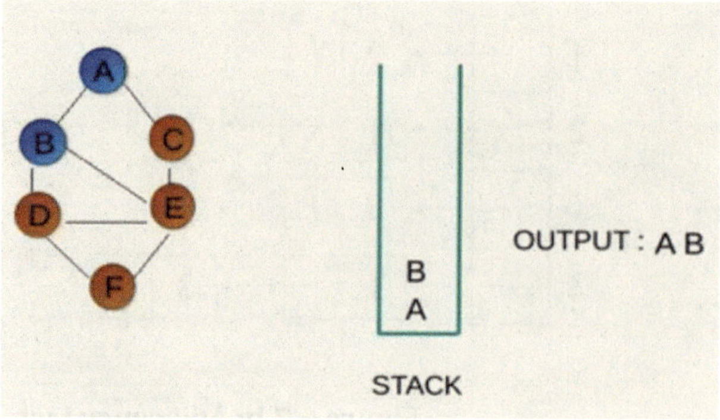
A
B
C
D
E
F
B
A
STACK
OUTPUT : A B

4.

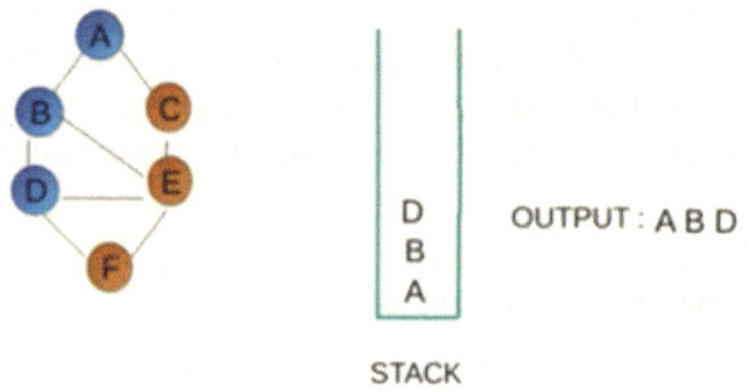
A
B
C
D
E
F
D
B
A
STACK
OUTPUT : A B D

5.

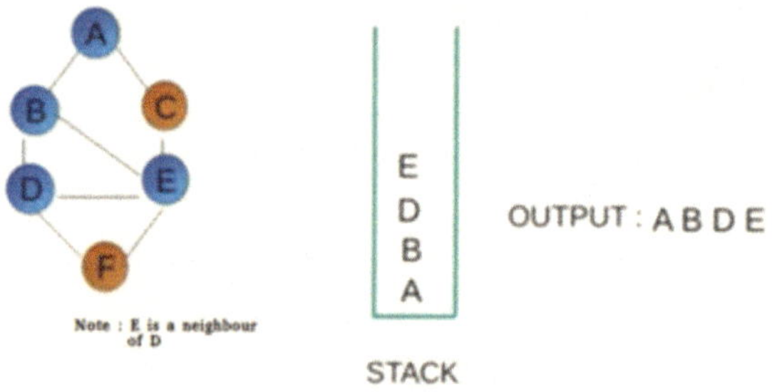
A
B
C
D
E
F
Note : E is a neighbour of D
E
D
B
A
STACK
OUTPUT : A B D E

6.

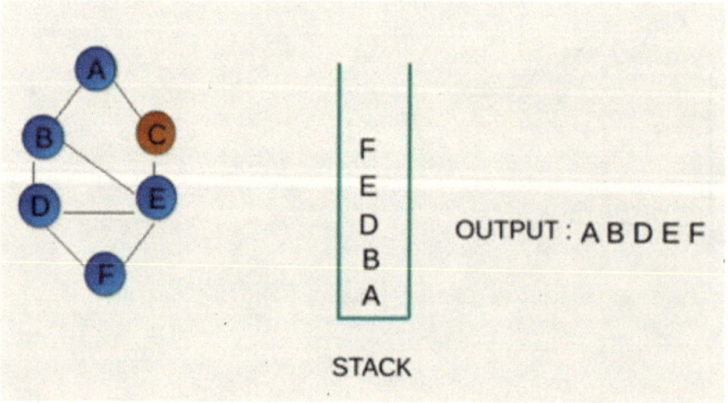
A
B
C
D
E
F
F
E
D
B
A
STACK
OUTPUT : A B D E F

7.

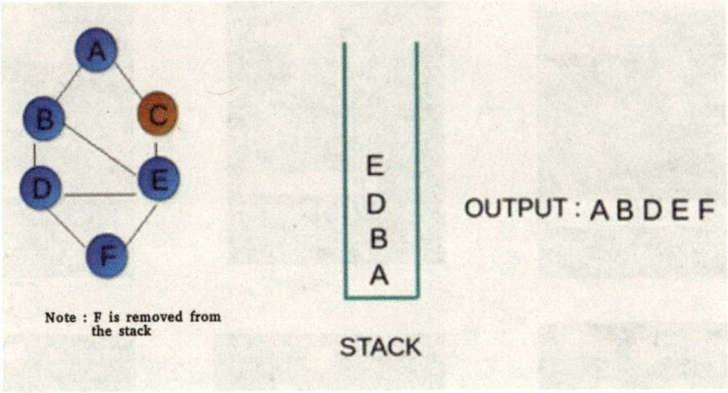

8.

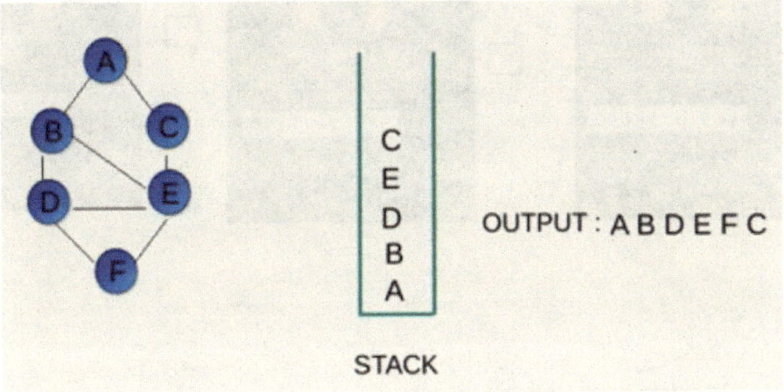

9.

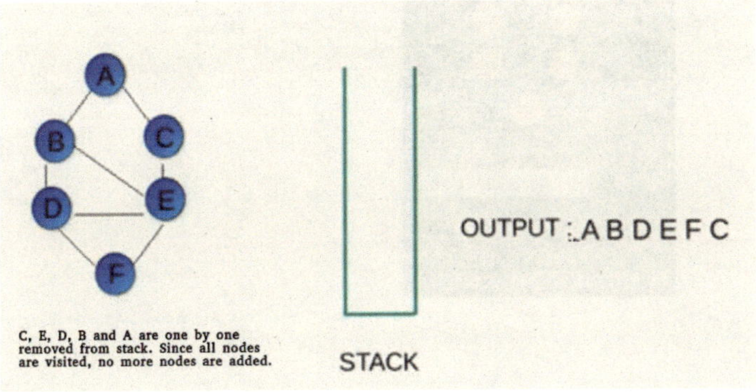

The BFS algorithm works as follows:

- Start by putting any one of the graph's vertices at the back of a queue.
- Take the front item of the queue and add it to the visited list.
- Create a list of that vertex's adjacent nodes. Add the ones which aren't in the visited list to the back of the queue.
- Keep repeating steps 2 and 3 until the queue is empty.

To understand it better let us take an example.

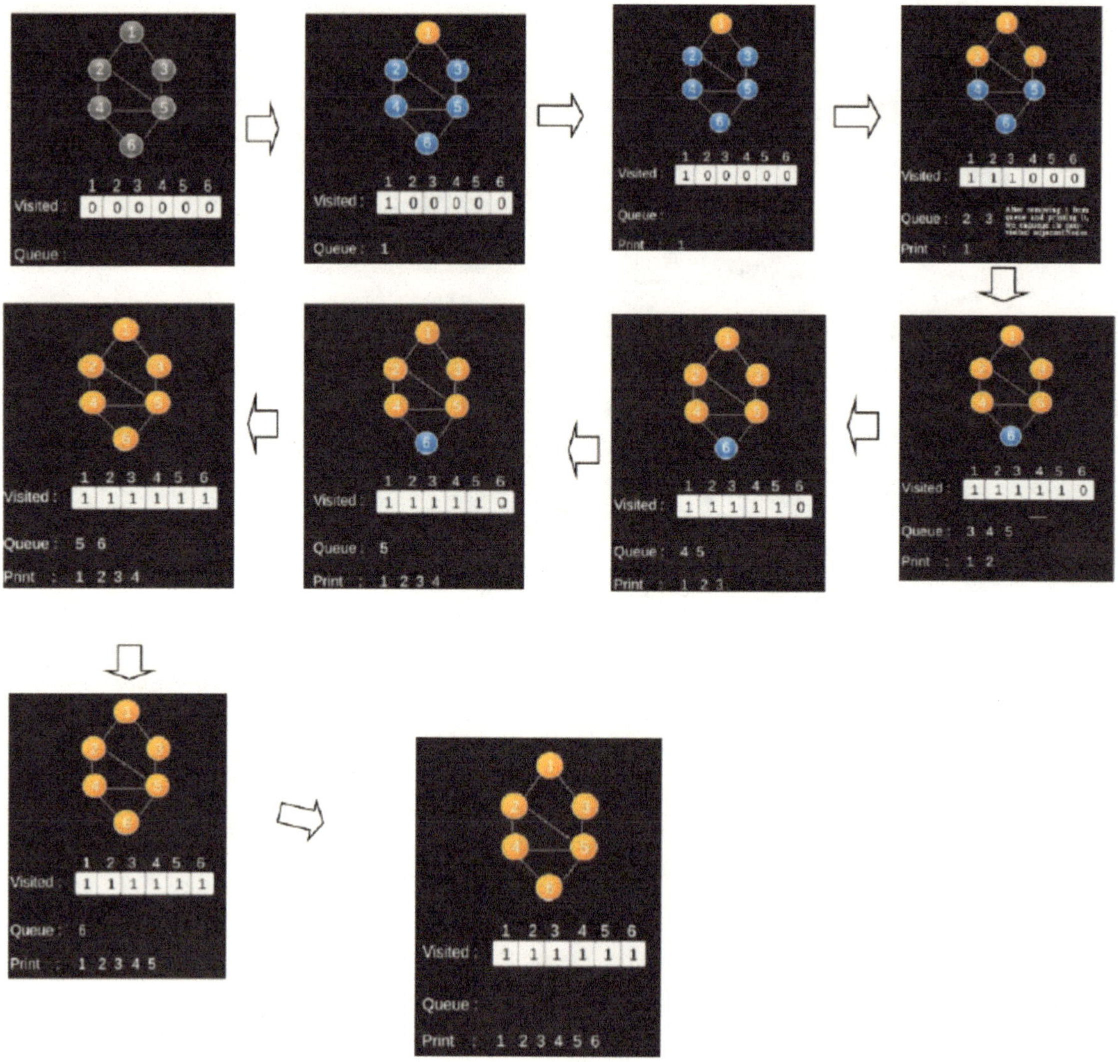

Programming Exercise 6.1

Write a program to implement DFS and BFS.

```
#include <iostream>
#include <list>
#include <queue>
using namespace std;

class Graph {
   int V; // Number of vertices
   list<int> *adj; // Adjacency list
```

```
public:
  Graph(int V);
  void addEdge(int v, int w);
  void BFS(int s);
  void DFS(int s);
  void DFSUtil(int v, bool visited[]);
};

// Constructor
Graph::Graph(int V) {
  this->V = V;
  adj = new list<int>[V];
}

// Add edge to the graph
void Graph::addEdge(int v, int w) {
  adj[v].push_back(w);
  adj[w].push_back(v); // Since it's an undirected graph
}

// BFS Implementation
void Graph::BFS(int s) {
  bool *visited = new bool[V]();
  queue<int> q;
  visited[s] = true;
  q.push(s);

  cout<< "BFS Traversal: ";
  while (!q.empty()) {
    int node = q.front();
    cout<< node << " ";
    q.pop();

    for (auto i :adj[node]) {
      if (!visited[i]) {
```

```
            visited[i] = true;
            q.push(i);
         }
      }
   }
   cout<<endl;
   delete[] visited;
}

// DFS Utility function (recursive)
void Graph::DFSUtil(int v, bool visited[ ]) {
   visited[v] = true;
   cout<< v << " ";

   for (auto i :adj[v]) {
      if (!visited[i]) {
           DFSUtil(i, visited);
      }
   }
}

// DFS Implementation
void Graph::DFS(int s) {
   bool *visited = new bool[V]( );
   cout<< "DFS Traversal: ";
   DFSUtil(s, visited);
   cout<<endl;
   delete[ ] visited;
}

int main( ) {
   int V, E;
   cout<< "Enter number of vertices: ";
   cin>> V;
   Graph g(V);
```

```
    cout<< "Enter number of edges: ";
    cin>> E;
    cout<< "Enter the edges (u v):\n";
    for (int i = 0; i< E; i++) {
        int u, v;
        cin>> u >> v;
        g.addEdge(u, v);
    }

    int startNode;
    cout<< "Enter starting node for traversal: ";
    cin>>startNode;

    g.BFS(startNode);
    g.DFS(startNode);

    return 0;
}
```

OUTPUT:

```
Enter number of vertices: 6
Enter number of edges: 7
Enter the edges (u v):
0 1
0 2
1 3
1 4
2 4
3 5
4 5
Enter starting node for traversal: 0

BFS Traversal: 0 1 2 3 4 5
DFS Traversal: 0 1 3 5 4 2
```

6.6. MINIMUM SPANNING TREE

A spanning tree is a subset of Graph G, which has all the vertices covered with minimum possible number of edges. Hence, a spanning tree does not have cycles and it cannot be disconnected. By this definition, we can draw a conclusion that every connected and undirected Graph G has at least one spanning tree. A disconnected graph does not have any spanning tree, as it cannot be spanned to all its vertices. We found three spanning trees off one complete graph. A complete undirected graph can have maximum n^{n-2} number of spanning trees, where n is the number of nodes. In the above addressed example, n is 3, hence $3^{3-2} = 3$ spanning trees are possible.

6.6.1 General Properties of Spanning Tree

We now understand that one graph can have more than one spanning tree. Following are a few properties of the spanning tree connected to graph G –

- A connected graph G can have more than one spanning tree.
- All possible spanning trees of graph G, have the same number of edges and vertices.
- The spanning tree does not have any cycle (loops).
- Removing one edge from the spanning tree will make the graph disconnected, i.e. the spanning tree is minimally connected.
- Adding one edge to the spanning tree will create a circuit or loop, i.e. the spanning tree is maximally acyclic.

6.6.2 Mathematical Properties of Spanning Tree

- Spanning tree has n-1 edges, where n is the number of nodes (vertices).
- From a complete graph, by removing maximum e - n + 1 edges, we can construct a spanning tree.
- A complete graph can have maximum n^{n-2} number of spanning trees.

Thus, we can conclude that spanning trees are a subset of connected Graph G and disconnected graphs do not have spanning tree.

6.6.3 Application of Spanning Tree

Spanning tree is basically used to find a minimum path to connect all nodes in a graph. Common application of spanning trees is –

- Civil Network Planning
- Computer Network Routing Protocol
- Cluster Analysis

Let us understand this through a small example. Consider, city network as a huge graph and now plans to deploy telephone lines in such a way that in minimum lines we can connect to all city nodes. This is where the spanning tree comes into picture.

6.6.4 Minimum Spanning Tree (MST)

In a weighted graph, a minimum spanning tree is a spanning tree that has minimum weight than all other spanning trees of the same graph. In real-world situations, this weight can be measured as distance, congestion, traffic load or any arbitrary value denoted to the edges.

Minimum Spanning-Tree Algorithm

We shall learn about two most important spanning tree algorithms that use greedy approach:

- Kruskal's Algorithm
- Prim's Algorithm

Kruskal's Algorithm Steps

1. Sort all the edges in non-decreasing order of their weight.
2. Pick the smallest edge. Check if it forms a cycle with the spanning tree formed so far. If cycle is not formed, include this edge. Else, discard it.
3. Repeat step2 until there are (V-1) edges in the spanning tree.

The algorithm is a Greedy Algorithm. The Greedy Choice is to pick the smallest weight edge that does not form a cycle in the MST constructed so far. Let us understand it with an example: Consider the following input graph.

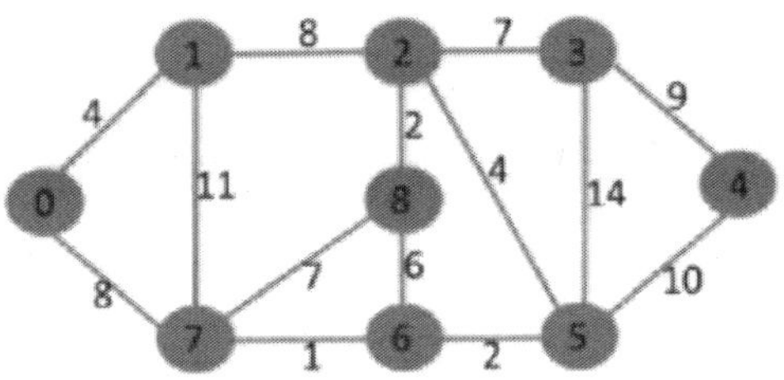

The graph contains 9 vertices and 14 edges. So, the minimum spanning tree formed will be having (9 – 1) = 8 edges.

After sorting:

Weight	Src	Dest
1	7	6
2	8	2
2	6	5
4	0	1
4	2	5
6	8	6
7	2	3
7	7	8
8	0	7
8	1	2
9	3	4
10	5	4
11	1	7
14	3	5

Now pick all edges one by one from sorted list of edges

1. *Pick edge 7-6:* No cycle is formed, include it.

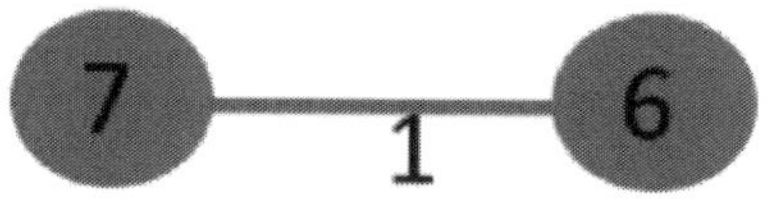

2. *Pick edge 8-2:* No cycle is formed, include it.

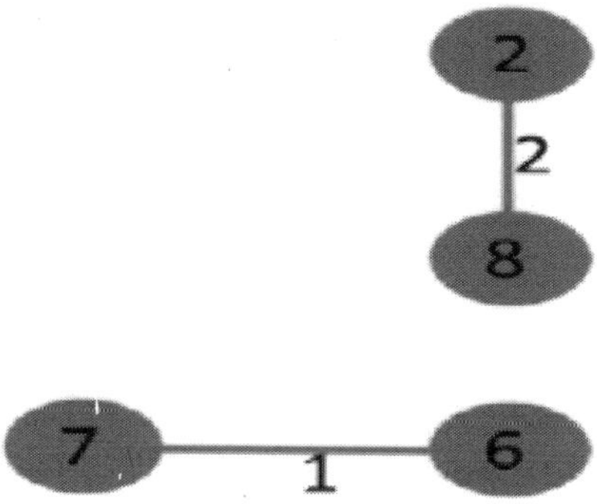

3. *Pick edge 6-5:* No cycle is formed, include it.

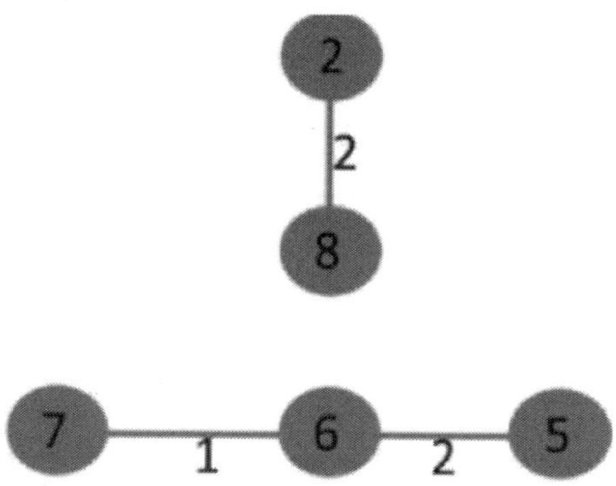

4. *Pick edge 0-1:* No cycle is formed, include it.

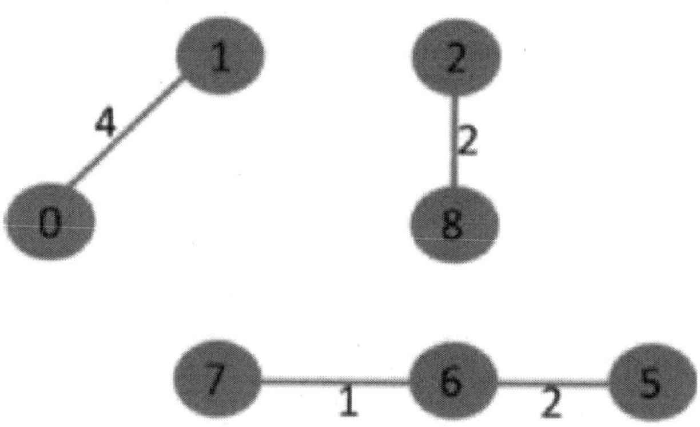

5. *Pick edge 2-5:* No cycle is formed, include it.

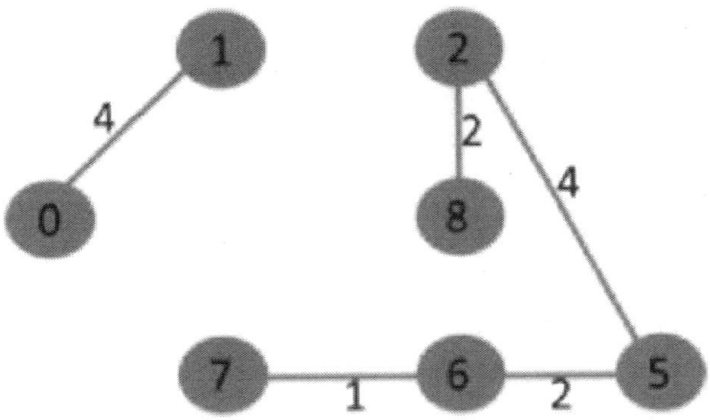

6. *Pick edge 8-6:* Since including this edge results in cycle, discard it.

7.*Pick edge 2-3:* No cycle is formed, include it.

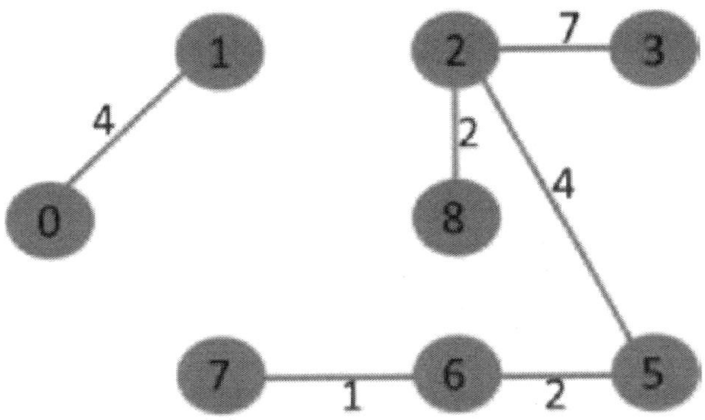

8.*Pick edge 7-8:* Since including this edge results in cycle, discard it.

9.*Pick edge 0-7:* No cycle is formed, include it.

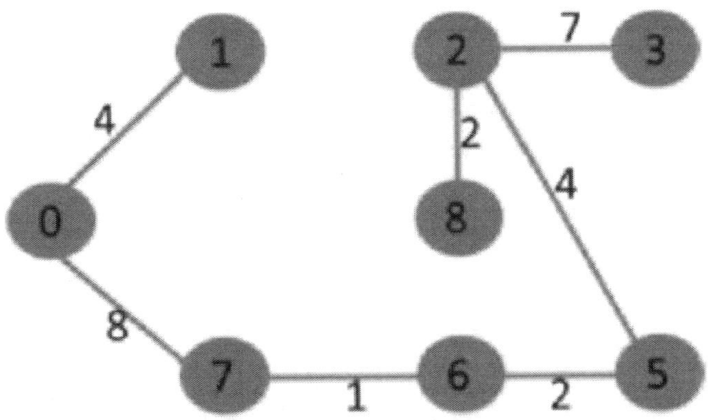

10.*Pick edge 1-2:* Since including this edge results in cycle, discard it.

11. *Pick edge 3-4:* No cycle is formed, include it.

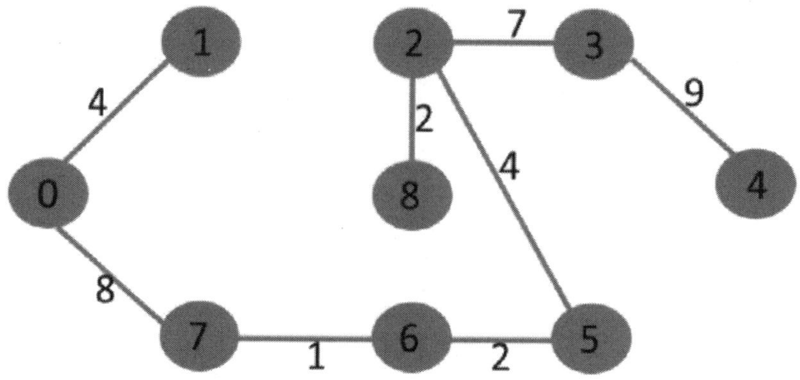

Since the number of edges included equals (V – 1), the algorithm stops here. So this is the minimum spanning tree.

Prim's algorithm

Prim's algorithm uses the greedy approach and shares a similarity with the **shortest path first** algorithms. Prim's algorithm, in contrast with Kruskal's algorithm, treats the nodes as a single tree and keeps on adding new nodes to the spanning tree from the given graph. To contrast with Kruskal's algorithm and to understand Prim's algorithm better, we shall use the same example –

Step 1 - Remove all loops and parallel edges

Remove all loops and parallel edges from the given graph. In case of parallel edges, keep the one which has the least cost associated and remove all others.

Step 2 - Choose any arbitrary node as root node

In this case, we choose **S** node as the root node of Prim's spanning tree. This node is arbitrarily chosen, so any node can be the root node. One may wonder why any video can be a root node. So the answer is, in the spanning tree all the nodes of a graph are included and because it is connected then there must be at least one edge, which will join it to the rest of the tree.

Step 3 - Check outgoing edges and select the one with less cost

After choosing the root node **S**, we see that S,A and S,C are two edges with weight 7 and 8, respectively. We choose the edge S,A as it is lesser than the other. Now, the tree S-7-A is treated as one node and we check for all edges going out from it. We select the one which has the lowest cost and include it in the tree. After this step, S-7-A-3-C tree is formed. Now we'll again treat it as a node and will check all the edges again. However, we will choose only the least cost edge. In this case, C-3-D is the new edge, which is less than other edges' cost 8, 6, 4, etc.

After adding node **D** to the spanning tree, we now have two edges going out of it having the same cost, i.e. D-2-T and D-2-B. Thus, we can add either one. But the next step will again yield edge 2 as the least cost. Hence, we are showing a spanning tree with both edges included. We may find that the output spanning tree of the same graph using two different algorithms is same.

Programming Exercise 6.2

Write a program to implement Prim's algorithm and Krushkal's algorithm to find minimum spanning tree of a graph.

```
#include <iostream>
#include <vector>
#include <algorithm>
#include <climits>

using namespace std;
// Structure to represent an edge
struct Edge {
   int src, dest, weight;
};

// Structure to represent a graph
struct Graph {
   int V, E;
   vector<Edge> edges;
};

// Find function for Disjoint Set (Used in Kruskal's Algorithm)
int find(vector<int>& parent, int i) {
   if (parent[i] == -1) return i;
   return find(parent, parent[i]);
}

// Union function for Disjoint Set
void unionSets(vector<int>& parent, int x, int y) {
   int xroot = find(parent, x);
   int yroot = find(parent, y);
   parent[xroot] = yroot;
}

// Compare function for sorting edges by weight
bool compare(Edge a, Edge b) {
```

```
    return a.weight<b.weight;
}

// Kruskal's Algorithm for MST
void kruskalMST(Graph& graph) {
    vector<Edge> result;
    vector<int>parent(graph.V, -1);

    // Sort edges based on weight
    sort(graph.edges.begin(), graph.edges.end(), compare);

    for (auto edge :graph.edges) {
        int x = find(parent, edge.src);
        int y = find(parent, edge.dest);

        // Include the edge if it does not form a cycle
        if (x != y) {
result.push_back(edge);
unionSets(parent, x, y);
        }
    }

    // Print MST
cout<< "Kruskal's MST:\n";
    for (auto edge : result) {
cout<<edge.src<< " - " <<edge.dest<<" : " <<edge.weight<< "\n";
    }
}

// Prim's Algorithm for MST
void primMST(vector<vector<int>>& graph, int V) {
    vector<int>parent(V, -1);
    vector<int>key(V, INT_MAX);
    vector<bool>inMST(V, false);
```

```
key[0] = 0;

  for (int count = 0; count < V - 1; count++) {
    int u = -1;
    for (int i = 0; i< V; i++) {
      if (!inMST[i] && (u == -1 || key[i] < key[u]))
        u = i;
    }

inMST[u] = true;

    for (int v = 0; v < V; v++) {
      if (graph[u][v] && !inMST[v] && graph[u][v] < key[v]) {
        key[v] = graph[u][v];
        parent[v] = u;
      }
    }
  }

  // Print MST
cout<< "Prim's MST:\n";
for (int i = 1; i< V; i++) {
  cout<< parent[i] << " - " <<i<<" : " << graph[i][parent[i]] << "\n";
  }
}

int main() {
  int V, E;

  cout<< "Enter number of vertices and edges: ";
  cin>> V >> E;

  Graph graph;
  graph.V = V;
  graph.E = E;
```

```
  cout<< "Enter edges (srcdest weight):\n";
  for (int i = 0; i< E; i++) {
    int src, dest, weight;
    cin>>src>>dest>> weight;
    graph.edges.push_back({src, dest, weight});
  }

  kruskalMST(graph);

  // Creating adjacency matrix for Prim's Algorithm
  vector<vector<int>>adjMatrix(V, vector<int>(V, 0));

  for (auto edge :graph.edges) {
    adjMatrix[edge.src][edge.dest] = edge.weight;
    adjMatrix[edge.dest][edge.src] = edge.weight;
  }

  primMST(adjMatrix, V);

  return 0;
}
```

OUTPUT:

```
Enter number of vertices and edges: 5 7
Enter edges (srcdest weight):
0 1 2
0 3 6
1 2 3
1 3 8
1 4 5
2 4 7
3 4 9

Kruskal's MST:
0 - 1 : 2
1 - 2 : 3
```

1 - 4 : 5

0 - 3 : 6

Prim's MST:

0 - 1 : 2

1 - 2 : 3

1 - 4 : 5

0 - 3 : 6

6.7 ALL-PAIRS SHORTEST PATHS

Here we consider the problem of finding shortest paths between all pairs of vertices in a graph. This problem might arise in making a table of distances between all pairs of cities for a road atlas. As we are given a weighted, directed graph G = (V, E) with a weight function w: E R that maps edges to real-valued weights. We wish to find, for every pair of vertices (u,v)€ V, a shortest (least-weight) path from u to v, where the weight of a path is the sum of the weights of its constituent edges. We typically want the output in tabular form: the entry in u's row and v's column should be the weight of a shortest path from u to v.

We can solve an all-pairs shortest-paths problem by running a single-source shortest-paths algorithm V times, once for each vertex as the source. If all edge weights are nonnegative, we can use Dijkstra's algorithm. If we use the linear-array implementation of the priority queue, the running time is $O(V^3 + VE) = O(V^3)$. The binary-heap implementation of the priority queue yields a running time of O(VE lg V), which is an improvement if the graph is sparse. Alternatively, we can implement the priority queue with a Fibonacci heap, yielding a running time of $O(V^2 \lg V + VE)$.

If negative-weight edges are allowed, Dijkstra's algorithm can no longer be used. Instead, we must run the slower Bellman-Ford algorithm once from each vertex. The resulting running time is $O(V^2 E)$, which on a dense graph is $O(V^4)$. Here we shall see how to do better. We shall also investigate the relation of the all-pairs shortest-paths problem to matrix multiplication and study its algebraic structure.

Unlike the single-source algorithms, which assume an adjacency-list representation of the graph, most of the algorithms in this chapter use an adjacency-matrix representation. (Johnson's algorithm for sparse graphs uses adjacency lists.) The input is an n n matrix W representing the edge weights of an n-vertex directed graph G = (V, E). That is, W = (wij), where

$$w_{ij} = \begin{cases} 0 & \text{if } i = j , \\ \text{the weight of directed edge } (i, j) & \text{if } i \neq j \text{ and } (i, j) \in E , \\ \infty & \text{if } i \neq j \text{ and } (i, j) \notin E . \end{cases}$$

The Floyd-Warshall Algorithm

Floyd-Warshall's algorithm is based upon the observation that a path linking any two vertices u and v may have zero or more intermediate vertices. The algorithm begins by disallowing all intermediate vertices. In this case, the partial solution is simply the initial weights of the graph or infinity if there is no edge.

The algorithm proceeds by allowing an additional intermediate vertex at each step. For each introduction of a new intermediate vertex x, the shortest path between any pair of vertices u and v, x,u,v∈V, is the minimum of the previous best estimate of δ(u,v), or the combination of the paths from u→x and x→v.

$$\delta(u,v) \leftarrow \min(\delta(u,v), \delta(u,x)+\delta(x,v))$$

Let the directed graph be represented by a weighted matrix W.

```
FLOYD-WARSHALL (W)
n ← rows [W]
D(0) ← W
for k← 1to n
do for i← 1to n
 do for j← 1to n
 do dij (k) ← MIN ( dij (k-1),dik (k-1) + dkj(k-1))
return D(n)
```

Time Complexity-

Floyd Warshall Algorithm consists of three loops over all nodes.

The inner most loop consists of only operations of a constant complexity.

Hence, the asymptotic complexity of Floyd-Warshall algorithm is O(n3), where n is the number of nodes in the given graph.

So, The time complexity of the algorithm above is $O(n^3)$.

Consider the following directed weighted graph. Let us find the shortest path distance between every pair of vertices using Floyd-Warshall Algorithm.

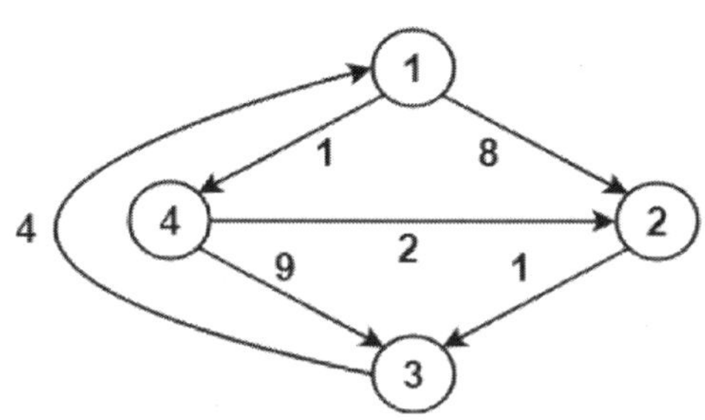

Step-01:

Remove all the self loops and parallel edges (keeping the edge with lowest weight) from the graph if any. In our case, we don't have any self edge and parallel edge.

Step-02:

Now, write the initial distance matrix representing the distance between every pair of vertices as mentioned in the given graph in the form of weights.

For diagonal elements (representing self-loops), value = 0

For vertices having a direct edge between them, value = weight of that edge

For vertices having no direct edges between them, value = ∞

D_0 =

	1	2	3	4
1	0	8	∞	1
2	∞	0	1	∞
3	4	∞	0	∞
4	∞	2	9	0

D_1 =

	1	2	3	4
1	0	8	∞	1
2	∞	0	1	∞
3	4	12	0	5
4	∞	2	9	0

D_2 =

	1	2	3	4
1	0	8	9	1
2	∞	0	1	∞
3	4	12	0	5
4	∞	2	3	0

D_3 =

	1	2	3	4
1	0	8	9	1
2	5	0	1	6
3	4	12	0	5
4	7	2	3	0

D_4 =

	1	2	3	4
1	0	3	4	1
2	5	0	1	6
3	4	7	0	5
4	7	2	3	0

Step-03:

Since, we have total 4 vertices in our given graph, so we will have total 4 matrices of order 4 x 4 in our solution. (excluding initial distance matrix)Diagonal elements of each matrix will always be 0.

Programming Exercise 6.3

Write a program to find the shortest path distance between every pair of vertices using Floyd-Warshall Algorithm.

```
#include <iostream>
#include <vector>
#include <limits.h>
#define INF INT_MAX // Define infinity as a large integer value
using namespace std;
// Function to implement Floyd-Warshall Algorithm
void floydWarshall(vector<vector<int>>& graph, int V) {
  vector<vector<int>>dist = graph; // Distance matrix initialized with graph weights
  // Applying Floyd-Warshall algorithm
  for (int k = 0; k < V; k++) {
    for (int i = 0; i< V; i++) {
      for (int j = 0; j < V; j++) {
        // If vertex k is on the shortest path from i to j, update dist[i][j]
        if (dist[i][k] != INF &&dist[k][j] != INF &&dist[i][k] + dist[k][j] <dist[i][j]) {
               dist[i][j] = dist[i][k] + dist[k][j];
        }
      }
    }
  }
  // Printing the shortest distance matrix
  cout<< "\nShortest distances between every pair of vertices:\n";
  for (int i = 0; i< V; i++) {
    for (int j = 0; j < V; j++) {
      if (dist[i][j] == INF)
        cout<< "INF" << "\t";
      else
        cout<<dist[i][j] << "\t";
    }
    cout<<endl;
  }
```

```
}
int main() {
  int V;
  cout<< "Enter the number of vertices: ";
  cin>> V;
  vector<vector<int>>graph(V, vector<int>(V));
  cout<< "Enter the adjacency matrix (use " << INF << " for infinity):\n";
  for (int i = 0; i< V; i++) {
    for (int j = 0; j < V; j++) {
        cin>> graph[i][j];
    }
  }
  floydWarshall(graph, V);
  return 0;
}
```

OUTPUT:

```
Enter the number of vertices: 4
Enter the adjacency matrix (use 2147483647 for infinity):
0 3 2147483647 7
8 0 2 2147483647
5 2147483647 0 1
2 2147483647 2147483647 00 3 2147483647 7

8 0 2 2147483647
5 2147483647 0 1
2 2147483647 2147483647 0

Shortest distances between every pair of vertices:
0    3    5    6
5    0    2    3
3    6    0    1
2    5    7    0
```

6.8 DIJKSTRA'S ALGORITHM

Given a graph G and a source node A, the Dijkstra's algorithm is used to find the shortest path between A and every other node. It does not work on a graph having negative weights. Objective of the Dijkstras Algorithm is to find the shortest path between any two vertices in a graph. It will find the shortest path from a given starting vertex to every other vertex in the graph.

Dijkstra algorithm steps:

1. Initialize:

   - Set distance[StartVertex] = 0
   - Set distance of all other vertices to ∞ (infinity)
   - Create an empty set of visited vertices

2. While there are unvisited vertices:

   a. Select the unvisited vertex with the smallest known distance (CurrentVertex)

   b. Mark CurrentVertex as visited

   c. Relaxation: For each unvisited neighbor (Neighbor) of CurrentVertex:

      i). Calculate new_distance = distance[CurrentVertex] + edge_weight(CurrentVertex, Neighbor)

      ii). If new_distance<distance[Neighbor]:

         - Update distance[Neighbor] = new_distance
         - Update previous[Neighbor] = CurrentVertex

3. Repeat until all vertices are visited

4. Output the shortest distances and paths from StartVertex to all other vertices

Example Find the shortest path from A to every other vertex using Dijkstra's algorithm.

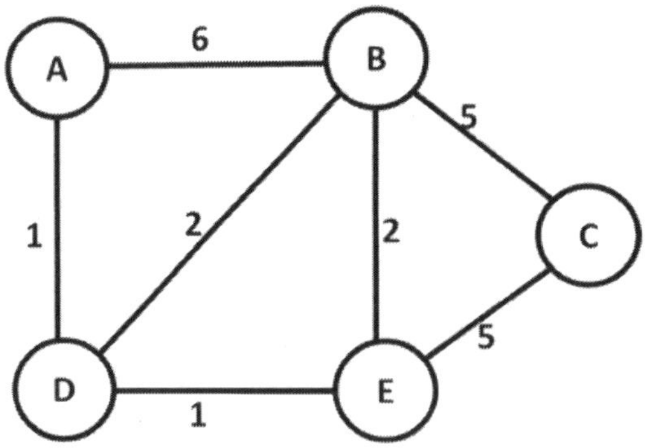

The start vertex is considered as A. Distance from A to A is 0. Distances from A to all other vertices are unknown, therefore infinity.

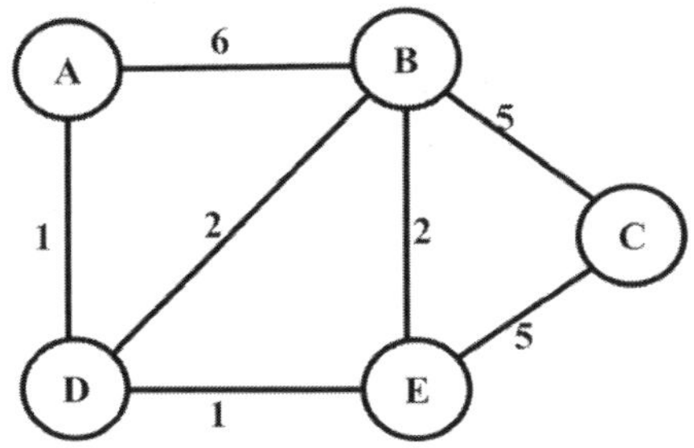

Visited=[ ]
Unvisited=[A,B,C,D,E]

Vertex	Shortest distance from A	Previous vertex
A	0	
B	∞	
C	∞	
D	∞	
E	∞	

We have to visit the unvisited vertex with the smallest distance from start vertex. In this case, vertex A satisfies this criteria, so A is selected. For this current vertex A, we examine its unvisited neighbbors B and D. We also find distance of each neighbor from start vertex. If the calculated distance of a vertex is less than the known distance, then we update the shortest distance. Next we update the previous vertex for each of the updated distances. Here, we visited B and D via A. Current vertex A is now visited.

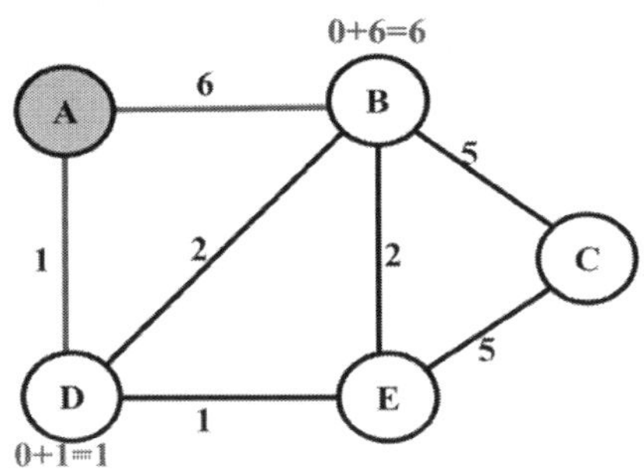

Visited=[A]
Unvisited=[B,C,D,E]

Vertex	Shortest distance from A	Previous vertex
A	0	
B	6	A
C	∞	
D	1	A
E	∞	

Next we visit D with smallest distance from start vertex. Unvisited neighbors of D are B and E. Distances of each neighbors from start vertex are also found. B and E are visited via D. Then we update the table.

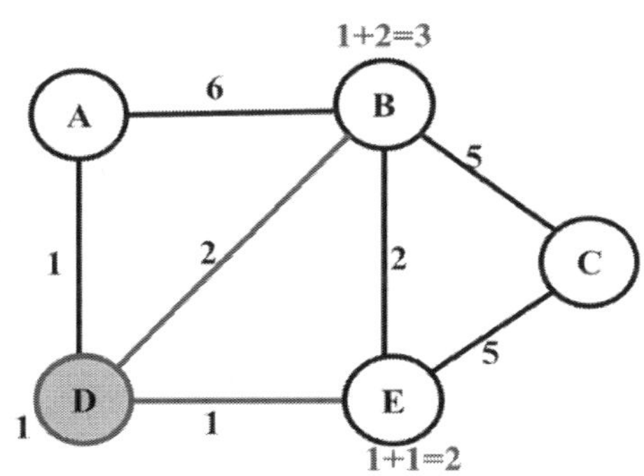

Visited=[A,D]
Unvisited=[B,C,E]

Vertex	Shortest distance from A	Previous vertex
A	0	
B	3	D
C	∞	
D	1	A
E	2	D

The unvisited vertex with smallest distance from start vertex is E. Unvisited neighbors of E are B and C. Distances of each neighbors from start vertex are also found. Here, calculated distance of B is greater than its known distance. So, we do not need to update the distance to B. We update value of C.

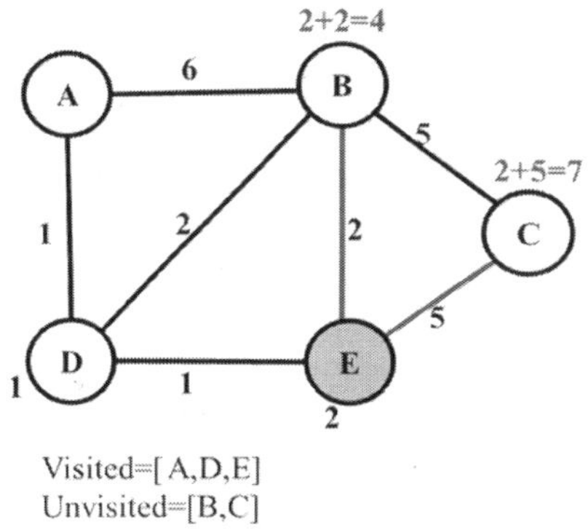

Vertex	Shortest distance from A	Previous vertex
A	0	
B	3	D
C	7	E
D	1	A
E	2	D

Next unvisited vertex with smallest known distance is B whose unvisited neighbor is C. We do not update vertex C. C has no unvisited vertices.

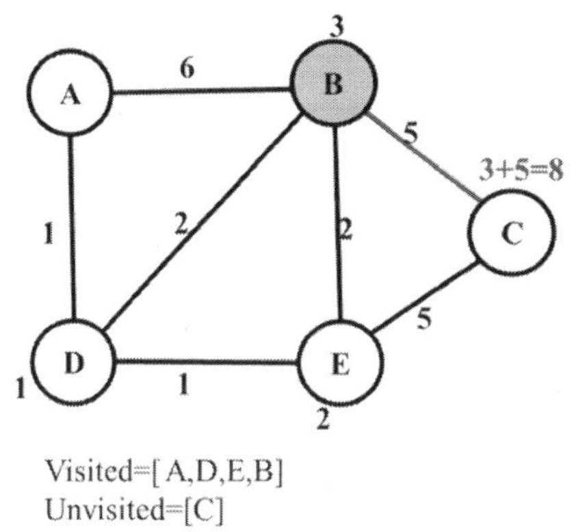

Vertex	Shortest distance from A	Previous vertex
A	0	
B	3	D
C	7	E
D	1	A
E	2	D

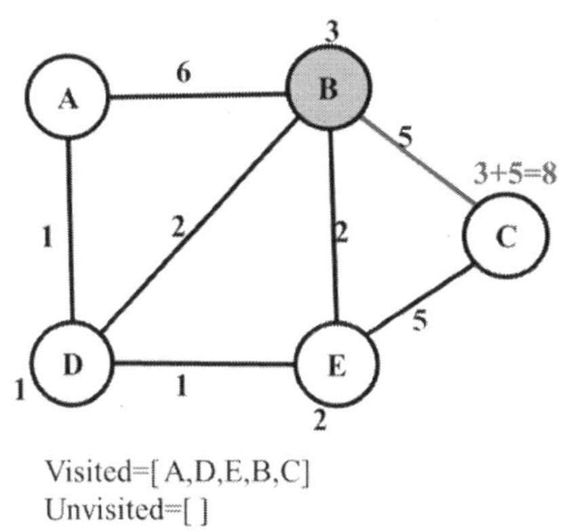

Vertex	Shortest distance from A	Previous vertex
A	0	
B	3	D
C	7	E
D	1	A
E	2	D

Example: Find the shortest path from A to every other vertex using Dijkstra's algorithm.

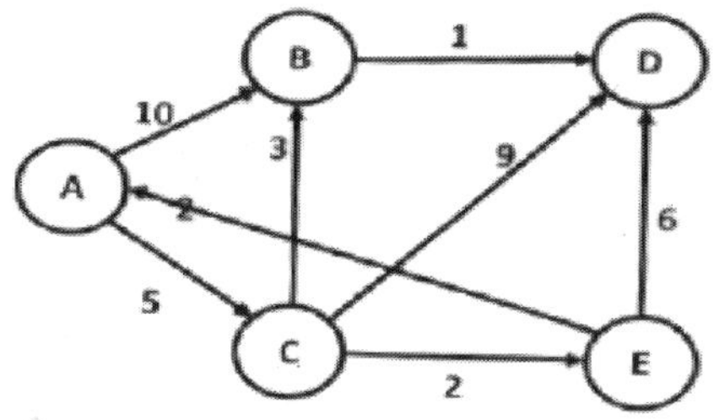

<u>Step 1</u>

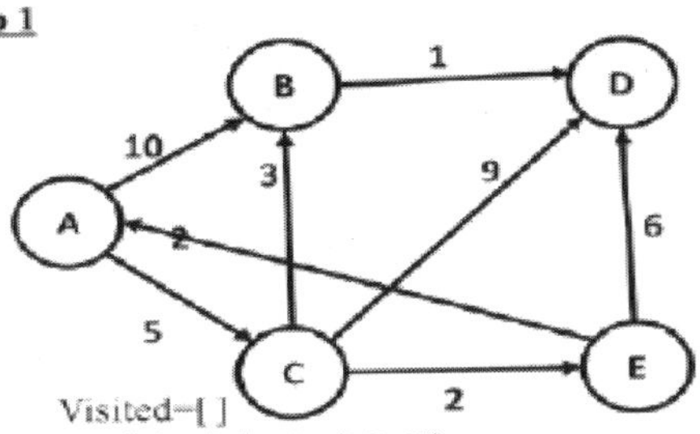

Visited=[ ]
Unvisited=[A,B,C,D,E]

Vertex	Shortest distance from A	Previous vertex
A	0	
B	∞	
C	∞	
D	∞	
E	∞	

<u>Step 2</u>

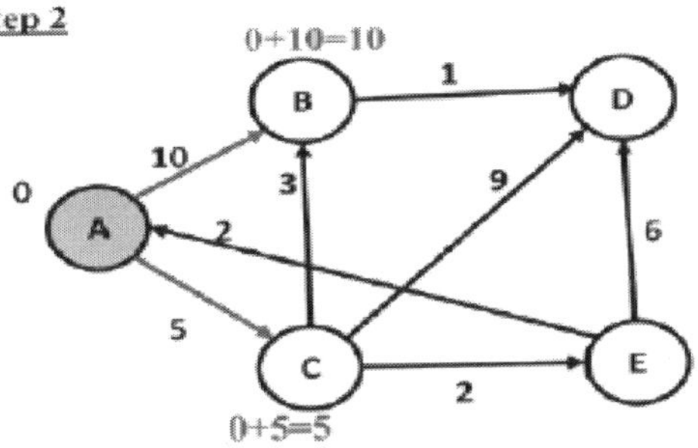

Visited=[A]
Unvisited=[B,C,D,E]

Vertex	Shortest distance from A	Previous vertex
A	0	
B	10	A
C	5	A
D	∞	
E	∞	

<u>Step 3</u>

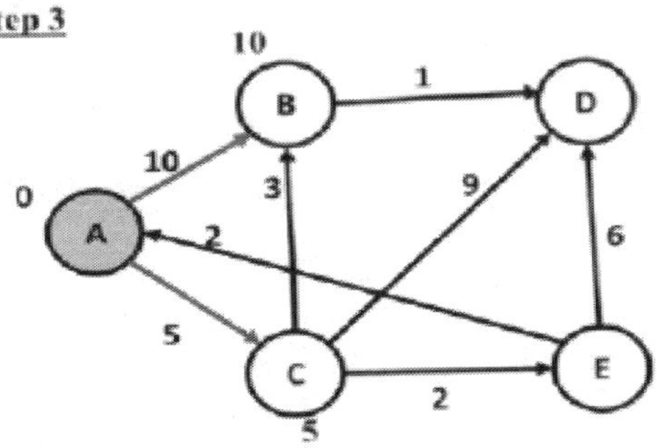

Visited=[A]
Unvisited=[B,C,D,E]

Vertex	Shortest distance from A	Previous vertex
A	0	
B	10	A
C	5	A
D	∞	
E	∞	

Step 4

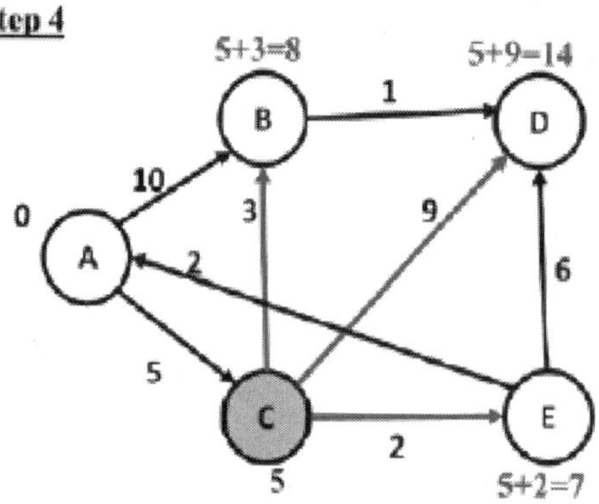

Visited=[A,C]
Unvisited=[B,D,E]

Vertex	Shortest distance from A	Previous vertex
A	0	
B	8	C
C	5	A
D	14	C
E	7	C

Step 5

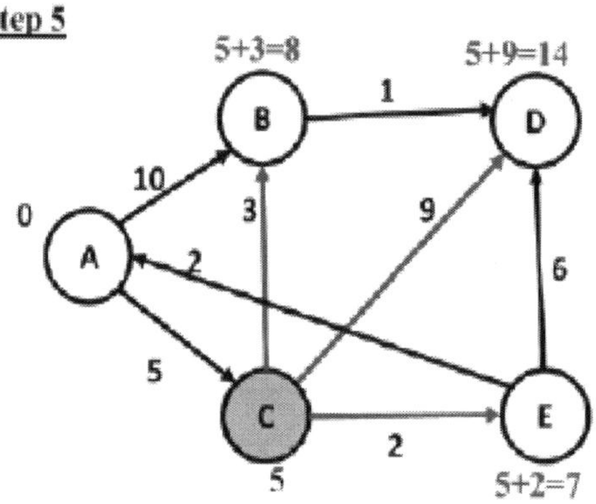

Visited=[A,C]
Unvisited=[B,D,E]

Vertex	Shortest distance from A	Previous vertex
A	0	
B	8	C
C	5	A
D	14	C
E	7	C

Step 6

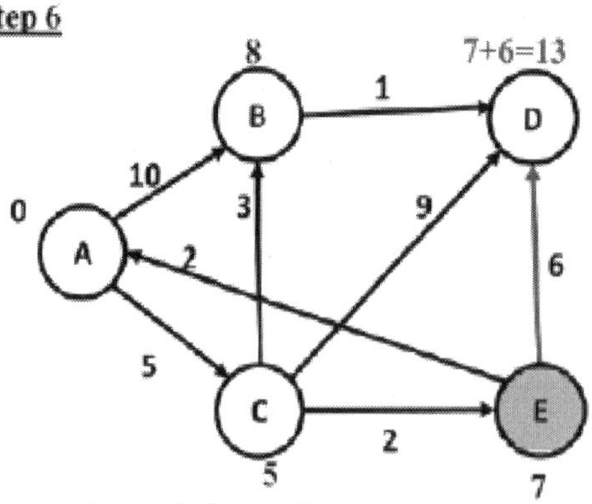

Visited=[A,C,E]
Unvisited=[B,D]

Vertex	Shortest distance from A	Previous vertex
A	0	
B	8	C
C	5	A
D	13	E
E	7	C

Step 7

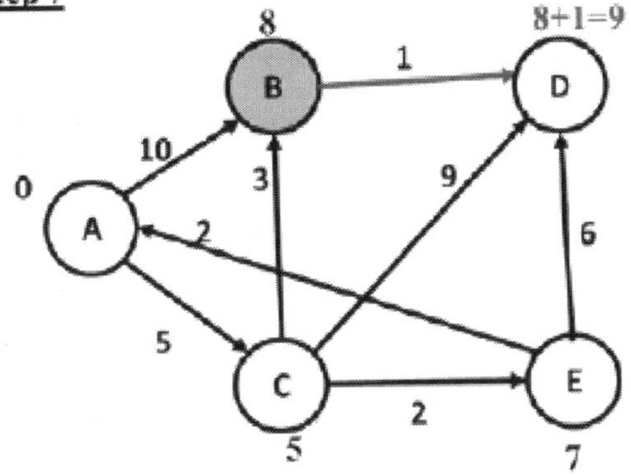

Visited=[A,C,E,B]
Unvisited=[D]

Vertex	Shortest distance from A	Previous vertex
A	0	
B	8	C
C	5	A
D	**9**	**B**
E	7	C

Step 8

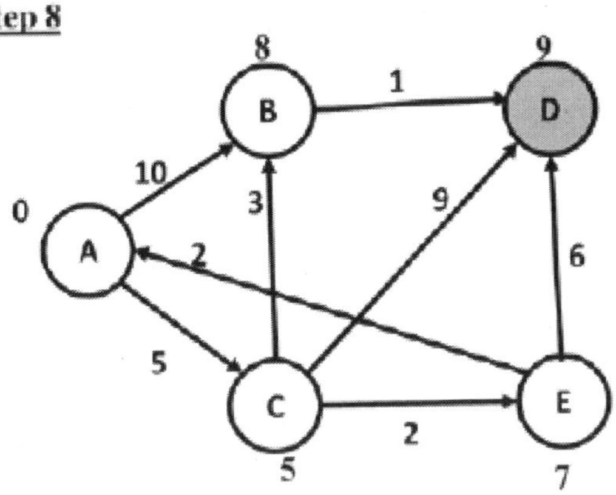

Visited=[A,C,E,B,D]
Unvisited=[ ]

Vertex	Shortest distance from A	Previous vertex
A	0	
B	8	C
C	5	A
D	9	B
E	7	C

6.9 BELLMAN FORD ALGORITHM

In a directed weighted graph we have to select one of the vertices as source vertex and find out the shortest path to all other vertices. To solve this problem, we already have Dijkstra's algorithm. However, Dijkstra's algorithm will not work if there are negative weights. Hence, we use Bellman Ford algorithm which states that we go on relaxing all the edges for n-1 times, where n is the number of vertices.

Bellman Ford algorithm finds the shortest distance from a single source vertex to all the other vertices of a weighted graph. It works on graph having negative weights. However, if a graph contains any cycle whose edges' sum is negative, then this algorithm will not work.

Example: Find the shortest path from A to every other vertex using Bellman Ford algorithm.

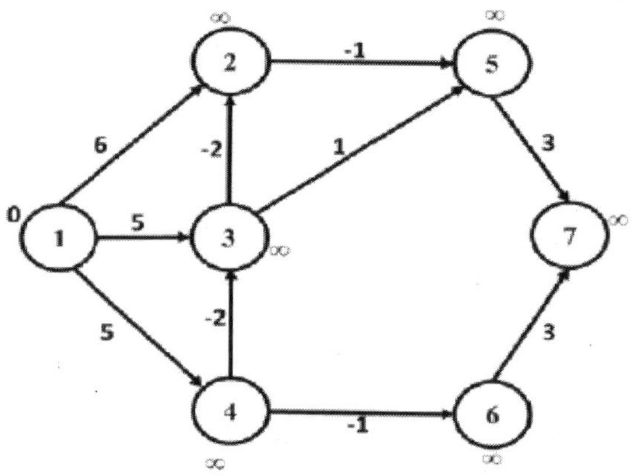

First we write down all the edges as: (1,2), (1,3), (1,4), (2,5), (3,2), (3,5),(4,3),(4,6),(5,7),(6,7)

These edges are relaxed for n-1=7-1=6 times.

1= Source vertex whose distance is zero.

Distance of all remaining edges will be infinity initially.

Number of iterations=7-1=6

1st Iteration

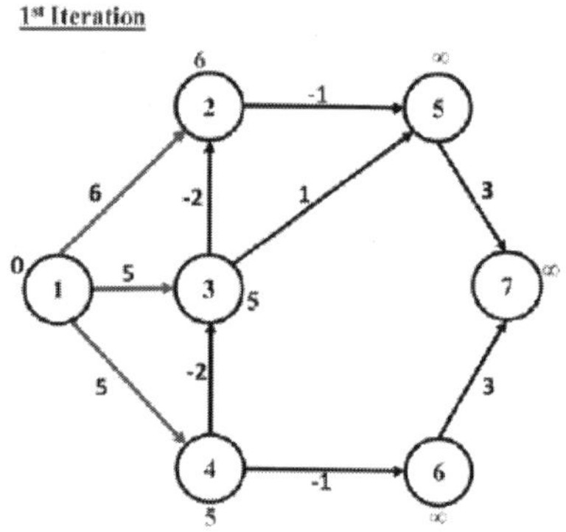

Edges are relaxed in the order (1,2), (1,3), (1,4)

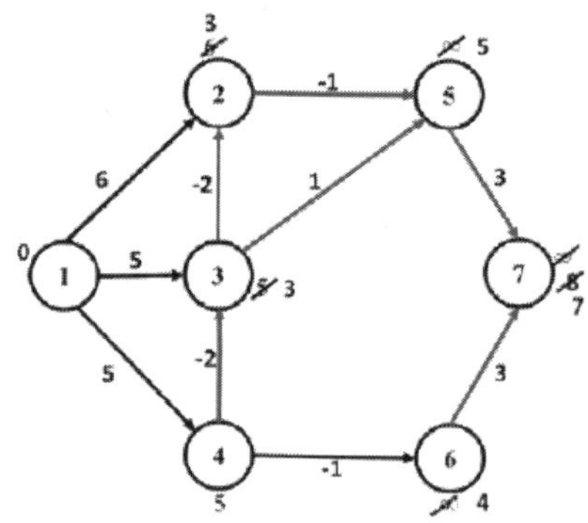

Edges are relaxed in the order (2,5), (3,2), (3,5), (4,3), (4,6), (5,7), (6,7)

2nd Iteration

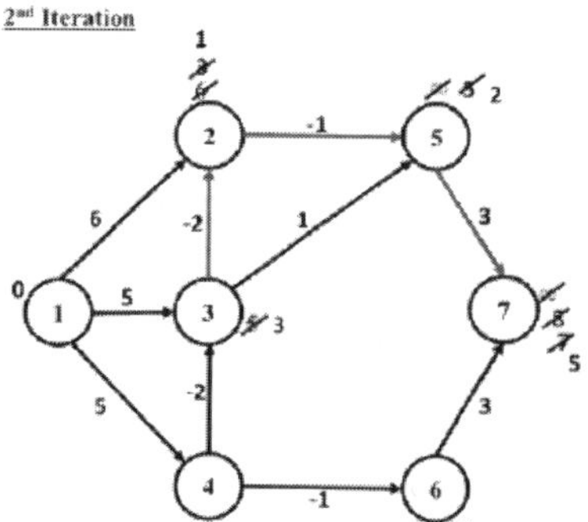

Edges are relaxed in their respective order

3rd Iteration

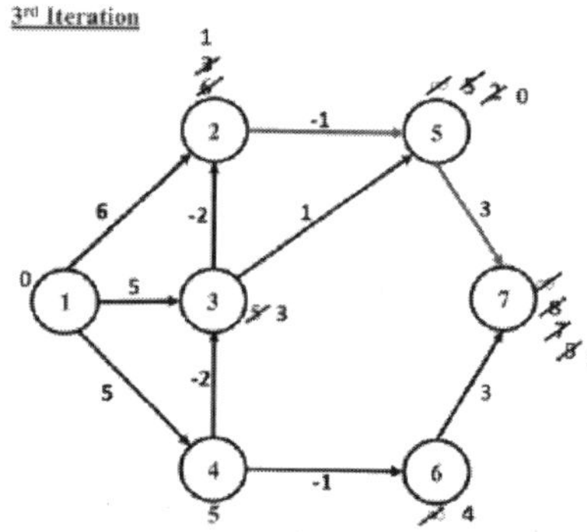

Edges are relaxed in their respective order

From 4th iteration onwards, there is no change in distances.

6.10 LET US SUM UP

- This chapter introduces the graph data structure. Basic terminologies associated with Graph are discussed. Various applications and representation of graph are discussed in detail.
- The chapter discusses about Traversal of a Graph using BFS and DFS techniques.
- In a weighted graph, a minimum spanning tree is a spanning tree that has minimum weight than all other spanning trees of the same graph. In real-world situations, this weight can be measured as distance, congestion, traffic load or any arbitrary value denoted to the edges.
- Two MST calculation algorithms are discussed in detail. All/Single pair shortest path algorithmsis also discussed in detail.

6.11CHECK YOUR PROGRESS

1. Consider the following graph
   i. Find the adjacency list
   ii. Draw the adjacency matrix

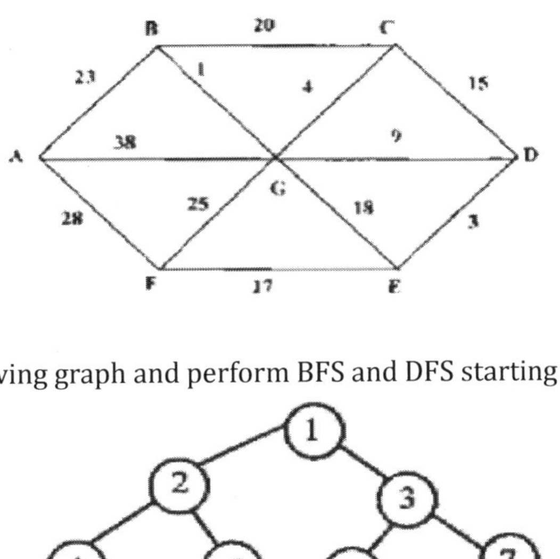

2. Consider the following graph and perform BFS and DFS starting with vertex '1'.

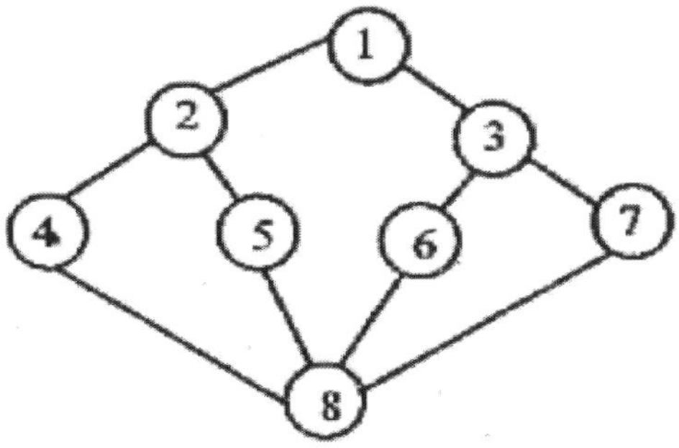

3. Write down the DFS and BFS algorithm for graph traversal.
4. Define spanning tree. What is minimum spanning tree? Explain Prims and Krushkals algorithm to find MST. Apply Krushkals and Prims algorithm to find MST from the following graph.

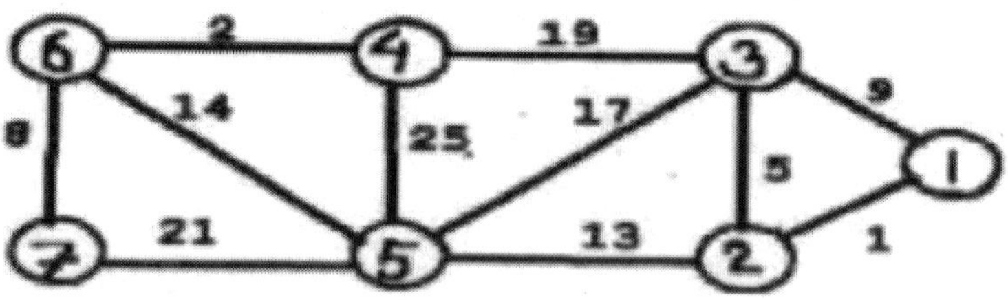

5. Consider the following weighted graph. Find the all pair shortest path.

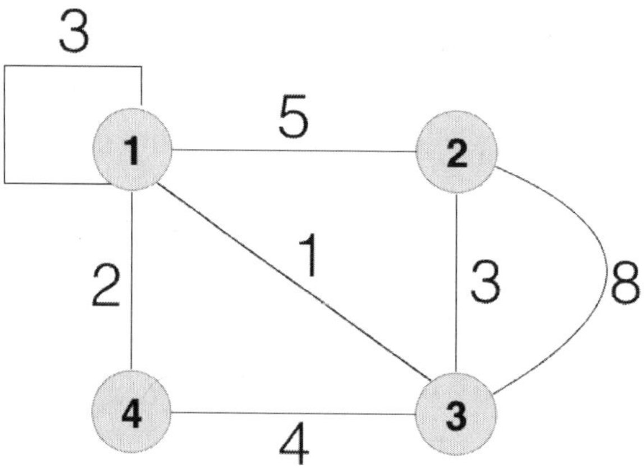

7

DESIGN AND ANALYSIS OF ALGORITHMS

7.1 INTRODUCTION TO ALGORITHM

An algorithm is an interpretable, finite step by step list of well-defined instructions for dealing with a particular problem with recognizable end points and end state or result for input given. Basically, an algorithm is seen as a tool for solving well specified computational problem. As the same problem may be solved by different ways, similarly same task may be performed by many different algorithms. In formal presentation an algorithm consists of two parts. The beginning part contains purpose of the algorithm, variable going to be used in the algorithm and list of input. The second part contains the list of steps required to be executed. Let us take a sorting algorithm to understand algorithmic notation better.

Algorithm INSERTION_SORT(A,n) ***part1**

This algorithm sorts the array A which contains 'n' number of elements

1. Assign A[0]:= -∞. ***part2**
2. Repeat Steps 3 to 5 for i=2 to n
3. Assign T:=A[i] and PTR:= i-1.
4. Repeat while T<A[PTR]
    a. Assign A[PTR+1]:= A[PTR]
    b. Assign PTR:=PTR-1.
5. Assign A[PTR+1]:=T
6. Exit

For a particular problem there are many ways to design algorithms for it. Some of the popular design techniques are:

- Brute force algorithm
- Divide and conquer
- Greedy Approach

- Dynamic Programming
- Branch and bound
- Backtracking

7.1.1 Brute Force Algorithm

Brute Force approach for solving any problem is the most straightforward way of solving a problem. It simply works by exhaustively trying out all the possible solutions until the right solution is identified. We can understand the approach of brute force algorithm with the following example.

Suppose a boy got a chance to win a cash briefcase with 100 million dollars in a game. But the box is locked with a safety four-digit combination code lock, and he is asked to just make the correct combination of the four-digit code. Now, he is not given any hint for solving the safety code lock problem. So, the last option if he wanted the 100 million dollars is to go with the brute force method in which he needs to go on trying for every possible four-digit combination of code from range 0-9. The total no of possible combinations he must try is 10,000 which is a very exhaustive approach to get the problem solved. Fig 7.1 shows the entire process of the game in which brute force technique is applied.

So, we can see that this process of solving a problem is not a optimal approach but it guarantees that the solution for the problem will be discovered as all possible solutions are identified in this approach.

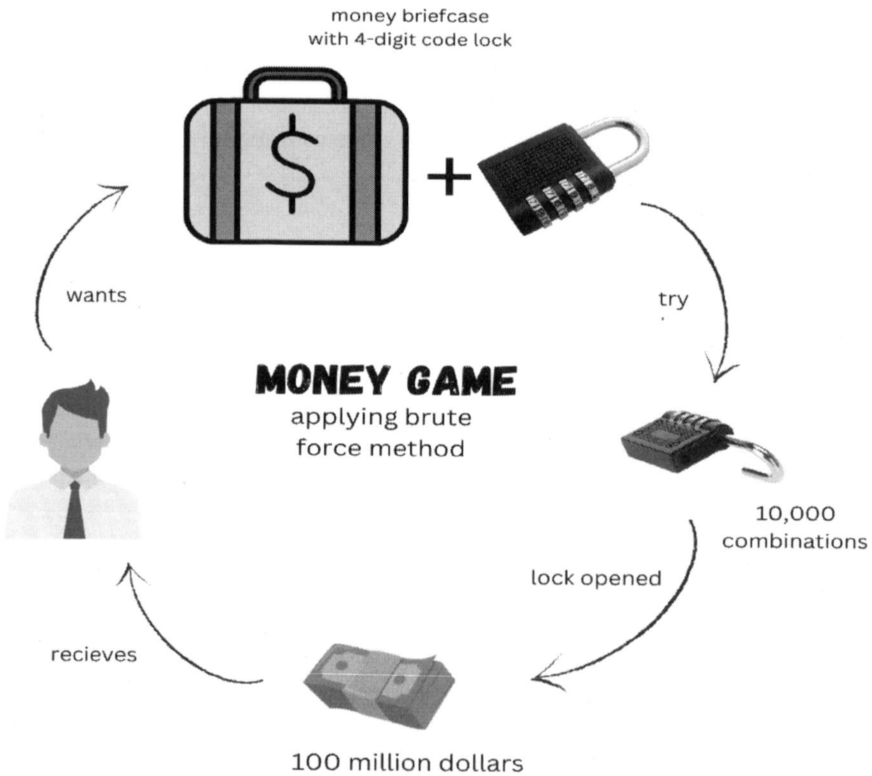

Fig 7.1 Money game in which brute force approach is applied

Fig 7.2 shows the working mechanism of brute force algorithms which just involves 2 basic steps – first to understand the problem and then to try all possible solutions.

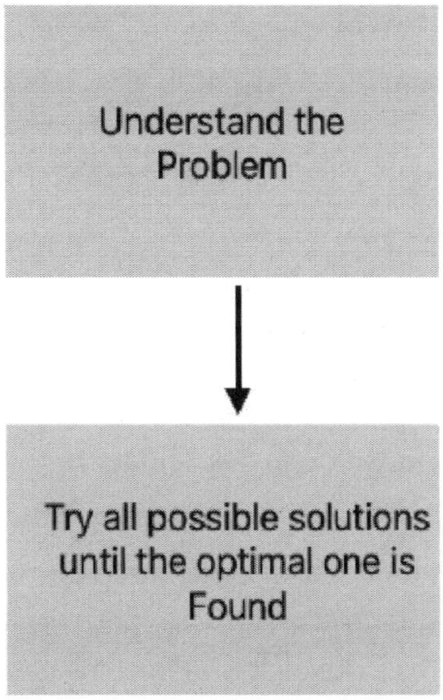

Fig 7.2 Brute force approach

Characteristics of brute force approach

- It is an approach in which all possible solutions are tried until the correct one is found.
- It is very simple to understand.
- It assures a correct solution (if one exists).
- This process is highly inefficient with a higher time complexity.
- It does not have an optimization approach.
- Best when the state space or input size of the problem is smaller.

Now, we will be discussing one problem which is called String Matching problem using brute force technique.

7.1.1.1 Brute Force String Matching

In this section we will be discussing one problem which is called String Matching problem using brute force technique.

What is String Matching Problem ?

It is a problem in which one needs to find a pattern in a text sequence (string). The task is to find a smaller string (substring or pattern) within a larger string. By applying brute force approach, it checks every possible position in the text, one by one, to see if the pattern matches. The brute force approach follows a straightforward "slide and compare" technique.

Steps involved in the procedure:

1. Given a text (T) with length n and a pattern (P) with length m.
2. Align the pattern with the text at index i = 0.
3. Then compare the first character of the pattern to be matched with the character in the text at that position.
4. If they match, we compare the next character of the pattern with the next character in text.
5. Continue step 4 until
   a. The pattern matches (string matching is successful).
   b. A mismatch occurs
6. If a mismatch occurs:
   a. Move the pattern one position forward in text.
   b. Again, compare the first character of pattern with the character in text.
7. Repeat until the pattern is found or the text ends.

Figure 7.3 shows an example of brute force string matching problem. In this example, there is a text "FINDINGFISHES" and pattern "FISH". The task is to find the pattern matching substring within the longer string text. The step wise procedure is shown in the figure.

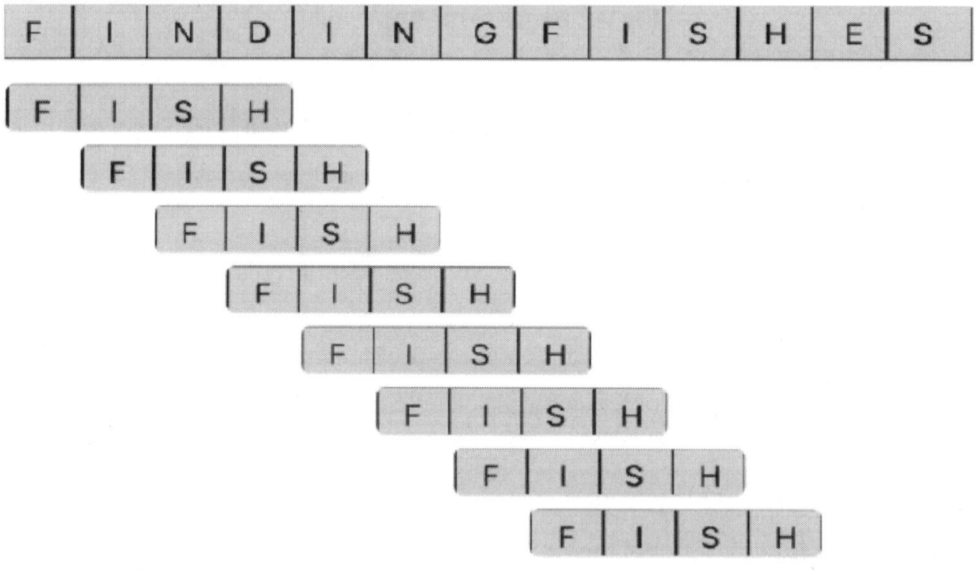

Fig 7.3 Example of brute force pattern matching problem

Brute force string matching algorithm

Algorithm BruteForceStringMatch(T, P)

input:

T ← text of length n

```
  P ← pattern of length m
output:
  list of indices where P occurs in T
initialize an empty list MATCHED_INDICES
for i ← 0 to (n - m) do  // slide pattern over text
  match ← true
  for j ← 0 to (m - 1) do  // compare characters of P with T
    if T[i + j] ≠ P[j] then
      match ← false
      break  // mismatch found, exit inner loop
  end for
  if match = true then
    append i to MATCHED_INDICES  // store matching index
end for
if MATCHED_INDICES is empty then
  return -1  // no match found
else
  return MATCHED_INDICES
```

The following C++ program shows the implementation of brute force method in solving string matching problem.

```
#include <iostream>
#include <vector>
using namespace std;
vector<int> BruteForceStringMatch(string T, string P) {
  int n = T.length();
  int m = P.length();
  vector<int> MATCHED_INDICES;
  // Slide the pattern over the text
  for (int i = 0; i <= n - m; i++) {
    bool match = true;

    // Compare characters of P with T
    for (int j = 0; j < m; j++) {
      if (T[i + j] != P[j]) {
        match = false;
```

```
            break;  // Mismatch found, exit inner loop
        }
    }
if(match){

 MATCHED_INDICES.push_back(i);
}
}

return MATCHED_INDICES.empty()?vector<int>{-1}:MATCHED_INDICES;
 }
int main() {
  string T, P;
  cout << "Enter the text: ";
  getline(cin, T);
  cout << "Enter the pattern: ";
  getline(cin, P);

  vector<int> result = BruteForceStringMatch(T, P);
  if (result[0] == -1) {
    cout << "Pattern not found in the text." << endl;
  } else {
    cout << "Pattern found at indices: ";
    for (int index : result) {
      cout << index << " ";
    }
    cout << endl;
  }

  return 0;
}
```

Output:

Enter the text: FINDINGFISHES

Enter the pattern: FISH

Pattern found at indices: 7

7.1.1.2 Drawbacks of Brute Force Approach

While brute force method is a simple and a straightforward approach of checking all possible solutions to find the best one for a given problem, but it comes with several drawbacks:

- Brute force algorithms have exponential or factorial time complexity making them unsuitable and impractical for larger inputs.
- As the problem size increases, its task of checking all possible solutions also increases and hence the process becomes slow and inefficient.
- Brute force process is not feasible for many real-world problems that require optimization.
- The Brute force approach also consumes excessive memory usage.

7.1.2 Divide and Conquer

Divide and Conquer approach is strategy of problem-solving in which the problem is divided into smaller sub-problems, each of those sub-problems are solved separately and finally the results of the individual sub-problems are combined to get the final solution to the problem. This approach, when used recursively, often yields efficient solutions to problems. Divide and Conquer method are usually recursive in nature.

Steps involved in Divide and Conquer:

- **Divide**: Split the original problem into smaller sub-problems.
- **Conquer**: Solve the sub-problems recursively.
- **Combine**: Merge the solutions of sub-problems to get the final answer.

We can understand it better with the help of a real-life example. Consider yourself in charge of a library with thousands of books that you must arrange alphabetically. It would be inefficient to sort every book individually. To speed up and improve efficiency, you can utilise Divide and Conquer instead. Let's apply divide and conquer approach to solve this problem.

- Divide: First, divide the entire collection of books into smaller sections (e.g., based on the first letter: A–M and N–Z) and continue dividing until each section has only one or a few books.
- Conquer: Sort each small section individually by only those books that belong to that specific section (this is much faster than sorting the entire library at once).
- Combine: All the sorted sections when merged turns into a single, fully correctly sorted library.

Why is divide and conquer used ?

The Divide and Conquer approach is widely used in algorithm design because it breaks down complex problems into smaller, manageable parts, making them easier to solve efficiently. Some of the key reasons of why this method is a preferred an effective problem solving method is given below.

- Many problems that take exponential time with brute force can be solved in polynomial or logarithmic time using Divide and Conquer.
- Divide and Conquer is a neat and organized method of designing solutions since many problems readily fit into a recursive structure.

- Instead of solving the problem multiple times (like brute force), divide and conquer breaks down the problem into independent units.
- Divide and conquer is used for designing efficient data structures for searching and sorting problems.

Analyzing divide and conquer algorithms.

The efficiency of a Divide and Conquer algorithm can be analyzed using a recurrence relation, which expresses the time complexity in terms of smaller sub-problems.

General Form of Recurrence Relation:

$T(n) = aT(n/b) + f(n)$

where

a = the number of sub-problems (a>=1)

n/b = size of the sub-problem (in terms of n)

f(n) = cost of work done outside the recursive calls like splitting into sub-problems and cost of combining them to get the solution.

7.1.2.1 Merge Sort

Merge sort is a sorting algorithm that uses the divide and conquer approach to sort an array of integers efficiently. The original array is divided into sub-arrays, recursively sorts them, and then merges the sorted sub-arrays. The steps involved are:

- Divide: an array with n-elements is divided into two n/2 sub-arrays.
- Conquer: recursively the sub-arrays are sorted
- Combine: the sorted sub-arrays are merged into the sorted array.

Algorithm for merge sort.

```
MergeSort(A, low, high)
  if low < high
    mid = (low + high) / 2          // Find the midpoint
    MergeSort(A, low, mid)          // Recursively sort the first half
    MergeSort(A, mid+1, high)       // Recursively sort the second half
    Merge(A, low, mid, high)        // Merge the two sorted halves
```

The MergeSort algorithm begins by dividing the original array into two halves i.e. into two sub-arrays. First, it generates the midpoint represented by mid using the formula (low + high) / 2, where low indicates starting index and high indicates the ending index of the current array segment. If the condition (low<high) is satisfied, then the segment consist of more than one element, the algorithm first proceeds by recursively calling itself on the left half of the array, which spans from low to mid. Then, it calls on the right half of the array, which spans from mid+1 to high. This is the process of recursively sorting the sub-arrays obtained after the dividing process. Finally, a merge function is invoked to combine the sorted sub-arrays into one sorted array. The Merge step compares the elements from each sorted half and merges them into a single sorted sequence, ensuring that the resulting array is ordered. This process continues recursively, breaking down the array into smaller

sub-arrays and merging them back together until the entire array is sorted.

Merge sort function

```
Merge(A, low, mid, high)
  n1 = mid - low + 1           // Length of left sub array
  n2 = high - mid              // Length of right sub-array

  L = new array of size n1     // Left sub-array
  R = new array of size n2     // Right sub-array

  // Copy data into temporary arrays
  for i = 0 to n1 - 1
    L[i] = A[low + i]

  for j = 0 to n2 - 1
    R[j] = A[mid + 1 + j]

  i = 0  // Initial index of left sub-array
  j = 0  // Initial index of right sub-array
  k = low // Initial index of merged sub-array

  // Merge the temporary arrays back into the original array A[]
  while i < n1 and j < n2
    if L[i] <= R[j]
      A[k] = L[i]
      i = i + 1
    else
      A[k] = R[j]
      j = j + 1
    k = k + 1 to j = j + 1

  // Copy the remaining elements of L[], if any
  while i < n1
    A[k] = L[i]
    i = i + 1
    k = k + 1
```

```
// Copy the remaining elements of R[], if any
while j < n2
  A[k] = R[j]
  j = j + 1
  k = k + 1
```

The Merge function is responsible for combining two sorted halves of an array into a single sorted array. n1 and n2 are the lengths of the two sub arrays:

- Left sub array: from low to mid
- Right sub array: from mid + 1 to high

The function begins by creating two temporary sub-arrays, L[] and R[], so that elements from left and right sub-arrays could be stored . Next, the function compares the elements of L[] and R[] one by one to check which element is smaller between the two. The smaller element between the compared elements is then placed into the original array A[]. This process continues until all elements from either L[] or R[] have been merge to sorted array A[]. If one sub-array has remaining elements while the other has been completely merged to A[], the remaining elements from the unfinished sub-array are directly copied into A[]. This ensures that the original array is merged in sorted order, completing the merging step of the Merge Sort algorithm.

Example: Given a unsorted array with elements {6,8,2,7,5,11,3,12}. Sort the unsorted array using divide and conquer approach of merge sort.

In the figure 7.4 , we see the application of merge sort algorithm to sort the unsorted array.

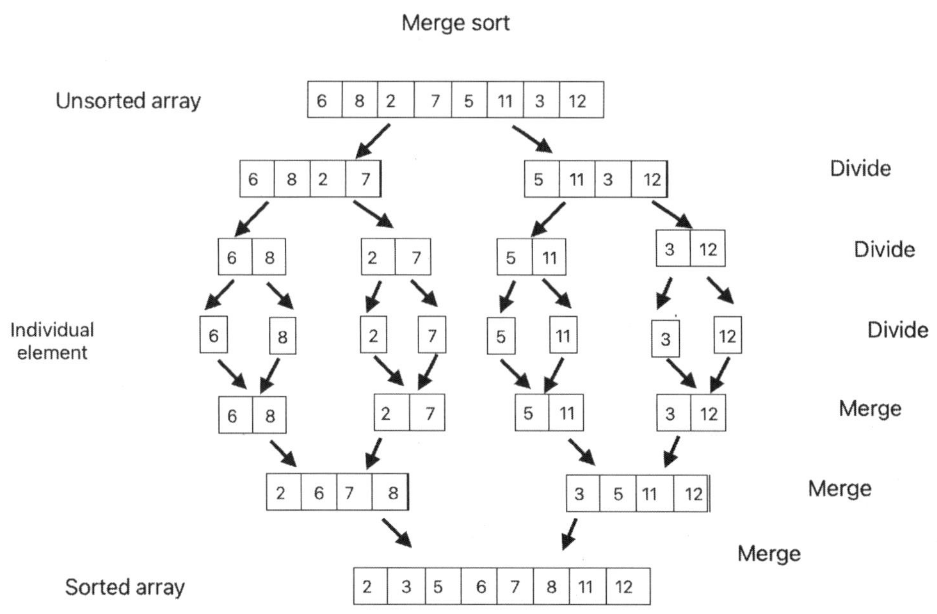

Fig 7.4 Merge Sort working

The following C++ program shows the implementation of merge sort.

```
#include <iostream>
using namespace std;
// Function to merge two subarrays into a single sorted array
void Merge(int A[], int low, int mid, int high) {
  int n1 = mid - low + 1;  // Length of the left sub-array
  int n2 = high - mid;    // Length of the right sub-array
  int L[n1], R[n2]; // Temporary arrays

  // Copy data into temporary arrays L[] and R[]
  for (int i = 0; i < n1; i++)
    L[i] = A[low + i];
  for (int j = 0; j < n2; j++)
    R[j] = A[mid + 1 + j];

  int i = 0, j = 0, k = low;

  // Merge the two sorted sub-arrays back into the original array
  while (i < n1 && j < n2) {
    if (L[i] <= R[j]) {
      A[k] = L[i];
      i++;
    } else {
      A[k] = R[j];
      j++;
    }
    k++;
  }

  // Copy the remaining elements of L[], if any
  while (i < n1) {
    A[k] = L[i];
    i++;
    k++;
  }
```

```
    // Copy the remaining elements of R[], if any
    while (j < n2) {
        A[k] = R[j];
        j++;
        k++;
    }
}

// Function to implement Merge Sort
void MergeSort(int A[], int low, int high) {
    if (low < high) {
        int mid = low + (high - low) / 2;

        // Recursively sort the first half
        MergeSort(A, low, mid);

        // Recursively sort the second half
        MergeSort(A, mid + 1, high);

        // Merge the two sorted halves
        Merge(A, low, mid, high);
    }
}

// Function to print the array
void PrintArray(int A[], int size) {
    for (int i = 0; i < size; i++) {
        cout << A[i] << " ";
    }
    cout << endl;
}

int main() {
    int n;
```

```
    // Ask the user for the number of elements in the array
    cout << "Enter the number of elements: ";
    cin >> n;

    int A[100]; // Fixed-size array (adjustable if needed)

    // Ask the user to input the array elements
    cout << "Enter " << n << " elements: ";
    for (int i = 0; i < n; i++) {
        cin >> A[i];
    }

    cout << "Original array: " << endl;
    PrintArray(A, n);

    // Call MergeSort to sort the array
    MergeSort(A, 0, n - 1);

    cout << "Sorted array: " << endl;
    PrintArray(A, n);

    return 0;
}
```

Output

```
Enter the number of elements: 8
Enter 8 elements: 6 8 2 7 5 11 3 12
Original array:
6 8 2 7 5 11 3 12
Sorted array:
2 3 5 6 7 8 11 12
```

Analysis of Merge Sort

The recurrence relation for Merge Sort is:

T(n) = 0 if n = 1

= 2T(n/2) + n otherwise

Where:

T(n) is the time complexity to sort an array of size *nn*n.

2T(n/2) represents the two recursive calls on subarrays of size n/2.

*O(n)*is the time spent on merging the two sorted halves.

Time complexity of Merge Sort :

Best case : O(nlogn)

Average case : O(nlogn)

Worst case : O(nlogn)

Space Complexity Analysis :

Merge sort requires additional space for merging the sorted left and right sub-arrays. The auxiliary space is used to store temporary sub-arrays during merging. The space complexity of merge sort is O(n).

7.1.2.2 Quick Sort

Quick sort is a highly efficient sorting algorithm based on divide and conquer approach. It works by partitioning the original array about a pivot element, recursively sorting left and right partitions and then later combining it back to the original array size in sorted manner. It involves the following steps :

a). Divide: Select a pivot element(can be the first element, last element or mid element, or any random element) and partition the original array based on the pivot element. All elements to the left of the pivot is smaller and all elements to the right of the pivot should be larger.

b). Conquer: recursively applying quick sort to left and right sub-arrays.

c). Combine: The sorted sub-arrays already combines to the original array size forming a single sorting array.

Algorithm for Quick sort:

```
QUICKSORT(A, p, r)
 if p < r then
  q = PARTITION(A, p, r)
  QUICKSORT(A, p, q - 1)
  QUICKSORT(A, q + 1, r)
 end if
```

```
PARTITION(A, p, r)
  pivot = A[r]
  i = p - 1
  for j = p to r - 1 do
    if A[j] ≤ pivot then
      i = i + 1
      swap A[i] with A[j]
    end if
  end for
  swap A[i + 1] with A[r]
  return i + 1
```

The QUICKSORT function sorts the array using divide and conquer technique. The function starts with checking if (p<r) where p is the starting index and r is the ending index. When p<r is satisfied, the function calls PARTITION function with A [p.....r]. It returns an index q where the element at q (represents the pivot element) is at its correct sorted position. All element left to q is less than q and all element right to q is greater than q. The QUICKSORT function then recursively sorts the 2 sub-arrays i.e. it calls itself on left sub-array A [p....q-1] and it calls itself on right sub-array A [q+1.....r].

The partition function performs rearrangement of A [p.....r] by choosing a pivot element to ensure that all elements less than pivot move to the left and all elements greater than pivot move to right. The pivot element can be chosen as the first element, last element, any random element or the median element. Here we have taken the last element A[r]. A variable i is initialized to p-1. A loop runs from j = p to r-1. For each element A[j], if A[j] is less than or equal to the pivot: increment i and then swap (A[i], A[j]). After coming out of the loop, the pivot element A[r] is swapped to A[i+1] ensuring pivot is in its correct array position. The function returns i+1 which is the newly located pivot element index.

Example: Given an unsorted array with elements {15,20,34,7,12,9,80,67}. Sort the unsorted array using divide and conquer approach of quick sort.

Solution : Fig 7.5 sorts the unsorted array using quick sort algorithm.

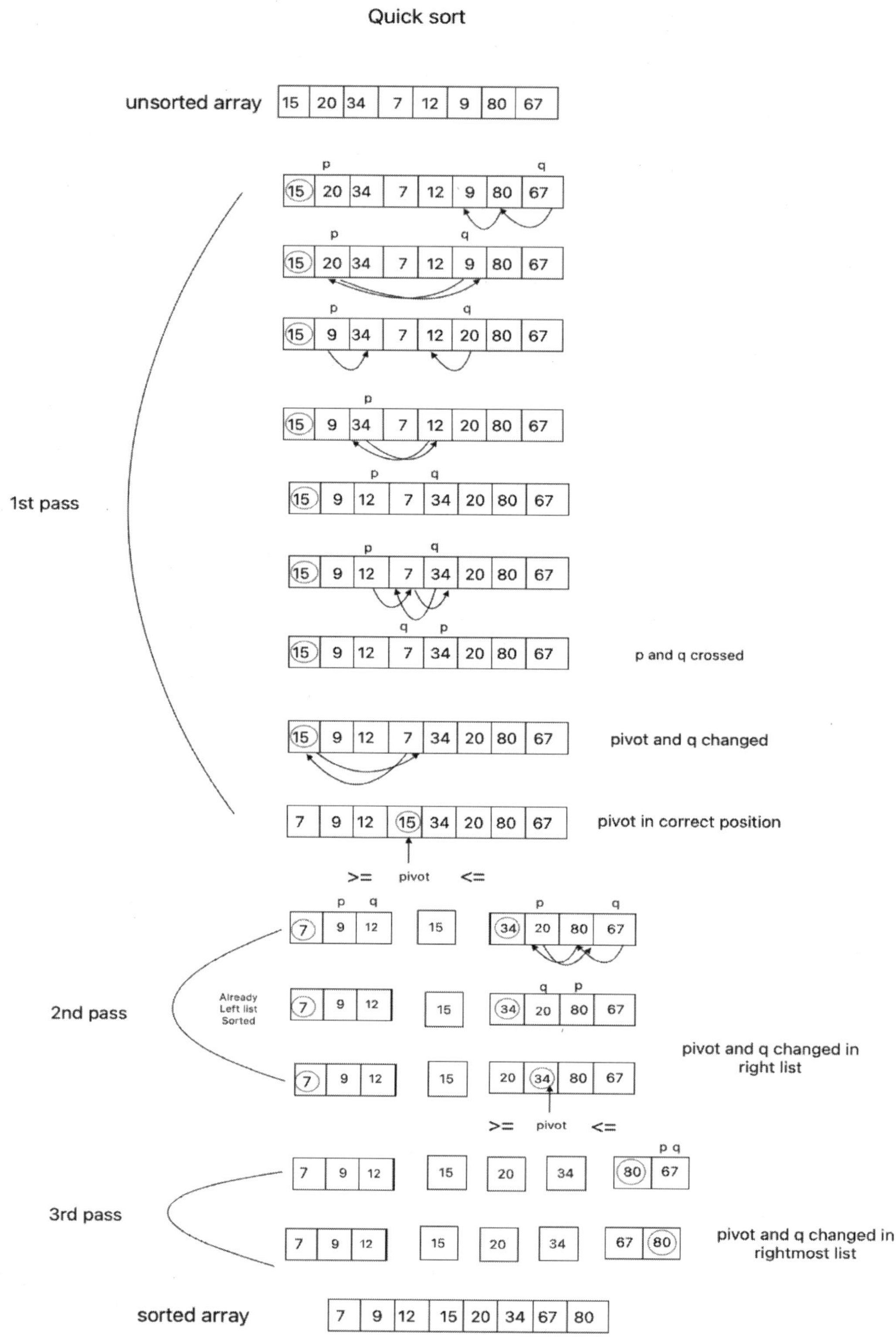

Fig 7.5 Quick Sort Working

The following C++ program shows the implementation of quick sort.

```
#include <iostream>
using namespace std;
// Function to partition the array
int partition(int arr[], int low, int high) {
  int pivot = arr[high];
  int i = low - 1;

  for (int j = low; j <= high - 1; j++) {
    if (arr[j] <= pivot) {
      i++;
      swap(arr[i], arr[j]);
    }
  }

  swap(arr[i + 1], arr[high]);
  return i + 1;
}

// QuickSort function
void quick_sort(int arr[], int low, int high) {
  if (low < high) {
    int pi = partition(arr, low, high);
    quick_sort(arr, low, pi - 1);
    quick_sort(arr, pi + 1, high);
  }
}

// Function to print the array
void print_array(int arr[], int size) {
  for (int i = 0; i < size; i++) {
    cout << arr[i] << " ";
  }
  cout << endl;
}
```

```
int main() {
  int n;

  // Ask user for the number of elements
  cout << "Enter the number of elements: ";
  cin >> n;

  int arr[100]; // Fixed-size array (can be adjusted if needed)

  // Ask user to enter the array elements
  cout << "Enter the elements of the array:" << endl;
  for (int i = 0; i < n; i++) {
    cin >> arr[i];
  }

  // Print the original array
  cout << "Original array:" << endl;
  print_array(arr, n);

  // Call quick_sort to sort the array
  quick_sort(arr, 0, n - 1);

  // Print the sorted array
  cout << "Sorted array:" << endl;
  print_array(arr, n);

  return 0;
}
```

Output

Enter the number of elements: 8

Enter the elements of the array:

15 20 34 7 12 9 80 67

Original array:

15 20 34 7 12 9 80 67

Sorted array:

7 9 12 15 20 34 67 80

Analysis of quick sort

1. **Best and Average Case analysis :**

In an ideal case, Quick Sort partitions the array into two perfect equal halves (balanced partition) at each step.

The recurrence relation is given by :

$$T(n)=2T(n/2)+O(n)$$

Quick sort selects a pivot and divide the array into two sub-array of size n/2. So, 2T(n/2) accounts for the recursive sorting of two sub-arrays. O(n) represents the time taken by the partitioning step (choosing pivot and reordering elements about the pivot), by scanning the array.

Using the Master Theorem :

$$T(n) = aT(n/b) + f(n) \text{ where}$$

a=2 (two recursive calls)

b=2 (each subproblem of size n/2)

f(n) = O(n) (partitioning takes linear time)

$f(n) = O(n^{\log_b a}) = O(n^{\log_2 2}) = O(n)$. Our function f(n) = O(n) matches $\Theta(n \log_b^a)$.

Since f(n) = Θ(nlogb a), we apply Case 2 of the master theorem :

$T(n) = O(n^{\log_b a} \log n) = O(n^1 \log n) = O(n\log n)$

2. **Worst Case :**

In worst case of quick sort occurs when the pivot is the smallest or the last element of the array i.e. the pivot consistently results in unbalanced partitions. One sub-array contains the smallest element and other contains all the remaining elements, hence not dividing the array evenly.

In this case, the recurrence relation changes to:

$T(n)=T(n-1)+O(n)$

Expanding the recurrence

$T(n)=T(n-1)+O(n)$

$T(n-1)=T(n-2)+O(n-1)$

$T(n-2)=T(n-3)+O(n-2)$

⋮

$T(2) = T(1) + O(2)$

Adding all of these

$T(n) = O(n)+O(n-1)+O(n-2)+\cdots+O(1)$

$T(n)=O(n+n-1+n-2+\cdots+1)$

This gives us arithmetic series with n terms , and the sum of first n integers is

$T(n)=O(n(n+1)/2) = O(n^2)$

Space Complexity :

- Best and Average Case : O(logn),
- Worst Case : O(n) .

7.1.2.3 Binary Search

Binary Search is an efficient searching algorithm which is developed in the concept of divide and conquer. It works by dividing the original array into two halved by calculating the middle value index. All element to the left of mid value is smaller than mid and all elements to the right of mid value are larger than mid value. Then, depending on in which sub-array the element being searched is, binary search is recursively applied until the element is found or the element is not present in the list. One important condition for a binary search is that the array need to be a sorted array. If not sorted, first the array is sorted and then binary search is applied.

The steps involved are :

- Divide: The array splits into two halves based on the mid value computed such at all elements to the left of mid are smaller than mid and all elements to the right of mode are larger than mid.
- Conquer: The search continues in the left or right half depending on whether the element to be searched is smaller or larger than the middle element.
- Combine: There is no combining operation. The search either find the element to be searched or returns –1 (element not found).

Binary Search Algorithm

```
FUNCTION BinarySearch(array, key)
  low ← 0
  high ← length(array) - 1

  WHILE low ≤ high DO
    mid ← FLOOR((low + high) / 2)
    IF array[mid] = key THEN
      RETURN mid
    ELSE IF array[mid] < key THEN
      low ← mid + 1
    ELSE
      high ← mid - 1
    END IF
  END WHILE

  RETURN -1
END FUNCTION
```

Binary Search function begins by defining two variables, low is assigned to the first index (0) of the array and high represents the last index. Then mid value index is calculated using (low + high) / 2. This divides the array into two halves. Left half consist of all elements smaller than mid value and right half consist of all elements greater than mid. Then comparison is made. If array[mid] == key(element which is being searched), then the element is found. If array[mid] < key, then the key is in the right subarray. Hence, low = mid + 1 updation is performed. Also, in this case the left subarray is completely ignored. If array[mid] > key, then the key is in the left subarray. Hence, high = mid - 1 updation is performed. Also, in this case the right subarray is completely ignored. This process repeats iteratively until the key element is found or the low surpasses high, indicating the element is not in the array.

Example: Given an array {15,20,34,7,12,9,80,67,22}. Binary search is implemented for searching the key element x = 12.

Solution : In the figure 7.6 , we see the implementation of binary search algorithm on the given array.

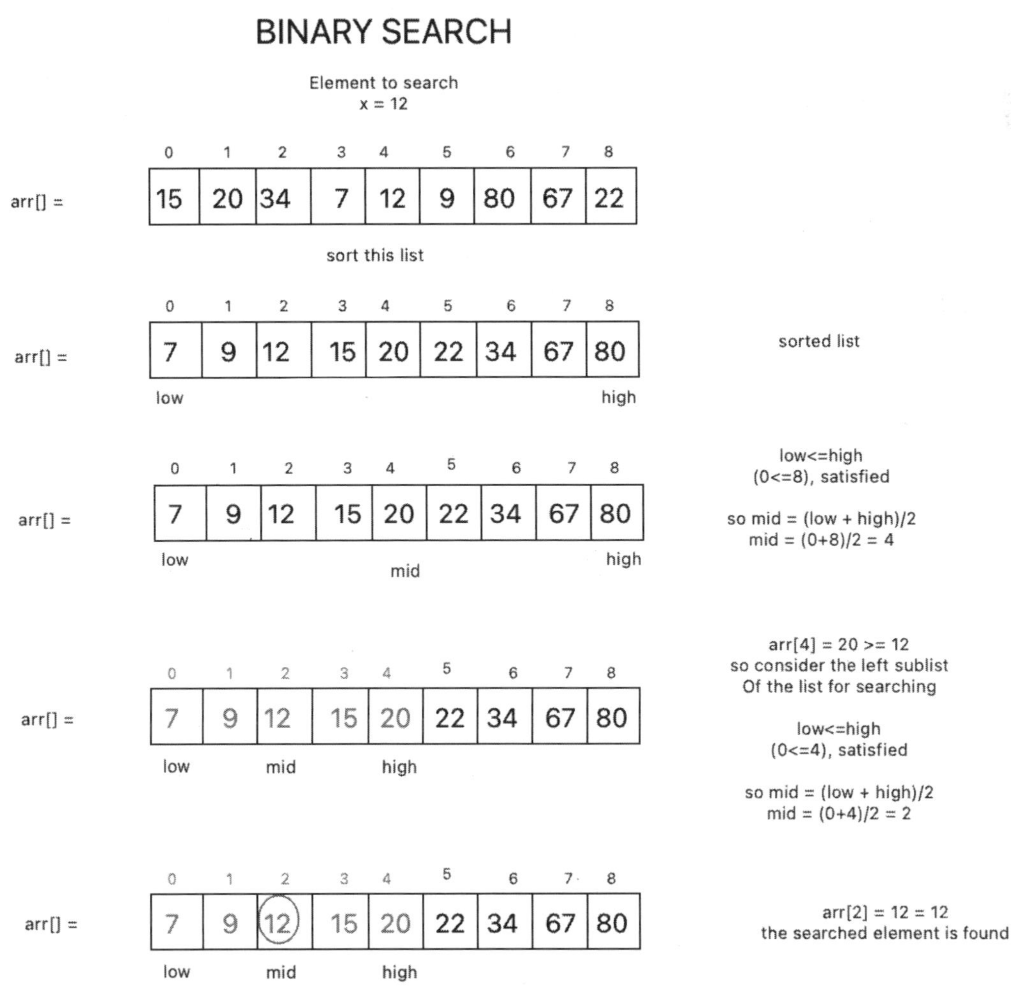

Fig 7.6 Binary Search Example

The following C++ program shows the implementation of binary search.

```
#include <iostream>
using namespace std;

// Function to perform binary search on a sorted array
int binarySearch(int arr[], int low, int high, int target) {
  while (low <= high) {
    int mid = (low + high) / 2;

    if (arr[mid] == target)
      return mid;  // Target found, return its index

    if (arr[mid] > target)
      high = mid - 1;  // Continue search in left half
    else
      low = mid + 1;   // Continue search in right half
  }
  return -1; // Target not found
}

// Function to perform Bubble Sort on an array
void bubbleSort(int arr[], int n) {
  for (int i = 0; i < n-1; i++) {
    for (int j = 0; j < n-i-1; j++) {
      if (arr[j] > arr[j+1]) {
        // Swap arr[j] and arr[j+1] if they are in the wrong order
        int temp = arr[j];
        arr[j] = arr[j+1];
        arr[j+1] = temp;
      }
    }
  }
}
```

```
int main() {
  int n;

  // Ask the user to enter the number of elements in the array
  cout << "Enter the number of elements in the array: ";
  cin >> n;

  int arr[n];

  // Ask the user to enter the elements of the array
  cout << "Enter the " << n << " elements of the array: ";
  for (int i = 0; i < n; i++) {
    cin >> arr[i];
  }

  // Sort the array using Bubble Sort
  bubbleSort(arr, n);

  // Ask the user to enter the target value
  int target;
  cout << "Enter the target value to search for: ";
  cin >> target;

  // Perform binary search to find the target element
  int result = binarySearch(arr, 0, n - 1, target);

  // Output the result of the binary search
  if (result != -1)
    cout << "Element " << target << " found at index " << result << " in the sorted array." << endl;
  else
    cout << "Element " << target << " not found in the array." << endl;

  return 0;
}
```

Output :

Enter the number of elements in the array: 9

Enter the 9 elements of the array: 15 20 34 7 12 9 80 67 22

Enter the target value to search for: 12

Element 12 found at index 2 in the sorted array.

Analysis of Binary Search

1. Time Complexity :

The recurrence relation for its time complexity can be defined as:

$T(n) = T(n/2) + O(1)$

where

$T(n/2)$: time to search a sub array of size *n/2n/2*n/2, reflecting the recursive call on the left or right half of the array.

$O(1)$: calculate middle element (constant time)

Solving this recurrence relation :

$T(n) = T(n/2) + O(1)$

Expanding it we get

$T(n)=(T(n/4)+O(1))+O(1)$ - by substituting $T(n/2)$ using the recurrence

$T(n)=((T(n/8)+O(1))+O(1))+2\cdot O(1)$ - by substituting $T(n/4)$ using the recurrence

$\vdots$

$T(n)=T(n/2k)+k\cdot O(1)$ - general expansion form

We stop the recursion when the size of the sub-problem becomes 1, i.e., when $n/2^k = 1$. Solving for k :

$n/2^k = 1$

Multiplying both sides by 2^k:

$n = 2^k$

Taking log on both side :

$k = \log_2 n$

Now, by substituting $k = \log_2 n$ in the general expansion

$T(n) = T(1) + O(\log_2 n)$

$T(n) = O(\log_2 n)$ since $T(1)$ is constant

- Best Case : O(1), occurs when the key matches to the first middle value in first step
- Average Case : $O(\log_2 n)$, the key value is found after searching through $\log_2 n$ level of recursion.
- Worst Case : $O(\log_2 n)$, occurs when the element is at extreme ends of the array.

2. **Space Complexity :**
   - **Iterative binary search**: Space complexity is O(1).
   - **Recursive binary search**: Space complexity is O(logn).

7.1.3 Greedy Algorithm

A greedy algorithm is a problem solving approach where decisions are taken at every step of processing by selecting the best option at that current moment, without thinking of global consequences. The goal of this approach is very simple – select the locally optimal solution (best solution at that current state) at each step with the hope that these locally optimal solution will eventually lead to the globally optimal solution (overall best solution for the problem). But, this approach does not guarantee the best solution (the best solution) for every problem. We can understand this with the help of a real-life example.

In a traffic scenario on road, a bike rider who has to reach his destination as fast as possible takes decision of moving through which route i.e. to take which route at that recent moment by having a look at the local traffic scenario. He takes local decision of best possible way at every step and decides the locally faster route with the hope of getting to his final destination as fast as possible. So, he applies a greedy approach of selecting the best solution depending on the local scenario with the hope of eventually taking the best route to reach to his final destination.

Why is Greedy Approach used?

Greedy Approach is used for solving problems efficiently, particularly when the problem exhibits certain properties that make the greedy choice effective. It provides quick solutions to many optimization problems by adopting the concept of local optimization leads to global optimization for finding solution to various problems.

- Greedy algorithms are simple to understand and implement as it takes decisions step-by-step based on local scenario of the problem.
- It does not require to look for the entire problem space or global problem space as it solves sub-problems at local space.
- Greedy Algorithms usually requires less memory and minimal resources than other methods such as dynamic programming.
- It provides a real-time problem-solving approach where decisions have to be made-on-the-spot.

When Greedy Algorithms works best?

Greedy algorithms work well for problems that exhibit:

- Greedy Choice Property: At every step, local optimal choice is taken that will lead to the global optimal solution.
- Optimal Substructure: The problem can be broken down into smaller, independent sub-problems and those sub-problems can be solved optimally.

7.1.3.1 Activity Selection Problem

It is a greedy algorithm problem that involves selecting the maximum number of non-overlapping activities that can be performed by a single person or resource. The problem statement is – Given

N activities, each with a start time and a finish time, choose the maximum number of activities than can be performed without overlapping.

Steps involved in solving this problem using greedy approach -

1. Sort the activities based on their end time.
2. Then select the first activity and mark its end time.
3. Iterate through the remaining activities and do this -
   a. If the start time of the current activity is greater than or equal to the end time of the previously chosen activity, then select that activity.
4. Repeat this process until all activities are checked.

Algorithm for Selection problem:

```
Greedy_Activity_Selector(s, f)
n ← length(s)
A ← {1}                  // Always select the first activity
j ← 1            // j stores the index of the last selected activity
for i ← 2 to n do
        if s[i] ≥ f[j] then
        A ← A ∪ {i}      // Select the i-th activity
        j ← i            // Update j to the newly selected activity's index
return A
```

The algorithm starts by setting the number of activities to n. Set A is initialized with the first activity as it has the earliest finish time (from the list of activities presorted by finish time). Setting j to 1 marks the index of the last selected activity. A loop runs from activity 2 to n to check if its start time s[i] is greater than or equal to finish time f[j] of the last selected activity. If the condition is satisfied, activity i is added to the set A and j is updated to i. After completion of the loop, the set A consist of the indices of set with highest number of non-overlapping activities.

Here in this example, there are some activities with their start time and their end time. The activities are first sorted according to the increasing order of their finish time.

Now, schedule A1.

Next, schedule A3 as it does not overlap with A1.

Next, as A2 is overlapping so we skip it (indicated by grey block).

Next, schedule A4 as it is non-overlapping activity.

Next, A6 also is non-overlapping, so schedule it.

Next, A5 is overlapping, so skip.

Next, schedule A7 as it not overlapping with other activities.

Next, schedule A8 as it is not overlapping with other activities.

Thus, the final list of activities scheduled is (A1, A3, A4, A6, A7, A8)

ACTIVITY SELECTION PROBLEM

Activity	A1	A3	A2	A4	A6	A5	A7	A8
Start	1	4	3	5	8	7	10	12
Finish	4	5	6	7	10	11	12	14

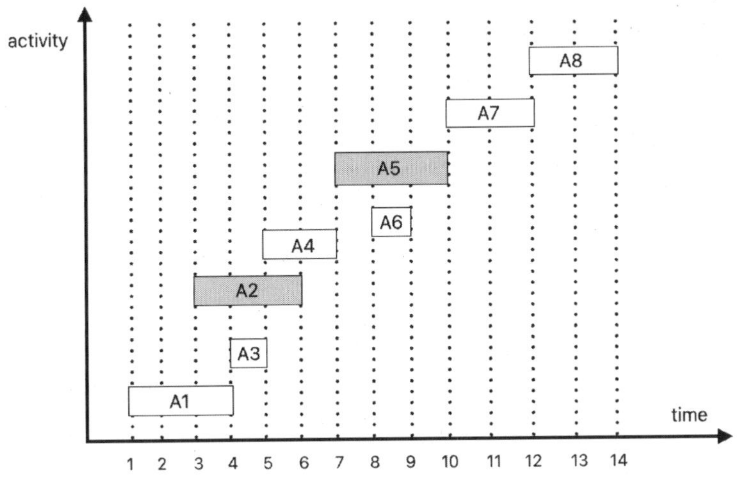

Final activity schedule = {A1,A3,A4,A6,A7,A8}

Fig 7.7 Activity selection problem example

The following C++ program shows the implementation of solving activity selection problem.

```
#include <iostream>
#include <vector>
#include <algorithm>
using namespace std;

// Function to solve the Activity Selection Problem
void activitySelection(const vector<int>& start, const vector<int>& finish) {
  int n = start.size();
// Create a vector of pairs to store both start and finish times along with the original index
vector<pair<pair<int,int>,int>>activities;
// Fill the activities vector with start, finish times and their original indices
for (int i = 0; i < n; i++) {
  activities.push_back({{finish[i], start[i]}, i}); // Store as (finish_time, start_time, original_index)
}
```

```
    // Sort activities based on finish times (primary) and start times (secondary)
    sort(activities.begin(), activities.end());

    // Array to store the indices of selected activities
    vector<int> A;
    // Step 1: Always select the first activity (sorted by finish time)
    A.push_back(activities[0].second); // Select first activity
    int j = activities[0].second; // Store the index of the last selected activity

    // Step 2: Process the remaining activities
    for (int i = 1; i < n; i++) {
        if (start[activities[i].second] >= finish[j]) { // If the current activity starts after or at the finish
time of the last selected activity
            A.push_back(activities[i].second);
            j = activities[i].second; // Update j to the index of the newly selected activity
        }
    }
    // Output the selected activities
    cout << "Selected activities (by index): ";
    for (int i = 0; i < A.size(); i++) {
        cout << A[i] + 1 << " "; // Displaying activities in 1-indexed format for readability
    }
    cout << endl;
}
int main() {
    int n;

    // User input for the number of activities
    cout << "Enter the number of activities: ";
    cin >> n;

    vector<int> start(n), finish(n);
    // User input for start and finish times
    cout << "Enter the start times of the activities: ";
    for (int i = 0; i < n; i++) {
```

```
        cin >> start[i];
    }

    cout << "Enter the finish times of the activities: ";
    for (int i = 0; i < n; i++) {
        cin >> finish[i];
    }

    // Step 3: Call the function to select activities
    activitySelection(start, finish);

    return 0;
}
```

Output

Enter the number of activities: 8

Enter the start times of the activities: 1 3 4 5 7 8 10 12

Enter the finish times of the activities: 4 6 5 7 11 10 12 14

Selected activities (by index): 1 3 4 6 7 8

7.1.3.2 Greedy Approach for Minimum Spanning Tree

Minimum spanning tree problem is a standard graph theory problem which requires to find the set of edges in a weighted, connected undirected graph that results to the minimum weight i.e., it requires to find the edges of a graph that connects all vertices without forming a cycle with minimized sum of edge weights.

Formal Definition :

Given a connected, undirected weighted graph G = (V,E) where V is the set of vertices, E is the set of weighted edges. Weight of an edge is nothing but the cost of each (u,v) where u and v are two distinct vertices.

Goal : To find $E' \subseteq E$ such that G' = (V,E') is a spanning tree (i.e., connected sub graph that includes all vertices without including a cycle), and the sum of the weights of edges included in the spanning tree is minimum with number of edges in the minimum spanning tree is $|V| - 1$.

The greedy approach is used to find the MST, where local optimal choices are made at every step in order to find the desired global optimal solution.

In the Fig 7.8, an example of minimum spanning tree is given. Given a graph with weighted edges, we need to find the MST. After generating all possible spanning tree and finding the sum of the edge weights of each of the spanning tree, it is observed that spanning tree SP2 has minimum weighted sum. So, the MST of the given graph is SP2.

Greedy Algorithm for finding MST

Two popular greedy approach based algorithm for finding an MST are:

- Kruskal's Algorithm
- Prim's Algorithm

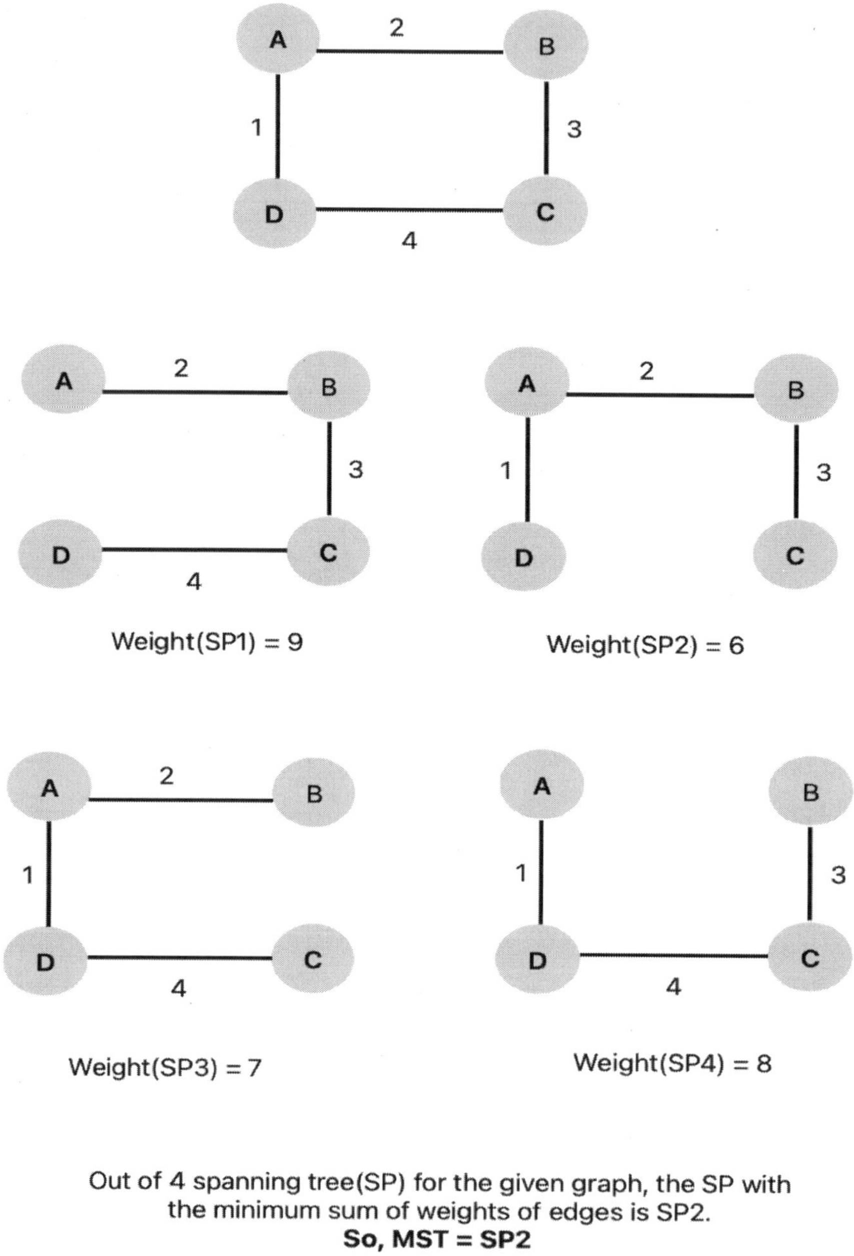

Fig 7. 8 Minimum Spanning tree example

Kruskal's Algorithm :

Kruskal's algorithm uses greedy approach to find the minimum spanning tree(MST) in a weighted, connected and undirected graph. Steps involved in Krushkal's algorithm are:

1. Sort edges of the graph in increasing order by their weight(cost).

2. Initialize an empty set for MST.

3. Iterate through the sorted edges starting from the edge with lowest cost until | V | - 1 edges are included in the set

   a). include the edge to the MST if it does not form a cycle.

   b). else, if it forms a cycle, do not include the edge in the MST.

4. The included edges form the minimum spanning tree ensuring all vertices are included in the MST.

Kruskal's algorithm using disjoint set:

A special data structure disjoint set (or union-find data structure) can be used to find the MST using kruskal's algorithm. It consists of two main operations: Find and Union. The find element to which the given element belongs, whereas Union operation merges two disjoint set. Three separate sets are created to maintain edge weights, tree hierarchy and rank of every node.

1. Sort all edges in increasing order of edge weight.
2. Initialize a disjoint set to keep track of connected components.
3. Create three distinct sets to maintain edge weights, tree hierarchy and rank of every node.
4. Initially, rank is marked to 0 and parent node value to –1 (each node as its own tree itself).
5. Iterate through sorted edges:
   a). If the inclusion of an edge does not create a cycle, then update the rank and parent of each node.
   b). Using union-find to merge or join the distinct nodes which are treated as different tree to form the MST.
6. Repeat step 5 until all | V | - 1 edges are included to the MST.

Algorithm:

```
KRUSKAL(G):
F = ϕ
for each vertex v ∈ G.V:
  MAKE-SET(v)
for each edge (u, v) ∈ G.E ordered by increasing order by weight(u, v):
  if FIND-SET(u) ≠ FIND-SET(v):
  F = F ∪ {(u, v)}
  UNION(u, v)
return F
```

KRUSKAL ALGORITHM

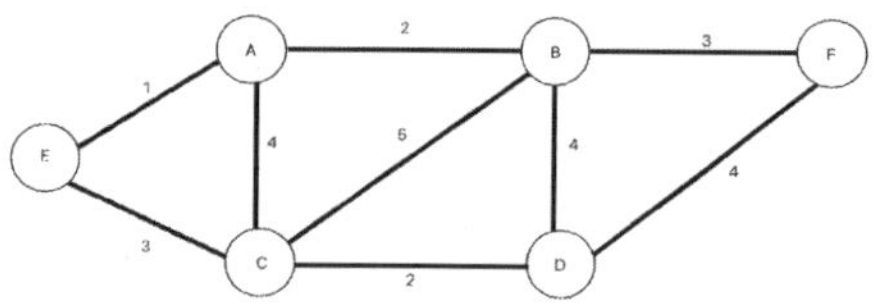

Edge	Weight
AE	1
AB	2
CD	2
EC	3
BF	3
AC	4
BD	4
DF	4
CB	5

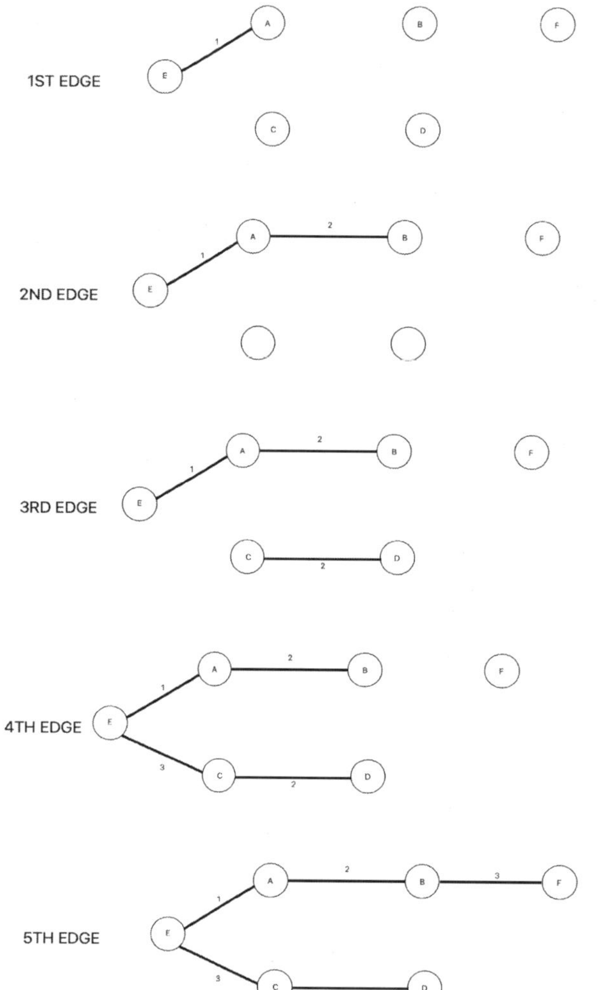

Included all vertices ,
so this is the minimum spanning tree.
Also addition of AC, BD, DF , CD will form a Cycle.

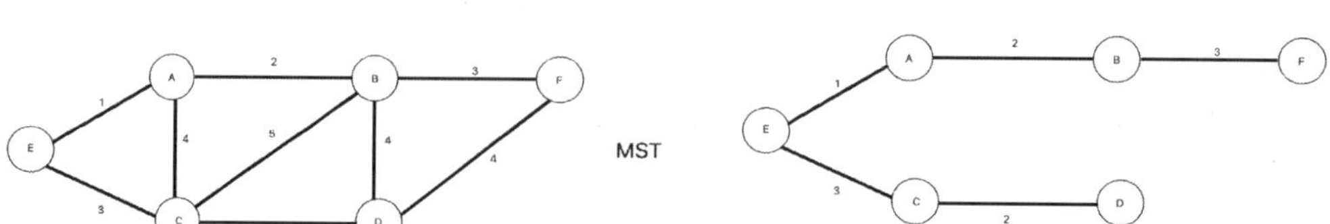

Fig 7.9 Kruskal's algorithm example

Time complexity:

Creating the disjoint set data structure i.e. rank, parent for every vertex takes V operations and O(V) times. Iteration through edge performs two operations – one union and two find operation per edge. These operations take $O(\alpha(V))$ time per operation, giving worst-case time $O(E\alpha(V))$, where α is the extremely slowly growing inverse Ackermann function. This part of the time bound is much smaller than the time for the sorting step, so the total time for the algorithm is simplified to the time for sorting step $O(ElogE) \sim O(Elog(V))$.

The following C++ program shows the implementation of Kruskal's algorithm to find MST using greedy approach.

```
#include <iostream>
using namespace std;
// Structure to represent an edge
struct Edge {
  int u, v, weight;
};
// Function to sort edges based on weight using Bubble Sort
void sortEdges(Edge edges[], int m) {
  for (int i = 0; i < m - 1; i++) {
    for (int j = 0; j < m - i - 1; j++) {
      if (edges[j].weight > edges[j + 1].weight) {
        Edge temp = edges[j];
        edges[j] = edges[j + 1];
        edges[j + 1] = temp;
      }
    }
  }
}

// Disjoint Set (Union-Find) with Path Compression and Union by Rank
class DisjointSet {
public:
  int parent[100], rank[100]; // Fixed-size arrays
DisjointSet(int n) {
    for (int i = 0; i < n; i++) {
      parent[i] = i; // Initially, each node is its own parent
      rank[i] = 0;
```

```
        }
    }

    int find(int node) {
        if (parent[node] != node)
            parent[node] = find(parent[node]); // Path compression
        return parent[node];
    }

    void unionSets(int u, int v) {
        int rootU = find(u);
        int rootV = find(v);

        if (rootU != rootV) {
            if (rank[rootU] > rank[rootV])
                parent[rootV] = rootU;
            else if (rank[rootU] < rank[rootV])
                parent[rootU] = rootV;
            else {
                parent[rootV] = rootU;
                rank[rootU]++;
            }
        }
    }
};

// Kruskal's Algorithm
void kruskal(int n, Edge edges[], int m) {
    Edge MST[100]; // Array to store the Minimum Spanning Tree
    int edgeCount = 0; // Track the number of edges in MST

    sortEdges(edges, m); // Step 1: Sort edges by weight
    DisjointSet ds(n);

    for (int i = 0; i < m; i++) {
```

```
        if (ds.find(edges[i].u) != ds.find(edges[i].v)) { // Step 2: Check if adding this edge creates a cycle
            MST[edgeCount++] = edges[i];
            ds.unionSets(edges[i].u, edges[i].v);
        }
        if (edgeCount == n - 1) break; // Stop when we have (V-1) edges in the MST
    }

    cout << "\nMinimum Spanning Tree Edges:\n";
    for (int i = 0; i < edgeCount; i++)
        cout << MST[i].u << " - " << MST[i].v << " : " << MST[i].weight << endl;
}

int main() {
    int n, m;
    cout << "Enter number of vertices: ";
    cin >> n;
    cout << "Enter number of edges: ";
    cin >> m;

    Edge edges[100]; // Fixed-size array for edges

    cout << "Enter edges in the format (u v weight):\n";
    for (int i = 0; i < m; i++) {
        cin >> edges[i].u >> edges[i].v >> edges[i].weight;
    }

    kruskal(n, edges, m);

    return 0;
}
```

Output:

Enter number of vertices: 4

Enter number of edges: 5

Enter edges in the format (u v weight):

0 1 1

0 2 4

1 2 2

1 3 3

2 3 2

Minimum Spanning Tree Edges:

0 - 1 : 1

1 - 2 : 2

2 - 3 : 2

Prim's Algorithm :

Prim's algorithm is a popular greedy algorithm to find minimum spanning tree of a connected, weighted undirected graph. It works by growing the MST by picking the lowest weight edge at a time, including it to MST if it does not form a cycle and then expanding the MST by choosing the next lowest weight edge from the selected edge. The steps involved in Prim's algorithm:

1. Start with any arbitrary vertex from the graph and include it to MST.
2. Select the lowest weight edge from the selected vertex that does not form a cycle.
3. Add that edge to the MST.
4. Repeat step 2 and step 4 until all vertices are included in the MST.
5. Once all vertices are included in the minimum spanning tree set, the algorithm is complete.

Finally, we obtain the spanning tree (sub graph) of a graph with the minimum sum of weights including all vertices using greedy approach by selecting the lowest edge weight from a connected selected edge as a local optimal solution which finally expands to the final minimum spanning tree (global solution).

Algorithm :

```
PRIM(V, E, r)
{for each u ε V do

key[u] <- ∞
π[u] <- Null
endfor
key[r] <- 0
Q <- V
while (Q ≠ Ø ) do
u <- extract_min(Q)
for each v ε adj[u] do
if (v ε Q and w (u, v) < key[v]) then
```

π[v] <- u

key[v] <- w(u,v)

endif

endfor

endwhile

}

Time Complexity:

The first for loop requires O(V) times. If Q is taken as binary min heap then O(V) time is taken to build the heap. The body of the while loop executes for O(V) times with each extract_min operation taking O(logV) times. Hence, the contribution of extract min operation during the execution of while loop takes O(V log V). The second for loop takes O(E) time. O(1) is used for membership check in Q. Changing the key value of v shows a decrease key operation in a min heap which takes O(log V) time. Since, this is performed within second loop, so total contribution in second loop is O(E log V).

Total time complexity of Prim's algorithm is O(V log V) + O(E log V) = O(E log V).

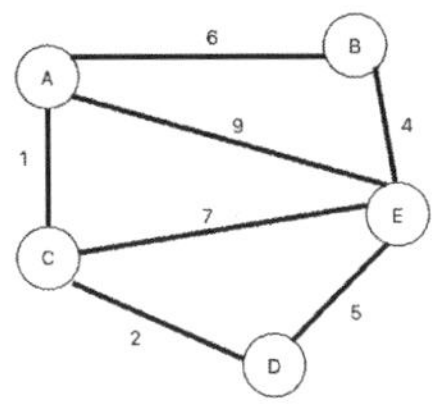

STEP 1

STEP 2

STEP 3

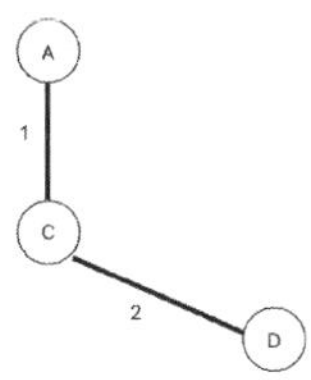

STEP 4

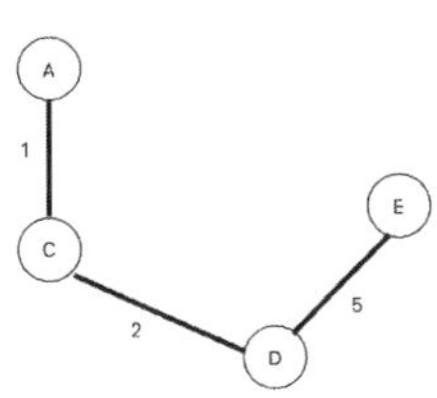

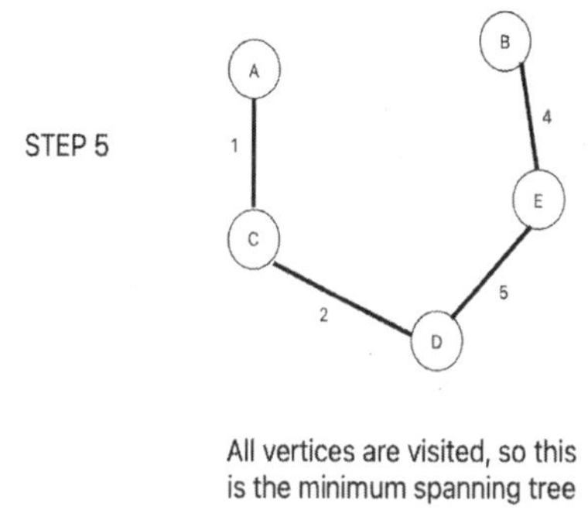

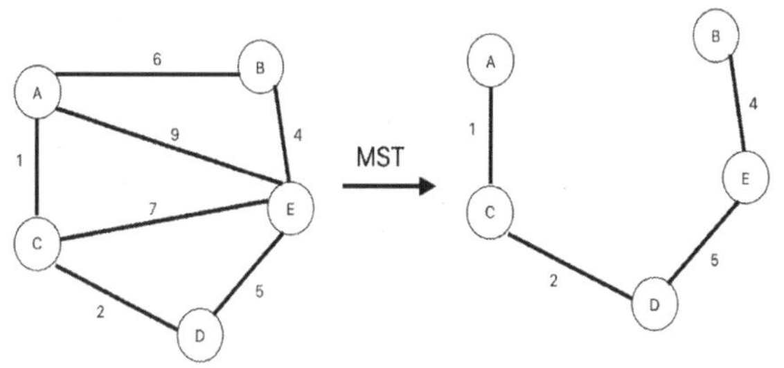

Fig 7.10 Prim's algorithm example

The following C++ program shows the implementation of Prim's algorithm to find MST using greedy approach.

```
#include <iostream>
using namespace std;
#define INF 999999 // Define a large number
// Function to find the vertex with the minimum key value
int minKey(int key[], bool mstSet[], int n) {
  int min = INF, min_index;


  for (int v = 0; v < n; v++) {
    if (!mstSet[v] && key[v] < min) {
      min = key[v];
      min_index = v;
    }
  }
  return min_index;
}
// Function to implement Prim's algorithm to find the MST
void primMST(int** graph, int n) {
 int parent[n];
```

```
    int key[n];    // Key values to select the minimum weight edge
    bool mstSet[n];   // Key values to select the minimum weight edge
     // Initialize all keys as "infinity" and mark all nodes as not included in MST
    for (int i = 0; i < n; i++) {
        key[i] = INF;
        mstSet[i] = false;
    }
    // Start from the first vertex
    key[0] = 0;
    parent[0] = -1;
// The MST will have n-1 edges
for (int count = 0; count < n - 1; count++) {
    // Pick the minimum key vertex that is not yet included in the MST
    int u = minKey(key, mstSet, n);

    // Add the selected vertex to the MST
    mstSet[u] = true;

    // Update the key values of adjacent vertices of the selected vertex
    for (int v = 0; v < n; v++) {
        if (graph[u][v] && !mstSet[v] && graph[u][v] < key[v]) {
            key[v] = graph[u][v];
            parent[v] = u;
        }
    }
}
    // Print the MST
    cout << "Edge \tWeight\n";
    for (int i = 1; i < n; i++) {
        cout << parent[i] << " - " << i << "\t" << graph[i][parent[i]] << endl;
    }
}
int main() {
 int n; cout << "Enter the number of vertices: ";
cin >> n;
```

```
// Dynamically allocate memory for the adjacency matrix
int** graph = new int*[n];
for (int i = 0; i < n; i++) {
  graph[i] = new int[n];
}  // Input the adjacency matrix
  cout << "Enter the adjacency matrix (0 for no edge):\n";
  for (int i = 0; i < n; i++) {
    for (int j = 0; j < n; j++) {
      cin >> graph[i][j];
    }
  }
// Call Prim's algorithm to find and display the MST
primMST(graph, n);

// Free the dynamically allocated memory
for (int i = 0; i < n; i++) {
  delete[] graph[i];
}
delete[] graph;
return 0;
}
```

Output:

```
Enter the number of vertices: 5
Enter the adjacency matrix (0 for no edge):
0 2 0 6 0
2 0 3 8 5
0 2 0 0 7
6 8 0 0 9
0 5 7 9 0
Edge   Weight
0 - 1  2
1 - 2  2
0 - 3  6
1 - 4  5
```

7.1.4 Dynamic Programming

Dynamic programming is used for solving optimization problems. The two characteristics that an optimization problem have:

1. Optimal substructure: A problem exhibits optimal substructure if optimal solution to a problem is constructed from optimal solutions to sub-problem.

2. Overlapping Sub-problem: An optimization problem is said to have overlapping sub-problem property when a recursive algorithm revisits the same sub problem over and over again. Dynamic problem uses the concept of overlapping sub-problem by solving a sub-problem once and then storing the result in a table where it can be looked up in future when needed.

Why dynamic programming is used?

Dynamic programming is an approach which is used to solve complex problems by breaking them into sub-problems and storing the results of solved sub-problems in a table with the goal of avoiding any redundant computations in an optimization problem.

- Dynamic programming is used for optimizing the recursive problems by solving them by avoiding unnecessary computation.
- Dynamic programming reduces the time complexity thus help in efficiently problem solving.
- In problems like Fibonacci numbers, solving fib(n) requires fib(n-1) and fib(n-2), which overlap in calculations, dynamic programming stores intermediate results thus avoiding re-computation.
- Dynamic programming is used in solving various problems such as fibonacci sequence, knapsack problem, longest common subsequence, matrix chain multiplication, traveling salesman problem, bellman ford algorithm, floyd-warshall's algorithm.

Types of dynamic programming?

1. Top-Down (Memoization): It is a recursive approach where results of the sub problems are stored in a table to avoid redundant calculations.

2. Bottom-up (Tabulation) : This approach iteratively computes and stores solutions of smaller subproblems in a table, which builds up to the final solution.

7.1.4.1 Longest Common Subsequence.

Longest Common Subsequence is a classic dynamic programming problem that finds the longest sequence of characters that appear in the same relative order in two given strings without necessarily being contagious. Suppose there are two strings X = "AGGTAB" and Y = "GXTXAYB". The longest common subsequence (LCS) is "GTAB". Hence, the length of the longest common subsequence is 4.

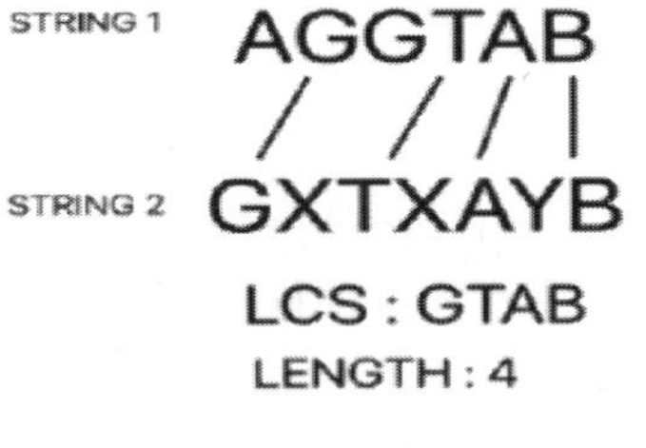

Algorithm for Longest Common Sequence

Algorithm LCS_Length(X, Y)

Input: Two sequences X and Y

Output: Table c containing LCS lengths and table b for backtracking

1. m ← length of X

2. n ← length of Y

3. Create tables c[m+1][n+1] and b[m+1][n+1]

4. Initialize base cases:

```
  for i = 0 to m do
    c[i,0] ← 0
  for j = 0 to n do
    c[0,j] ← 0
```

5. Compute LCS length:

```
  for i = 1 to m do
    for j = 1 to n do
      if X[i-1] = Y[j-1] then
        c[i,j] ← c[i-1, j-1] + 1
        b[i,j] ← "↖" (Diagonal move, meaning characters match)
      else if c[i-1, j] ≥ c[i, j-1] then
        c[i,j] ← c[i-1, j]
        b[i,j] ← "↑" (Move up, meaning take LCS from the above cell)
      else
        c[i,j] ← c[i, j-1]
        b[i,j] ← "←" (Move left, meaning take LCS from the left cell)
```

6. Return c and b

The algorithm starts with defining two sequence X and Y and m = length(X) and n = length(Y). A table is constructed c[m+1][n+1] where : c[i][j] stores the length of LCS of X[0..i-1] and Y[0..j-1]. Another table b[m+1][n+1] is used for backtracking to generate the LCS.

Base Case:

Since the LCS of any string with an empty string is 0, we initialize:

c[i][0] = 0 for all i (first column is 0)

c[0][j] = 0 for all j (first row is 0)

We iterate over both sequences and compute the LCS length as follows:

1. When character matches i.e., X[i-1] == Y[j-1] then compute c[i][j] = c[i−1][j−1]+1. c[i,j] values are computed in row major order i.e. the 1st row is filled from left to right, and then the second row and so on. b[i,j] points to the table entry corresponding to the optimal subproblem solution chosen when computing c[i,j]. It stores diagonal move (↖) in b[i][j].

2. When character does not match, the maximum LCS length from the previous value is chosen:
   a). If c[i-1][j] ≥ c[i][j-1]: choose the value from above **(c[i-1][j])** and store up move (↑) in b[i][j].
   b). Else choose the value from left **(c[i][j-1])** and store left move (←) in b[i][j].
3. After filling the entire table, c[m][n] stores the length of LCS.

Construction of LCS:

- Start from b[m,n] and trace the cells of the table using arrows.
- Whenever a ↖ is seen it implies that $x_i = y_j$, which indicates that that element in the cell belongs to the LCS.
- The elements are generated in the reverse sequence.

Example: Let there be two sequences **X = "ABCBDAB", Y = "BDCAB".** Find the LCS using dynamic programming.

	Yj	B	D	C	A	B
Xi	0	0	0	0	0	0
A	0	0 ↑	0 ↑	0 ↑	1 ↖	1 ←
B	0	1 ↖	1 ←	1 ←	1 ←	2 ↖
C	0	1 ↑	1 ←	2 ↖	2 ←	2 ←
B	0	1 ↖	1 ←	2 ↑	2 ←	3 ↖
D	0	1 ↑	2 ↖	2 ←	2 ←	3 ↑
A	0	1 ↑	2 ↑	2 ←	3 ↖	3 ↑
B	0	1 ↖	2 ↑	2 ←	3 ↑	4 ↖ ← c[m][n]

LCS LENGTH c[m][n] = 4

LCS extracted = "BDAB"

Fig 7.11 Longest common subsequence example

The following C++ program shows the implementation of dynamic programming in finding longest common subsequence from two strings.

```
#include <iostream>
using namespace std;
// Function to find the LCS length and construct the LCS string
string LCS(string X, string Y) {
    int m = X.length();
    int n = Y.length();
```

```
// Dynamically allocate a 2D array
int** dp = new int*[m + 1];
for (int i = 0; i <= m; i++) {
  dp[i] = new int[n + 1];
}
  // Filling the DP table
  for (int i = 0; i <= m; i++) {
    for (int j = 0; j <= n; j++) {
      if (i == 0 || j == 0)
        dp[i][j] = 0;  // Base case
      else if (X[i - 1] == Y[j - 1]) // Characters match
        dp[i][j] = dp[i - 1][j - 1] + 1;
      else // Take the maximum of left or top
        dp[i][j] = (dp[i - 1][j] > dp[i][j - 1]) ? dp[i - 1][j] : dp[i][j - 1];
    }
  }
  // Backtracking to find the LCS string
  int i = m, j = n;
  string lcs = "";

  while (i > 0 && j > 0) {
    if (X[i - 1] == Y[j - 1]) { // Match found, add to result
      lcs = X[i - 1] + lcs;
      i--;
      j--;
    } else if (dp[i - 1][j] > dp[i][j - 1]) {
      i--; // Move up
    } else {
      j--; // Move left
    }
  }
  // Free dynamically allocated memory
  for (int i = 0; i <= m; i++) {
    delete[] dp[i];
  }
```

```
    delete[] dp;

    return lcs;
}
int main() {
    string X, Y;
    cout << "Enter first string: ";
    cin >> X;
    cout << "Enter second string: ";
    cin >> Y;

    string lcs = LCS(X, Y);
    cout << "Longest Common Subsequence: " << lcs << endl;
    cout << "Length of LCS: " << lcs.length() << endl;

    return 0;
}
```

Output:

Enter first string: ABCBDAB

Enter second string: BDCAB

Longest Common Subsequence: BDAB

Length of LCS: 4

7.1.4.2 Matrix Chain Multiplication

Matrix Chain Multiplication is a classic dynamic programming problem that finds the most efficient way to multiply a given sequence of matrices. It selects the most effective (optimal) order to reduce the number of scalar multiplications rather than carrying out the multiplication.

Suppose, given matrices A, B, C, different multiplication orders yield different computational costs. It can be order in the following sequence

1. $(A \times B) \times C$
2. $A \times (B \times C)$

Computational cost varies depending on the order and so the goal is to find the best order that tends to reduce computational cost for large matrices.

Matrix Chain Multiplication applies the principle of optimality concept of dynamic programming which states "An optimal solution to a problem contains optimal solutions to its sub-problems."

If (A1 x (A2 x A3)) x A4 is optimal order of multiplication for A1 x A2 x A3 x A4, then (A1 x (A2 x A3)) is optimal order of multiplication for A1 x A2 x A3.

If we split the matrix chain at some index k, then:

- The sub-problem of multiplying matrices A_1 to A_k must be solved optimally.
- The sub-problem of multiplying matrices A_{k+1} to A_n must also be solved optimally.
- The overall solution uses the results of these optimal sub-problems to determine the minimum cost.

Mathematical Formulation:

Suppose we are given two matrices A (p × q) and B (q × r), the cost of multiplying these two matrices is **p × q × r** scalar multiplications.

M[i,j] defines minimum number of scalar multiplications required for multiplying matrices from Ai to Aj.

Using dynamic programming, we use the recurrence relation:

m[i, j] = min (m[i, k] + m[k+1, j] + p[i-1] * p[k] * p[j])

where the base case is m[i][i] = 0 .

Time Complexity:

- Brute Force (Recursive): The brute force method involves trying every possible split for each sub-problem, leading to an exponential number of calls. $O(2^n)$ where n is the number of matrices.
- In dynamic programming, the problem is solved in bottom-up fashion and intermediate results are stored to avoid redundant calculations. The idea is to fill a 2D table m[][], where m[i][j] represents the minimum number of scalar multiplications needed to multiply matrices from A_i to A_j.

Nested loop structure is used :

- The outer loop runs for each chain length from 2 to n.
- For each chain length, the two inner loops iterate over all sub-problems. Thus the time complexity is : $O(n^3)$.

Given n matrices with dimensions $p_0 \times p_1, p_1 \times p_2, ..., p_{n-1} \times p_n$, find the optimal way to parenthesize them to minimize the number of scalar multiplications.

Example

Consider 4 matrices:

- A_1: **5 × 3**
- A_2: 3 × 6
- A_3: **6 × 4**
- A_4: 4 × 7

The number of multiplications depends on how we parenthesize the matrices:

- $(A_1 \times A_2) \times (A_3 \times A_4)$
- $((A_1 \times A_2) \times A_3) \times A_4$
- $A_1 \times ((A_2 \times A_3) \times A_4)$ ... and more possibilities.

Each order results in a different number of scalar multiplications.

Algorithm for Matrix Chain Order:

```
Matrix-Chain-Order(p, n)
Create a table m[n+1][n+1] to store the minimum multiplication costs.
    Create a table s[n+1][n+1] to store the split points.
    for i = 1 to n do
    m[i, i] = 0 // Cost of multiplying a single matrix is zero.
    for len = 2 to n do // Length of the subchain being evaluated.
    for i = 1 to n - len + 1 do
    j = i + len - 1 // Compute the ending index of the chain.
    m[i, j] = ∞ // Initialize with a large value.
    for k = i to j - 1 do // Try all possible partition points.
            q = m[i, k] + m[k+1, j] + p[i-1] * p[k] * p[j]
            if q < m[i, j] then
                m[i, j] = q // Store the minimum cost.
                s[i, j] = k // Store the best partition index.
    return s // Table containing the optimal split points.
```

In this algorithm, firstly, two tables, m[n+1][n+1] and s[n+1][n+1], are created. The table m[i][j] stores the minimum number of multiplications needed to multiply matrices from i to j, while s[i][j] stores the index at which the optimal split occurs. The algorithm initializes m[i][i] = 0 for all i, since the cost of multiplying a single matrix is always zero. It then evaluates matrix sub chains of increasing lengths, starting from 2 up to n, iterating over all possible starting indices i. The ending index j is computed as j = i + len - 1. Initially, m[i][j] is set to infinity to ensure we can find the minimum value. For each sub chain (i to j), all possible split points k between i and j-1 are considered. The cost of splitting at k is computed using the formula:

$$q = m[i,k] + m[k+1,j] + p[i-1] \times p[k] \times p[j]$$

If this cost is smaller than the current stored value of m[i][j], it is updated, and s[i][j] is set to k, marking the best place to split. Finally, the table s is returned, which assist in reconstructing the optimal order of matrix multiplication. This specific approach ensures the number of scalar multiplications used is minimum thus preserving the order of the matrix.

Example: Given sequence {5,4,4,6,6,2,2,7}. The matrices have sizes 5×4, 4×6, 6×2, 2×7. Compute M[i,j], 0<= i, j<= 5. M[i][i] = 0 for all i.

Solution : Fig 7.12 shows the implementation of matrix chain multiplication using dynamic programming

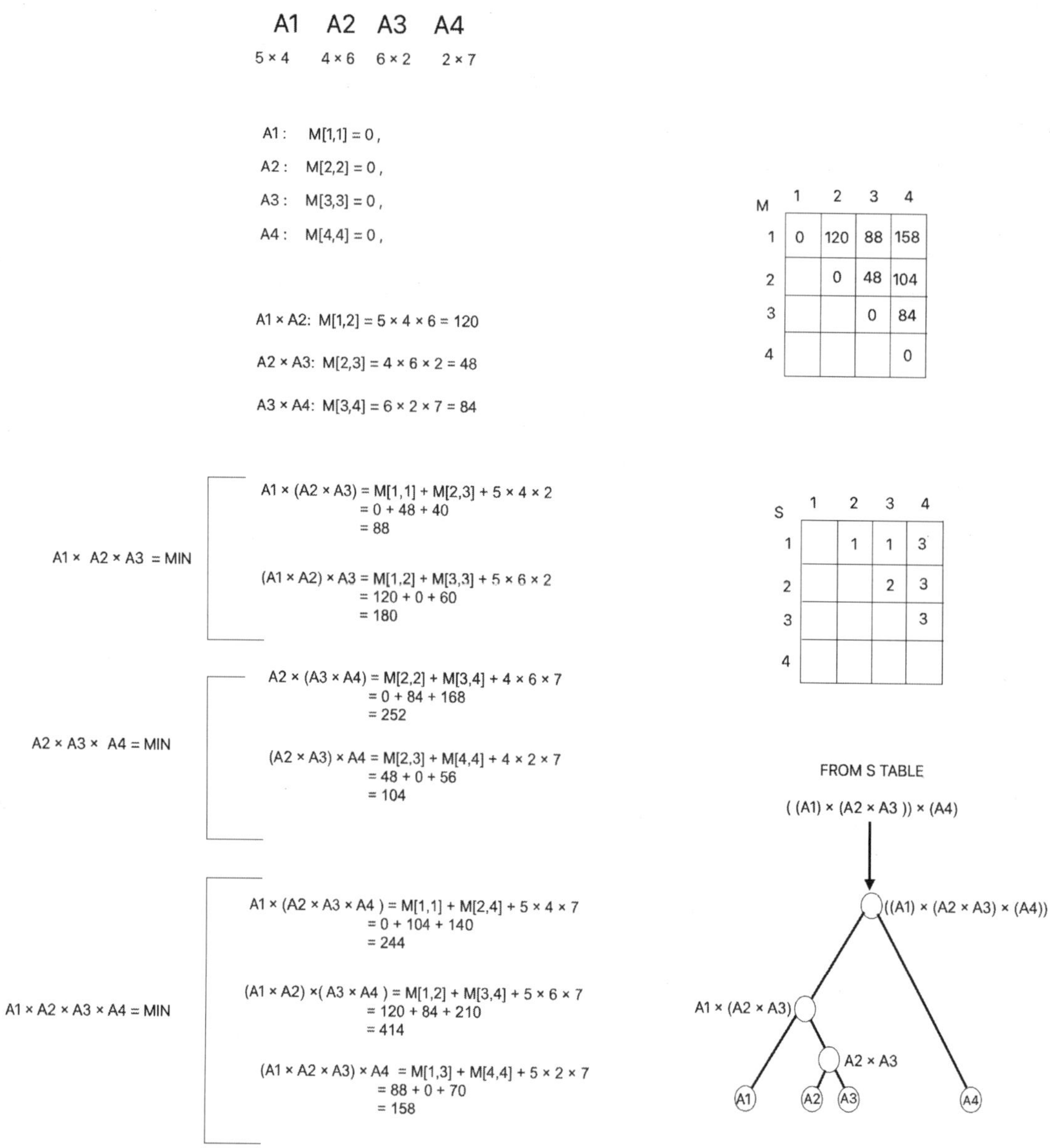

Fig 7.12 Matrix multiplication example

The following C++ program shows the implementation of dynamic programming in performing matrix chain multiplication.

```
#include <iostream>
using namespace std;
// Function to compute the minimum number of scalar multiplications
int matrixChainMultiplication(int dims[], int n) {
  int dp[n][n]; // DP table to store minimum multiplication costs
```

```
// Initialize the diagonal elements to zero (single matrix cost is zero)
for (int i = 1; i < n; i++)
  dp[i][i] = 0;
// L is the chain length (starting from 2 matrices up to n-1 matrices)
for (int L = 2; L < n; L++) {
  for (int i = 1; i < n - L + 1; i++) {
    int j = i + L - 1;
    dp[i][j] = 1e9; // A large value (instead of using INT_MAX)
// Try different partitions (splitting at k)

  for (int k = i; k < j; k++) {
    int cost = dp[i][k] + dp[k+1][j] + dims[i-1] * dims[k] * dims[j];
if (cost < dp[i][j]) {
        dp[i][j] = cost;
              }
      }
    }
}
return dp[1][n-1]; // Minimum cost to multiply the entire chain
}
int main() {
  int numMatrices;
  cout << "Enter the number of matrices: ";
  cin >> numMatrices;
   int dims[numMatrices + 1]; // Array to store dimensions
  cout << "Enter the dimensions of matrices:\n";
   for (int i = 0; i <= numMatrices; i++) {
     cin >> dims[i];
  }
  int minMultiplications = matrixChainMultiplication(dims, numMatrices + 1);
  cout << "Minimum number of scalar multiplications: " << minMultiplications << endl;
 return 0;
 }
```

Output :

Enter the number of matrices: 4

Enter the dimensions of matrices:

5 4 6 2 7

Minimum number of scalar multiplications: 158

7.1.5 Backtracking

Backtracking method of problem-solving is a very efficient method which recursively go on exploring the possible solutions. It starts with an empty solution. It goes on incrementally build the solution by adding elements. If an added element leads to a valid solution, then proceed further. If it leads to an invalid solution, backtrack (move to the previous solution state) and try other possibility. This process is repeated until all possibilities are explored, or an optimal solution is found. A state space tree is used which represents nodes as a state or partial solution. There are constraints that a partial solution must satisfy. When a current path does not lead to a valid or optimal solution, then pruning is performed i.e. no exploration is taken forward from that node. Backtracking is an effective algorithmic method for resolving combinatorial optimization and constraint satisfaction issues.

Characteristics of backtracking algorithm:

- **Systematic Search (State Space Tree):** Examines all possible potential solutions in a tree-like structure.
- **Incremental Solution Construction:** Builds solutions step by step while checking constraints.
- **Constraint-Based Search:** Verifies partial solutions meet problem constraints before moving further.
- **Pruning (Early Termination):** Reduces computation by removing infeasible solutions early.

7.1.5.1 Sum of subset problem:

Given a set of n distinct positive integers w_1, w_2,.....w_n. The problem is to find a subset of {w_1, w_2,..... w_n} whose sum is exactly equal to a positive integer M. Subsets can be represented in Boolean form with arrays of fixed size n. A valid solution is of the form {x_1, x 2, ...x_n} where each x_i can either take value 1 if that integer is included in the subset or take value 0 if that integer is excluded from the subset.

Suppose there is a set {1,2,4,5,6,7,8} with n = 7. The subset {2,4,6} can be represented as the following binary array 0110100. The position marked 1 represent that particular element is included in the subset and other positions are marked as 1 represents exclusion of the element from that subset.

The steps involved in finding the solution is given below:

- Arranging the integers in an ascending order.
- The algorithm goes on expanding the tree.
- If at any node, it can be concluded that the current path will not lead to a solution then expansion in that branch of the tree is stopped. Using bounding functions, the algorithm stops expanding the tree downwards at certain nodes.

The bounding function used is:

1. At a node corresponding to the partial solution $(x_1, x_2, ...x_k)$ the function is

$$\sum_{i=1}^{k} w_i\ x_i + \sum_{i=k+1}^{n} w_i \geq m.$$

$(x_1, x_2, ...x_k)$ cannot lead to an answer node if this condition is not satisfied.

2. Another bounding function is

$$\sum_{i=1}^{k} w_i\ x_i + w_{k+1} \leq m$$

These two bounding functions are used to prune the node.

Algorithm for Sum of Subset problem:

In this algorithm, parameter s is the sum of the partial solution obtained so far, k represents the current place of the binary array x. r represent the remaining total sum.

So $s = \sum_{i=1}^{k} w_i\ x_i$ and $r = \sum_{i=k+1}^{n} w_i$

Algorithm:

```
sumofsubs(s, k, r)
{
  x[k] ← 1 // Include w[k] in the subset

  if (s + w[k] == M)
    print x[1] to x[k] // Found a valid subset

  if ((s + w[k] + w[k+1]) ≤ M)
    sumofsubs(s + w[k], k+1, r - w[k]); // Recur with included element

  if ((s + r - w[k] ≥ M) and (s + w[k+1] ≤ M))
  {
    x[k] ← 0; // Exclude w[k] from the subset
    sumofsubs(s, k+1, r - w[k]); // Recur without the element
  }
}
```

Given set of weights {5,10,12,13,15,18}. Find the subsets of weight whose sum is exactly equal to M = 30 using backtracking technique.

In the figure 7.13, we can see the solution of sum of the subset problem using backtracking technique . This is represented by forming a state space tree which consist of nodes. It is a binary tree which either includes the weight by assigning $x_i = 1$ or excluding the weight assigning $x_i = 0$. Initially, the root node does not include any weight in the subset, so left part is 0 and total sum of all weights is 73. Then on including the w1 = 5, represented by x1=1 tree is expanded to left sub tree.

Now partial solution part of the node is updated to 5 and total remaining sum of weight is 68. On including the w2 = 10, represented by x2=1 tree is expanded to left sub tree. Now partial solution part of the node is updated to 5+10 = 15 and total remaining sum of weight is 58. On including the w3 = 12, represented by x3=1 tree is expanded to left sub tree. Now partial solution part of the node is updated to 15+12 = 27 and total remaining sum of weight is 46. Now, next if we include w4, the partial sum becomes 27 + 13 = 40, which exceeds the target 30. This branch cannot lead to a valid solution, so it is pruned (marked with a cross in the figure). As from that node no more branching is possible, so we backtrack to the previous node. We then exclude w3 = 12 in the subset represented by x3 = 0. Now, the partial solution is 15+0 = 15 and remaining sum of weight is 46. Then we include w4 = 13 in the subset represented by x4 =1, so partial solution 15 + 13 = 28 and remaining solution is 33. Now, next if we include w5, the partial sum becomes 28 + 15 = 43, which exceeds the target 30. This branch cannot lead to a valid solution, so it is pruned (marked with a cross in the figure). So, we backtrack and excluding w4 = 13 represented by x4 = 0, we find the partial solution is 15 + 0 = 15 and remaining weight is 33. Now, we include w5 = 15 represented by x5 = 1 from this new node and find partial solution 15 + 15 = 30 which matches our target. Now if we trace the route from the root node and including the weights inclusion and exclusion data given by x_i value, we can find a valid subset of weights which is exactly equal to M. A valid subset of weight represented by binary string x_i {1,1,0,0,1,0} So this says that w1, w2 and w5 weights form a valid subset {w1 ,w2 ,w5}. Checking the validity = 5 + 15 + 15 = 30. In this way by backtracking and expanding the branches of the tree, we can find other valid subset of weights equal to the target.

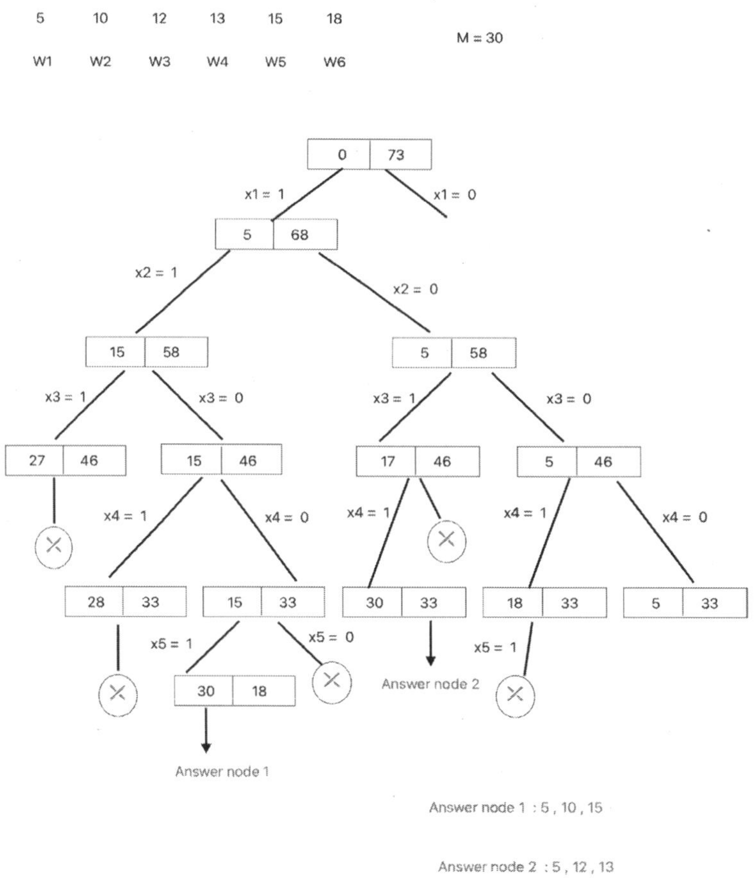

Fig 7.13 Sum of subset problem (backtracking technique)

The following C++ program shows the implementation of backtracking method in solving sum of subset problem.

```
#include <iostream>
#include <algorithm> // For sorting
using namespace std;
#define MAX 100  // Maximum number of elements

int w[MAX]; // Weight array
int x[MAX]; // Solution array
int M, n;   // Target sum and number of elements

void sumofsubs(int s, int k, int r) {
  x[k] = 1; // Include w[k] in the subset

  if (s + w[k] == M) { // If subset sum matches target
    cout << "Subset found: ";
    for (int i = 0; i <= k; i++) {
      if (x[i] == 1) cout << w[i] << " ";
    }
    cout << endl;
  }
  if (k + 1 < n && (s + w[k] + w[k + 1]) <= M)
    sumofsubs(s + w[k], k + 1, r - w[k]); // Recur with inclusion

  if (k + 1 < n && (s + r - w[k] >= M)) {
    x[k] = 0; // Exclude w[k] from the subset
    sumofsubs(s, k + 1, r - w[k]); // Recur with exclusion
  }
}

int main() {
  cout << "Enter the number of elements: ";
  cin >> n;

  cout << "Enter the elements: ";
```

```
    int totalSum = 0;
    for (int i = 0; i < n; i++) {
        cin >> w[i];
        totalSum += w[i];
    }

    cout << "Enter the target sum: ";
    cin >> M;

    // Sorting the array for correctness
    sort(w, w + n);

    cout << "Subsets summing to " << M << " are:\n";
    sumofsubs(0, 0, totalSum); // Start recursion
    return 0;
}
```

Output :

Enter the number of elements: 6

Enter the elements: 5 10 12 13 15 18

Enter the target sum: 30

Subsets summing to 30 are:

Subset found: 5 10 15

Subset found: 5 12 13

Subset found: 12 18

7.1.6. Branch and Bound

Branch and bound is a problem-solving technique which systematically explores a solution space while using bounding technique to prune optimal solutions of subproblems. It goes searching a state space tree with the final goal of reaching to a desired solution. Steps involved branch and bounding technique:

- The problem to be solved is divided into smaller sub-problems i.e. the child nodes of the state space tree which is the technique of branching.
- Each sub-problem define a partial solution.
- Each sub-problem is associated with a bound (upper and lower) that is used to estimate the optimal solution for that sub-problem. This defines the bounding mechanism.
- If the bound of the sub-problem is worse than the best-known solution, it is pruned i.e. discarded.

- A sub-problem is pruned when it violates the problem constraint, or its bound is worse than the best solution found so far, or it gets to a complete feasible solution.

7.1.6.1 Job Sequencing Problem

It is an optimization problem which aims to schedule jobs with the objective of finding a feasible solution (minimum overall job completion time) with minimum penalty. Given n jobs in a set J where each job is represented by a 3-tuple (p_i, d_i, t_i) where $t_i >= 0$ is the unit of processing time required for job i, d_i is the deadline for job i, p_i is the penalty incurred if the job is not completed within the stipulated deadline. The jobs are executed in a sequential manner. A feasible solution to this problem means all the jobs n in the set of jobs J are successfully completed within the deadlines. For this solution penalty is incurred only for those jobs from that are not in the set J.

To solve this problem, we represent the solution space in form of a state space tree starting from a root node. The nodes in the tree are generated in a level wise fashion. In this method, using some bounding functions, the expansion of the tree could be stopped earlier in many nodes. For, any node x, let S_x be the subset of jobs selected from set J at node x. Let $q = \max \{i \mid i \in S_x\}$.

Let m(x) be the minimum cost result node in the subtree with root at x. A node is considered a result/answer node if a path from the root to that particular node defines a tuple that belongs to the set of feasible solutions. Let,

$$n(x) \sum_{i \notin S_x, i \leq m} pi. \quad n(x) \leq m(X)$$

$$u(x) \sum_{i \notin S_x} pi. \; m(x) \leq u(X)$$

An upper bound U is maintained simultaneously with the construction of the tree. Initially, U defines the sum of all penalty score. Updation of U is done when the condition u(x) < U is obtained. A node is pruned (stopping the expansion in that branch) when the condition n(x) > U is meet for a node or if it becomes infeasible.

Let us consider an example to solve the problem of job sequencing using branch and bound technique. Given four jobs {J1, J2, J3, J4} with their processing time, deadline and penalty for each job in the following table.

j_i	p_i	d_i	t_i
J1	5	1	1
J2	10	3	2
J3	6	2	1
J4	3	1	1

Here, we can see J1 has a penalty of 5 unit if not finished with its deadline 1. Similarly, for J2 incurs a penalty of 10 if it job is not finished within its deadline i.e. 3, J3 incurs penalty of 6 if its job is not done by deadline 2 and J4 gets a penalty of 3 if it does not finish its job by deadline 1. Let's see how we can find the feasible solution.

Initially we consider the starting time is from 0. Now if the J1 is done first it consumes time 1 as its processing time is 1 and completes its job within its deadline 1. Then if J2 is done then, it consumes 2 units of processing time and completes its job within its stipulated deadline 3. So {J1, J2} is a feasible job sequence. In this case, penalty will be incurred from the jobs not in the set of feasible solution i.e. penalty of J3 and J4 which is 6+3 = 9. In this way, with the help of state space tree given below we find the feasible solutions possible.

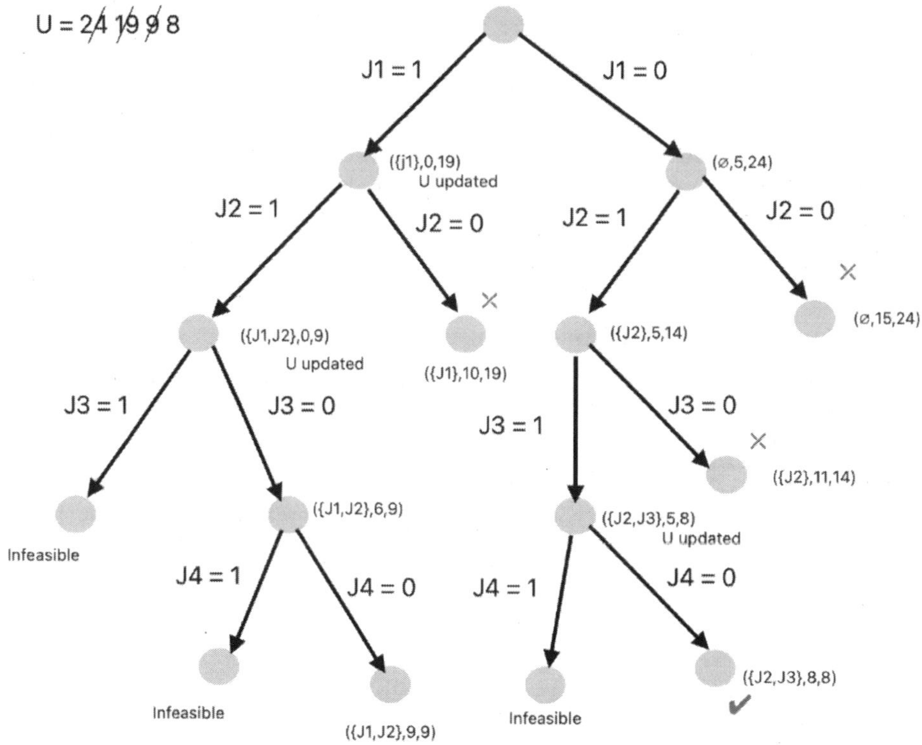

Fig 7.14 Job Sequencing problem solved using branch and bound

The following C++ problem shows the implementation of branch and bound method to solve job sequencing problem.

```
#include <iostream>
#include <vector>
#include <algorithm>

// Structure to represent a job
struct Job {
  int id;      // Job ID
  int deadline; // Deadline of job
  int profit;  // Profit if job is completed before the deadline
  int processingTime; // Time required to complete the job
};
```

```
// Comparison function to sort jobs in descending order of profit
bool compare(Job a, Job b) {
  return (a.profit > b.profit);
}

// Function to find the maximum profit using Job Sequencing with Processing Time
void jobSequencing(vector<Job> &jobs, int n) {
  // Sort jobs by profit in descending order
  sort(jobs.begin(), jobs.end(), compare);

  int maxDeadline = 0;
  for (Job j : jobs) maxDeadline = max(maxDeadline, j.deadline); // Find max deadline

  vector<int> slot(maxDeadline, -1); // Time slots available for scheduling
  vector<bool> occupied(maxDeadline, false); // Track occupied slots
  int totalProfit = 0;

  // Place jobs in available slots
  for (int i = 0; i < n; i++) {
    int startSlot = jobs[i].deadline - jobs[i].processingTime; // Find available time slot

    // Find a slot where the job can fit
    while (startSlot >= 0 && occupied[startSlot]) {
      startSlot--;
    }

    if (startSlot >= 0) { // If a valid slot is found
      for (int t = startSlot; t < startSlot + jobs[i].processingTime; t++) {
        occupied[t] = true;
      }
      slot[startSlot] = jobs[i].id;
      totalProfit += jobs[i].profit;
    }
  }
```

```
// Print the scheduled job sequence
  cout << "Job Sequence: ";
  for (int i = 0; i < maxDeadline; i++) {
    if (slot[i] != -1)
      cout << "J" << slot[i] << " ";
  }
  cout << "\nTotal Profit: " << totalProfit << endl;
}

// Driver function
int main() {
  int n;
  cout << "Enter number of jobs: ";
  cin >> n;
  vector<Job> jobs(n);

  cout << "Enter Job ID, Deadline, Profit, and Processing Time:\n";
  for (int i = 0; i < n; i++) {
    cin >> jobs[i].id >> jobs[i].deadline >> jobs[i].profit >> jobs[i].processingTime;
  }
  jobSequencing(jobs, n);
  return 0;
}
```

Output :

```
Enter number of jobs: 4
Enter Job ID, Deadline, Profit, and Processing Time:
1 1 5 1
2 3 10 2
3 2 6 1
4 1 3 1
Job Sequence: J3 J2
Total Profit: 16
```

7.2 COMPLEXITY OF ALGORITHM

In algorithm design two things are of major concern. First is correctness of the algorithm and the second is efficiency of the algorithm. As we know that there are many different ways to write algorithm that gives correct ouput for a particular problem, which among those will be used, depends upon the efficiency of the algorithm. Space and Time are two key measures for evaluating efficiency of an algorithm. The space is calculated by counting the maximum memory needed by the algorithm. While the time complexity is measured by counting the number of elementary operation. To understand it better let us take the example of the Algorithm 7.1. Let us calculate the time taken by the given algorithm in Table 7.1 . The number of execution taking place for each of the step is shown in the table. Important point here to note is that Step 4, 4.a and 4.b executes different number of time for different sets of input.

Say, the list is in desending order. In that case the inner loop i.e Step 4, 4.a and 4.b will execute k-1(k varies from 1 to n) time. Which will lead to: 1+2+3...+(n-1)=n(n-1)/2 number of execution of the Step 4, 4.a and 4.b. In this scenario the total complexity of the algorithm T(n) is =1+(n-1)+(n-1)+ n(n-1)/2+ n(n-1)/2+ n(n-1)/2+(n-1)+1= 3 n(n-1)/2 +3n-1. This is the worst case scenario.

Steps	Numbers of execution
1. Assign A[0]:= -∞.	1
2. Repeat Steps 3 to 5 for i=2 to n	n-1
3. Assign T:=A[i] and PTR:= i-1.	n-1
4. Repeat while T<A[PTR]	(n-1)x***[0 to n-1]***
a. Assign A[PTR+1]:= A[PTR]	(n-1)x[***0 to n-1]***
b. Assign PTR:=PTR-1.	(n-1)x***[0 to n-1]***
5. Assign A[PTR+1]:=T	n-1
6. Exit	1

Table 7.1 Time complexity calculation

Now let's assume that the list is already in ascending order. In that case the inner loop i.e Step 4, 4.a and 4.b will never execute. So time taken by the algorithm T(n) is 1+(n-1)+(n-1)+(n-1)+1=3n-1. This is the best case scenario. However, it is observed that on an average approximately k-1/2 executions will be made of the Steps 4, 4.a and 4.b. Which will lead to n(n-1)/4+ n(n-1)/4+ n(n-1)/4 coparisons. And the complexity of the algorithm T(n) is 1+(n-1)+(n-1)+ n(n-1)/4+ n(n-1)/4+ n(n-1)/4+(n-1)+1= 3 n(n-1)/4 +3n-1.The average case time complexity calculation is a much complex task to do, in comparison to worst case complexity calculation. In general complexity of an algorithm usually means the function which gives the running time of worst case in terms of input size.

Typical Algorithm Complexities

This table will explain what every type of complexity (running time) means:

Complexity	Running Time	Description
constant	O(1)	It takes a **constant number of steps** for performing a given operation (for example 1, 5, 10 or other number) and this count does not depend on the size of the input data.

Complexity	Running Time	Description
logarithmic	O(log(N))	It takes the order of **log(N) steps**, where the base of the logarithm is most often 2, for performing a given operation on N elements. For example, if N = 1,000,000, an algorithm with a complexity O(log(N)) would do about 20 steps (with a constant precision). Since the base of the logarithm is not of a vital importance for the order of the operation count, it is usually omitted.
linear	O(N)	It takes nearly the **same amount of steps as the number of elements** for performing an operation on N elements. For example, if we have 1,000 elements, it takes about 1,000 steps. Linear complexity means that the number of elements and the number of steps are linearly dependent, for example the number of steps for N elements can be N/2 or 3*N.
loglinear	O(n*log(n))	It takes **N*log(N) steps** for performing a given operation on N elements. For example, if you have 1,000 elements, it will take about 10,000 steps.
quadratic	$O(n^2)$	It takes the order of **N^2 number** of steps, where the N is the size of the input data, for performing a given operation. For example, N = 100, it takes about 10,000 steps. Actually we have a quadratic complexity when the number of steps is in quadratic relation with the size of the input data. For example for N elements the steps can be of the order of $3*N^2/2$.
cubic	$O(n^3)$	It takes the order of **N^3 steps**, where N is the size of the input data, for performing an operation on N elements. For example, if we have 100 elements, it takes about 1,000,000 steps.
exponential	$O(2^n)$, O(N!), $O(n^k)$, ...	It takes a number of steps, which is with an **exponential** dependability with the size of the input data, to perform an operation on N elements. For example, if N = 10, the exponential function 2^N has a value of 1024, if N = 20, it has a value of 1 048 576, and if N = 100, it has a value of a number with about 30 digits. The exponential function N! grows even faster: for N = 5 it has a value of 120, for N = 10 it has a value of 3,628,800 and for N = 20 – 2,432,90,008,176,640,000.

When evaluating complexity, constants are not taken into account, because they do not significantly affect the count of operations. Therefore an algorithm which does N steps and algorithms which do N/2 or 3*N respectively are considered linear and approximately equally efficient, because they perform a number of operations which is of the same order.

7.3 ASYMPTOTIC NOTATIONS

From the above discussions it is clear that when we analyze any algorithm, we generally get a formula to represent the amount of time required for execution or the time required by the computer to run the lines of code of the algorithm, number of memory accesses, number of comparisons etc. When the size of input tends to infinity some of the details contained in the formulae become redundant while telling us about the running time.

Let us take an example, if some algorithm has a time complexity of f(n) = (n^3 + 5n + 10), which is a quadratic equation. For large values of n, the "5n + 10" part will become insignificant compared to the n^2 part. So, the n^2 term dominates the expression, and this is the main factor for comparing algorithm costs. From the discussions it is quite clear that asymptotic notations indicate about bounds on the performance of algorithms, rather than giving exact speeds. Following are the commonly used asymptotic notations to calculate the running time complexity of an algorithm.

- O Notation (Big Oh Notation)
- Ω Notation (Big Omega Notation)
- θ Notation (Theta Notation)
- o Notation (Little-O Notation)
- ω Notation (Little Omega Notation)

7.3.1 Big Oh Notation, O

The notation O(n) is the formal way to express the upper bound of an algorithm's running time. Say an algorithm has a time complexity f(n), then:

O(g(n)) = { f(n) : there exists c > 0 and k such that 0≤f(n) ≤ c.g(n) for all n > k. }

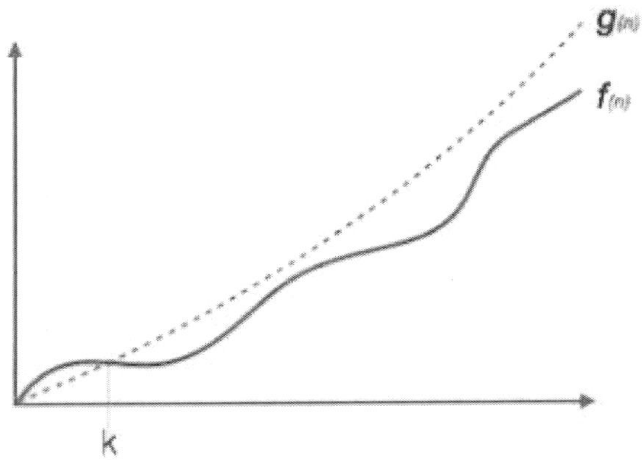

Figure 7.15: Big Oh Notation

In Figure 7.15 f(n) represents a complexity function of an algorithm and g(n) is an upper bound to the function f(n). So g(n) is also a Big O of f(n).

7.3.2 Big-Omega Notation, Ω

The notation Ω(n) is the formal way to express the lower bound of an algorithm's running time. Say an algorithm has a time complexity f(n), then:

Ω(*g*(n)) ≥ {*f*(n) : there exists c > 0 and k such that 0≤ c.*g*(n) ≤ *f*(n) for all n > k. }

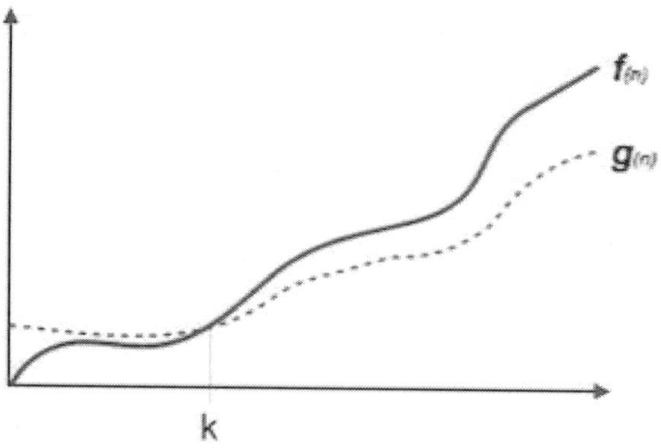

Figure 7.16: Big Omega Notation

In Figure 7.16 f(n) represents a complexity function of an algorithm and g(n) is an lower bound to the function f(n). So g(n) is also a Big omega of f(n).

7.3.3 Theta Notation, θ

The notation **θ** (n) is the formal way to express the functions that bound the complexity function from both above and below. Basically it tells about the exact asymptotic behavior. Say an algorithm has a time complexity f(n), then:

Θ(g(n)) = {f(n): there exist positive constants c1, c2 and n0 such

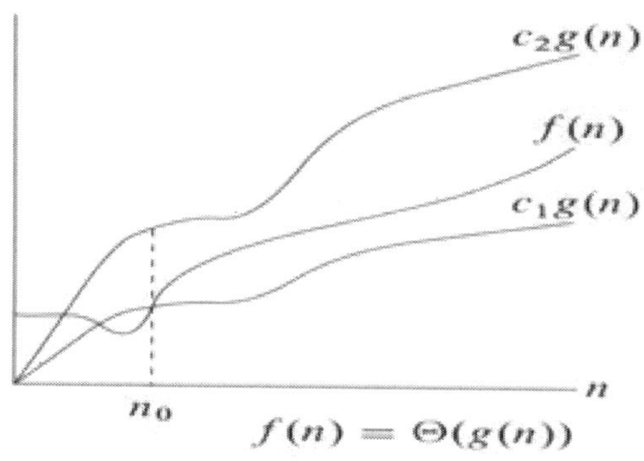

that 0 <= c1*g(n) <= f(n) <= c2*g(n) for all n >= n0}

Figure 7.17 Big Theta Notation

7.3.4 Little o-notation, o

Little o –notation is used to denote an upper bound that is not asymptotically tight. Basically little o means loose upper-bound.

o(g(n)) = { f(n) : for any positive constant c > 0 there exist a k>0, such that 0 ≤ f(n) <cg(n) for all n > k. }

Primarily , in o-notation, the function f (n) becomes insignificant relative to g(n) , as n approaches infinity; that is,

$$\lim_{n \to \infty} f(n)/g(n) = 0$$

7.3.5 Little omega notation, ω

Little **ω** –notation is used to denote a lower bound that is not asymptotically tight. Basically little **ω** means loose lower-bound.

ω (g(n)) = { f(n) : for any positive constant c > 0 there exist a k>0, such that $0 \le cg(n) < f(n)$ for all n > k. }

Primarily , in **ω** -notation, the function g (n) becomes insignificant relative to f(n) , as n approaches infinity; that is,

$$\lim_{n \to \infty} g(n)/f(n) = 0$$

7.4 ANALYSIS OF ALGORITHM BY SOLVING RECURRENCES

Many algorithms are recursive in nature. When we analyse them, we get a recurrence relation for time complexity. We get running time on an input of size n as a function of n and the running time on inputs of smaller sizes. For example in Merge Sort, to sort a given array, we divide it in two halves and recursively repeat the process for the two halves. Finally we merge the results. Time complexity of Merge Sort can be written as T(n) = 2T(n/2) + cn. There are many other algorithms like Binary Search, Tower of Hanoi, etc. Two different ways for solving recurrences are explained here

1) Substitution Method: We make a guess for the solution and then we use mathematical induction to prove the guess is correct or incorrect.

For example consider the recurrence T(n) = 2T(n/2) + n

We guess the solution as T(n) = O(nLogn). Now we use induction to prove our guess.

We need to prove that T(n) <= cnLogn. We can assume that it is true for values smaller than n.

T(n) = 2T(n/2) + n

<= cn/2Log(n/2) + n

= cnLogn - cnLog2 + n

= cnLogn - cn + n

<= cnLogn

Let us consider one more recurrence relation, which shows up fairly frequently for some types of algorithms:

T(1) = 1

T(n) = 2T(n−1) + c1

By expanding this out a bit (using the "iteration method"), we can guess that this will be $O(2^n)$. To use the substitution method to prove this bound, we now need to guess a closed-form upper bound based on this asymptotic bound. We will guess an upper bound of $k2^n - b$, where b is some constant. We include the b in anticipation of having to deal with the constant c1 that appears in the recurrence relation, and because it does no harm. In the process of proving this bound by induction, we will generate a set of constraints on k and b, and if b turns out to be unnecessary, we will be able to set it to whatever we want at the end.

Our property, then, is $T(n) \le k2^n - b$, for some two constants k and b. Note that this property logically implies that T(n) is $O(2^n)$, which can be verified with reference to the definition of O.

Base case: n = 1. $T(1) = 1 \le k2^1 - b = 2k - b$. This is true as long as $k \ge (b + 1)/2$.

Inductive case: We assume our property is true for n – 1. We now want to show that it is true for n.

$$
\begin{aligned}
T(n) &= 2T(n-1) + c1 \\
&\le 2(k2^{n-1} - b) + c1 \quad \text{(by IH)} \\
&= k2^n - 2b + c1 \\
&\le k2^n - b
\end{aligned}
$$

This is true as long as $b \ge c1$.

So we end up with two constraints that need to be satisfied for this proof to work, and we can satisfy them simply by letting b = c1 and k = (b + 1)/2, which is always possible, as the definition of O allows us to choose any constant. Therefore, we have proved that our property is true, and so T(n) is $O(2^n)$.

The biggest thing worth noting about this proof is the importance of adding additional terms to the upper bound we assume. In almost all cases in which the recurrence has constants or lower-order terms, it will be necessary to have additional terms in the upper bound to "cancel out" the constants or lower-order terms. Without the right additional terms, the inductive case of the proof will get stuck in the middle, or generate an impossible constraint; this is a signal to go back to your upper bound and determine what else needs to be added to it that will allow the proof to proceed without causing the bound to change in asymptotic terms.

2) Master Method:

Master Method is a direct way to get the solution. The master method works only for following type of recurrences or for recurrences that can be transformed to following type.

T(n) = aT(n/b) + f(n) where a >= 1 and b > 1

There are following three cases:

1. If $f(n) = \Theta(n^c)$ where $c < \text{Log}_b a$ then $T(n) = \Theta(n^{\text{Log}_b a})$

2. If $f(n) = \Theta(n^c)$ where $c = \text{Log}_b a$ then $T(n) = \Theta(n^c \text{Log } n)$

3. If $f(n) = \Theta(n^c)$ where $c > \text{Log}_b a$ then $T(n) = \Theta(f(n))$

Example 1: Say you have derived the recurrence relation $T(n) = 8T(n/2) + cn^2$, where c is some positive constant. We see that this has the appropriate form for applying the master method, and that a=8, b=2, and $h(n) = cn^2$. cn^2 is $O(n^{\log_2 8-\epsilon}) = O(n^{3-\varepsilon})$ for any $\varepsilon \le 1$, so this falls into case 1. Therefore, T(n) is $\Theta(n^3)$.

Example 2: Say you have derived the recurrence relation T(n) = T(n/2) + cn, where c is some positive constant. We see that this has the appropriate form for applying the master method, and that a=1, b=2, and h(n) = cn. Then h(n) is $\Omega(n^{\log_2 1+\varepsilon}) = \Omega(n^\varepsilon)$ for any $\varepsilon \le 1$, so this falls into case3. and ah(n/b) = cn/2 = ½h(n), therefore T(n) is $\Theta(n)$.

Example 3: Say you have derived the recurrence relation $T(n) = 8T(n/4) + cn^{3/2}$, where c is some positive constant. We see that this has the appropriate form for applying the master method, and that a=8, b=4, and $h(n) = cn^{3/2}$. $cn^{3/2}$ is $\Theta(n^{\log_4 8}) = \Theta(n^{3/2})$, so this falls into case 2. Therefore, T(n) is $\Theta(n^{3/2}\log n)$

7.5 P, NP, NP – HARD AND NP-COMPLETE PROBLEM

In this section, we will discuss on the problems that have a polynomial time algorithms giving solutions to problem and problem for which there is no known polynomial time algorithm.

- **P(polynomial time):** An algorithm is said to be a polynomial time algorithm if given an instance of size k, the algorithm solves the problem i.e gives an answer in $O(n^k)$ for some constant k. The class P consists of all decision problems (yes/no problems) that can be solved in polynomial time, i.e., in $O(n^k)$ for some constant k. Example problems:

  a). Sorting (Merge Sort, Quick Sort) → O(n log n)

  b). Finding the shortest path in a graph (Dijkstra's Algorithm) → $O(V^2)$

- **NP(Nondeterministic polynomial time):** Problems for which there exist polynomial time verification algorithms for all "Yes" instance of the decision problem are said to belong to class of NP i.e., the class NP consists of decision problems for which a solution can be verified in polynomial time. Example problem :

  a). Hamiltonian Cycle Problem (given a cycle, check if it visits all vertices exactly once).

  b). Traveling Salesman Problem (TSP) (given a path, check if its cost is below a threshold).

- **NP – hard(Non-Deterministic Polynomial-Hard):** A problem is NP-Hard if it is at least as hard as any problem in NP, meaning every NP problem can be reduced to it in polynomial time. A problem A is NP-Hard if, for every problem B in NP, there exists a polynomial-time reduction from B to A. Reduction means that if we can solve A, we can use it to solve any problem B in NP. Some NP-Hard problems may not be in NP. Example problems:

  a). TSP optimization: Finding the shortest route.

  b). Halting Problem(Given a program and input, determine if it will halt): Not in NP because we can't verify a solution in polynomial time.

- **NP-Complete (NPC):** A problem is NP-Complete (NPC) if:

  a). It is in NP (i.e., a given solution can be verified in polynomial time).

  b). It is NP-Hard (i.e., every NP problem can be reduced to it in polynomial time).

NP-Complete problems are the "hardest" problems in NP. If any NP-Complete problem is solved in polynomial time, then P = NP. Example problems.

a). Vertex Cover Problem: Given a graph G = (V,E) and an integer k, the vertex cover problem ask whether there exist a subset $V' \subseteq V$ of size at most k such that every edge in E has at leasr one endpoint in V' i.e Given G and k, is there any vertex cover of size ≤ k.

b). Satisfiability problem (SAT) : Given a Boolean expression E, is it satisfiable?

Diagrammatic Representation:

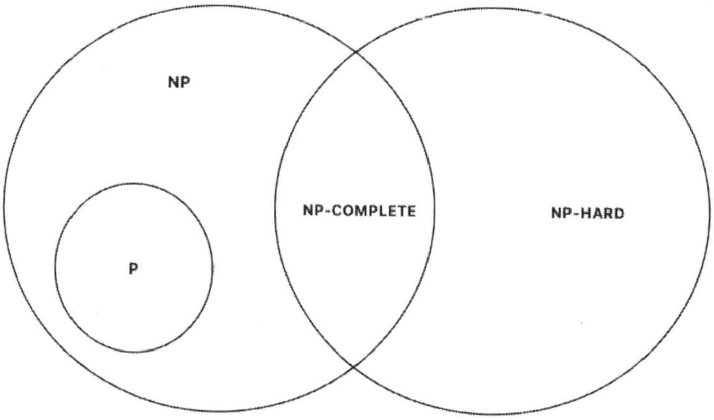

Fig 7.18 Diagrammatic representation of different classes

7.6 LET US SUM UP

- Design and Analysis of Algorithm focuses on systematically designing efficient computational procedures and evaluating their performance in terms of time and space complexity.
- An algorithm in Design and Analysis of Algorithm is a well-defined, step-by-step computational procedure that transforms input into output while ensuring correctness and efficiency.
- Characteristics of an algorithm include well-defined inputs and outputs, clear and unambiguous steps, a finite execution time, and correctness in solving the given problem.
- The Brute Force Method is a straightforward approach that systematically explores all possible solutions to find the correct answer, often resulting in high computational costs.
- Problems in the Brute Force Method include inefficiency due to the exponential number of possibilities, making it impractical for large inputs requiring optimized solutions.
- Brute Force String Matching sequentially compares each character of a given pattern with the text, sliding through the text one character at a time to find occurrences.
- Divide and Conquer is an algorithmic paradigm that breaks a problem into smaller sub-problems, solves them recursively, and then merges their solutions for the final result.
- Merge Sort is a comparison-based sorting algorithm that recursively divides an array, sorts the smaller parts, and then merges them back together in O(n log n) time complexity.
- Quick Sort is a highly efficient sorting algorithm that selects a pivot, partitions the array into smaller and larger elements, and recursively sorts the partitions for optimal performance.
- The Master Theorem provides a mathematical formula to determine the time complexity of recursive algorithms by analyzing their recurrence relations.
- Binary Search is an efficient searching technique that repeatedly divides a sorted array in half to locate an element, achieving an O(log n) time complexity.
- Greedy Algorithm solves problems by making the locally optimal choice at each step with the hope of finding a globally optimal solution in a computationally efficient manner.

- The Activity Selection Problem uses a greedy approach to maximize the number of non-overlapping activities that can be scheduled within a given time frame.
- The Minimum Spanning Tree (MST) is a sub graph that connects all vertices with the least total edge weight while avoiding cycles in a weighted graph.
- Prim's Algorithm is a greedy algorithm that constructs an MST by starting from a single vertex and adding the smallest available edge at each step.
- Kruskal's Algorithm finds the MST by sorting all edges in ascending order and adding them one by one, ensuring no cycles are formed while maintaining connectivity.
- Dynamic Programming is a powerful optimization technique that breaks problems into overlapping sub-problems, stores their solutions, and reuses them to avoid redundant computations.
- The Longest Common Subsequence (LCS) finds the longest sequence of characters that appear in the same order in two given strings using a dynamic programming approach.
- Memoization is a top-down dynamic programming technique that stores the results of sub-problems in a table to avoid re-computation and enhance efficiency.
- Tabulation is a bottom-up dynamic programming approach that pre computes solutions for smaller sub-problems and builds up to the final solution iteratively.
- Matrix Chain Multiplication determines the most efficient way to multiply a sequence of matrices by optimizing the order of multiplication to minimize computational cost.
- Backtracking is a recursive problem-solving technique that explores all possible solutions and abandons non-promising paths to efficiently find valid answers.
- The Sum of Subset Problem uses backtracking to explore all subsets of a given set and identify those whose sum matches a given target value.
- Branch and Bound is an optimization strategy that systematically eliminates non-promising solution branches to find the best possible answer in problems like TSP and knapsack.
- Job Sequencing by Branch and Bound determines the optimal order of executing jobs with deadlines and profits to maximize the total profit while meeting time constraints.
- An algorithm is an efficient method that can be expressed within finite amount of time and space.
- The important aspects of algorithm design include creating an efficient algorithm to solve a problem in an efficient way using minimum time and space.
- To solve a problem, different approaches can be followed. Some of them can be efficient with respect to time consumption, whereas other approaches may be memory efficient. However, one has to keep in mind that both time consumption and memory usage cannot be optimized simultaneously.
- If we require an algorithm to run in lesser time, we have to invest in more memory and if we require an algorithm to run with lesser memory, we need to have more time. We cannot talk about efficiency of algorithms and data structures without explaining the term "algorithm complexity", which we have already mentioned several times in one form or another. We will avoid the mathematical definitions and we have given a simple explanation of what the term means.

- Algorithm complexity is a measure which evaluates the order of the count of operations, performed by a given or algorithm as a function of the size of the input data. To put this simpler, complexity is a rough approximation of the number of steps necessary to execute an algorithm. When we evaluate complexity we speak of order of operation count, not of their exact count. For example if we have an order of N^2 operations to process N elements, then $N^2/2$ and $3*N^2$ are of one and the same quadratic order.
- Algorithm complexity is commonly represented with the O(f) notation, also known as asymptotic notation or "Big O notation", where f is the function of the size of the input data. The asymptotic computational complexity O(f) measures the order of the consumed resources (CPU time, memory, etc.) by certain algorithm expressed as function of the input data size.
- Complexity can be constant, logarithmic, linear, n*log(n), quadratic, cubic, exponential, etc. This is respectively the order of constant, logarithmic, linear and so on, number of steps, are executed to solve a given problem. For simplicity, sometime instead of "algorithms complexity" or just "complexity" we use the term "running time". For solving recurrent relations which may arise in finding complexity of many divide and conquer based algorithm the procedure to solve them is discussed in details.
- P focuses on solving problems efficiently within polynomial time, ensuring practical feasibility for large inputs.
- NP includes problems where solutions can be verified in polynomial time, but finding a solution may still be computationally hard.
- NP-Hard represents problems that are at least as difficult as NP problems, though they may not belong to NP themselves.
- NP-Complete consists of the most challenging problems in NP, as they are both NP and NP-Hard, meaning solving one efficiently would solve all NP problems.

7.7 CHECK YOUR PROGRESS

1. What are the main criteria used to evaluate an algorithm's efficiency?
2. How do time complexity and space complexity impact algorithm performance?
3. What are the essential properties of a well-defined algorithm?
4. What are the five key characteristics that define an algorithm?
5. Why must an algorithm have a finite number of steps?
6. What is the brute force approach, and when is it used?
7. Give an example where brute force is inefficient compared to optimized approaches.
8. Why is brute force not suitable for large input sizes?
9. How does brute force compare to dynamic programming in terms of efficiency?
10. Explain how the brute force string matching algorithm works.
11. What are the three main steps in the divide and conquer approach?
12. How does divide and conquer improve efficiency compared to brute force?
13. Explain how merge sort works with an example.

14. What is the worst-case and best-case time complexity of merge sort?
15. Explain how quick sort works with an example.
16. What is the role of the pivot in quick sort?
17. What is the general form of recurrence relations solved using the Master Theorem?
18. Use the Master Theorem to solve the recurrence relation $T(n) = 2T(n/2) + O(n)$.
19. Why is binary search more efficient than linear search?
20. What is the precondition for applying binary search on an array?
21. What is the greedy choice property in greedy algorithms?
22. Why does a greedy algorithm not always guarantee an optimal solution?
23. How does the greedy algorithm help in solving the activity selection problem?
24. What is a Minimum Spanning Tree, and how is it different from a regular spanning tree? What are two standard algorithms for finding MSTs?
25. How does Prim's algorithm select edges while constructing an MST?
26. What data structure is used in Kruskal's algorithm to check for cycles?
27. How does Kruskal's algorithm differ from Prim's algorithm?
28. How does dynamic programming improve upon divide and conquer?
29. What is the main difference between dynamic programming and greedy algorithms?
30. How longest common subsequence is solved using dynamic programming.
31. How is tabulation different from memoization in dynamic programming?
32. What is the goal of the matrix chain multiplication problem?
33. Why do we use dynamic programming to solve matrix chain multiplication?
34. How does backtracking solve the sum of subsets problem?
35. How does branch and bound differ from backtracking?
36. What constraints are considered in the job sequencing problem?
37. How does branch and bound ensure an optimal job sequencing solution?
38. What is the Average case complexity of merge sort algorithm?
39. $f(n)=3n+7$, express $f(n)$ in terms of all the complexity notations.
40. What is meant by complexity analysis of an algorithm? What is asymptotic analysis and why it is important? Explain all the asymptotic notations in detail.
41. Write down your own algorithm to create a sorted list by combining two sorted list. Do the complexity analysis of this algorithm.
42. What is P, NP, NP-hard, NP-complete problem. Describe the relationship between them.
43. Give examples of NP-hard and NP-complete problem.
44. Find the complexity of the following in terms of Big O notation

    (A) $T(n)=T(n-1)+n$

    (B) $T(n)=4T(n/2)+n^2$

7.8 EXERCISES

Q.1 Write an algorithm to find the sum of the first n natural numbers.

Q.2 Design an algorithm to find the maximum element in an unsorted array.

Q.3 How many comparisons are required to find the maximum number in an array of size n using brute force?

Q.4 If we check all possible subsets of a set of size n, how many total subsets will be checked?

Q.5 Apply the brute force string matching algorithm to T = "ABABABA" and P = "ABA" and list the matching indices.

Q.6 Find the number of shifts required when matching "ABCD" in "ABCDABCDABCD".

Q.7 Sort the array [38, 27, 43, 3, 9, 82, 10] using merge sort. Show all the steps of dividing and merging.

Q.8 Sort the array {14, 7, 3, 12, 9, 11, 6, 2} using merge sort and show the merging steps.

Q.9 Given an array [15, 9, 12, 3, 7, 18, 11], determine how many total comparisons will be made during the merge sort process.

Q.10 Sort [10, 80, 30, 90, 40, 50, 70] using quick sort with the first element as the pivot.

Q.11 Apply quick sort on the array [25, 35, 10, 15, 40, 20] using the last element as the pivot. Write the sorted sequence after each partition step.

Q.12 If quick sort is applied to a sorted array [1, 2, 3, 4, 5, 6, 7, 8, 9, 10] with the first element as the pivot, how many comparisons will be made?

Q.13 Sort the array [12, 7, 14, 9, 10, 11] using quick sort with the first element as the pivot. Show all partitioning steps.

Q.14 Search for 23 in {3, 9, 15, 23, 27, 34, 41} using binary search and count the number of comparisons.

Q.15 Search for 15 in {2,4, 8,11, 15, 22, 28, 44, 54} using binary search and count the number of comparisons.

Q.16 Solve the activity selection problem for activities with start times {1, 3, 0, 5, 8, 5} and finish times {2, 4, 6, 7, 9, 9}.

Q.17 Consider a weighted undirected graph with 5 vertices and the following edges:

Edge	Weight
A–B	1
A–C	3
B–C	1
B–D	4
C–D	2
C–E	5
D–E	6

Use Kruskal's Algorithm to determine the MST and its total weight.

Q.18 A transportation network connects 8 cities with the following road construction costs (in millions):

Edge	Weight
A–B	2
A–C	6
B–C	3
B–D	8
C–D	5
C–E	7
D–E	9
D-F	12
E-F	4
E-G	11
F-G	10

Find the MST and its total cost using Kruskal's Algorithm.

Q.18 Given a weighted graph, find MST using Prim's algorithm.

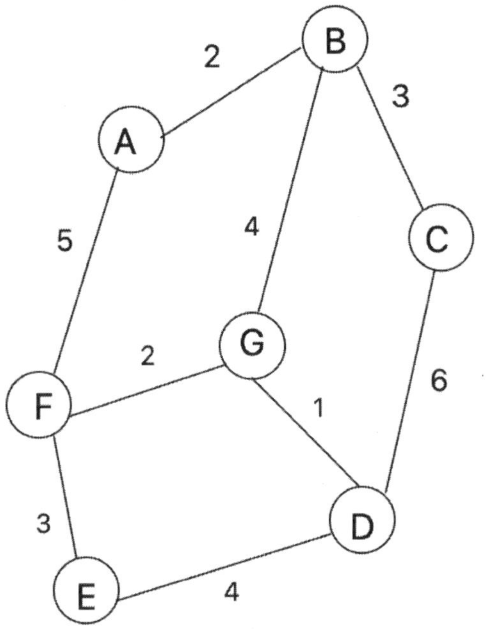

Q.19 A graph with 4 vertices (A, B, C, D) has the following weighted edges:

A–B: 1, A–C: 3, B–C: 1, B–D: 4, C–D: 2

Apply Prim's Algorithm, starting from vertex A, and determine the total weight of the MST.

Q.20 Given a weighted graph, find MST using Prim's algorithm and Kruskal's algorithm.

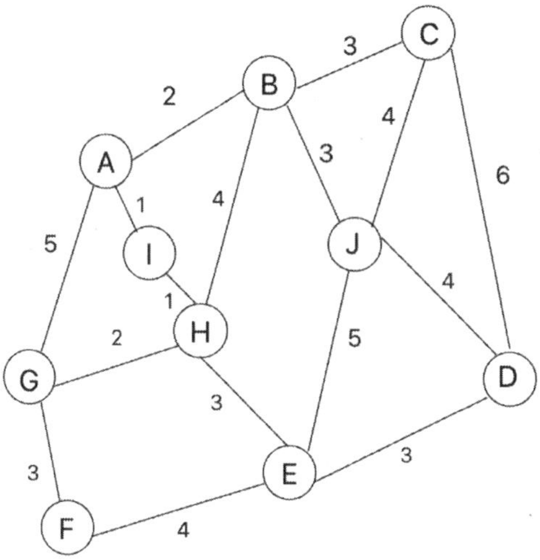

Q.21 Find the Longest Common Subsequence (LCS) of the strings:

X="AGGTABABTX" and

Y="GXTXAYBATB"

What is the length of the LCS and the actual subsequence?

Q.22 Find the Longest Common Subsequence (LCS) of the strings:

X="ACGTACGTGAC"

Y="GTCGTAGTAC"

What is the length of the LCS and the actual subsequence?

Q.23 Find the Longest Common Subsequence (LCS) of the strings:

X="DYNAMIC"

Y="PROGRAMMING"

What is the length of the LCS and the actual subsequence?

Q.24 Given the matrices with dimensions A1 (10×20), A2 (20×30), A3 (30×40), A4 (40×30), A5 (30×10). Determine the minimum number of scalar multiplications required to compute their product using Matrix Chain Multiplication.

Q.25 A set of matrices A1 (4×5), A2 (5×7), A3 (7×10), A4 (10×15), A5 (15×20) are given. Find the optimal multiplication order and the minimum number of scalar multiplications required.

Q.25 Given S = {3, 5, 6, 7, 9, 12, 14} and M = 21. Determine all subsets whose sum is exactly 21 using backtracking.

Q.26 For the set S = {5, 8, 10, 12, 15, 18, 20, 25} and M = 35, Find:

- All possible subsets whose sum is 35.
- The total number of valid subsets found.

Q.27 Using the Branch and Bound technique, determine the optimal job sequence that minimizes the total penalty.

Job	**Processing Time (hours)**	**Deadline (hours)**	**Penalty (units)**
J1	2	4	70
J2	1	2	60
J3	3	3	50
J4	2	1	40

Q.28 Find the maximum number of jobs that can be scheduled before their deadlines while minimizing the penalty.

Job	Processing Time (hours)	Deadline (hours)	Penalty (units)
J1	2	4	100
J2	3	3	90
J3	1	1	50
J4	4	2	70
J5	2	5	60

Q.29 Find the complexity of

```
    for (i = 1; i <= n; i++)
{
  for (j = 1; j <= i; j++)
  {
    a = a + 1;
  }
}
```

Q.30 What is the time, space complexity of following code:

```
int a = 0, b = 0;
for (i = 0; i < N; i++) {
                    a = a + rand();
}
for (j = 0; j < M; j++) {
                    b = b + rand();
}
```

Q.31 What is the time complexity of following code

```
int a = 0;
for (i = 0; i < N; i++) {
```

```
  for (j = N; j > i; j--) {
                        a = a + i + j;
                        }
}
```

Q.32 Find the complexity of

```
for (i = 1; i <= n; i++)
{
  for (j = 1; j <= n; j++)
  {
    for (k = 1; k <= n; k++)
    {
      a = a + 1;
    }
  }
}
```

Q.33 Find the complexity of the program

```
for (i = 1; i <=n; i = 2*i)
{
          a=a+1;
}
```

Q.34 Determine the complexity of

```
for (i = 1; i <= n; i++)
{
  for (j = 1; j <= n; j *= 2)
  {
    a = a + 1;
  }
}
```

Q.35 Solve the recurrence using master's theorem:

1. $T(n) = 9T(n/3) + O(n^2)$.
2. $T(n) = 5T(n/4) + O(n^2)$.
3. $T(n) = 2T(n/2) + O(n\log n)$.
4. $T(n) = 3T(n/2) + O(n\log^2 n)$.
5. $T(n) = 6T(n/3) + O(n^2)$.

8

SORTING AND SEARCHING ALGORITHMS

8.1 INTRODUCTION

Sorting and Searching are fundamental operations in Computer Science. Sorting is the rearranging of the data elements into ascending or desending order.

Say, we have a list of 10 elements:

LIST before sorting: 12 9 100 20 200 205 708 28 920 103

After soting the list will become:

LIST after sorting: 9 12 20 28 100 103 200 205 708 920

Most of the sorting algorithms are comparison-based sorting. Normally the three basic operations in these algorithms are:

- **Comparisons:** check wheather $L_i > L_j$
- **Interachange :** Exchange the contents of L_i and L_j based on comparison outcome
- **Assignment:** Assign values to variables

8.2 SORTING ALGORITHMS

Let us consider some of the comparison-based sorting algorithm. In this section we will discuss Inscrtion sort, selection sort, buuble sort, heap sort, quick sort and merge sort algorithm.

8.2.1 Insertion sort

Suppose we have a list of n numbers. For performing Insertion sort, first things are to place the list of numbers in an array A of size n. Insertion sort scans the array A from A[1] to A[n] inserting each element A[i] into proper location(on i^{th} pass) in previously sorted part of the array, i.e A[1] to A[i-1]. Here we assume that the array A[0] to A[i-1] is sorted and we insert A[i] on i^{th} pass. The algorithm completes the job of sorting in 'n' paases. The various passes are explanied below:

Pass1: A[1] in a list of one element i.e by itself is trivially sorted.

Pass2: for inserting A[2] compare with A[1] and place in sorted order.

Pass 3: Compare with the sorted list containing A[1], A[2] and place in such a way that A[1], A[2] and A[3] is sorted.

.....

......

Pass n: Compare with the sorted list containing A[1], A[2]...A[n-1] and place in such a way that A[1], A[2] ...A[n] is sorted.

Algorithm 8.1: INSERTION_SORT(A,n)

This algorithm sorts the array A which contains 'n' number of elements

1. Assign A [0]:= -∞.
2. Repeat Steps 3 to 5 for i=2 to n
3. Assign T:=A[i] and PTR:= i-1.
4. Repeat while T<A[PTR]
   a. Assign A[PTR+1]:= A[PTR]
   b. Assign PTR:=PTR-1.
5. Assign A[PTR+1]:=T
6. Exit

To understand it better let us take an example. Say the list is (-1, 4, 0, 25, 17, 1) using insertion sort. In this example, the bold numbers are the ones that we are inserting the current step. Firstly the list is placed in the array A[6].

List before ordering ⇒

-1	4	0	25	17	1

Pass 1:

i. Check wheather 4 < -1? No

-1	4	0	25	17	1

Pass 2:

i. Check 0 < 4? Yes

-1	4	0	25	17	1

ii. 0 < -1? No => Shift 4. Move 0.

-1	0	4	25	17	1

Pass 3:

i. 25 < 4? No

-1	0	4	25	17	1

Pass 4:

i. 1 7 < 25? Yes

-1	0	4	25	17	1

ii. 1 7 < 4? No => Shift 25. Move 7

-1	0	4	17	25	1

Pass 5:

i. 1 < 25? Yes

-1	0	4	17	25	1

ii. 1 <17? Yes

-1	0	4	17	25	1

iii. 1 < 4? Yes

-1	0	4	17	25	1

-1	0	4	17	25	1

iv. Check 1 < 0? No => Shift 4, 17, 25, Move 1

-1	0	1	4	17	25

Complexity Analysis

In Best case

The best possible dataset is a sorted list. In that case the iner loop will never execute as once a comprison will be made. So the time complexity will be O(n).

Worst Case

Inner loop executes for all previous elements. This is the case when numbers are in opposite order i. e. if ascending order is desired and numbers are in desending order and vice versa. So total number of comparisons will be

$1+2+3......+(n-1)=n*(n-1)/2= O(n^2)$

Average Case

Assuming all types of inputs to be equally likely, the expected number of comparisons for a number in ith location is:

$$(1+2+..i)/i = (i+1)/2$$

So total expected number of comparisons are $= \sum_{k=1}^{n-1} (i+1)/2$

$$=(n^2+n-2)/4$$

$$=O(n^2)$$

Assignment 8.1: Write a program to implement Insertion Sort algorithm.

```
#include <iostream>
using namespace std;
void insertionSort(int A[], int n) {
A[0] = -1e9; // Sentinel value (-∞)
  for (int i = 2; i <= n; i++) {
    int T = A[i];
    int PTR = i - 1;
    while (T < A[PTR]) {
A[PTR + 1] = A[PTR];
      PTR--;
    }
A[PTR + 1] = T;
  }
}
int main() {
  int n;
  cout << "Enter the number of elements: ";
  cin >> n;
  int A[n + 1]; // Extra space for A[0] as a sentinel
  cout << "Enter " << n << " elements: ";

  for (int i = 1; i <= n; i++) {
    cin >> A[i];
  }
```

```
insertionSort(A, n);
  cout << "Sorted array: ";
  for (int i = 1; i <= n; i++) {
    cout << A[i] << " ";
  }
  return 0;
}
```

Output:

Enter the number of elements: 5

Enter 5 elements: 76

32

56

88

12

Sorted array: 12 32 56 76 88

8.2.2 SELECTION SORT

The basic objective of selection sort is to minimize the data movement. Let us write down the **SELECTION SORT** in a more formal algorithmic way.

Algorithm 8.2: SELECTION_SORT(A,n)

This algorithm sorts the array A which contains 'n' number of elements.

1. Repeat steps 2 to 7 for i = 1 to n – 1
2. Set min := i
3. Repeat steps 4 and 5 for j = i+1 to n
4. if A[j] < A[min] then
5. min := j
6. if **index** of the ***min*** element != i then
7. swap A[min] and A[i]
8. Exit

To illustrate its working let us consider an array A[n] with n elements A[1],A[2]...,A[n]. In the first pass the algorithm will find the smallest element A[LOC1] and exchange it with first element A[1]. In the next step it will find the second smallest element A[LOC2] and exchange it with the second element A[2]. This continues for all the elements. Let us take an example:

List before ordering

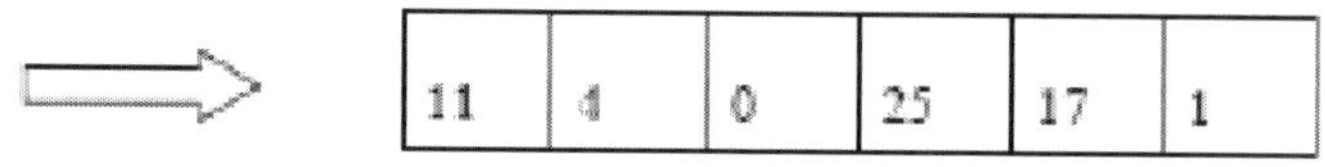

Pass 1:

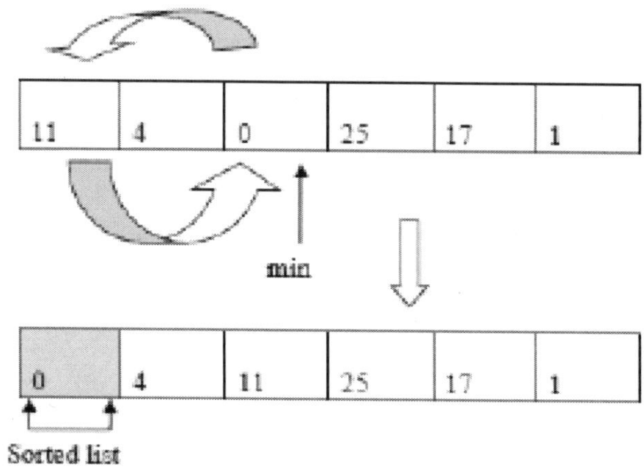

Pass 2:

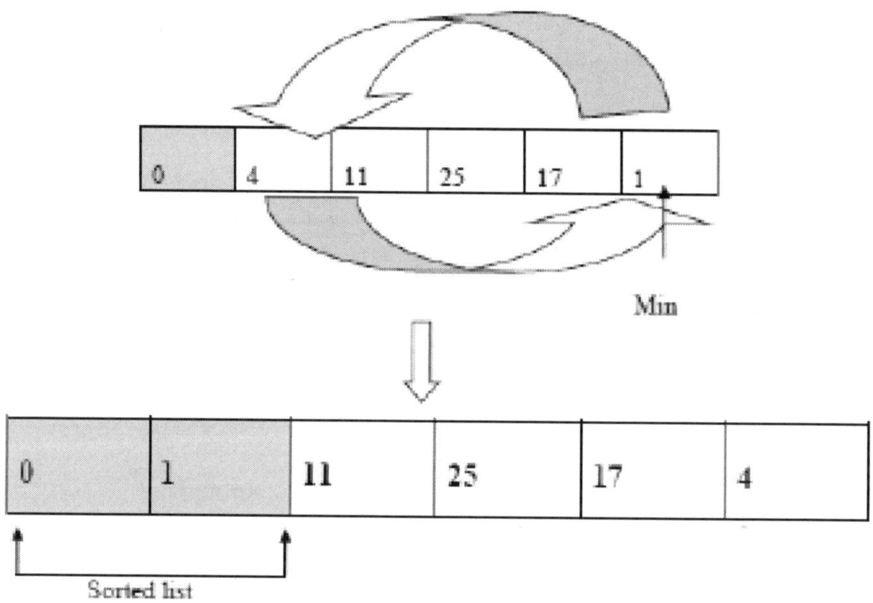

Pass 3:

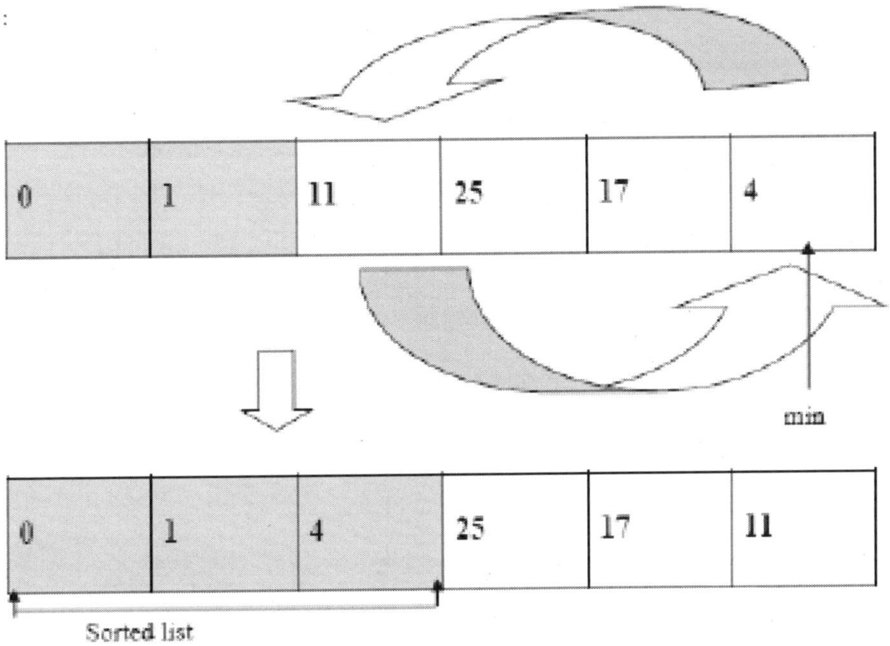
0
1
11
25
17
4
min
0
1
4
25
17
11
Sorted list

Pass 4:

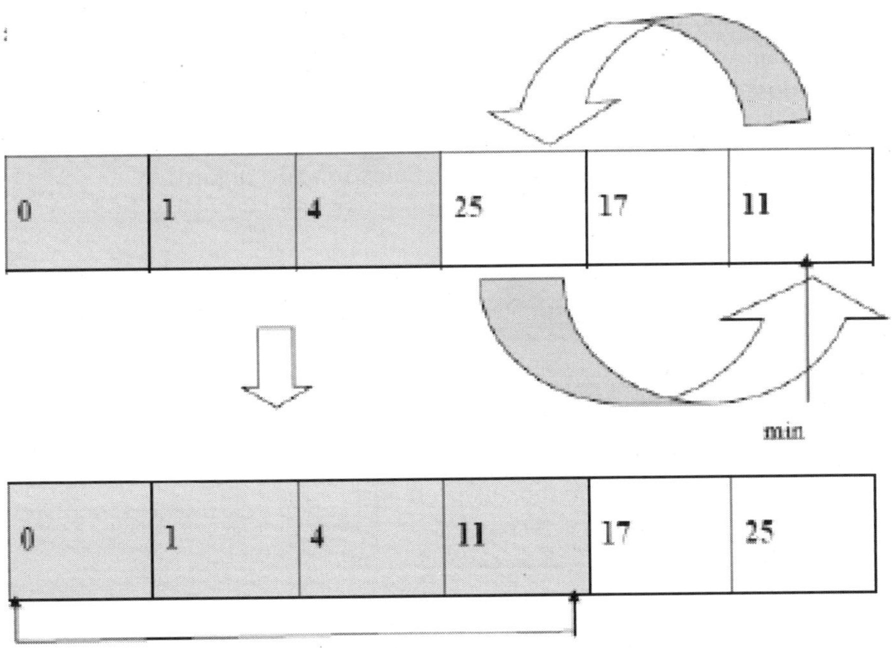
0
1
4
25
17
11
min
0
1
4
11
17
25

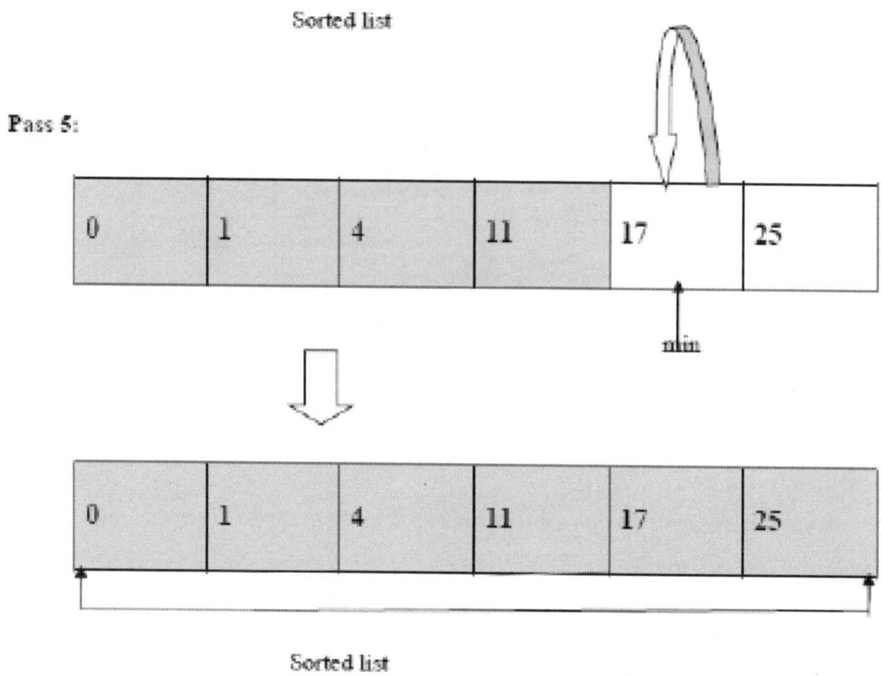

Complexity Analysis

The number of iterations of the outer loop is n time. The inner loop makes n-1 comparisons in the first call, then n-2 in second pass, then n-3 and so on, irrespective of permutations of elements. So the time required is: 1 + 2 + ..+ (n-1) and it evaluates to n(n-1)/2 i.e $O(n^2)$, which is true for best, worst and average case.

Assignment 8.2: Write a program to implement Selection Sort algorithm.

```
#include <iostream>
using namespace std;
// Function to perform Selection Sort
void selectionSort(int A[], int n) {
  for (int i = 0; i < n - 1; i++) {
    int minIndex = i; // Assume the first element is the minimum
    // Find the minimum element in the unsorted part
    for (int j = i + 1; j < n; j++) {
      if (A[j] < A[minIndex]) {
        minIndex = j;
      }
    }
    // Swap the found minimum element with the first element
```

```
        if (minIndex != i) {
            swap(A[i], A[minIndex]);
        }
    }
}
// Function to print the array
void printArray(int A[ ], int n) {
    for (int i = 0; i < n; i++) {
        cout << A[i] << " ";
    }
    cout << endl;
}
// Main function
int main() {
    int A[ ] = {64, 25, 12, 22, 11};
    int n = sizeof(A) / size of (A[0]);
    cout << "Original array: ";
printArray(A, n);
selection Sort(A, n);
    cout << "Sorted array: ";
printArray(A, n);
    return 0;
}
```

Output:

Original array: 64 25 12 22 11

Sorted array: 11 12 22 25 64

8.2.3 BUBBLE SORT

Bubble sort algorithm starts by comparing the first two elements of an array and swapping if necessary, i.e., if you want to sort the elements of array in ascending order and if the first element is greater than second then, you need to swap the elements but, if the first element is smaller than second, you mustn't swap the element. Then, again second and third elements are compared and swapped if it is necessary and this process go on until last and second last element is compared and swapped. This completes the first step of bubble sort.

If there are n elements to be sorted then, the process mentioned above should be repeated n-1 times to get required result. But, for better performance, in second step, last and second last elements are not compared because; the proper element is automatically placed at last after first step. Similarly, in third step, last and second last and second last and third last elements are not compared and so on. Bubble Sort in a formal algorithmic way is explained in Algorithm 8.3.

Algorithm 8.3: BUBBLE_SORT(A,n)

This algorithm sorts the array A which contains 'n' number of elements.

```
1. Repeat steps 2 to 3  for i = 1 to n – 1
2.       Set Ptr:=1
3.             Repeat steps 4,5 and 6 while Ptr<= n-i
4.                    if A[Ptr] > A[Ptr+1] then
5.                                   swap A[Ptr] and A[Ptr+1]
6.                   Set Ptr:=Ptr+1
7. Exit
```

Let's try to understand the algorithm with an example: A [6] = { 9, 1, 5, 3,7,2}

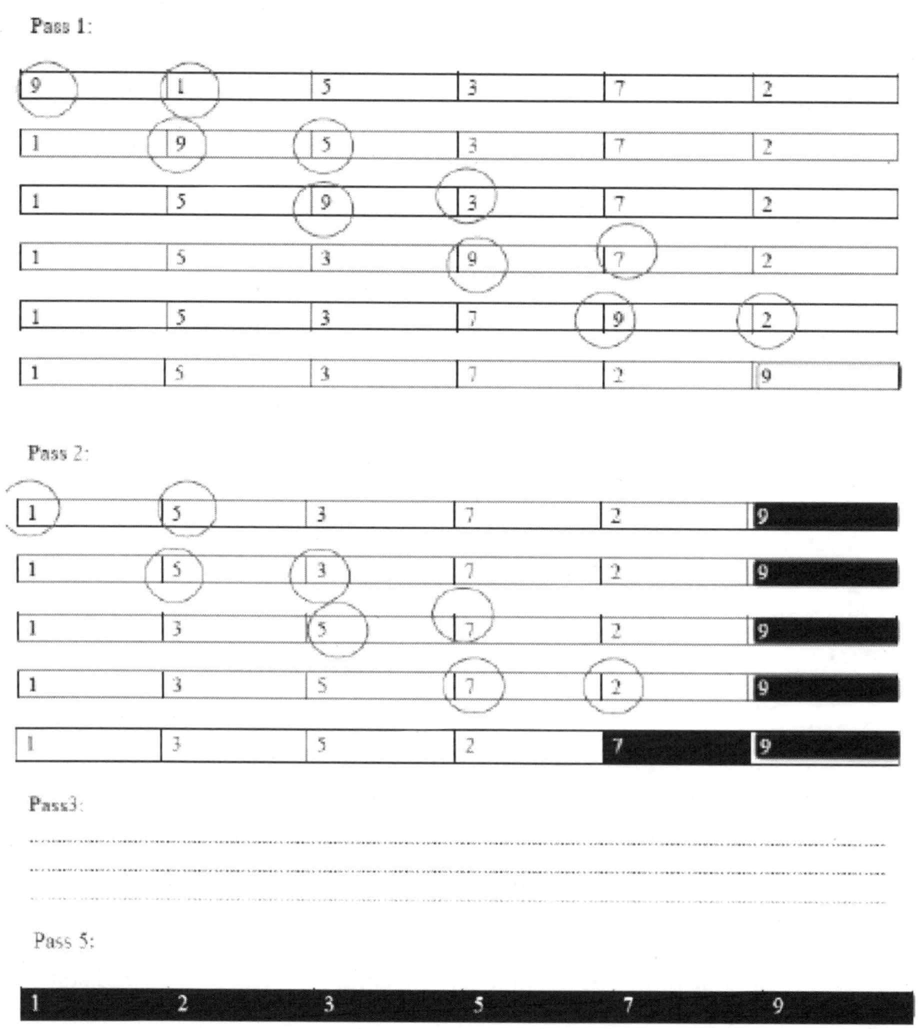

Complexity Analysis

The number of iterations of the outer loop is n-1 time. The inner loop makes n-1 comparisons in the first call, then n-2 in second pass, then n-3 and so on, irrespective of permutations of elements. So the time required is: 1 + 2 + ..+ (n-1) and it evaluates to n(n-1)/2 i.e $O(n^2)$, which is true for best, worst and average case.

Assignment 8.3: Write a program to implement Bubble Sort algorithm.

```
#include <iostream>
using namespace std;
// Function to perform Bubble Sort
void bubbleSort(int A[], int n) {
  for (int i = 0; i < n - 1; i++) { // Step 1: Loop through array n-1 times
    int Ptr = 0; // Step 2: Initialize Ptr
    // Step 3: Iterate while Ptr <= n - i - 1
    while (Ptr < n - i - 1) {
      // Step 4: Compare adjacent elements
      if (A[Ptr] >A[Ptr + 1]) {
        // Step 5: Swap if the left element is greater
        swap(A[Ptr], A[Ptr + 1]);
      }
      // Step 6: Increment Ptr
      Ptr++;
    }
  }
}
// Function to print the array
void print Array(int A[], int n) {
  for (int i = 0; i < n; i++) {
    cout << A[i] << " ";
  }
  cout << endl;
}
// Main function
int main() {
  int A[] = {64, 34, 25, 12, 22, 11, 90};
  int n = sizeof(A) / sizeof(A[0]);
```

```
    cout << "Original array: ";
    printArray(A, n);
    bubbleSort(A, n);
    cout << "Sorted array: ";
    printArray(A, n);
    return 0;
}
```

Output:

Original array: 64 34 25 12 22 11 90

Sorted array: 11 12 22 25 34 64 90

8.2.4 MERGE SORT

It is a sorting algorithm that follows divide-and-conquer approach. Accordingly the approach involves three major steps.

STEP1 Divide: two subsequences of n/2 elements each needs to be created out of the sequence of n-element to be sorted.

STEP2 Conquer: perform the merge sort over the two subsequences recursively.

STEP3 Combine: the two sorted subsequences have to be merged for producing the sorted list using merge function call.

Let's try to understand the algorithm with an example: A [6] = { 6,5,12,10,9,1}. In step1 the array keeps dividing recurrently till it is divided into 1 element list. Once we have one list we try to merge two adjacent nodes and from a sorted array of two elements using merge function call.

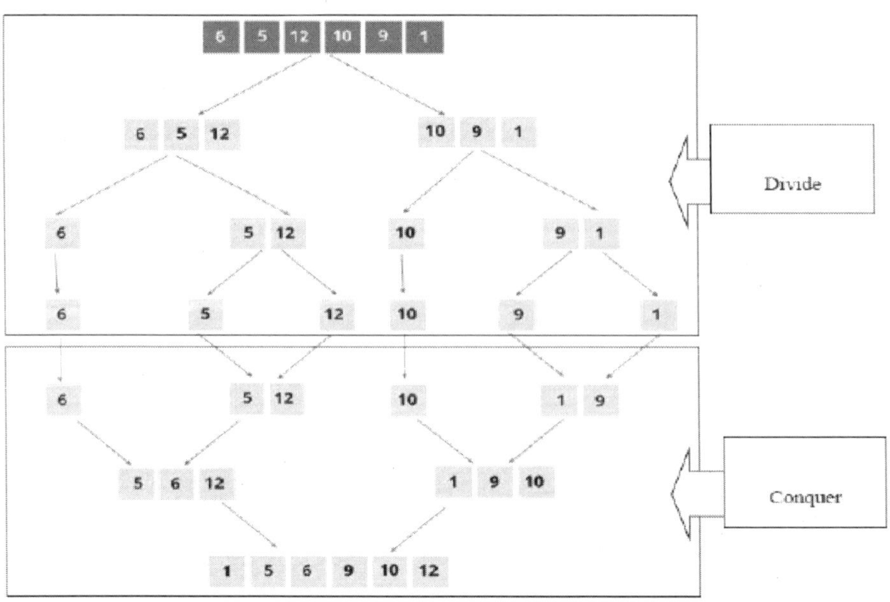

The merge function combines two sorted lists to build one sorted list. Let us take the example of two sorted lists A1=5,6,12 and A2=1,9,10.

Compare "5" with "1", 1 is smaller so move it to new list and shift j right.

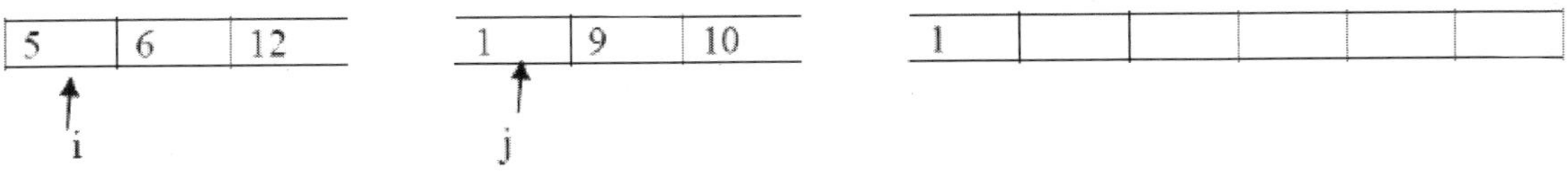

Compare "5" with "9", 5 is smaller so move it to new list and shift i right.

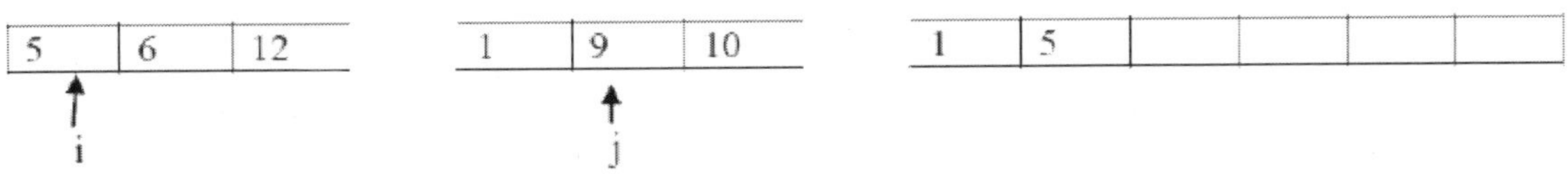

Compare "6" with "9", 6 is smaller so move it to new list and shift i right.

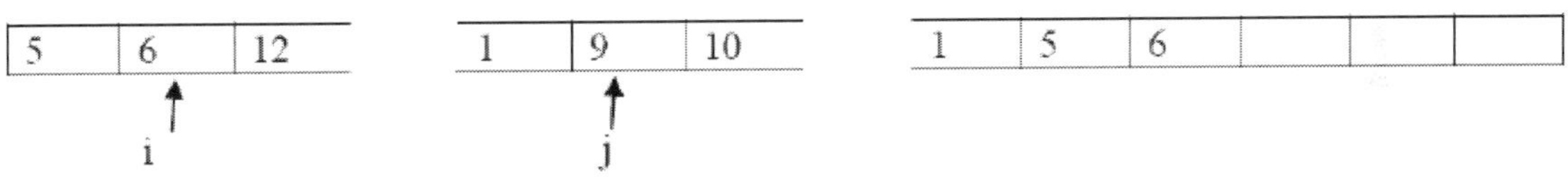

Compare "12" with "9", 9 is smaller so move it to new list and shift j right.

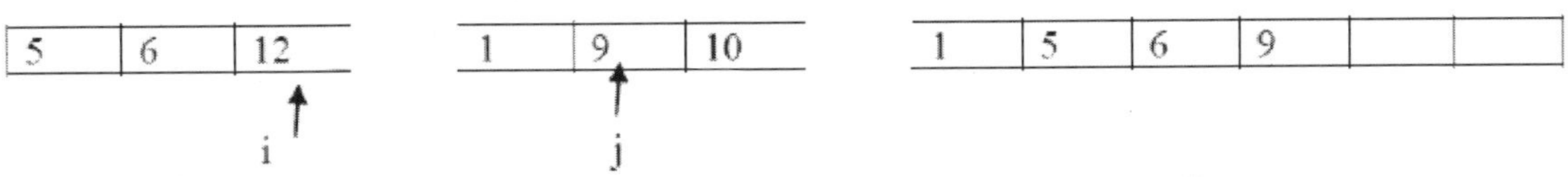

Compare "12" with "10", 10 is smaller so move it to new list.

"j" has reached maximum index so bring the items in first list as it is in the new list. The final result is shown below.

Assignment 8.4: Write a program to implement Merge Sort algorithm.

```
#include <iostream>
using namespace std;
void merge(int arr[], int left, int mid, int right) {
   int n1 = mid - left + 1; int n2 = right - mid;
```

```
    int leftArray[n1], rightArray[n2];
    // Copy data to temp arrays leftArray[] and rightArray[]
    for (int i = 0; i < n1; i++)
      leftArray[i] = arr[left + i];
    for (int j = 0; j < n2; j++)
      rightArray[j] = arr[mid + 1 + j];
    int i = 0, j = 0, k = left;
    // Merge the temp arrays back into arr[left..right]
    while (i < n1 && j < n2) {
      if (leftArray[i] <= rightArray[j]) {
        arr[k] = leftArray[i];
        i++;
      } else {
        arr[k] = rightArray[j];
        j++;
      }
      k++;
    }
    // Copy the remaining elements of leftArray[], if any
    while (i < n1) {
      arr[k] = leftArray[i];
      i++;
      k++;
    }
    // Copy the remaining elements of rightArray[], if any
    while (j < n2) {
      arr[k] = rightArray[j];
      j++;
      k++;
    }
}
// Function implementing Merge Sort
void mergeSort(int arr[], int left, int right) {
    if (left < right) {
      int mid = left + (right - left) / 2;
```

```
    // Recursively sort first and second halves
mergeSort(arr, left, mid);
mergeSort(arr, mid + 1, right);
    // Merge the sorted halves
merge(arr, left, mid, right);
  }
}
// Function to print the array
void printArray(int arr[], int size) {
  for (int i = 0; i < size; i++)
    cout << arr[i] << " ";
  cout << endl;
}
int main() {
  int arr[] = {6, 5, 12, 10, 9, 1};
  int size = sizeof(arr) / sizeof(arr[0]);
  cout << "Original array: ";
printArray(arr, size);
mergeSort(arr, 0, size - 1);
cout << "Sorted array: ";
printArray(arr, size);
  return 0;
}
```

Output:

Original array: 6 5 12 10 9 1

Sorted array: 1 5 6 9 10 12

8.2.5 Quick Sort

The **quick sort** uses divide and conquer to gain the same advantages as the merge sort, while not using additional storage. As a trade-off, however, it is possible that the list may not be divided in half. When this happens, we will see that performance is diminished.

A quick sort first selects a value, which is called the **pivot value**. Although there are many different ways to choose the pivot value, we will simply use the first item in the list. The role of the pivot value is to assist with splitting the list. The actual position where the pivot value belongs in the final sorted list, commonly called the **split point**, will be used to divide the list for subsequent calls to the quick sort.

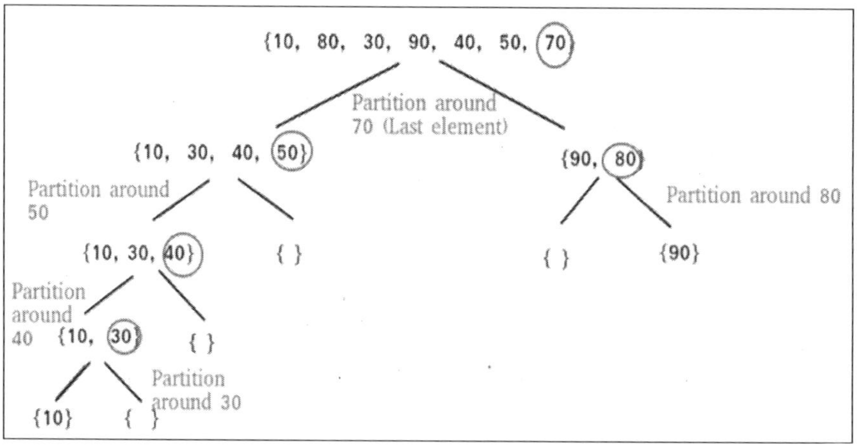

Following are the steps involved in Quick Sort Algorithm.

Quick Sort

1. Choose the highest index value to be the pivot element
2. Take two variables to point left and right of the List excluding pivot
3. left points to the low index
4. right points to the high
5. while value at left is less than pivot move right
6. while value at right is greater than pivot move left
7. if both step 5 and step 6 does not match swap left and right
8. if left ≥ right, the point where they met is new pivot

Assignment 8.5: Write a program to implement Quick Sort algorithm.

```
#include <iostream>
using namespace std;
// Function to partition the array
int partition(int arr[], int low, int high) {
    int pivot = arr[high]; // Choosing the highest index as pivot
    int left = low, right = high - 1;
    while (true) {
        while (left <= right && arr[left] < pivot) left++; // Move right if value at left is less than pivot
        while (right >= left && arr[right] > pivot) right--; // Move left if value at right is greater than pivot
        if (left >= right) break; // If left is greater or equal to right, partition is done
        swap(arr[left], arr[right]); // Swap left and right elements
        left++;
```

```
      right--;
    }


  swap(arr[left], arr[high]); // Swap pivot with the partition point
  return left; // Return the partition index
}
// Function to perform Quick Sort
void quickSort(int arr[], int low, int high) {
  if (low < high) {
    int pivotIndex = partition(arr, low, high); // Partitioning the array
    quickSort(arr, low, pivotIndex - 1);  // Recursively sort the left part
    quickSort(arr, pivotIndex + 1, high); // Recursively sort the right part
  }
}
// Function to print the array
void printArray(int arr[], int size) {
  for (int i = 0; i < size; i++) {
    cout << arr[i] << " ";
  }
  cout << endl;
}
int main() {
  int arr[] = {10, 7, 8, 9, 1, 5};
  int size = sizeof(arr) / sizeof(arr[0]);

  cout << "Original array: ";
  printArray(arr, size);

  quickSort(arr, 0, size - 1);

  cout << "Sorted array: ";
  printArray(arr, size);
  return 0;
}
```

Output:

Original array: 10 7 8 9 1 5

Sorted array: 1 5 7 8 9 10

8.3 SEARCHING ALGORITHM

One most basic algorithm in computer science is searching, which is the method of finding the position of a target among a list of objects. In the case of a list, searching means that given a value, we want to find the location of the first element in the list that contains that value.

There are two basic searches for lists:

- sequential search: can be used to locate an item in any list
- binary search: requires the list to be sorted

Sequential search

Sequential search is used if the list to be searched is not an ordered list. Generally, we use this technique only for small lists, or lists that are not searched often. In a sequential search, we start searching for the target from the beginning of the list. We continue until we either find the target or reach the end of the list.

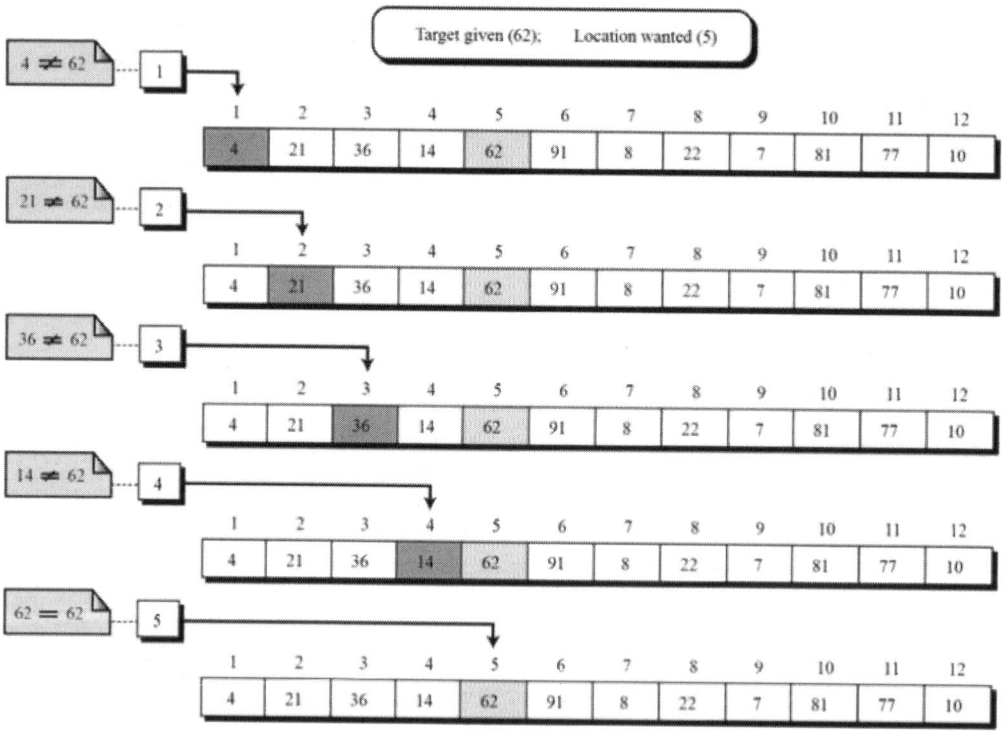

Binary search

In case of a sorted list binary search is a more efficient algorithm. Programmers use a binary search when a list is large and sorted. A binary search starts by testing the data in the element at the middle of the list. This determines whether the target is in the first half or the second half of the list. If it is in the first half, there is no need to further check the second half. If it is in the second half, there is no need to further check the first half. In other words, we eliminate half the list from further consideration.

Let the array to be searched is as follows:

10 13 32 33 65 68 71 89 100

Now let the element to be searched is key = 32.

- hi=8 low=0 so mid=4 and x[mid]= 65 is the center element but 65 > 32. So now hi = 4-1=3. Now mid= (0 + 3)/2 = 1, so x[mid]= 23 < 32.
- again low= 1 + 1 = 2. Now mid = (3 + 2)/2 = 2 & x[mid]= 32 = key. So the search is successful and is performed in two comparisons .

Complexity:

This is highly efficient than linear search. Each comparision in the binary search reduces the no. of possible candidates by a factor of 2. So the maximum no. of key comparisions is equal to $\log_2 n$ approx. So the complexity of binary search is O(log n).

Limitations:

Binary search algorithm can only be used if the list to be searched is in array form and not linked list. This is because the algorithm uses the fact that the indices of the array elements are consecutive integers. This makes this algorithm useless for lists with many insertions and deletions which can be implemented only when the list is in the form of a linked list.

8.4 Hashing

The problem at hands is to speed up searching. Consider the problem of searching an array for a given value. If the array is not sorted, the search might require examining each and all elements of the array. If the array is sorted, we can use the binary search, and therefore reduce the worse-case runtime complexity to O(log n). We could search even faster if we know in advance the index at which that value is located in the array. Suppose we do have that magic function that would tell us the index for a given value. With this magic function our search is reduced to just one probe, giving us a constant runtime O(1). Such a function is called a hash function . A hash function is a function which when given a key, generates an address in the table.

The example of a hash function is a book call number. Each book in the library has a unique call number. A call number is like an address: it tells us where the book is located in the library. Many academic libraries in the United States, uses Library of Congress Classification for call numbers. This system uses a combination of letters and numbers to arrange materials by subjects.

A hash function that returns a unique hash number is called a universal hash function. In practice it is extremely hard to assign unique numbers to objects. The later is always possible only if you know (or approximate) the number of objects to be proccessed.

Thus, we say that our hash function has the following properties

- it always returns a number for an object.
- two equal objects will always have the same number
- two unequal objects not always have different numbers

The procedure of storing objects using a hash function is the following.

Create an array of size M. Choose a hash function h, that is a mapping from objects into integers 0, 1, ..., M-1. Put these objects into an array at indexes computed via the hash function index = h(object). Such array is called a hash table. So, Hash Table is a data structure which stores data in an associative manner. In a hash table, data is stored in an array format, where each data value has its own unique index value. Access of data becomes very fast if we know the index of the desired data. Thus, it becomes a data structure in which insertion and search operations are very fast irrespective of the size of the data. Hash Table uses an array as a storage medium and uses hash technique to generate an index where an element is to be inserted or is to be located from.

Hashing Operation

Hashing is a technique to convert a range of key values into a range of indexes of an array. We're going to use modulo operator to get a range of key values. Consider an example of hash table of size 20, and the following items are to be stored. Item are in the (key,value) format.

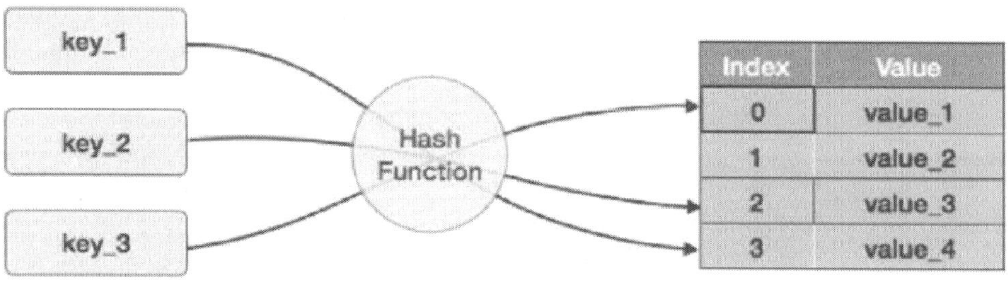

Let us take an example to understand it better. Say we need to store the following nine key value pairs.

1. (1,20)
2. (2,70)
3. (42,80)
4. (4,25)
5. (12,44)
6. (14,32)
7. (17,11)
8. (13,78)
9. (37,98)

Sr. No.	Key	Hash	Array Index
1	1	1 % 20 = 1	1
2	2	2 % 20 = 2	2
3	42	42 % 20 = 2	2
4	4	4 % 20 = 4	4
5	12	12 % 20 = 12	12

6	14	14 % 20 = 14	14
7	17	17 % 20 = 17	17
8	13	13 % 20 = 13	13
9	37	37 % 20 = 17	17

Hash function

A function that can take a key value and compute an integer value (or an index in a table) from it is called a hash function.

For example, student records for a class could be stored in an array C of dimension 10000

by truncating the student's ID number to its last four digits:

H(IDNum) = IDNum % 10000

Given an ID number X, the corresponding record would be inserted at C[H(X)].

Basically, a hash function, f, transforms an identifier, x, into a bucket address in the hash table. We want to hash function that is easy to compute and that minimizes the number of collisions. Although the hash function we used in above example was easy to compute, using only the first character in an identifier is bound to have disastrous consequences. We know that identifiers, whether they represent variable names in a program, word in a dictionary, or names in a telephone book, cluster around certain letters of the alphabet. To avoid collisions, the hash function should depend on all the characters in an identifier. It also should be unbiased. That is, if we randomly choose an identifier, x, from the identifier space (the universe of all possible identifiers), the probability that f(x) = i is 1/b for all buckets i. This means that a random x has an equal property a uniform hash function.

There are several types of uniform hash functions, and we shall describe four of them. We assume that the identifiers have been suitably transformed into a numerical equivalent.

Mid-square:

The middle of square hash function is frequently used in symbol table application. We compute the function f_m by squaring the identifier and then using an appropriate number of bits from the middle of the square to obtain the bucket address. Since the middle bits of the square usually depend upon all the characters in an identifier, there is a high probability that different identifiers will produce different hash addresses, even when some of the characters are the same. The number of bits used to obtain the bucket address depends on the table size. If we use r bits, the range of the values is 2^r. Therefore, the size of the hash table should be a power of 2 when we use this scheme.

Steps:

- square the key, then use the middle part as the result

  - e.g., 3121 -> 9740641 -> 406 (with a table size of 1000)
- a string would first be transformed into a number, say by folding
- idea is to let all of the key influence the result
- if table size is a power of 2, this can be done efficiently at the bit level:

3121 ->100101001010000101100001 ->0101000010 (with a table size of 1024)

Division:

This hash function is using the modulus (%) operator. We divide the identifier x by some number M and use the remainder as the hash address of x. The hash function is: f_D (x) = x % M This gives bucket address that range from 0 to M-1, where M = the table size. The choice of M is critical. In the division function, if M is a power of 2, then f_D (x) depends only on the least significant bits of x. Such a choice for M results in a biased use of the hash table when several of the identifiers in use have the same suffix. If M is divisible by 2, then odd keys are mapped to odd buckets, and even keys are mapped to even buckets. Hence, an even M results in a biased use of the table when a majority of identifiers are even or when majorities are odd.

Steps:

- The first order of business for a hash function is to compute an integer value.
- If we expect the hash function to produce a valid index for our chosen table size, that integer will probably be out of range.
- That is easily remedied by modding the integer by the table size.
- There is some reason to believe that it is better if the table size is a prime, or at least has no small prime factors.

Folding:

In this method, we partition the identifier x into several parts. All parts, except for the last one have the same length. We then add the parts together to obtain the hash address for x. There are two ways of carrying out this addition. In the first method, we shift all parts except for the last one, so that the least significant bit of each part lines up with the corresponding bit of the last part. We then add the parts together to obtain f(x). This method is known as shift folding. The second method, know as folding at the boundaries, reverses every other partition before adding

Steps:

- Portions of the key are often recombined, or folded together

  e.g - shift folding: 123-45-6789 -> 123 + 456 + 789

  - boundary folding: 123-45-6789 -> 123 + 654 + 789
- Can be efficiently performed using bitwise operations.
- The characters of a string can be xor'd together, but small numbers result.
- "chunks" of characters can be xor'd instead, say in integer-sized chunks

Digit Analysis:

The last method we will examine, digit analysis, is used with static files. A static file is one in which all the identifiers are known in advance. Using this method, we first transform the identifiers into numbers using some radix, r. We then examine the digits of each identifier, deleting those digits that have the most skewed distributions. We continue deleting digits until the number of remaining digits is small enough to give an address in the range of the hash table. The digits used to calculate the hash address must be the same for all identifiers and must not have abnormally high peaks or valleys (the standard deviation must be small).

So from the above discussion it has been noted that a good hash function should:

- Be easy and quick to compute
- Achieve an even distribution of the key values that actually occur across the index range supported by the table.
- Ideally be mathematically one-to-one on the set of relevant key values Collisions handling

When we put objects into a hash table, it is possible that different objects might have the same hash code. This is called a collision. Following are some of the strategy to overcome collision.

1. Linear Probing

As discussed earlier, it may happen that the hashing technique is used to create an already used index of the array. In such a case, we can search the next empty location in the array by looking into the next cell until we find an empty cell. This technique is called linear probing.

Sr.No.	Key	Hash	Array Index	After Linear Probing, Array Index
1	1	1 % 20 = 1	1	1
2	2	2 % 20 = 2	2	2
3	42	42 % 20 = 2	2	3
4	4	4 % 20 = 4	4	4
5	12	12 % 20 = 12	12	12
6	14	14 % 20 = 14	14	14
7	17	17 % 20 = 17	17	17
8	13	13 % 20 = 13	13	13
9	37	37 % 20 = 17	17	18

Following are the basic primary operations of a hash table.

- **Search** – Searches an element in a hash table.
- **Insert** – Inserts an element in a hash table.
- **Delete** – Deletes an element from a hash table.

To implement the linear probing strategy, we first compute f (x) for identifier x and them examine the hash table buckets ht[(f(x) + j) % TABLE_SIZE], 0 ≤ j ≤TABLE_SIZE in this order. Four outcomes result from the examination of a hash table bucket:

(1). The bucket contains x. In this case, x is already in the table. Depending on the application, we may either simply report a duplicate identifier, or we may update information in the other fields of the element.

(2). The bucket contains the empty string. In this case, the bucket is empty, and we may insert the new element into it.

(3). The bucket contains a nonempty string other than x. In this case we proceed to examine the next bucket.

(4). We return to the home bucket ht [f (x)] (j = TABLE_SIZE). In this case, the home bucket is being examined for the second time and all remaining buckets have been examined. The table is full and we report an error condition and exit.

We can summarise the *Insertion algorithm* as follows:

1. Calculate a hash code from the key

2. Access that hash element

   a. If the hash element is empty, add straight away

   b. If not, probe through subsequent elements (looping back if necessary), trying to find a free place

      i). If a free place is found, add the data at that position.

      ii). if no free place is found, the add will fail.

We can summarise the *retrieval algorithm* as follows:

1. Calculate the hash code for the given search key

2. Access the hash element

3. If the hash element is empty, the search has immediately failed.

4. Otherwise, check for a match between the search and data key

   a. If there is a match, return the data.

   b. If there is no match, probe the table until either:

      i). An match is found between the search and data key.

      ii). A completely empty hash element is found.

A summary of the *deletion algorithm* is below. Note that it is very similar to that of the retrieve -- this is because the data must be found before it can be deleted.

1. Calculate the hash code for the given target key

2. Access the hash element

3. If the hash element is empty, the deletion has immediately failed.

4. Otherwise, check for a match between the target and data key

   a. If there is a match, delete the hash element (and set the flag)

   b. If there is no match, probe the table until either:

      i). An match is found between the target key and the data's key; the data can be deleted, and the deleted flag set.

      ii). A completely empty hash element is found.

2. Chaining

Linear probing and its variations perform poorly because inserting an identifier requires the comparison of identifiers with different hash values. To insert a new element we would only have to compute the hash address f (x) and examine the identifiers in the list for f (x). Since we would not know the sizes of the lists in advance, we should maintain them as linked chains. We now require additional space for a link field. Since we will have M lists, where M is the desired table size, we employ a head node for each chain. These head nodes only need a link field, so they are smaller than the other nodes. We maintain the head nodes in ascending order, 0,........, M-1 so that we may access the lists at random.

Basically in this strategy, when a collision occurs, elements with the same hash key will be chained together. A chain is simply a linked list of all the elements with the same hash key. The hash table slots will no longer hold a table element. They will now hold the address of a table element.

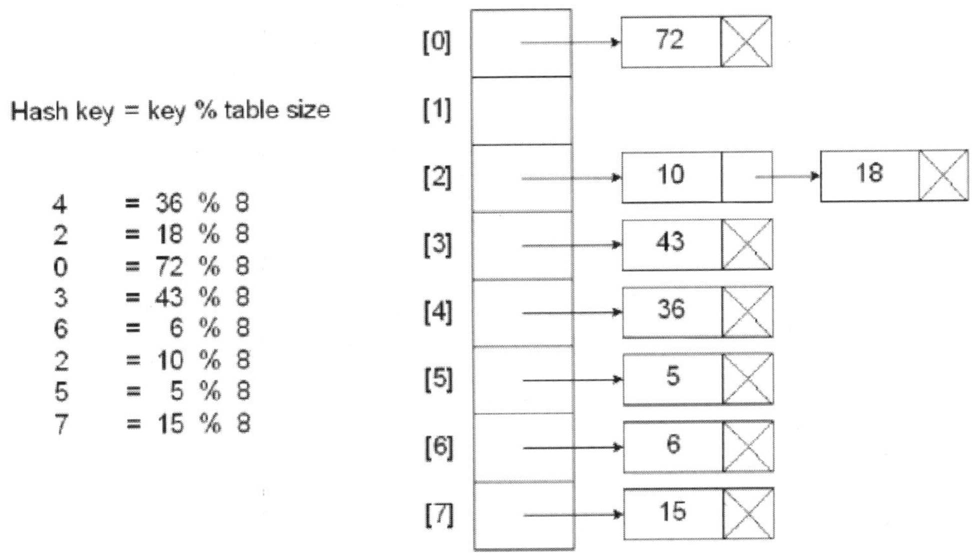

Let us consider a simple hash function as "key mod 7" and sequence of keys as 50, 700, 76, 85, 92, 73, 101 to understand it better.,

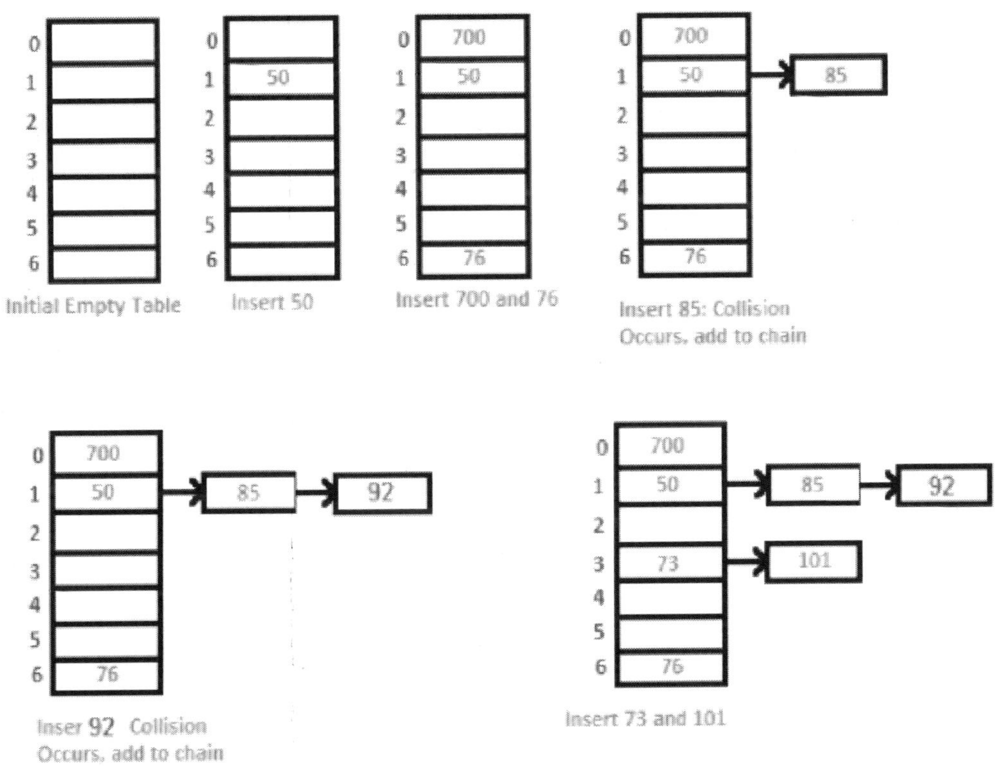

Advantages:

- Simple to implement.
- Hash table never fills up, we can always add more elements to chain.
- Less sensitive to the hash function or load factors.
- It is mostly used when it is unknown how many and how frequently keys may be inserted or deleted.

Disadvantages:

- Cache performance of chaining is not good as keys are stored using linked list. Open addressing provides better cache performance as everything is stored in same table.
- Wastage of Space (Some Parts of hash table are never used)
- If the chain becomes long, then search time can become O(n) in worst case.
- Uses extra space for links.

Performance of Chaining:

Performance of hashing can be evaluated under the assumption that each key is equally likely to be hashed to any slot of table (simple uniform hashing).

m = Number of slots in hash table

n = Number of keys to be inserted in hash table

Load factor $\alpha = n/m$

Expected time to search = $O(1 + \alpha)$

Expected time to insert/delete = $O(1 + \alpha)$

Time complexity of search insert and delete is

O(1) if α is O(1)

8.5 LET US SUM UP

- This chapter discusses various Sorting and Searching are fundamental operations. Various increamental sorting opeartions like insertion, selection, bubble sort and various divide and conquer sorting like merge sort, quick sort are also discussed in detail with examples.
- It has been observed that comparison based sorting takes minmum O(nlogn) amount of time.
- Similarly comparison based searching takes minimum O(log n) amount of time.

- To make the searching more faster people came up with the idea of hashing. Various hashing techniques and removal of collision process is discussed in the later part of the chapter.

8.6 CHECK YOUR PROGRESS

1. Choose the correct option

1) The worst case occur in linear search algorithm when:

a). Item is somewhere in the middle of the array

b). Item is not in the array at all

c). Item is the last element in the array

d). Item is the last element in the array or item is not there at all

2) Which of the following is not a limitation of binary search algorithm?

a). must use a sorted array

b). requirement of sorted array is expensive when a lot of insertion and deletions are needed

c). there must be a mechanism to access middle element directly

d). binary search algorithm is not efficient when the data elements more than 1500

3) The Average case occurs in linear search algorithm ....

a). when item is somewhere in the middle of the array

b). B. when item is not the array at all

c). when item is the last element in the array

d). Item is the last element in the array or item is not there at all

4) Binary search algorithm cannot be applied to ...

a). sorted linked list

b). sorted binary trees

c). sorted linear array

d). pointer array

5) Complexity of linear search algorithm is ....

a). O(n)

b). O(logn)

c). O(n^2)

d). O(n logn)

6) The complexity of bubble sort algorithm is

a). O(n)

b). O(logn)

c). O(n^2)

d). O(n logn)

7) The complexity of merge sort algorithm is

a). O(n)

b). O(logn)

c). $O(n^2)$

d). O(n logn)

8) .... is the method used by card sorter.

a). Radix sort

b). Insertion

c). Heap

d). Quick

9) Which of the following sorting algorithm is of divide and conquer type?

a). Bubble sort

b). Insertion sort

c). Merge sort

d). Selection sort

10) Partition and exchange sort is ....

a). quick sort

b). tree sort

c). heap sort

d). bubble sort

2. Discuss how one can handle overflow in hashing.

3. Write a program in C++ for binary search. What is the worst case time complexity of binary search?

4. How the choice of pivot element affect the running time of quick sort algorithm? – Explain.

5. Write Heapsort algorithm. Analyze the running time of your algorithm.

6. Use merge sort algorithm to sort

15,22,30,10,15,64,1,3,9,2. Is it a stable sorting algorithm? – Justify.

7. Use quick sort algorithm to sort

15,22,30,10,15,64,1,3,9,2. Is it a stable sorting algorithm? – Justify

8. Write mergesort algorithm. Analyze the running time of your algorithm.

9. Write insertion sort algorithm. Analyze the running time of your algorithm.

10. Write selection sort algorithm. Analyze the running time of your algorithm.

11. What is a hash function? Give some examples.

12. Calculate hash values of keys: 1892, 1921, 2007, 3456 using different methods of hashing.

13. Consider a hash table with size=10. Using linear probing, insert keys 27, 72, 63, 42, 36, 18, 29 and 101 into the table.

14. What is hashing? Give its applications. Also, discuss the pros and cons of hashing.
15. How is a hash table better than a direct access table (array)?
16. Define sorting. What is the importance of sorting?
17. Explain the difference between bubble sort and quick sort. Which one is more efficient?
18. Quick sort shows quadratic behaviour in certain situations. Justify.
19. If the following sequence of numbers is to be sorted using quick sort, then show the iterations of the sorting process. 42, 34, 75, 23, 21, 18, 90, 67, 78.

Bibliography

[1] Lipschutz, S. (2011) Data Structures with C. New York, US: The McGraw-Hill Companies.

[2] Siddiqui, A.T. and Siddiqui, S.A. (2024) Data structure using C: Theory and program. Boca Raton, FL: CRC Press.

[3] PAWAR, L.B., ROHIT (2023) Data structure. S.l.: LAP LAMBERT ACADEMIC PUBL.

[4] Sharma, A.K. (2010) Data structure using C. Pearson India.

[5] Thareja, Reema. Data structures using C. 2nd ed. New Delhi: Oxford University Press, 2011. Text.

[6] Langsam, Y., Augenstein, M. and Tenenbaum, A.M. (2012) Data structures using C and C++. New Delhi: Prentice-Hall of India.

[7] Koffman, E.B. (2021) Data Structures. New York: John Wiley & Sons, Incorporated.

[8] Kaur, S., Sharma, S. and Singh, P.P. (2006) Data Structure: Complete Course Book. New Delhi: Deep & Deep Publications.

[9] Cormen, Thomas H., Leiserson, Charles E., Rivest, Ronald L., and Clifford-Stein. Introduction to Algorithms. Cambridge, MA: The MIT Press, 2001.

[10] Karumanchi, N. (2023) Data Structures and algorithms made easy: To all my readers and parents: Concepts, problems, Interview Questions. Madinaguda, Hyderabad, India: CareerMonk Publications.

[11] https://www.tutorialspoint.com

[12] http:// www.btechsmartclass.com

[13] http://www.cs.cmu.edu